"In what may be the best book yet written on early Jewish and Christian concepts of election, Chad Thornhill provides clear and compelling evidence for the view that election in early Jewish and Christian circles was both corporate and conditional, and that the focus of election language was *not* on the salvation of particular individuals from before the foundations of the world. In short, election and salvation were not synonymous terms in either early Judaism or the writings of Paul. Thornhill covers a wide swath of early Jewish material and convincingly situates Paul's discussion—especially Romans 9–11—within it. Thornhill's careful and compelling exposition should be a game changer in the age-old battles over the relationship of God's unconditional love and choice of a people and the issue of human freedom when it comes to the matter of individual salvation."

Ben Witherington III, Jean R. Amos Professor of New Testament for Doctoral Studies, Asbury Theological Seminary

"The welcome emphasis on Jewish backgrounds that now permeates the field of New Testament scholarship has rekindled a number of traditional discussions surrounding Pauline theology. Among the most illuminating developments is a renewed interest in the notion of corporate election. Based on evidence from the Old Testament and Second Temple Jewish literature, many scholars now insist that the time-worn debate over the relative importance of divine sovereignty versus human responsibility in God's salvific economy must be reframed in collectivist—rather than individualist—terms. The challenge, of course, is to appropriate these background materials in a way that (1) makes sense of the particularity of Paul's social location while (2) still supporting a close reading of the apostle's letters. Chad Thornhill's book is a welcome contribution to the conversation on both counts. Thornill thoroughly surveys Second Temple Jewish thinking about election and then interprets key Pauline texts against this background. Those interested in a fresh and intriguing solution to a familiar theological puzzle will find much to think about in these well-written pages."

Joe Hellerman, professor of New Testament language and literature, Talbot School of Theology

"It is a distinct pleasure to recommend to the Christian reading public this book by Dr. A. Chadwick Thornhill. By a thorough examination of Second Temple and Pauline texts, Dr. Thornhill has demonstrated that the center of gravity of both resides in the corporate or collective dimension of ancient Israel and latter-day Israel (the church) as the elect people of God. Particularly as regards the Jewish materials, he has filled a gap in our appreciation of Paul's predecessors and contemporaries. This volume will serve as both a cover-to-cover read and a ready reference work for all who take an interest in this important subject."

Don Garlington, author of *The Obedience of Faith*

The
Chosen People

Election, Paul and Second Temple Judaism

A. Chadwick Thornhill

IVP Academic

An imprint of InterVarsity Press
Downers Grove, Illinois

InterVarsity Press
P.O. Box 1400, Downers Grove, IL 60515-1426
ivpress.com
email@ivpress.com

InterVarsity Press® is the book-publishing division of InterVarsity Christian Fellowship/USA®, a movement of students and faculty active on campus at hundreds of universities, colleges and schools of nursing in the United States of America, and a member movement of the International Fellowship of Evangelical Students. For information about local and regional activities, visit intervarsity.org.

All Scripture translations, unless otherwise indicated, are the author's own.

Cover design: Cindy Kiple

Interior design: Beth McGill

Images: Byzantine plaque of St. Paul: Werner Forman Archive / British Museum, London. Location: 12 / Glow Images
    biblical temple: Model of the city of Jerusalem. Israel. / Photo © Tarker / Bridgeman Images

ISBN 978-0-8308-4083-0 (print)
ISBN 978-0-8308-9915-9 (digital)

Printed in the United States of America ∞

g green press INITIATIVE   As a member of the Green Press Initiative, InterVarsity Press is committed to protecting the environment and to the responsible use of natural resources. To learn more, visit greenpressinitiative.org.

Library of Congress Cataloging-in-Publication Data

Thornhill, A. Chadwick, 1983-
  The chosen people : election, Paul, and Second Temple Judaism / A. Chadwick Thornhill.
    pages cm
  Includes bibliographical references and index.
  ISBN 978-0-8308-4083-0 (pbk. : alk. paper)
  1. Election (Theology) 2. Jews—Election, Doctrine of. 3. Bible. Epistles of Paul—Theology. 4. Judaism—Influence.
  5. Judaism—History—Post-exilic period, 586 B.C.-210 A.D. I. Title.
  BS2655.J4T55 2015
  231.7'6—dc23

                                                                                                2015027568

P   23   22   21   20   19   18   17   16   15   14   13   12   11   10   9   8   7   6   5   4   3   2   1

Y   34   33   32   31   30   29   28   27   26   25   24   23   22   21   20   19   18   17   16   15

For Caroline, my dearest friend,

and Josiah and Adelyn, my energetic sources of joy.

Contents

Acknowledgments

A great many conversations, personal and literary, have gone into this work. I am indebted to a great number of friends, colleagues and professors who have invested in me. I would be remiss to not first and foremost thank my wife, Caroline, children, Josiah and Adelyn, and parents, Bobby and Darlene, for their support through this endeavor, which began as my doctoral dissertation.

Dr. Leo Percer was instrumental in my coming to this topic in the first place. I would like to thank him for spurring on my interest in Second Temple Judaism, which proved to be integral to this project, and for the many discussions we have had on this and many related topics. I would also like to thank Dr. Gary Yates, for his influence on my understanding of the Old Testament, and Dr. Michael Heiser, for his comments and questions, which were extremely valuable in shaping my thinking and articulation of these ideas. Both of these men graciously served on my dissertation committee.

I must also thank Dr. Jim Freerksen for the enduring influence he has had on my understanding of the New Testament through his excellent instruction in New Testament Greek, as well as Dr. Gary Habermas, Dr. John Morrison and Dr. Ed Smither, each of whom played a key role in my academic development. Dr. Don Garlington also provided helpful comments on the overall shape of the manuscript, which assisted in further refining my thinking. Dr. Craig Evans also must be thanked for recommending this project to InterVarsity Press in its early stages. Any errors in exegesis or interpretation are my own.

Finally, I am incredibly grateful for the work of the good people at InterVarsity Press with whom I have had the privilege of interacting. In particular, I'd like to thank Brannon Ellis (now with Lexham Press), who advocated for this project in its initial stages and also helped shape its style and form. In addition, Andy Le Peau has provided invaluable guidance for much of the duration of this project, and I am grateful for his helpful direction.

I pray that this book both faithfully represents the world and the words of the New Testament and that it might be used "to equip the saints for the work of ministry" (Eph 4:12).

Abbreviations

JSP	*Journal for the Study of the Pseudepigrapha*
JSS	*Journal of Semitic Studies*
JSSSup	Journal of Semitic Studies Supplement
KD	*Kerygma und Dogma*
L&N	Johannes P. Louw and Eugene A. Nida, eds. *Greek-English Lexicon of the New Testament: Based on Semantic Domains.* 2nd ed. New York: United Bible Societies, 1989
LSJ	Henry George Liddell, Robert Scott and Henry Stuart Jones. *A Greek-English Lexicon.* 9th ed. with revised supplement. Oxford: Clarendon, 1996
NAC	New American Commentary
NCB	New Century Bible
NICNT	New International Commentary on the New Testament
NIGTC	New International Greek Testament Commentary
NIVAC	NIV Application Commentary
NovT	*Novum Testamentum*
NTL	New Testament Library
NTS	*New Testament Studies*
PEQ	*Palestine Exploration Quarterly*
PIBA	*Proceedings of the Irish Biblical Association*
PRSt	*Perspectives in Religious Studies*
RevExp	*Review and Expositor*
RevQ	*Revue de Qumran*
SBLDS	Society of Biblical Literature Dissertation Series
SJT	*Scottish Journal of Theology*
SwJT	*Southwestern Journal of Theology*
TNTC	*Tyndale New Testament Commentaries*
TS	*Theological Studies*
UBCS	*Understanding the Bible Commentary Series*
VT	*Vetus Testamentum*
WW	*Word and World*

ANCIENT WRITINGS

1 En.	*1 Enoch*
Ant.	*Josephus, Antiquities of the Jews*
Bib. Ant.	*pseudo-Philo, Biblical Antiquities*
CD	*Cairo Genizah copy of the Damascus Document*
Jub.	*Jubilees*
Odes Sol.	*Odes of Solomon*
Ps. Sol.	*Psalms of Solomon*
Sib. Or.	*Sibylline Oracles*
T. Ash.	*Testament of Asher*
T. Benj.	*Testament of Benjamin*
T. Dan	*Testament of Dan*
T. Gad	*Testament of Gad*
T. Iss.	*Testament of Issachaar*
T. Jos.	*Testament of Joseph*
T. Jud.	*Testament of Judah*
T. Levi	*Testament of Levi*
T. Naph.	*Testament of Naphtali*
T. Sim.	*Testament of Simeon*
T. Reu.	*Testament of Reuben*
T. Zeb.	*Testament of Zebulun*

The Missing Link
in Election

Halfway through my seminary studies, I was sitting in a class titled Patristics and Ancient Heresies (my wife always joked about the odd titles of the courses I took) when a shift began for me. A substitute professor, who would later be my doctoral mentor, was introducing us to Greek philosophy and Jewish sectarianism. He made the suggestion, perhaps even implicitly, that understanding these ancient belief systems could actually aid us in understanding the New Testament and Christian theology. Though others had likely offered that suggestion to me before, something clicked that day. I began a series of conversations with this professor that eventually led to a course of study on the Apocrypha.

I had prior to that class only heard the term *Apocrypha* used as a mild expletive in reference to "those" books filled with heresies and thus shunned by "good Christians." (I'm only half kidding.) The journey accelerated in that course because of a very simple task. I actually read the Apocrypha. I began to see connections. I started to understand the value. I realized that there actually is quite a lot to glean from reading "those" books. From that beginning with the Apocrypha, I set out on a trajectory through the remainder of my seminary program and through my PhD to explore in more detail the "intertestamental" writings, which most now refer to as "Second Temple" or "early Jewish" texts. What began with the Apocrypha continued with the Pseudepigrapha, Dead Sea Scrolls and rabbinic writings. Through the journey, I was able to get a better sense of what Jews were thinking during and around the time of the New Testament.

THE "NEW PERSPECTIVE" ON PAUL

In combination with exploring Judaism, I was likewise introduced to the "new perspective on Paul" (NPP). Most credit E. P. Sanders with igniting somewhat of a revolution among New Testament interpreters in his *Paul and Palestinian Judaism*. Sanders, and the NPP in general, contends that Second Temple Judaism, more or less indicating the period from 500 B.C.E. to 70 C.E., did not view "works" as determinative for salvation, as many Pauline interpreters understand in Paul's contrast between "works" and "faith." Rather, some form of "covenantal nomism," Sanders argued, better described what Jews during the Second Temple period understood as "how to be saved" (though they would not have used that language). For Sanders, covenantal nomism puts the covenant at the center of our understand of what "keeping Torah" meant. This would not have meant "earning salvation" but rather represented the appropriate response to God's offer of the covenant, which was graciously given. Though critiques of Sanders's view have been offered, myself included in this work, it seems to me the correction prevails.

The NPP contains a good bit of diversity, and its three central figures, E. P. Sanders, James D. G. Dunn and N. T. Wright, certainly have their own share of differences. These differences primarily lie in how to tease out the relationship between Paul and Judaism rather than how to discern the nature of Judaism itself. What interested me at this intersection between Paul and Judaism was the question of election. But whereas the NPP debate has often centered on the question of the meaning of "works of the law," the "faithfulness of Jesus," the "righteousness of God" and what Paul's "justification" language means, "election" itself, something all three authors assume to be vital to the nature of Jewish thought, has received less attention. I was surprised to find many works at the intersection between Paul and Judaism talking "around" election rather than "about" it, which largely prompted my own approach.[1] The question this book explores concerns how Jewish authors spoke of election and how this background knowledge relates to Paul.

---

[1]N. T. Wright has offered significant contributions in this area, in particular in his recent two-volume work *Paul and the Faithfulness of God* (Minneapolis: Fortress, 2013).

ELECTION IN JUDAISM

I will spend a great deal of time laying out the various Jewish perspectives on election. Here, and briefly, I wish to tease out some general patterns among scholars concerning Jewish views of election. The headings here are my own, and I intend for them to represent as best as possible the views of the authors represented. There seem to be three basic camps among scholars as to the extent of Israel's election and the means by which it receives it: "national and unconditional," "national and cooperative" and "remnant-oriented and conditional."

G. F. Moore's summary in *Judaism in the First Centuries of the Christian Era* (1927) is frequently referenced in addressing the "national and unconditional" view of Israel's election. He states, "Salvation, or eternal life, is ultimately assured to every Israelite on the ground of the original election of the people by the free grace of God, prompted not by its merits, collective or individual, but solely on God's love."[2] W. D. Davies largely echoes this view in his *Paul and Rabbinic Judaism*, as does also, more recently, E. P. Sanders. Often those who hold this view rely heavily on the rabbinic materials, which many now hesitate to employ as sources for understanding the first century because of their late dating. Sanders's reason for relying more heavily on the rabbinic materials was primarily pragmatic.[3] The central point to his approach was that the view of Judaism as a merit-based religion, proposed by Ferdinand Weber, Emil Schürer and Wilhelm Bousset, among others, was misguided. Sanders's (now quite famous) explanation of the relationship between election and covenant was that "one is put in the covenant by the gracious election of God; one stays in it by observing the law and atoning for transgression."[4] S. Leyla Gürkan's more recent work reaffirms the idea of unconditional national election.[5] Gürkan envisions election as signifying "that 'all Israel,'

---

[2]G. F. Moore, *Judaism in the First Centuries of the Christian Era* (1927–1930; repr., Peabody, MA: Hendrickson, 1997), 2:94-95. See also 1:398-400; 1:542; 2:341.

[3]E. P. Sanders, *Paul and Palestinian Judaism* (Minneapolis: Fortress, 1970), pp. 24-25.

[4]E. P. Sanders, *Paul, the Law, and the Jewish People* (Minneapolis: Fortress, 1985), p. 45. He argues against the notion that what brought one into the covenant of the elect was works rather than election (of grace) (ibid., p. 50).

[5]Joel Lohr's text also works within a similar framework though he does not address the Second Temple background (see Joel N. Lohr, *Chosen and Unchosen: Conceptions of Election in the Pen-*

i.e. the descendants of Jacob, are chosen through 'an everlasting covenant,'"[6] and that "unlike the writings of the Qumran community, the notion of 'true Israel' as associated with a particular group within the people of Israel does not appear in the apocryphal and pseudepigraphal books."[7] This statement is, however, in tension with her recognition of the presence of the remnant motif in that body of literature, which of course asserts primarily that there is a particular group within Israel that is the "true Israel."

Favoring the "national and cooperative" view, Joseph Bonsirven, in his 1964 work *Palestinian Judaism in the Time of Jesus Christ*, primarily employed the rabbinic sources and used only a handful of texts from the Apocrypha and Pseudepigrapha. Bonsirven suggested the rabbis understood Abraham's election as a reward for his righteousness and noted that the same theme is present in the Apocrypha, Philo and Josephus.[8] The merits of the patriarchs, and of later Israel, as well as the gratuity of God (what Bonsirven refers to as a "reciprocal choice"[9]), together brought about Israel's election, which was of a national nature.[10] Bonsirven understands this as a national/ethnic concept, and notes a tension within the Jewish writings between understanding this election as conditional (i.e., dependent on keeping Torah) and unconditional. Simon Gathercole[11] seeks to counter the view that Jewish "boasting" was primarily because of either their "works-righteousness" or their "*national* righteousness" received through their election.[12] Gathercole argues that both election and

---

tateuch and Jewish-Christian Interpretation [Winona Lake, IN: Eisenbrauns, 2009]).

[6]S. Leyla Gürkan, *The Jews as a Chosen People: Tradition and Transformation* (New York: Routledge, 2009), p. 22.

[7]Ibid., p. 24.

[8]Joseph Bonsirven, *Palestinian Judaism in the Time of Jesus Christ* (New York: Holt, Rinehart & Winston, 1964), p. 43.

[9]Ibid., p. 46.

[10]Ibid., pp. 44-45. Köhler sees a deep connection between the election and mission of Israel and, similar to Bonsirven, notes that this election is rooted in the merits of the patriarchs as well as in God's love (Kaufmann Köhler, *Jewish Theology: Systematically and Historically Considered* [New York: Macmillan, 1918], p. 406). Köhler affirmed the centrality of election to the Jewish religion and recognized it as the key to understanding the nature of Judaism (ibid., p. 323).

[11]Simon J. Gathercole, *Where Is Boasting? Early Jewish Soteriology and Paul's Response in Romans 1–5* (Grand Rapids: Eerdmans, 2002).

[12]Ibid., p. 263.

obedience were a part of the Jewish confidence. Gathercole sees election and obedience as compatible when obedience is understood as the "basis for vindication at the *eschaton*,"[13] a theme he also sees in Paul.

The late Mark Adam Elliott, in his 2000 publication *The Survivors of Israel: A Reconsideration of the Theology of Pre-Christian Judaism*, offered a significant critique of Sanders's view by calling "a third 'pillar' belief to the bench. This is the doctrine, widely assumed to belong *universally* to Judaism, of the *irrevocable national election of Israel*."[14] Elliott contended that, due to poor historical methodology, the standard interpretation of Second Temple Judaism's beliefs concerning election has been seen primarily as nationalistic and unconditioned due to an anachronistic projection of the beliefs of rabbinic Judaism onto the Second Temple materials. In his study, Elliott examined the Dead Sea Scrolls and the Pseudepigrapha, to argue that an unconditional, nationalistic view of Israel's election cannot sufficiently account for the preponderance of evidence. He instead contends, rightly in my mind, that a conditional view of covenant was predominant,[15] rooted in a soteriological dualism in which the unrighteous are composed of both the nations and apostate Israel while the righteous/elect are members of the preserved "remnant" who are faithful to the covenant. As he summarizes, "*The conventional nationalistic view of election theology is not accurately reflective of at least some important pre-Christian Jewish groups*; in contradistinction to past treatments, moreover, one must conclude from such evidence that a *Jewish theology of special election existed well in advance of the New Testament period*."[16] Likewise, Sigurd Grindheim has concluded that election was associated closely with law observance, and was frequently pictured as relevant only to a faithful remnant and not to the whole nation of Israel.[17] Grindheim concludes that Paul, at least in part, critiques the idea

---

[13]Ibid., pp. 263-64.
[14]Mark Adam Elliott, *The Survivors of Israel: A Reconsideration of the Theology of Pre-Christian Judaism* (Grand Rapids: Eerdmans, 2000), p. 28.
[15]Ibid., p. 639.
[16]Ibid., p. 640 (emphasis original).
[17]Sigurd Grindheim, *The Crux of Election: Paul's Critique of the Jewish Confidence in the Election of Israel* (Tübingen: Mohr Siebeck, 2005), pp. 2, 75-76.

that visible status claims among the Jewish people acted as evidence of membership in the elect.[18] More radically, Chris VanLandingham argues that, within late Second Temple Judaism, "election (like salvation) is *not* a gift of God's grace, but a reward for proper behavior."[19] VanLandingham sees the foundation of the argument as resting with Abraham. If Abraham received the covenant by God's gratuity then Israel likewise receives it as such, but if he received the covenant because of his righteous merits, then Israel has likewise received it. God's bestowal of the covenants came because of God's response to Abraham's righteousness, and "the mercy God grants to Israel is not given to each individual, but only to the entity of Israel."[20]

Elliott, Grindheim and VanLandingham rightly recognize that Sanders may have swung the pendulum too far as it relates to Jewish beliefs concerning election. Elliott in particular demonstrates the extent to which a conditional/remnant-focused view of election persisted throughout Judaism. This does not, however, return us to a pre-Sanders understanding of Second Temple Judaism according to which salvation can be earned by tipping the scales of judgment through good behavior. But rather it recognizes that there were both conditional and unconditional elements to the covenant in the thinking of many, if not most, Jewish authors of this time, something that resonates with the Old Testament itself and that I will suggest also helps us make better sense of Paul.[21]

METHOD AND APPROACH

The basic thrust of this study will be to answer two key questions: (1) How did Jews during the Second Temple period understand the nature

---

[18]Ibid., p. 196.

[19]Chris VanLandingham, *Judgment and Justification in Early Judaism and the Apostle Paul* (Grand Rapids: Baker Academic, 2006), p. 18.

[20]Ibid., p. 65.

[21]It seems best to view the covenant as unconditional in terms of God's commitment to it, but conditional in terms of how Israel relates to God through it. Kessler helpfully suggests, "Thus, while Yahweh's election of Israel is unconditional, an ongoing experiential covenantal relationship with Yahweh is conditioned upon the willingness of Israel to 'abide within the covenant's demands'" (John Kessler, *Old Testament Theology: Divine Call and Human Response* [Waco: Baylor University Press, 2013], p. 267).

of their election? And (2) how does one's understanding of Jewish idea(s) of election influence how one might understand the key Pauline texts that address election? The first question contains several subquestions, which I will address to various degrees. I will primarily focus on Jewish concepts of the nature of election as they relate to the questions of "extent" (ethnic/national or remnant?), the relationship to the individual (corporate or individual in focus?) and the relationship to salvation (divine/human agency and the presence of "conditions"). I will likewise address whether these authors viewed election as merited or given graciously, but only as it connects to the primary questions noted above.

Before beginning our examination, I must make some summary statements about how we might make such a comparison. First, I recognize Paul operated within a historical and cultural context that shaped his thinking and influenced how he might have expressed certain ideas. This notion comes with less controversy now than perhaps it did in the past, but we must remind ourselves of it nonetheless. Paul reacts against "Jewish theology" (or we might say Christless Jewish theology—Paul would have considered himself a Jewish "theologian"), but he himself is also a product of it, steeped both in the Old Testament and in the traditions of first-century Jews. We should not, then, expect Paul always to run counter to Jewish ideas. Much more often the influence of those ideas stands out.

We must also recognize that when we speak of "Judaism" we do not speak of a monolithic entity in which everyone believes the same way. Certain core ideas resonate with all Jews, no doubt (e.g., monotheism, election, Torah), but great variety is present as well. As such, I will attempt to recognize the variations present in the literature when they exist, while also recognizing the commonalities. As much as possible I will attempt to let the texts "speak for themselves," meaning I will attempt to engage with the interests of these texts as they relate to the questions rather than to foist these questions on them. Gathercole suggested such an approach in arguing, "If one is exploring the dispute between Paul and Judaism, we need to understand not only the Jewish texts on their own terms, but also Judaism *on Paul's terms*."[22] This is certainly sound advice. We cannot only consider Jewish beliefs, but from there we must also consider in what ways Paul interacts with those beliefs. The proper approach is thus to understand these texts as separate entities before asking how they relate to Paul rather than adopting some preconceived framework about Paul's beliefs and then seeking to justify it by finding supporting literature from Jewish sources.

As it concerns the examination of these specific texts, I will seek to approach them with sensitivity to social, historical and literary factors in the text. Since these texts come to us from different centuries within the late Second Temple period and address different events that motivated their composition, we must consider the historical background of each text in both an immediate and extended sense, in order to properly contextualize its contents. In addition to historical concerns, we must consider the literary and social setting of each text. Here genre and form certainly come to bear on the meaning of the text as well as a consideration of why the author wrote and what they originally intended to accomplish. By social analysis, I will attempt to attend to the social factors that may have influenced the development of a particular theological expression.[23] I will not seek, as do many who focus on social factors, to uphold or apply a particular "model" of sociological theory in relation to the texts and movements studied herein,[24] but rather to operate with an awareness of the underlying social factors that are at work in the various texts under examination.[25] Elliott's approach offers a helpful model. He

---

[22]Gathercole, *Where Is Boasting?*, p. 26.

[23]As Elliott has stated, "it is nevertheless important to acknowledge that the influences of social factors in the Second Temple period have been more or less proven to possess real (only some would say predominating) significance for the formation and explication of Jewish theology" (Elliott, *Survivors of Israel*, p. 7).

[24]For background information on social models and New Testament studies, see John Hall Elliott, "Social-Scientific Criticism of the New Testament: More on Methods and Models," *Semeia* 35 (1986): 1-33.

[25]As Horrell has recognized, "Those who advocate a model-based approach insist that their use of models is heuristic and not prescriptive, and that only if the data fit the model will its use be justified. . . . But any particular model *shapes* the way in which evidence is selected and interpreted" (David G. Horrell, "Social-Scientific Interpretation of the New Testament: Retrospect and Prospect," in *Social-Scientific Approaches to New Testament Interpretation*, ed. David G. Horrell [Edinburgh: T&T Clark, 1999], pp. 19-20).

speaks of a "socioliterary" function, which he defines as follows: "texts not only *say* something, they also *do* something. Not only do religious authors intend to express theological teachings or propositions by writing, in other words, but consistently (if unconsciously) there would appear to be some *purpose* for their writing in the first place, and this purpose forms an essential part of the communication."[26] The basic question to ask is, What did the author seek to accomplish in composing this text in this way? To some extent, then, we will seek to understand the "thought world" of late Second Temple Judaism concerning the theme of election. Though I will obviously not be able to create a complete picture of this thought world, I do seek to deal with all of the available evidence that comes to bear on the issue. So we must construct this thought world in order to consider what a text could have meant within that thought world and exclude what it could not have meant to those who may have read it in the late Second Temple setting. I will thus aim to examine the materials selected with sensitivity to these issues.

SOURCES

The sources I will examine in this study are both chronologically and theologically diverse. Since I will examine Jewish beliefs during the Second Temple period (and specifically the late Second Temple period) concerning election, I will focus on the literature of this period that gives a glimpse into the thought world of first-century Jews. The sources I will consider primarily date to pre-70 C.E. in their composition and come from Jewish origins. Our ultimate goal is, again, to gain an understanding of Jewish perspectives[27] of election leading up to the time in which the New Testament, and specifically Pauline materials, came about. I will

---

[26]Elliott, *Survivors of Israel*, p. 9. This is, in general, a recognition of the basic principles of "speech-act" theory in which it is argued that texts are written not only to inform, but to bring about some action on the part of the intended reader. This is the distinction made between the illocution (the intended message) and perlocution (the intended result of the message). Thus it is argued that words don't just have intended meaning, but also intended actions or results.

[27]It is common to speak now of "Judaisms" rather than of Judaism, recognizing the variety that existed within Jewish monotheistic beliefs during this time. See James H. Charlesworth, *The Old Testament Pseudepigrapha and the New Testament* (Cambridge: Cambridge University Press, 1985), p. 56.

examine various texts from the Dead Sea Scrolls (DSS),[28] Apocrypha and Pseudepigrapha.

Dead Sea Scrolls. The writings found at Qumran in the mid-twentieth century have provided new and important insights into both the world of Second Temple Judaism and have shed new light on certain areas of New Testament studies (e.g., the Jewish concepts of Messiah, apocalypse, Torah, soteriology). We can place these writings with fair certainty in the late Second Temple period, as most scholars date the bulk of the materials to the first century B.C.E., with some texts dated at various points between the third century B.C.E. and the first century C.E.[29] We should first consider several questions about the nature of the community. The primary question at hand is how the beliefs of the scrolls community related to the larger picture of Second Temple Palestinian Judaism, though we must also ask who the members of this community were and what connection they had with Jews outside of their community.

Concerning the first question, of the identity of the DSS community, several suggestions have been proposed. The dominant view among scholars today, however, identifies the scrolls community as some sort of Essenic sect given the numerous similarities between what we know of this community through their own texts and what we know of the Essenes in Josephus.[30] Concerning "outsiders," the documents of the sect

---

[28]Though there were nonsectarian documents found at Qumran, such as copies of Old Testament books and noncanonical writings such as *Jubilees*, I employ the designation DSS to refer specifically to the sectarian documents found at Qumran.

[29]See Geza Vermes, *An Introduction to the Complete Dead Sea Scrolls* (Minneapolis: Fortress, 2000), pp. 11-12.

[30]As Vermes asserts, "If its intricacies are handled with sophistication, it is still the best *hypothesis* today. . . . Indeed, it accounts best for such striking peculiarities as common ownership of property and the lack of reference to women in the Community Rule; the probable co-existence of celibate and married sectaries . . . and the remarkable coincidence between the geographical setting of Qumran and Pliny the Elder's description of an Essene establishment near the Dead Sea between Jericho and Engedi" (ibid., p. 12). For their relevance to this study, Elliott helpfully puts the debate into perspective in summarizing, "Even if the scrolls were penned or edited by more than one specific group, they nonetheless preserve a more or less *common point of view*" (Elliott, *Survivors of Israel*, p. 21). Schiffman has argued that the community is connected to the Sadducees, and Golb has suggested a single sect was not responsible for them (Lawrence H. Schiffman, *Reclaiming the Dead Sea Scrolls: Their True Meaning for Judaism and Christianity* [New York: Doubleday, 1995]; Norman Golb, *Who Wrote the Dead Sea Scrolls? The Search for the Secret of Qumran* [New York: Scribner, 1995]).

seem to indicate a definitive sense of separation from the temple establishment.[31] There was general disdain among the community for the priesthood in Jerusalem, which they viewed as corrupt. The location of the community also isolated them from outsiders.[32] As David Flusser has demonstrated, interaction with and possible persecution from the Pharisees and Sadducees and the Essenes prior to their (partial?) withdrawal to the desert existed, as we see in several of the pesher scrolls found at Qumran.[33] Some of the "rules" of the community, however, indicate there was contact, albeit limited, with outsiders, which we might imagine must be necessary for a remote desert group.[34] According to Josephus, the Essenes still interacted at the Jerusalem temple, though they refused to sacrifice there (*Ant.* 18.1.5). Josephus also demonstrated some knowledge, though limited, of the beliefs of the sect, such as their proneness to "determinism" (*Ant.* 13.5.9), their reclusive lifestyle and their strict rules concerning money and property (*Ant.* 18.1.5).[35]

"Apocryphal" texts. The writings of the Apocrypha can generally be dated with fair confidence to the late Second Temple period, prior to the composition of the New Testament and primarily of Palestinian provenance. Those whose contents bear on the questions addressed in this study are Tobit (ca. 200 B.C.E.), the Wisdom of Ben Sira (ca. 175 B.C.E.),[36] Baruch (ca. 150 B.C.E.), 1 and 2 Maccabees (both ca. 125 B.C.E.) and

---

[31]See Lawrence H. Schiffman, *Qumran and Jerusalem: Studies in the Dead Sea Scrolls and the History of Judaism* (Grand Rapids: Eerdmans, 2010), pp. 86-87.

[32]David Flusser, *Judaism of the Second Temple Period* (Grand Rapids: Eerdmans, 2007), 1:9.

[33]Ibid., 1:224-35.

[34]See Florentino García Martínez, *Echoes from the Caves: Qumran and the New Testament* (Leiden: Brill, 2009), p. 219; Marcus K. M. Tso, *Ethics in the Qumran Community* (Tübingen: Mohr Siebeck, 2010), p. 117. Harrington likewise affirms, "Labelling outsiders ritually as well as morally impure helped to preserve the group's identity as a community set apart to maintain holiness in Israel" (Hannah K. Harrington, *The Purity Texts* [New York: T&T Clark, 2004], p. 112). Baumgarten also sees it likely that there was some inevitable contact with outsiders among members of the community (Joseph M. Baumgarten, *Studies in Qumran Law* [Leiden: Brill, 1977], p. 73).

[35]See Alison Schofield, *From Qumran to the Yahad: A New Paradigm of Textual Development for The Community Rule* (Leiden: Brill, 2009), p. 204. Flusser suggests that the Qumran community likely, at least at points in their history, intended to eventually reform Jewish life and persuade the people to stop following the errant teachings of the Pharisees (Flusser, *Judaism*, 1:244).

[36]This text is sometimes referred to by the titles Sirach, Ecclesiasticus, the Wisdom of Sirach or the Wisdom of Ben Sira.

Wisdom of Solomon[37] (near the end of the first century B.C.E. or the
beginning of the first century C.E.). Though some books were more influential in Second Temple Judaism than others (Ben Sira, for example,
is frequently afforded fairly prominent status), I will examine these texts
together, seeking to identify areas of commonality and disagreement in
the realm of Jewish literature during this period.[38]

"Pseudepigraphical" texts. Like the apocryphal writings, the pseudepigraphical materials do not belong to a single period or provenance.[39]
Their contents must thus be treated with care as it concerns the significance of an individual writing in relation to the "whole" of Judaism at
the time. Within the pseudepigraphical "Old Testament" writings, we
can identify a number of texts within the late Second Temple period. For
our purposes, this includes *Jubilees* (ca. 150 B.C.E.), *Testaments of the
Twelve Patriarchs* (ca. 150 B.C.E.),[40] the additional Psalms of David (151A,
152, 153 and 155 [5ApocSyrPs 3], ca. first century B.C.E. or earlier), the
Psalms of Solomon (ca. 100 B.C.E.), the *Sibylline Oracles* (near the end of
the first century B.C.E. or the beginning of the first century C.E.),[41] *Biblical*

---

[37]The Wisdom of Solomon is a text of Egyptian provenance that was heavily influenced by Greek
literature and philosophy. This text has been included in this study because it appears to have
been widely circulated across the Roman Empire by the end of the first century and it may have
also had some influence on some New Testament passages (see Lester Grabbe, *Wisdom of Solomon* [New York: T&T Clark, 1997], pp. 28-29).

[38]All translations of the Apocrypha are taken from the NRSV.

[39]For OT Pseudepigraphal texts, all translations are taken from James H. Charlesworth, ed., *The
Old Testament Pseudepigrapha*, vols. 1-2 (Peabody, MA: Hendrickson Publishers, 2010), unless
otherwise noted.

[40]The *Testaments of the Twelve Patriarchs* is a text of Jewish origin likely dating to the Maccabean
period. The textual history of this testament is complex, with at least two recensions of the text
available, having been translated into Armenian, Slavonic, late Hebrew and Aramaic, though the
text itself is likely of Greek origin (see H. C. Kee, "Testaments of the Twelve Patriarchs," in *The Old
Testament Pseudepigrapha*, vol. 1, *Apocalyptic Literature and Testaments*, ed. James H. Charlesworth [1983; repr., Peabody, MA: Hendrickson, 2011], pp. 775-77). The text contains later Christian interpolations, though it is clearly of an original Jewish origin that predates the composition
of the New Testament. As Elliott has summarized, "The continuity in subject matter and unifor-
mity of structure within and throughout the present *Testaments* suggests a basic unity of composition . . . [with a preferred] Hasmonean date" (Elliott, *Survivors of Israel*, p. 25).

[41]The collection known as the *Sibylline Oracles* has a wide range of compositional dates assigned to
its various books, ranging somewhere from the second century B.C.E. to the seventh century C.E.
(John J. Collins, "Sibylline Oracles," in Charlesworth, *Apocalyptic Literature and Testaments*, p.
317. The later books in the collection are primarily Christian in nature and postdate the period
under examination in this study). Of the fourteen books and fragments included in the collection,
four can be dated to the period under examination (i.e., books 3 [ca. 163-45 B.C.E.], 4 [ca. 80 C.E.]

Antiquities (*Pseudo-Philo*) (early first century C.E.),[42] the *Testament of Moses* (early first century C.E.)[43] and *1 Enoch*.[44]

SUMMARY OF CHAPTERS

Preliminaries aside, we will begin our journey in chapter two by looking at how various Jewish sources and Paul's letters discuss the concept of election as it relates to specific individuals, which I will argue typically either emphasizes the character or designated role of the "chosen one" or depicts him as a "representative head." The third chapter will show that the Jewish emphasis typically falls on the collective, illustrated through various corporate metaphors and the remnant motif, and suggest Paul shares a similar emphasis. In chapter four, I will seek to tease out how the various groups and Paul defined the parameters of God's people via what "markers" or "conditions" defined these various groups, both implicitly and explicitly. The fifth chapter will look at how our Jewish texts view Jew and Gentile inclusion and exclusion before examining the same discussion in Paul's writings. Chapter six will then look at the issue of divine agency and human responsibility across these writings. In chapter seven, I will offer a rereading of Romans 8:26–11:36 based on my examination of Jewish theology and Paul's thought. Finally, in chapter eight, after a summary of my findings I will ask what we gain from this view and also suggest further work that needs to be done in this area. This is where we are headed, but first we begin with election and the individual.

---

and 5 [ca. 80 C.E.]). Book 11 was likely composed near the turn of the era (see ibid., pp. 430-32), but its contents are not relevant to the focus of this study. Books 1 and 2, though likely of early origin, contain later Christian interpolations. The Jewish phases of books 1 and 2 can be placed near the end of the first century B.C.E. or the beginning of the first century C.E. (ibid., p. 331).

[42]See Daniel J. Harrington, "Pseudo-Philo," in Charlesworth, *Apocalyptic Literature and Testaments*, p. 299.

[43]See Johannes Tromp, "Moses, Assumption of," in *The Eerdmans Dictionary of Early Judaism*, ed. John J. Collins and Daniel C. Harlow (Grand Rapids: Eerdmans, 2010), p. 971.

[44]The book known as *1 Enoch*, like many of this period, has a complex compositional history. The majority of the text is dated by a consensus to before 160 B.C.E. (John J. Collins, "Enoch, Ethiopic Apocalypse of (1 Enoch)," in *The Eerdmans Dictionary of Early Judaism*, ed. John J. Collins and Daniel C. Harlow [Grand Rapids: Eerdmans, 2010], p. 585). See also George W. E. Nickelsburg, *Jewish Literature Between the Bible and the Mishnah* (Minneapolis: Fortress, 2005), p. 255; Michael A. Knibb, "Enoch, Similitudes of (1 Enoch 37–71)," in Collins and Harlow, *Eerdmans Dictionary of Early Judaism*, p. 587.

God Chose Whom?

Election and the Individual

As we begin our examination of Paul's thought in light of Judaism, my goal is to lay out the Jewish framework for thinking about "election" and to explore its implications for our understanding of Paul. From the outset, I admit the categories of thinking about election in terms of "individuals" and "collectives" are *in a sense* artificial, since the texts themselves do not speak in these terms. However, there are themes that come into view when individuals are in focus but vary when the collective is in focus, and so I maintain the importance if not the necessity of the distinction. These themes at times, of course, overlap, but the uniquenesses are enough that it merits their separate examination.

THE CHARACTER OF THE ELECT

One of the features Second Temple literature sometimes emphasizes is the character of the elect.[1] The general piety, or specific covenant faithfulness, of certain individuals, or at times even of the elect in general, is often on display. To be elect, as will be argued below, is more commonly not associated with a "soteriological" status (Jews did not necessarily think in those categories) but rather with the quality of the individual (or sometimes group) in view.

---

[1] I should note from the outset that there are genuine disagreements concerning the dating of some of these texts. I have attempted to adopt the dating schemes employed by a majority of scholars in selecting which materials may best represent the world of Judaism with which Paul would have been familiar (i.e., not those texts written after his lifetime).

Wisdom of Ben Sira. The book of Ben Sira (also known as Sirach or Ecclesiasticus) is perhaps the most well-known of the extrabiblical Jewish wisdom texts. The bulk of the contents of the book present the application of wisdom in social scenarios, primarily in the family, community and marketplace. The book contributes to the wisdom genre with its personification of Wisdom, which it connects deeply to Torah,[2] and its "hymn" directed to the ancestors of Israel. Like other texts in the wisdom tradition, Ben Sira's focus is not "otherworldly," and there is scant evidence that he envisions any sort of afterlife.[3] Thus his treatment of election must be set in such a context. The issue in Ben Sira is further complicated by his frequent oscillation between the general and the particular, at times speaking directly of Israel and at times of humanity in general.

We find the fullest discussion of election in Ben Sira (outside of, perhaps, Sir 24) in the hymn of Sirach 44:1–50:29. Scholars have debated the "genre" of this hymn.[4] The hymn opens with a summary of the legacy left by these "famous men" (Sir 44:1-15), and traces Israel's history through select ancestors from Adam to the author's contemporary Simon son of Onias. According to Burton Mack, the hymn follows a certain pattern of description. Mack recognizes the individual's office, election, relationship to covenant, character, work, historical situation and rewards as recurring themes in the hymn.[5] For Mack the office of these

---

[2]There is some disagreement, as Goering traces, as to which element controls the other: whether Torah is dominant over wisdom, or wisdom over Torah. Goering's suggestion is that the two are correlated, that wisdom is a "general revelation" given by Yahweh to all humanity, while Torah is special revelation, given to the chosen people of Israel (Greg S. Goering, *Wisdom's Root Revealed: Ben Sira and the Election of Israel,* JSJSup 139 [Leiden: Brill, 2009], pp. 5-9). Goering thus suggests, "Ben Sira maintains a focus upon the universal concern of the wisdom tradition for the well-being of all humanity and also upon the particular traditions of Israel's own national heritage contained within its ancient literature" (ibid., p. 14).

[3]As Gilbert states quite bluntly, "Because Ben Sira has no idea of an afterlife, man is called to praise the Lord during his time on earth" (Maurice Gilbert, "God, Sin and Mercy: Sirach 15:11-18:14," in *Ben Sira's God: Proceedings of the International Ben Sira Conference,* ed. Renate Egger-Wenzel [Berlin: de Gruyter, 2002], p. 130).

[4]As Collins summarizes, this includes a remembrance of heroes, exemplum, *De Viris Illustribus,* succession, epic poem and encomium, which he favors (John J. Collins, *Jewish Wisdom in the Hellenistic Age* [Louisville: Westminster John Knox, 1997], pp. 98-100).

[5]See Burton L. Mack, *Wisdom and the Hebrew Epic: Ben Sira's Hymn in Praise of the Fathers* (Chicago: University of Chicago Press, 1986), p. 18. These elements are not present, at least fully, in each individual described.

men determines the pattern to the extent that the "greatness of these heroes is directly related to the great significance of these offices."[6] While that may be true to an extent, what is mentioned of nearly every individual, even of those who held no formal office, is their work or character.[7] As he recounts Israel's men of fame, Ben Sira presents their righteous behavior before recognizing God's gracious response to or blessing of them.[8] God's choosing is mentioned explicitly only in the cases of Moses (Sir 45:4), Aaron (Sir 45:16) and David (Sir 47:2). Moses' election is described in connection with his faithfulness and meekness,[9] while God's choice is simply affirmed of Aaron and David with no emphasis on sequence or causation. The emphasis in this chapter on the deeds and piety of these characters thus makes it plausible to understand, as Sigurd Grindheim has suggested, "divine election as based on the ethical and religious quality of the elect."[10]

The climax of the hymn is in Ben Sira's praise of Simon, son of Onias, the high priest (Sir 50:1-29). Though the author lauds David's descendants in several places in the hymn, it seems that Ben Sira, as Greg Goering states, "indicates that the high priest had assumed some of the functions previously performed by the king."[11] Don Garlington affirms this interpretation in suggesting that "for Ben Sira Simon is the Messiah. . . . The priest is depicted as possessing messianic traits; his priesthood is

---

[6]Ibid., p. 19.

[7]Only Isaac and Jacob are not mentioned in connection with any praise of their works or character for whom it is said only that God upheld his covenant and blessings to them and their children (Sir 44:22-23).

[8]Enoch pleased the Lord, and then was taken up (Sir 44:16); Noah was righteous and then received a covenant (Sir 44:17-18); Abraham kept the law and then received the covenant (Sir 44:19-21); Isaac received the covenant for Abraham's sake (Sir 44:22); Moses was merciful and highly favored and was then made God's spokesman (Sir 45:1-5); Aaron was a holy man and received an everlasting covenant (Sir 45:6-22); Phineas had zeal and courage and was then given a covenant of peace (Sir 45:23-26). This pattern repeats throughout the hymn of the ancestors. The only exception when the character or work of the man is mentioned along with God's benevolence toward him (whether through blessing, reward, covenant, etc.) is David, whose being "set apart from the Israelites" is the first detail mentioned in his section of the hymn (Sir 47:2).

[9]The LXX reads, ἐν πίστει καὶ πραΰτητι αὐτὸν ἡγίασεν, ἐξελέξατο αὐτὸν ἐκ πάσης σαρκός. The question here is how to read the preposition ἐν and the participle ἐξελέξατο.

[10]Sigurd Grindheim, The Crux of Election: Paul's Critique of the Jewish Confidence in the Election of Israel (Tübingen: Mohr Siebeck, 2005), p. 37.

[11]Goering, Wisdom's Root Revealed, p. 123.

the guarantee of the continued existence and peace of Israel. . . . He stands in the line of David and Hezekiah . . . [and] salvation is present" in him, though in a "'this-worldly' way."[12] Wisdom and election thus have culminated in Israel's history, for Ben Sira, in the current peace enjoyed under Simon, which he prays is sustained in the future of Israel (Sir 50:23). God's choice, in these examples, is fundamentally connected to their character, role and pious deeds.

Additional Psalms of David. Prior to their discovery at Qumran, the additional psalms of David survived primarily through Syriac copies, and scholars referred to them as the Syriac noncanonical psalms.[13] Of these psalms, Psalms 151A, 151B and 155 are present within the Qumran Psalms Scroll (11QPs[a]), and are thus clearly pre-Christian in their composition. Psalms 152 and 153 were not contained in the Psalms Scroll, though this does not exclude the possibility that they are pre-Christian in origin. While scholars have given the most attention to their compositional history, and especially to the relationship between the Hebrew, Greek and Syriac versions in light of the discovery of the Qumran Psalms Scroll,[14] their content nonetheless contributes to an understanding of Second Temple Jewish beliefs.

---

[12]Don B. Garlington, *The Obedience of Faith: A Pauline Phrase in Historical Context* (Tübingen: Mohr Siebeck, 1991), p. 48.

[13]Though discovered at Qumran, these psalms, and specifically Psalms 151 and 155, are thought to predate the Qumran community and thus are not necessarily sectarian or Essenic in origin. Charlesworth and Sanders write, "Some distinguished scholars [Philonenko, Delcor and Dupont-Sommer] have argued that one or more of these pseudepigraphical psalms were composed by the Essenes, the authors of the Dead Sea Scrolls. Most scholars, however, conclude correctly that while some passages can be interpreted in line with Essene theology, this possibility does not indicate that these psalms were composed by the Essenes, who shared ideas with other Jews contemporaneous with them" (James H. Charlesworth and James A. Sanders, "More Psalms of David," in *The Old Testament Pseudepigrapha*, vol. 2, *Expansions of the "Old Testament" and Legends, Wisdom and Philosophical Literature, Prayers, Psalms, and Odes, Fragments of Lost Judeo-Hellenistic Works*, ed. James H. Charlesworth [1985; repr., Peabody, MA: Hendrickson, 2011], p. 610).

[14]For discussions, see Hans Debel, "De psalm die 'buiten het getal valt': Psalm 151 in de Septuaginta en in de rollen van de Dode Zee," *Collationes* 1, no. 1 (2010): 7-20; Florentino García Martínez, "Salmos Apócrifos en Qumran," *Estudios* 40, nos. 3-4 (1982): 197-220; Elisha Qimron, "Some Remarks on the Apocryphal Psalm 155 (11QPs[a] Column 24)," *JSP* 5, no. 57 (1992): 57-59; James A. Sanders, *The Dead Sea Psalms Scroll* (Ithaca, NY: Cornell University Press, 1967); Sanders, "Two Non-Canonical Psalms in 11QPs," *Zeitschrift für die alttestamentliche Wissenschaft* 76 (1964): 64-76; John Strugnell, "Notes on the Text and Transmission of the Apocryphal Psalms 151, 154 (=Syr. II) and 155 (=Syr III)," *HTR* 59, no. 3 (1966): 257-81; Herrie F. Van Rooy, ed., *Studies on the Syriac Apocryphal Psalms*, JSSSup 7 (Oxford: Oxford University Press, 2000).

Psalm 152 is contained in the Syriac collection but did not exist (or survive) at Qumran and is not found in the Qumran Psalms Scroll. The original provenance, authorship and date of the psalm are thus indeterminable.[15] This Syriac psalm describes an encounter between David and a lion and wolf that had attacked his flocks. In Psalm 152:4, the psalmist declares, "Spare, O Lord, your elect one;[16] and deliver your holy one from destruction." The main theme of the psalm is rescue from danger and death, and the psalmist here seems to plea to God for salvation based on his standing before God. As an "elect one" and a "holy one," David's plea rests on God's calling of him, presumably for the role of ruler and king. It is noteworthy here that "elect one" and "holy one" are offered as parallel terms and again likely emphasize character over soteriological status. The underlying expectation seems to be that if David dies, God's purposes for him (and his kingdom) will be thwarted. The explicit purpose is that, through continuing in life, the psalmist may continue to praise the name of God (Ps 152:4), thus validating the need for God's intervention.

Like Psalm 152, the date and provenance of Psalm 153 are not determinable. It might, like Psalm 152, be originally Hebrew and from the Hellenistic period, but this is determined more by association than internal evidence.[17] Also like Psalm 152, the psalm's reference to David's election occurs in the context of deliverance from danger, though here it is retrospective. God has "delivered the physical life of his elect one from the hands of death; and he redeemed his holy one from destruction" (Ps 153:2). Here again "elect" and "holy" are paralleled, and the result of David's deliverance is that he will continue to praise and exalt God (Ps 153:6).

Like Psalm 151, Psalm 155 is most certainly Jewish in its original composition in that it is included in the collection of the Qumran Psalms

---

[15]As Charlesworth and Sanders suggest, "It is impossible to date this psalm. The general tone, Jewish but non-rabbinic character, and association with Psalms 151, 154, and 155 indicate that it was probably composed by a Palestinian Jew during the hellenistic period" (Charlesworth and Sanders, "More Psalms of David," p. 615). See also Van Rooy, *Studies on the Syriac Apocryphal Psalms*, p. 122.

[16]"Your elect one" is omitted outside of the Syriac manuscripts.

[17]Charlesworth and Sanders, "More Psalms of David," p. 616. See also Van Rooy, *Studies on the Syriac Apocryphal Psalms*, p. 132.

Scroll. While the Hebrew text lacks a title, the Syriac version (5Apoc-SyrPs 3) situates the psalm with Hezekiah's request for deliverance from the Assyrians. The end of the Hebrew version is lost due to the decay of the manuscript prior to its discovery. The Syriac version, however, which closely parallels the extant portions of the Hebrew version, concludes with a plea to "Save Israel, your elect one; and those of the house of Jacob, your chosen one" (Ps 155:21). James Charlesworth and James Sanders add that one could render "chosen one" here as "tried (or approved) one."[18] God's choice in Psalm 155 of Israel and the house of Jacob serves as the basis for the plea for deliverance. It is possible that "those of the house of Jacob" is a reference to faithful Israel, and that "elect one" and "chosen one" act as descriptors of the faithfulness of the people, or more narrowly of Jacob/Israel as God's chosen channel of the covenant.[19]

Though brief, these noncanonical psalms appear to emphasize the *character* or *office* of the elect rather than their soteriological status. The psalmist portrays David as a pious young man rewarded for his character, a message that resonated strongly with many Jewish people of the period.[20] It is not David's physical abilities, but his piety and pure heart, that establish him as the "right man for the job." Psalm 152 and Psalm 153 likewise emphasize the ethical aspect of election in that the psalmist employs "elect" and "holy" as parallel terms. Though less obvious than the examples above, Psalm 155 may also plea for God's salvation of Israel based on their faithfulness to him or based on his covenant with Jacob. This again shows that election in Second Temple Jewish thought represented more than God's uninfluenced and predetermined choice of in-

---

[18]Charlesworth and Sanders, "More Psalms of David," p. 624 n. v. Falk states that "the psalmist offers no personal qualifications to elicit God's help, but appeals only to God's reputation, his simple trust, and God's election of Israel/Jacob (Syriac 10, 17, 21; 11QPsᵃ 24:9, 15)" (Daniel Falk, "Psalms and Prayers," in *Justification and Variegated Nomism*, vol. 1, *The Complexities of Second Temple Judaism*, ed. D. A. Carson, Peter T. O'Brien and Mark A. Seifrid [Grand Rapids: Baker Academic, 2001], p. 23). This assumes that the purpose of God teaching him Torah is not to aid him in covenant obedience.

[19]Abegg, Flint and Ulrich translate "elect one" here as "faithful one" (Martin Abegg Jr., Peter Flint and Eugene Ulrich, eds., *The Dead Sea Scrolls Bible* [New York: HarperCollins, 1999], p. 580).

[20]See Natalio Fernández-Marcos, "David the Adolescent: On Psalm 151," in *The Old Greek Psalter: Studies in Honor of Albert Pietersma*, ed. Robert J. V. Hiebert, Claude E. Cox and Peter J. Gentry (Sheffield: Sheffield Academic, 2001), p. 216.

dividuals for a particular soteriological standing, but rather involved his response to their obedience to the covenant or character.

1 Enoch. The book of *1 Enoch*, like many of the period, is a composite text, with five widely recognized divisions to the book. While the majority of the work was composed prior to the first century C.E., Enochic scholars generally think the lengthy Similitudes of Enoch (*1 En.* 37–71) come from some point in the first century.[21] The work has survived fully only in Ethiopic, though some portions of the text also exist in Greek, and Aramaic fragments of all sections of the book except the Similitudes were extant at Qumran.[22] The book is replete with the theme and language of election.

The Book of Watchers (*1 En.* 1–36)[23] opens with the introduction of Enoch, who receives a "vision from the heavens" and records it to bless the "elect and the righteous" (*1 En.* 1:1-7). At the day of judgment, God vindicates the elect and destroys the wicked "on account of everything that they have done" (*1 En.* 1:8-9). The author(s) uses the term "the elect" frequently in the Book of Watchers, numerously in the Similitudes and twice in the Epistle of Enoch (*1 En.* 91–108). They frequently pair it with the terms "the righteous" or "the holy."[24] The term emphasizes the relationship of the community (the "true Israel") to God,[25] and *not* a predetermined individual soteriological status. In Enoch's vision, the people have not done what God has intended for them because they have trans-

---

[21]See John J. Collins, *The Apocalyptic Imagination* (Grand Rapids: Eerdmans, 1998), p. 43.

[22]See ibid., p. 43. For a study of the history of and relationship between the Aramaic, Greek and Ethiopic texts, see Michael A. Knibb, "The Book of Enoch or Books of Enoch? The Textual Evidence for 1 Enoch," in *The Early Enoch Literature*, ed. Gabriele Boccaccini and John J. Collins (Leiden: Brill, 2007), pp. 21-40.

[23]The Book of Watchers is typically dated to the third century B.C.E. (see Ryan E. Stokes, "Watchers, Book of the (1 Enoch 1–36)," in *The Eerdmans Dictionary of Early Judaism*, ed. John J. Collins and Daniel C. Harlow [Grand Rapids: Eerdmans, 2010], p. 1333).

[24]So VanLandingham writes, "The term emphasizes the community's faithful obedience to God, especially considering that the righteous are often compared with sinners, oppressors, evil, or ungodly ones, terms equally descriptive of human conduct" (Chris VanLandingham, *Judgment and Justification in Early Judaism and the Apostle Paul* [Grand Rapids: Baker Academic, 2006], p. 87).

[25]Nickelsburg agrees in noting, "In 1 Enoch 1:8 the ancient priestly blessing of the nation is interpreted as the eschatological blessing to a part of that nation, the *true* Israel, here called 'righteous and chosen.' . . . The biblical technical term 'chosen' (בחר and cognates) originally denoted God's election of the nation, but it came to designate the remnant or portion of Israel that lived out its covenantal responsibilities" (George W. E. Nickelsburg, *1 Enoch*, Hermeneia [Minneapolis: Fortress, 2001], 1:147).

gressed the commandments, and thus God will judge them and show them no mercy (*1 En.* 5:4-6). The elect, however, will be blessed and will "all live and not return again to sin, either by being wicked or through pride; but those who have wisdom shall be humble and not return again to sin," enjoying peace through the remainder of their days (*1 En.* 5:7-10).[26] The wisdom here given to the elect is, as Grindheim suggests, "a reward that will be revealed in the end times (5:8)."[27]

The Epistle of Enoch[28] begins in the manner of the testamentary literature of the period in that Enoch calls all of his sons together to impart his knowledge to them (*1 En.* 91:1-2). Enoch instructs his children to love uprightness and walk in righteousness, for great evil approaches the earth and God's judgment will follow it (*1 En.* 91:3-9). The Righteous/ Wise One will arise to judge the sinners, and their deeds will depart from the earth (*1 En.* 91:10-14). Since the Righteous One receives "eternal uprightness" and "authority," E. P. Sanders suggests from this verse that "the author characteristically thinks that the reward of the righteous in the resurrection will not be earned by works, but be given by the mercy of God; even the righteous man's continuing uprightness in the new life will be by grace."[29] Clearly, however, the purpose of this verse is not to offer a general soteriological principle, but rather to show that the authority to judge humanity given to the Righteous One comes from God. Contra Sanders, Simon Gathercole notes, "The author of the epistle affirms both realities [i.e., election and obedience] by defining the righteous both in terms of their election and in terms of their works (91:3-4; 91:13)."[30] In Enoch, then, the author(s) emphasizes the character of the elect. The elect are those faithful to YHWH's covenant expectations.

---

[26]Nickelsburg notes here that this may have been intended as an appeal for "sinners to repent and become a part of the chosen" (ibid., 1:133).

[27]Grindheim, *Crux of Election*, p. 44.

[28]Stückenbruck affirms the second-century-B.C.E. date in noting, "Except for the *Eschatological Admonition* [108:1-15], which was composed during the late first century C.E., the other works originated during the second century B.C.E." (Loren T. Stückenbruck, "Enoch, Epistle of (1 Enoch 91-108)," in Collins and Harlow, *Eerdmans Dictionary of Early Judaism*, p. 583).

[29]E. P. Sanders, *Paul and Palestinian Judaism* (Minneapolis: Fortress, 1970), p. 356.

[30]Simon J. Gathercole, *Where Is Boasting? Early Jewish Soteriology and Paul's Response in Romans 1-5* (Grand Rapids: Eerdmans, 2002), pp. 48-49.

CHOSEN FOR A PURPOSE

While some writings focus on the chosen people's piety, other Second Temple texts describe elect individuals in terms of the task or position to which God has appointed them. Most commonly these texts refer to David's appointment to Israel's throne, though God's choice of other key leaders in Israel's history are also included. Such an emphasis is in keeping with what we find in the Old Testament as well, in particular of the kings, priests and leaders of Israel.

Wisdom of Ben Sira. We previously saw how Ben Sira traced the history of Israel through their ancestors. Of particular significance, Ben Sira recognizes Moses, Aaron, David and Simon the high priest as chosen by God. While the author highlights the faithfulness of each, as discussed above, Ben Sira also has their selection for a particular role or task (leader, priest and king) in view, something seen with some frequency in the Old Testament as well.[31]

Ben Sira states that God chose Moses from all of humankind because of his faithfulness and meekness (Sir 45:4), and that God equipped him "so that he might teach Jacob the covenant, and Israel his decrees" (45:5). Aaron is given "the priesthood of the people" (Sir 45:7) and chosen "out of all the living to offer sacrifice to the Lord" and "to make atonement for the people" (45:16). God also gave him authority "to teach Jacob the testimonies, and to enlighten Israel with his law" (Sir 45:17). Likewise, God set apart David from the Israelites (Sir 47:2), and he received "a covenant of kingship and a glorious throne in Israel" (47:11). In each of these cases, God chooses these ancestors of Israel to fill a particular role (teacher, priest and king), and to fulfill the mission associated with it (instruct, offer sacrifices, rule). Ben Sira clearly links their election with the position they occupy and the activities they perform.[32]

---

[31]For a brief summary, see A. Chadwick Thornhill, "Election," in *Lexham Bible Dictionary*, ed. John D. Barry et al. (Bellingham, WA: Lexham Press, 2012). For an extended discussion of the election of individuals in the Old Testament, see H. H. Rowley, *The Biblical Doctrine of Election* (London: Lutterworth, 1964), pp. 95-120. As noted above, Mack suggests that the significance of these individuals lies primarily in their office (Mack, *Wisdom and the Hebrew Epic*, pp. 18-19).

[32]Garlington has suggested, "More often than not, election throughout the 'praise' has to do with consecration for special service (cf. 45.16; 47.2)" (Garlington, *Obedience of Faith*, p. 40). Goering similarly concludes concerning the relationship of election and piety that Israel's election is

Additional Psalms of David. Psalm 151 recounts God's choice of David over his brothers. In Qumran Psalms Scroll 151:6-7, David declares, "(Although) their stature was tall, (and) their hair handsome, the Lord God did not choose [לוא בחר] them, but he sent and took me [ויקחני] from behind the flock, and he anointed me with holy oil, and he made me leader for his people, and ruler over the sons of his covenant." Here the author contrasts God's choice of David with the stature of his brothers, who presumably would have made more "natural" choices for a warrior-king than the scrawny, young musician David. As Sanders describes, "Even though David is insignificant in external appearance, he, in his soul or heart to himself, has said the significant thing: he would give glory to the Lord (verse 2); and the Lord who can see into the heart has seen and heard everything David has done and said (verse 4)."[33] The psalmist presents David's selection for the role of king as an irony, contrary to common human intuitions. His election is also office-oriented in that God chose him for the task of ruling, and the psalmist makes no soteriological connections.[34] Furthermore, God's choice of David is precipitated by his pious disposition, indicating that God has chosen a king who was worthy of choosing because of his righteous character rather than his physical capabilities.

Psalms of Solomon. Scholars of both the New Testament and Judaism have given much attention to the *Psalms of Solomon* because they contain early Jewish ideas about messianism, and some believed, especially prior to the Qumran discovery, they were a product of the Pharisees. These psalms, unlike many texts of the Pseudepigrapha, place themselves within a relatively precise historical situation. With the discovery of the

---

rooted in the primordial existence of wisdom, and as the elect, they are charged to enact the "ethical and ritual commandments of the Torah," and thus "benefit the whole of humankind, indeed the whole world" by renewing and sustaining "the primeval order upon which the world is built." In this way, "Israel's chosenness is intended to achieve goals greater than the covenant community" (Goering, *Wisdom's Root Revealed*, pp. 185-86).

[33]Sanders, *Dead Sea Psalms Scroll*, p. 95.

[34]Miura agrees in noting, "11QPs[a] 28 refers to David's anointing in terms of *his receiving kingship in the eyes of God*" (Yuzuru Miura, *David in Luke-Acts: His Portrayal in the Light of Early Judaism* [Tübingen: Mohr Siebeck, 2007], p. 71).

DSS, most now question identifying the author(s) with the Pharisees,[35] and many conclude that we cannot identify the group beyond that they were a devout Jewish sect who had separated themselves, either physically or in terms of their identity, from the Jerusalem establishment.[36] Scholars generally date the *Psalms* to the first century B.C.E., based on both internal and external evidence.[37]

There is more agreement over the purpose of the *Psalms*.[38] The community apparently existed in close proximity to Jerusalem, or within the city itself, and they considered themselves as *the* pious/devout Jews and all or most outsiders as sinners.[39] As Brad Embry argues, the *Psalms*

---

[35]Lane, for example, defended the Pharisaical authorship of the *Psalms of Solomon* and saw it as valuable for placing Paul within a Jewish context (William L. Lane, "Paul's Legacy from Pharisaism: Light from the Psalms of Solomon," *Concordia Journal* 8 [1982]: 130-40). The assumed Pharisaical origin, or at least Pharisaic tone, of the *Psalms of Solomon* has led to several comparisons with Paul's own theology of justification (see, e.g., Jens Schröter, "Gerechtigkeit und Barmherzigkeit: Das Gottesbild der Psalmen Salomos in seinem Verhältnis zu Qumran und Paulus," *NTS* 44 [1998]: 557-77; or Mikael Winninge, *Sinners and the Righteous: A Comparative Study of the Psalms of Solomon and Paul's Letters* [Stockholm: Almqvist & Wiksell International, 1995]).

[36]Trafton, for example, notes that the position that the Pharisees were responsible for these psalms is questioned by a number of recent scholars (see Joseph L. Trafton, "The Psalms of Solomon: New Light from the Syriac Version?," *JBL* 105, no. 2 [1986]: 227-37). Atkinson states emphatically, "There is virtually no evidence, however, that supports maintaining the Pharisaical authorship of these psalms" (Kenneth Atkinson, "Toward a Redating of the Psalms of Solomon: Implications for Understanding the *Sitz im Leben* of an Unknown Jewish Sect," *JSP* 17 [1998]: 112), and surmises that "the group responsible for these psalms should be situated within the confines of the city, since they suffer the effects of corrupt Jewish leadership, know of the activities of the Jerusalem Sanhedrin, and experience first-hand the siege of the city" (ibid., p. 107). See also Paul N. Franklyn, "The Cultic and Pious Climax of Eschatology in the Psalms of Solomon," *JSJ* 18, no. 1 (1987): 1-17; Robert B. Wright, "Psalms of Solomon," in Charlesworth, *Expansions*, p. 639.

[37]Lattke affirms, "If *1 Baruch* 5:5-8 is dependent on *Psalms of Solomon* 11:2-5 the Greek version must have existed before the end of the first century A.D." (Michael Lattke, "Psalms of Solomon," in *Dictionary of New Testament Background*, ed. Craig A. Evans and Stanley E. Porter [Downers Grove, IL: InterVarsity Press, 2000], p. 853). The references to Pompey, and possibly Herod, in the *Psalms* places their writing at earliest between ca. 62 B.C.E. and ca. 30 B.C.E. (see Atkinson, "Toward a Redating," pp. 95-112).

[38]For discussion of debated issues in *Psalms of Solomon* research, see Joseph L. Trafton, "The *Psalms of Solomon* in Recent Research," *JSP* 12 (1994): 5-7.

[39]Atkinson has suggested that "the *Pss. Sol.* does not represent Judaism at large" but rather "depicts a group in isolation from the temple community, which denounced as sinners virtually every individual and institution of the day (*Pss. Sol.* 17.19-20), including the temple establishment (*Pss. Sol.* 2.3; 8.11-13), the Sanhedrin (*Pss. Sol.* 4.1), the king, local judges, and the common people (*Pss. Sol.* 17.20)" (Atkinson, "Toward a Redating," pp. 110-11). Embry, on the other hand, disagrees, noting, "A good case can be made for viewing *Pss. Sol.* as appealing to the mass of loyal Jews over and above the various 'sects' or 'associations' which happened to exist. The terms 'sinner' and 'righteous' are used by *Pss. Sol.* to explain the reason for the invasion and punishment of Israel

functioned to instill hope or give encouragement to the reader[40] while also both affirming the "rightness" of the community and informing the reader of how to remain in right standing with God. The *Psalms* provide an important contribution to our understanding of election in Second Temple Judaism.

Of any psalm in the collection, *Psalms of Solomon* 17 has received the most attention, particularly because of its messianic convictions and the framework it offers for understanding Jewish expectations. The psalmist begins with recognition of God's choice of David as king over Israel and his promise that his kingdom would not fail, stating, "You, O Lord, choose David to be king over Israel" (*Pss. Sol.* 17:4). The psalmist indicates, however, that the sinners eventually caused Jerusalem to fall,[41] and that hope for restoration lies in a Davidic king taking the throne and the unrighteous being destroyed (*Pss. Sol.* 17:21-26). Here again, God's choice of David was role-oriented, specifically directed toward his rule over Israel.

Corporate Representation

The final major category in which Second Temple texts identify individuals as "elect" is through the concept of corporate representation. Though the motif also contains implications for the elect "collective," it focuses on the relationship of the group to the representative individual. In these examples, the individual represents the larger collective in that the collective in some sense must reflect the character and actions of the individual. The concept applies to those both inside and outside of God's people, as will be seen in the following discussions.

---

from the standpoint of purity as defined by the Hebrew Bible" (Brad Embry, "The *Psalms of Solomon* and the New Testament: Intertextuality and the Need for a Re-Evaluation," *JSP* 13, no. 2 [2002]: 121). While the collection may have been intended for an isolated or small community, the message of the collection resonates quite well with other literature in that it draws a sharp distinction between the faithful and unfaithful based on the community's understanding of what faithfulness to the Torah means.

[40]See Embry, "*Psalms of Solomon,*" pp. 132-35.

[41]According to Winninge, "Apparently, the designations οἱ υἱοὶ τῆς διαθήκης (17:15) and ὁ λαός (17:20) formerly had been theirs, but now they appear to have lost their covenantal status and become ἄνομοι (17:18)" (Winninge, *Sinners and the Righteous*, p. 127).

Jubilees. Jubilees retells the book of Genesis and portions of Exodus through an encounter between God and Moses. The book rearranges and expands on these biblical materials. Though sharing some features with apocalyptic writings, the book does not preoccupy itself with the typical imagery and eschatological emphases usually found in the genre.[42] The author's purpose resonates with that of 1 Maccabees, calling on pious Jews to avoid adopting Gentile customs and thus violate the Torah.[43] The book holds great significance, as it relates to the issues of covenant and election, and thus we must give it careful and thorough treatment.

Much conversation has taken place concerning chapter 15 of *Jubilees* as to the exact relationship between election and covenant obedience. Most scholars agree that according to the author of *Jubilees*, disobeying certain commands, such as circumcision, at times results in the expelling of the guilty party from the covenant community and its benefits.[44] Scholars disagree, however, concerning the basis of the nature of election. Sanders contended that *Jubilees* portrays an election availed to Abraham's seed by God's grace and not works. Thus, for Sanders, breaking the covenant means forfeiting one's status in the covenant community, though God's gracious election is the means by which they entered.[45] Chris VanLandingham disagrees, suggesting that both entering into and breaking the covenant are dependent on obedience/disobedience.[46] First, election in

---

[42]See Orval S. Wintermute, "Jubilees," in Charlesworth, *Expansions*, p. 37.

[43]As VanderKam summarizes, "The author's penchant for antedating Mosaic legislation so that the patriarchs become practitioners of the law can be seen as countering the Hellenizers' assumption that there had been a golden age when the laws of Moses were not yet in effect and Jew and non-Jew lived in the same way and in unity. . . . *Jubilees* is an all-out defense of what makes the people of Israel distinctive from the nations and a forceful assertion that they were never one with them" (James VanderKam, *The Book of Jubilees* [Sheffield: Sheffield Academic, 2001], p. 140).

[44]Thus, as VanderKam again notes, "Naturally, when members of the chosen line sinned, punishment awaited them, but that did not mean the end of their membership in the covenantal community where forgiveness was possible. However, if a member of the elect violated certain laws, then that person was to be removed from the relationship. Examples are omitting circumcision and marrying a gentile (15.34; 30.7-10, 15-16, 21-22)" (ibid., p. 122).

[45]Thus, as he states, "Rejection of any one of these commandments, like transgression of the commandment to circumcise, was regarded by the author as forsaking the covenant and thus forfeiting one's status as a member of Israel and one destined for eternal salvation" (Sanders, *Paul and Palestinian Judaism*, p. 368).

[46]VanLandingham, *Judgment and Justification*, p. 79. Christiansen seems to agree in noting, "Circumcision is a covenant obligation, by means of which Israel affirms and accepts the covenant

Jubilees focuses on Jacob/Israel rather than Abraham, since the author castigates both Ishmael and Esau, who seem to represent for him Gentiles and uncircumcised (and thus unfaithful) Jews (see *Jub.* 15:28-30). God's rejection of Ishmael and Esau is based on the fact that God "knew them" (*Jub.* 15:30), which seems in the context to indicate that God knew they would be unfaithful (i.e., lack of proper circumcision observance, marriage of foreign wives, etc.) and thus did not include them as covenant members (see *Jub.* 16:26; 19:13-31; 20:14-20; 35:9-17).[47] Second, it seems clear from this passage that entry into the covenant requires obeying (at least on the part of one's parents for males) the covenant stipulations. Covenant obedience thus begins shortly after birth, and disobeying this first command assigns one "to be destroyed and annihilated from the earth and to be uprooted from the earth because he has broken the covenant of the LORD our God" (*Jub.* 15:26). Thus, in *Jubilees*, the text emphasizes covenant faithfulness rather than a nationalistic arrangement of election.[48] God does not "save" apart from his power or mercy, but also not apart from obedience to the covenant stipulations.

The author further explicates this in *Jubilees* 16:15-19, in which the angels reveal to Abraham that all of his sons would be fathers of nations, but

> from the sons of Isaac one would become a holy seed and he would not be counted among the nations because he would become the portion of the Most High and all his seed would fall (by lot) into that which God will

---

(Jub 15:25)" (Ellen Juhl Christiansen, *The Covenant in Judaism and Paul: A Study of Ritual Boundaries as Identity Markers* [Leiden: Brill, 1995], p. 80).

[47]Thus, VanLandingham argues, "the phrase 'for he knew them' suggests that God knew that Ishmael and Esau would be disobedient and so did not choose them" (VanLandingham, *Judgment and Justification*, p. 37). See also *Jub.* 24:1-13; 26:34-35; 27:8-9; 33:10-14, 18-20; 36:9-11; 37:6–38:3. Here again Esau's reckless and unrighteous character is portrayed as the basis for his rejection from the covenant community. Thus Elliott asserts, commenting on *Jub.* 25:28, "The implication here is accordingly clear: all who follow the spirit of Mastema—the opponents of the order prescribed in *Jubilees*—are disqualified from the 'seed' of Abraham. Their 'seed' will not be saved anymore than that of Esau, who forsook God—'both he and his sons'—apparently by seeking Gentile wives (35:14)" (Mark Adam Elliott, *The Survivors of Israel: A Reconsideration of the Theology of Pre-Christian Judaism* [Grand Rapids: Eerdmans, 2000], p. 321).

[48]Or, as Segal describes, "Verse 26 describes the dualism in earthly terms: every person belongs to one of the two groups, either those who are part of the covenant with the Lord and who therefore benefit from his protection, or those who are destined for destruction because they do not" (Michael Segal, *The Book of Jubilees: Rewritten Bible, Redaction, Ideology, and Theology* [Leiden: Brill, 2007], p. 237).

rule so that he might become a people (belonging) to the LORD, a (special) possession from all people, and so that he might become a kingdom of priests and a holy people.

This clearly shows that the author of *Jubilees* sees Jacob, not Abraham alone, as the chosen heir of the promises, and those outside of his line, those who failed to fulfill the covenant obligations as Jacob did, are doomed as outsiders. The author portrays this in *Jubilees* 19:13-31, where Esau is depicted as an unruly and unrighteous man from his earliest days, a trait Abraham perceives and communicates to Sarah in order to ensure Jacob will inherit the promise and blessings. Here the text connects membership in the covenant community more with obedience to the commandments and righteous character than to unconditional election or progeny. Brian Abasciano makes a similar observation: "Jacob was chosen as the covenant heir because of his goodness and . . . Esau was rejected because of his wickedness. . . . It is apparently the Lord's knowledge of Esau's character as wicked that served as the basis of his covenantal rejection of him."[49] While clearly true of Esau, Michael Segal notes also of Ishmael, "The story in *Jub.* 15 seeks to remove the possibility that Ishmael was circumcised immediately, and as a result he is not considered a member of the covenant."[50]

Sanders, in contrast, largely reads the whole book through the lens of *Jubilees* 1:17-29, a section he sees as ensuring the future salvation of national Israel. Sanders recognizes that *Jubilees* indicates that some Israelites will "be damned." As such, he asserts, *"Physical descent is the basis of the election, and the election is the basis of salvation, but physical descent from Jacob is not the sole condition of salvation."*[51] He does not here include how God's choice of Jacob over Esau was based on Esau's reckless and unrighteous reputation or how the author recognizes circumcision as necessary for "entering" the covenant, as is explicit in *Jubilees* 15. Sanders correctly notes that the position of *Jubilees* does not constitute "works

---

[49]Brian J. Abasciano, *Paul's Use of the Old Testament in Romans 9.10-18: An Intertextual and Theological Exegesis* (New York: T&T Clark, 2011), p. 24.

[50]Segal, *Book of Jubilees*, p. 243.

[51]Sanders, *Paul and Palestinian Judaism*, p. 368 (emphasis original).

righteousness,"[52] as the author does not depict salvation as something
Jews earn. However, defining it as "salvation depends on the grace of
God"[53] fails to recognize the author's emphasis on the necessity of
keeping the covenant (e.g., circumcision or refusing to marry Gentiles),
by both initially accepting the covenant and continuing to obey it.

The election of Jacob is unique since *Jubilees* does not describe it in
terms of his own standing before God, but rather because he stands as a
representative of the people and because his chosen seed "will be one
which fills all of the earth" (*Jub.* 19:21). Thus, Abasciano again writes,
"Jacob's is a corporate election, for he is chosen 'as a people' (19.18)."[54] This
"corporate" nature of Jacob's election does not, however, guarantee that
all of Jacob's seed have a guaranteed final verdict, something the book
holds out for the faithful alone.[55] Those who are of Jacob, however, alone
fulfill the covenant since its promise and blessings are for him and his
faithful descendants.[56]

The text further develops the concept in *Jubilees* 21:21-26, where, as
Abraham gives his "final" advice to Isaac, he instructs him to be faithful
to God so that he will experience his blessings and so that "he will raise
up from you a righteous plant in all the earth throughout all the generations of the earth; and my name and your name shall not cease from
beneath heaven forever." Abraham displays the necessity of faithfulness
to receive the covenant blessings, while forsaking the covenant by committing "a mortal sin"[57] (*Jub.* 21:22) will result in the wiping out of his

---

[52]Ibid., p. 383.

[53]Ibid.

[54]Abasciano, *Paul's Use*, p. 23.

[55]Thus, Grindheim states, "It is unwarranted to see in the election of Jacob's seed an election of
the nation Israel as a whole. One of the main points of the entire narrative of the patriarchs is
that election is not tied to physical descent but is instead contingent upon religious purity"
(Grindheim, *Crux of Election*, p. 48).

[56]Hanneken adds, "one should not deny that the author of Jubilees has a contemporary people
in mind in Jub. 8:14. . . . On the other hand, one should not think that Jubilees is primarily
concerned with contemporary politics in its treatment of Esau and his descendants. . . . Israel is
an absolute category for the division of humanity. There is no partial credit for brothers or
cousins of Jacob" (Todd R. Hanneken, *The Subversion of the Apocalypses in the Book of Jubilees*
[Atlanta: Society of Biblical Literature, 2012], pp. 163-64).

[57]These mortal sins in *Jubilees* have been referenced above as including omitting circumcision,
marrying foreign wives, worshiping idols, etc. Elliott notes that the appeal here to Abraham,
Enoch and the heavenly tablets in *Jub.* 21:10-11 is likely to give greater weight or authority to

"name and seed . . . from all the earth" (*Jub.* 21:22). That not all of Isaac's descendants will endure is expressed apparently by Abraham asking that God would "bless all of your seed and the remnant of your seed for eternal generations" (*Jub.* 22:25).[58]

As Abraham's farewell blessings continue, he calls Jacob to his side and prays:

> May the God of all bless you and strengthen you to do righteousness and his will before him. And may he elect you and your seed so that you become a people for him who always belong to his inheritance according to his will. . . . May the LORD give you righteous seed, and may he sanctify some of your sons in the midst of all the earth. . . . And may he renew his covenant with you, so that you might be a people for him, belonging to his inheritance forever, and he will be God for you and for your seed in truth and righteousness throughout all the days of the earth. . . . Separate yourself from the gentiles, and do not eat with them, and do not perform deed like theirs. . . . Do not take a wife from any of the seed of the daughters of Canaan. (*Jub.* 22:10-20)

Here again the conditional nature of the covenant is emphasized. In order for Jacob (i.e., faithful Israel) to enjoy the blessings, he must avoid certain sins that would cause separation from the community. The author also presents Jacob's "election" here as representative. His election represents and establishes the seed that will come from him (*Jub.* 22:10), though not all of this seed will remain faithful since the author calls only some "sanctified" (22:11).[59]

---

certain laws that he deemed paramount for Jewish faithfulness (Elliott, *Survivors of Israel*, p. 255).

[58]Sanders here curiously asserts, "Thus we see that all Israel will be saved. Excluded from Israel are those who transgress a commandment which is, in the author's view, tantamount to denying the covenant (not circumcising, not keeping the Sabbath, intermarrying or permitting intermarriage with Gentiles, not keeping the Passover, devising evil against fellow Israelites) or those who blatantly commit a heinous transgression which is, by inference, a denial of the God who gave the commandment (eating blood, having intercourse with one's father's wife and perhaps with one's mother-in-law or daughter-in-law)" (Sanders, *Paul and Palestinian Judaism*, p. 370). The long list of exceptions here should surely give pause to accepting the notion that the author believed "all Israel will be saved" since he excludes such a great number of Israelites from those who are truly in Israel.

[59]This is contra Sanders, who suggests, "We should not take the phrase 'some of thy sons' to indicate that only a portion of Jacob's descendants is elect. This is negated by the prayer that 'thy sons' should become 'a holy nation' in the same passage and by the reference to 'all his seed' in 16.18" (ibid., p. 363).

While individuals are spoken of in the book in the context of election (e.g., Abraham, Isaac, Jacob, etc.), this is *always* in light of their relationship to the group they represent. Jacob and some of his sons stand for faithful Israel, while Ishmael, Esau and others represent those Gentiles and Jews outside of the covenant. Thus with Abasciano it can be affirmed, "As for the election of Israel, it is clearly a corporate matter. It is obviously assumed that the corporate election of Israel is in the individual Jacob, but its corporate nature comes out all the more clearly when the text contrasts the rejection of Ishmael and Esau with the election of the people of Israel and omits mention of Jacob."[60]

Testaments of the Twelve Patriarchs. Scholars frequently recognize the difference between the content of the *Testaments* and many other texts of the Second Temple period. The *Testaments* contain only a few references to specific commands found in the Torah and emphasize instead moral principles.[61] Some have seen this as indicating Hellenistic Jewish influence since the themes involved often overlap with those found in Stoicism.[62] To view it, however, as outside of the mainstream of Judaism is unwarranted since references to the law are found, specifically as it relates to circumcision (*T. Levi* 6:3-6), sacrifices (*T. Reu.* 6:8; *T. Levi* 9:7-14; 16:1; *T. Jud.* 18:5), and intermarriage with Gentiles (*T. Levi* 9:10), and since the text references the law as something to be read (*T. Levi* 13:1-3).[63] Other writings from the postbiblical period

---

[60]Abasciano, *Paul's Use*, p. 25.

[61]Concerning their general structure, Kugler summarizes, "each testament in this collection follows more or less a familiar pattern: it begins with the patriarch's summons to his children to his bedside, continues with his autobiographical reflections, moral exhortation, and future prediction, and concludes with an account of the man's death and burial" (Robert A. Kugler, "Testaments," in Collins and Harlow, *Eerdmans Dictionary of Early Judaism*, p. 1296).

[62]See H. C. Kee, "Testaments of the Twelve Patriarchs," in *The Old Testament Pseudepigrapha*, vol. 1, *Apocalyptic Literature and Testaments*, ed. James H. Charlesworth (1983; repr., Peabody, MA: Hendrickson, 2011), p. 780.

[63]Thus Slingerland has argued, "These authors conceive of the law as a written body of jurisprudence to be read, studied, and taught; they hold the role of Israel's traditional teachers in high regard; they refer to the 'Law and the Prophets'; they call for obedience to *all* this legal matter; and they reflect much interest in several aspects of Israel's ritual laws. There is no reason to think otherwise, therefore, than that when these writers speak of *nomos* they have in mind Israel's traditional legal corpus understood in its wholeness" (Dixon Slingerland, "The Nature of *Nomos* (Law) Within the *Testaments of the Twelve Patriarchs*," *JBL* 105, no. 1 [1986]: 46, 48). See also Gathercole, *Where Is Boasting?*, p. 76.

(e.g., Ben Sira) also reflect a more generic view of the law as equated with wisdom and applicable to all humanity without disregarding the Jewishness of the Torah.

The *Testaments* contain several important themes relevant to understanding Jewish thoughts about election; in particular, what scholars refer to as the Levi and Judah passages (LJ), descriptions of Israel's disobedience, judgment and repentance (often termed as S-E-R [sin-exile-return] passages), and the fate of the nations.[64] Particular difficulty exists with the LJ texts[65] since they contain several Christian interpolations. Scholars also observe an unevenness present concerning the relationship between Levi and Judah as it relates to the role of the messiah(s). In *Testament of Reuben* 6:6-12, the author describes Levi and Judah as holding God-given authority, though he seems to elevate Levi since God will reign among the people through him.[66] In *Testament of Simeon* 5:1-6, the author seems to indicate that Levi and Judah, though small in number, represent the faithful who have remained true to God.[67] In *Testament of Levi* 2:10-12, the author portrays Levi as the priestly leader who will bring about Israel's redemption, though Judah also plays a role in restoring the nation. Though this prediction finds no precedent in the Aramaic *Testament of Levi* (4Q213-14), that text does speak of a righteous seed coming from Levi, and Levi enters into heaven where the vision in *Testament of Levi* 2 takes place before the fragment ends.

In *Testament of Judah* 21:1-6 another interesting, and here more deci-

---

[64]These categories are commonly discussed in *Testaments* literature. See John J. Collins, "Testaments," in *Jewish Writings of the Second Temple Period*, ed. Michael E. Stone (Philadelphia: Fortress, 1984), 2:337.

[65]Relevant here for the purpose of this study are *T. Reu.* 6:6-12; *T. Sim.* 5:1-6; 7:1-3; *T. Levi* 2:10-12; 4:2-6; 8:11-19; 14:4–19:3; *T. Jud.* 21:1-6; *T. Dan* 5:1–6:11; *T. Naph.* 8:1-5; *T. Gad* 8:1-3; *T. Jos.* 19:1–20:1.

[66]This is often seen, and certainly may be, a reference solely to Christ inserted by a Christian redactor. Like many of the messianic texts in the *Testaments*, though certainly not all of them, there is nothing overtly Christian about this particular passage that necessitates its not possibly being a part of an original Jewish text or tradition. Occurrences of clear Christian redaction in the LJ portions in the *Testaments* are evident in *T. Levi* 8:11-19.

[67]*T. Sim.* 7:1-3 also mentions the ruling of Levi and Judah, though here apparently a reference to a single individual. The passage is most certainly Christian, either in origin or redaction, and several lengthy and overt references to Jesus make it difficult to determine what may have been original in any Jewish source material for this section.

sively divided, portrayal of the messianic role(s) occurs as Levi receives the priesthood to oversee heavenly matters and Judah the kingship to oversee earthly matters. Judah's kingdom, much like David's, exists eternally, though currently interrupted until God rescues Israel (*T. Jud.* 22:1-3). Again in *Testament of Dan* 5:1-13 (as well as *T. Gad* 8:1-3 and in *T. Jos.* 19:1-12), salvation arises from Levi and Judah, and they are granted victory over Beliar. In *Testament of Naphtali* 8:1-5, it is Judah from whom salvation will arise, and he will bless Jacob. Though the text mentions Levi, here the *Testaments* elevate Judah, who has prominence, rather than Levi.[68] Marinus de Jonge has suggested the dual portrayal of messiahs from Levi and Judah should be taken to refer to a single figure, namely Jesus as intended by the Christian author(s)/redactor(s).[69] Elliott agrees the passages likely have a single referent but suggests that this may have (at least originally) described the original Jewish community itself rather than Jesus. As he writes, "The exhortations to honor Levi and Judah in the above passages would suit better their role as patrons of the *Testaments* community, figureheads representing the corporate identity of the group who *believed themselves alone to emulate the ideals expressed by these figures*."[70] As he goes on to explain concerning *Testament of Simeon* 5:4-6,

> Here it is particularly notable how the pair "Jacob and Israel" has been subtly replaced by "Levi and Judah," thus suggesting that the author of the *Testaments* took "Levi and Judah" to be a designation for the righteous in

---

[68]It is also worth noting that in *T. Benj.* 11:4-5 the messiah from Judah and Levi is called "God's Chosen One forever." Of this reference, Hollander and de Jonge note, "like ἀγαπητός κυρίου (cf. v. 2), ἐκλεκτὸς (τοῦ) θεοῦ/κυρίου is used as an epithet of righteous individuals (besides the more common use of the plural οἱ ἐκλεκτοὶ [τοῦ] θεοῦ/κυρίου indicating the group of true worshippers)" (Harm W. Hollander and Marinus de Jonge, *The Testaments of the Twelve Patriarchs: A Commentary* [Leiden: Brill, 1985], p. 444).

[69]"We should stress that these views do not necessarily lead to the expectation of two messianic figures, as is found in some Qumran texts. . . . There is no 'double messianism' in the Testaments. Whenever a savior figure occurs in the LJ [Levi-Judah] passages, there is only one" (ibid., pp. 60-61).

[70]Elliott, *Survivors of Israel*, p. 450 (emphasis original). He continues, "The *Testaments* community was accordingly composed of supporters of a legitimate priesthood and of a legitimate Davidic government in Jerusalem—not because they belonged to the Levi and Judah tribes, but because they recognized these offices to be essential to the religion and welfare of the state. It was also a highly consequential fact that *this order of things, a legitimate priesthood and a Davidic government, was presently not experienced in Jerusalem*" (ibid., p. 451 [emphasis original]; see also pp. 324, 370, 424 and 555).

Israel with which he replaced the more nationalistic term "Jacob and Israel" as found in Genesis. . . . Taken together, therefore, these passages suggest that while "Levi and Judah" represented the righteous, the other tribes cumulatively represented the unrighteous.[71]

Though he is hesitant to assert that Levi and Judah became a sort of self-identification for the community, Elliott's suggestion is intriguing. Elliott's theory gives credence to Levi and Judah's prominence in the book and recognizes that, for the author(s), to be in the people of God for the *Testaments* requires submission to and emulation of them.

1 Enoch. Book two, also known as the Similitudes of Enoch, abounds with election language; the author uses the term "elect" twenty-five times in this section of the book.[72] The author introduces the Similitudes as a revelation of wisdom to Enoch, who received it "in accordance with the will of the Lord of the Spirits" (*1 En.* 37:4). Though some have argued for a second- or third-century date of the work and view it as Christian in origin, general consensus today among Enoch scholars holds that the book, as Matthew Black states, "was a pre-Christian Jewish apocalypse,"[73] for which a pre-70-C.E. dating "for at least some of the oldest traditions in the Book" cannot be ruled out.[74]

As John Collins has noted, "The Similitudes of Enoch consist of three 'parables' (chaps. 38–44, 45–57, and 58–69) and a double epilogue in chaps. 70 and 71."[75] At the beginning of the first parable, Enoch declares,[76] "When the congregation of the righteous shall appear, sinners shall be judged for their sins, they shall be driven from the face of the earth, and when the Righteous One shall appear before the face of the righteous, those elect ones, their deeds are hung upon the Lord

---

[71]Ibid., pp. 453-54.

[72]This is compared with only eight times in book 1 and twice in book 5, with no occurrences in books 3 and 4.

[73]Matthew Black, *The Book of Enoch or I Enoch: A New English Edition* (Leiden: Brill, 1985), p. 182.

[74]Ibid., pp. 187-88. See also Nickelsburg, *1 Enoch*, 2:58-66; Nickelsburg, *Jewish Literature Between the Bible and the Mishnah* (Minneapolis: Fortress, 2005), p. 255. Nickelsburg dates the work to the first half of the first century C.E.

[75]Collins, *Apocalyptic Imagination*, p. 178.

[76]Here, as elsewhere in *1 Enoch*, Enoch is the bearer of the special revelation necessary for inclusion in the community of the elect. See ibid., p. 182.

of the Spirits, he shall reveal light to the righteous and the elect who dwell upon the earth" (*1 En.* 38:1-2). The terms "righteous ones," "holy ones" and "elect ones" occur throughout the Similitudes in various combinations, with a clear emphasis on the quality of the community.[77] Here, as throughout the book, a close relationship is maintained between the community of the righteous/elect and the Righteous/Elect One who serves as their vindicator and the judge of the sinners (*1 En.* 38:3-6).[78] This Righteous/Elect One ensures the salvation and blessing of the righteous/elect ones (*1 En.* 39:6). The righteous ones will dwell among the holy angels in the days of the Elect One "underneath the wings of the Lord of the Spirits" (*1 En.* 39:7).

Enoch introduces the second parable by stating that it concerns "those who deny the name of the Lord of the Spirits and the congregation of the holy ones" (*1 En.* 45:1).[79] Enoch sees here a transformed heaven and earth, ruled over by the Elect One, and free from sinners who have been destroyed "from before the face of the earth" (*1 En.* 45:2-6). This "One" is described in *1 Enoch* 47 as the "Son of Man," in whom righteousness dwells and whom the Lord of Spirits has chosen to unseat kings and rulers, shame the strong and end oppression.[80] These unjust rulers, though they practice injustice and worship idols, "like to congregate in his houses and (with) the faithful ones who cling to the Lord of the

---

[77]Nickelsburg suggests, "Their righteousness refers to their lifestyle as the obedient people of God, as opposed to 'the sinners' (see esp. 38:1-3). Their status as 'the chosen' involves their relationship to God. As 'the holy' they are destined to live with the holy ones in heaven. They are oppressed by the kings and the mighty, although there is no evidence that this is a function of their status and lifestyles as the chosen and the righteous" (Nickelsburg, *1 Enoch*, 2:46-47).

[78]As Nickelsburg summarizes, "Moreover, of the seven occurrences of 'the chosen' in the Parables, six of them are found in contexts that refer to God's agent, 'the Chosen One' (40:5; 45:3, 5; 62:7, 8, 11). Additionally, the combined form 'the righteous and chosen' occurs six times in such context (39:6, 7; 51:5; 62:12, 13, 15). Thus, in part, the term 'the chosen' emphasizes the status of the author's people as clients of 'the Chosen One.' The Chosen One is related to the chosen as the Righteous One is related to the righteous" (ibid., 2:100). See also Collins, *Apocalyptic Imagination*, p. 184.

[79]So a failure to recognize the elect community as *the* people of God is subsequently a denial of God himself.

[80]On the identity of the sinners, Knibb writes, "It appears that the *Parables* stem from a dissident group that were being oppressed by the ruling powers and their supporters, and one of the main aims of the work is to assure the righteous that they will ultimately enjoy salvation" (Michael A. Knibb, "Enoch, Similitudes of (1 Enoch 37-71)," in Collins and Harlow, *Eerdmans Dictionary of Early Judaism*, p. 586).

Spirits" (*1 En.* 46:8). It is likely that these represent the powerful leaders in Israel, perhaps along with the Gentiles with whom they conspire.

In chapter 47, the righteous are a persecuted group, whose prayers, along with the hosts of the heavens, fervently petition the Lord of the Spirits to bring judgment on their tormentors. The Son of Man—the Before-Time—will act as a staff for the righteous to lean on, and he also is "the light of the gentiles and he will become the hope of those who are sick in their hearts" (*1 En.* 48:4).[81] It is he, as the Chosen One before creation, who will save the righteous and holy ones and bring about the destruction of those who oppress the righteous (*1 En.* 48:6-10; 50:1-2). The coming judgment of the sinners will bring an occasion for repentance, effecting the salvation of the penitent by the Lord of the Spirits, but the unrepentant will perish (*1 En.* 50:2-5).[82]

The Elect One is also present when the righteous/elect ones are raised back to life and inherit the earth (*1 En.* 51:1-5). As the scene of judgment is prepared (*1 En.* 52), it is again the wicked sinners who will be destroyed by the Lord of the Spirits, included among them the kings and rulers of earth (53:1-5), and after this, "this Righteous and Elect One will reveal the house of his congregation," and give the righteous ones "rest from the oppression of sinners" (*1 En.* 53:6-7). The judgment (again) takes the form of the flooding of the world, which obliterates those who "did not recognize their oppressive deeds which they carried out on the earth" (*1 En.* 54:10). The wicked angels, and Azaz'el chief among them, are likewise bound and thrown into the abyss along with "their elect and beloved ones,"[83] and their influence on the earth will come to an end (*1 En.* 56:3-4).

---

[81]Nickelsburg notes that "the Chosen One combines the titles, attributes, and functions of the one like a son of man in Daniel 7, the Servant of YHWH in Second Isaiah, and the Davidic Messiah" (Nickelsburg, *Jewish Literature*, p. 249). The notion of a heavenly eschatological Messiah figure is present in other literature of the period, such as in *4 Ezra* and at Qumran. See Knibb, "Enoch, Similitudes of," p. 587.

[82]For a discussion on the presence of the notion here of salvation without honor, see Ronald Herms, "'Being Saved Without Honor': A Conceptual Link Between 1 Corinthians 3 and *1 Enoch* 50?," *JSNT* 29, no. 2 (2006): 187-210.

[83]Of the identity of these "elect ones" of Azaz'el, Black notes, "Dillmann interprets, in the light of 90.26,27, of the 'blinded sheep,' the apostate Israel, and Schodde thinks of the 'kings and the mighty'" (Black, *Book of Enoch*, p. 221). The use of the title here is no doubt intended to be ironic and to contrast Azaz'el's "elect ones" with those of the Son of Man.

The third and final parable of the Similitudes begins with the blessing of the righteous and elect ones, who will enjoy innumerable days full of righteousness and peace (*1 En.* 58:1-6). Enoch witnesses a disturbing violence in the heavens in which the cosmic forces are greatly agitated. Michael explains to him that the day of judgment approaches (*1 En.* 59:1–60:5), which the Lord of Spirits prepared for those who do not worship "the righteous judgment" and who "take his name in vain." The day of judgment will bring a "day of covenant for the elect and inquisition for the sinners" (60:6). The judgment of the Elect One will be just, and all the creatures of heaven and the elect ones will glorify God because of his mercy and justice (*1 En.* 61:7-13). The Son of Man/Elect One who comes to judge the oppressors is revealed only to the holy and elect ones, and God will save them alone on the day of judgment, never again to see "the faces of the sinners and the oppressors" (*1 En.* 62:7-16).

The oppressors will plead for mercy and seek to worship God, but because "our Lord is faithful in all his works, his judgments, and his righteousness; and his judgments have no respect of persons," their judgment-day confessions will do them no good (*1 En.* 63:1-12). Again the Son of Man is the instrument by which the corruption of the world will cease, as the fallen angels and their followers are bound and the Son of Man rules from his glorious throne (*1 En.* 69:26-29). Following this, the heavenly tour guide shows Enoch the secrets of heaven and righteousness (*1 En.* 70:1–71:13), and the angel assures him that all who will follow Enoch's path will find peace and length of days (*1 En.* 71:14-17).

Here, as throughout *1 Enoch*, the elect are seen as a righteous and chosen community, a subgroup, the remnant of Israel, which represents the true people of God.[84] What separates them from the sinners in the Similitudes is their relation to the Chosen One/Son of Man and their avoidance of sins, such as blasphemy and what may be termed as "practical atheism."[85] The guilty also include the powerful,[86] who lord their

---

[84]See Grindheim, *Crux of Election*, p. 43. Collins recognizes that the group, in its conviction that it is the only true expression of God's people, shares some characteristics of the community at Qumran (Collins, *Apocalyptic Imagination*, p. 192).

[85]See Collins, *Apocalyptic Imagination*, p. 182.

[86]Knibb suggests that "'the kings and the mighty' represent the Roman authorities, and a good

power over the righteous and oppress them. God has given the judgment of those who oppress the elect ones to the Elect One/Son of Man, who ensures that the elect will receive a favorable outcome.

PAUL AND CHOSEN INDIVIDUALS

With this background in mind, we can see more clearly Paul's own discussion of "individual election." The basic categories outlined above appear to varying degrees in Paul's writings. Sometimes Paul describes "chosen" individuals by focusing on their character quality rather than soteriological status. Further, Paul at times also specifically has the calling or role of the individual in mind. Finally, we also find in his writings the concept of corporate representation, where an individual stands for a collective, with an emphasis on the relationship between the two.

Galatians 1:15-16. Paul's main discussion of God's choosing an individual focuses on none other than God's choice of Paul himself.[87] In Galatians 1:15-16, Paul recounts, "But when he was pleased, the one who set me apart from my mother's womb and called me through his grace, to reveal his son to me, so that I might proclaim his good news to the Gentiles, immediately I did not consult with flesh and blood."[88] Paul includes this in order to defend the divine nature of his calling and his gospel, which he did not receive from the apostles or any other human, but from God's revealing Jesus to Paul directly. That Paul is speaking specifically of his calling as apostle to the Gentiles is clear when he states that God's revealing act was ἵνα εὐαγγελίζωμαι ("in order to proclaim the good news"), with ἵνα indicating the purpose of God's action. Likewise, as Brendan Byrne and William Baird both recognize, the terminology Paul uses reflects God's call of the prophets in the Old Testament, an

---

case has been made for the view that the *Parables* date from around the turn of the era" (Knibb, "Enoch, Similitudes of," p. 587).

[87]The Pastoral Epistles evidence a similar understanding of Paul's calling. Paul is "appointed to service" (1 Tim 1:12) and "made a preacher and apostle . . . and a teacher of the Gentiles" (1 Tim 2:7; 2 Tim 1:11). Here God's choice of Paul is connected to his service or role, and specifically to his fulfillment of that role to the Gentiles.

[88]All translations from the New Testament are my own.

"election" unto office and service rather than a soteriological decision.[89] It is reasonable to conclude, then, with James Dunn that Paul is describing "primarily a commissioning (apostle-making) experience."[90]

Romans 16:13. At the end of Paul's letter to the Romans (Rom 16:13), Paul commends several believers living in Rome. He includes the request to "greet Rufus the chosen/choice one in the Lord and his mother and mine." Paul probably does not intend to indicate by ἐκλεκτὸν here that he thought God had predetermined Rufus for a certain, final eschatological fate, but rather that the local body respected him as an "excellent" or "prominent" member.[91] While some have suggested that this indicates "individual election unto salvation," it seems more likely that Paul simply recognizes the quality character of Rufus, a phenomenon also observed in the Second Temple literature surveyed above.[92]

1 Corinthians 15:20-24. The concept of "corporate representation" becomes significant in several Pauline letters. The concept is present in 1 Corinthians 15. Having defended the centrality for believers of God's raising Jesus, Paul explicates the order of the resurrection. Here he asserts:

> Since death came through a man, resurrection from among the dead ones

---

[89]"The language in which Paul describes his call ('from my mother's womb . . . set me apart') consciously echoes the call of prophetic figures in the Old Testament (Jer 1:4-5; Isa 49:1, 5-6). In line with these biblical figures, Paul sees himself as divinely chosen from the earliest moment of his existence for a saving role in regard to the nations of the world" (Brendan Byrne, *Galatians and Romans* [Collegeville, MN: Liturgical Press, 2010], p. 12). Baird likewise concludes that "Gal 1:11-17 echoes the main themes of the prophetic call narratives" (William Baird, "Visions, Revelation, and Ministry: Reflections on 2 Cor 12:1-5 and Gal 1:11-17," *JBL* 104, no. 4 [Dec 1985]: 657).

[90]James D. G. Dunn, *The Theology of Paul's Letter to the Galatians* (Cambridge: Cambridge University Press, 1993), p. 26.

[91]See Robert H. Mounce, *Romans*, NAC (Nashville: Broadman & Holman, 1995), p. 277. See also Frank J. Matera, *Romans*, Paideia Commentary on the New Testament (Grand Rapids: Baker Academic 2010), p. 342; Leon Morris, *The Epistle to the Romans*, Pillar New Testament Commentary (Grand Rapids: Eerdmans, 1988), p. 536. Toews suggests that it is probably that Rufus was chosen for a particular task that Paul does not specify (John E. Toews, *Romans*, BCBC [Scottdale, PA: Herald, 2004]). This interpretation also has good standing in church history as Ambrosiaster's commentary on Romans suggests that Rufus is "chosen to work for the grace of God" and "chosen and promoted by the Lord to care for his own work."

[92]Demarest and Schreiner in contrast suggest that this is an indication of the presence of "individual election unto salvation" in the New Testament (Bruce Demarest, *The Cross and Salvation: The Doctrine of Salvation* [Wheaton, IL: Crossway, 1997], p. 133; Thomas R. Schreiner, *Romans*, BECNT [Grand Rapids: Baker Academic, 1998], p. 791).

also came through a man. For just as in Adam all are dying, so also in the Christ all will be made alive. But each in their own order; Christ as first-fruits, then the ones who are of Christ at his coming, then the end, when he is going to deliver the kingdom to the God and Father, when he has abolished all rule and all authority and power.

First, I should note Paul, in describing Christ as the "firstfruits," indicates Christ's resurrection both represents and guarantees that the full harvest will be brought in at the appointed time.[93] Paul here portrays both Adam and Jesus as representing humanity: Adam of the decomposing and Jesus of the restored.[94] Here we find typical "representative" language since the activities of the representative reflect on those whom they represent.[95] Adam represents a humanity unavoidably susceptible to death. Jesus represents a humanity, those who find their life in him, whom he will rescue from death. Only being "in Christ" and belonging to him delivers the benefits of his victory. Though we do not find "election terminology" here, the concept is clearly transferrable since those associated with the "right" representative will find blessings and life in the eschaton.

2 Corinthians 5:14-21. Another Pauline passage conceptually connected to the "representative" images seen in texts like *Jubilees* and *Testaments* is 2 Corinthians 5. As Paul describes and defends his ministry to the Corinthians, he elaborates on the essence of the message of reconciliation that he preached. Here he declares, beginning in 2 Corinthians

---

[93]See David E. Garland, *1 Corinthians*, BECNT (Grand Rapids: Baker Academic, 2003), pp. 705-6; Marion L. Soards, *1 Corinthians*, UBCS (Grand Rapids: Baker Books, 2011), p. 331; Anthony C. Thiselton, *The First Epistle to the Corinthians: A Commentary on the Greek Text*, NIGTC (Grand Rapids: Eerdmans, 2000), pp. 1223-24. Thiselton summarizes well that "firstfruits" entails "(1) prior *temporality*; (2) *representation* of the same quality or character; and (3) *promise* or *pledge* of *more of the same kind to come*" (ibid., p. 1224).

[94]Campbell writes, "Nevertheless, it is more likely that v. 22 is not simply supplying the names of the two 'men' of v. 21, but is also delimiting those to whom death comes—those 'in Adam'—and those who will be made alive—those 'in Christ.' Consequently it may be better to regard 'in Adam' and 'in Christ' as expressing the realms under which each group respectively belongs. The representative nature of Adam and Christ is commonly understood in this verse; 'Adam is, for Paul, both an individual and a corporate entity' [quoting Thiselton, *First Epistle to the Corinthians*, p. 1125], and Christ likewise" (Constantine R. Campbell, *Paul and Union with Christ: An Exegetical and Theological Study* [Grand Rapids: Zondervan, 2012]).

[95]As Garland describes it, "Paul assumes that the representative determines the fate of the group" (Garland, *1 Corinthians*, p. 707). See also Thiselton, *First Epistle to the Corinthians*, pp. 1224-26.

5:14, "one died for all; therefore all died; and he died for all, so that the ones who are living are no longer living for themselves but for the one who died for them and was raised." Commentators have discussed what Paul means here with his "all" (πάντων) language. As Morna Hooker suggests, Paul does not specify in what sense Christ's death results (ἄρα) in all dying.[96] Clearer, however, is Paul seeing Christ's death as somehow representatively connected to the death of "all."[97] As a result, all who live (presumably believers) live not for themselves but for Christ.

Scholars have proposed, of course, a number of models for how the atonement "works."[98] Dunn suggests Paul has in mind both a representative and atoning death of sorts, arguing that "Paul's teaching is *not* that Christ dies 'in the place of' others so that they *escape* death (as the logic of 'substitution' implies). It is rather that Christ's sharing *their* death makes it possible for them to share *his* death. 'Representation' is not an adequate single-word description, nor particularly 'participation' or 'participatory event.'"[99] Though Paul does not specify the "mechanism" by which this works, it is clear that he is working with a representative and participatory construct.[100] Those who are "in Christ" are those who identify with and benefit from what Christ has done by his entering into

---

[96]She says, "The fact that Christ died for all means, first, that 'all have died': in other words, his death was not a substitute for theirs, but in some sense brought it about" (Morna D. Hooker, "On Becoming the Righteousness of God: Another Look at 2 Cor 5:21," *NovT* 50 [2008]: 366).

[97]Belleville suggests the "all" here is intended as believers who have died to their old life and been raised in Christ (see Linda L. Belleville, *Second Corinthians*, IVP New Testament Commentary [Downers Grove, IL: InterVarsity Press, 1996], p. 151).

[98]For an introduction to the discussion, see James Beilby and Paul R. Eddy, eds., *The Nature of the Atonement: Four Views* (Downers Grove, IL: IVP Academic, 2006).

[99]Dunn, *Theology of Paul the Apostle*, p. 223. Harris seems to offer a similar reading (Murray J. Harris, *The Second Epistle to the Corinthians: A Commentary on the Greek Text*, NIGTC [Grand Rapids: Eerdmans, 2005], p. 421). Bell similarly argues, "According to Gese and Janowski, the sin offering does not simply remove sin but is an event of salvation which brings renewal to the Israelite. By participating in the death of the animal through the laying on of a hand, the Israelite enjoys fellowship with God. The animal's death is therefore the Israelite's death. Paul in 2 Cor. 5:14-21 has applied these ideas to the death of Christ. First in v. 14b Paul declares that Christ has died, therefore all have died and in v. 15 expresses the goal of his sacrificial death: those who live (i.e. those who come to life through Christ's atoning death) live not for themselves but for Christ who died and was raised for them. We see here that the atonement for Paul is achieved by the death *and* resurrection of Christ" (Richard H. Bell, "Sacrifice and Christology in Paul," *JTS* 53, no. 1 [2002]: 8).

[100]See Belleville, *Second Corinthians*, pp. 150-51.

and overcoming humanity's fatal flaw. Paul explains the logical out-working in 2 Corinthians 5:16-18: "From now on we know no one according to flesh; even though we have known Christ according to flesh, but now we are knowing *him that way* no longer.[101] Therefore if anyone is in Christ, they are a new creation, the old things passed away, behold they have become new things." This change in perspective for the believer must totally transform how they view not only Christ, but everything. As a result, in Christ and echoed in prophetic expectations,[102] they become a new creation through their identification with Christ.[103]

Paul concludes in 2 Corinthians 5:18-21 that "all things are from God who reconciled us to himself through Christ and gave to us the ministry of reconciliation."[104] This reconciliation occurs because God made Christ, the sinless one, "sin."[105] As a result, those "in Christ" now represent "Christ, as God is making an appeal through us." God has called those now in right standing with him, because of Christ's representative activity, to be his representatives. These must work to bring others into a reconciled relationship. Here N. T. Wright states, "This is 'election theology': the divine choice of Israel, in order that *through* Israel the covenant God may work his saving purposes for the whole world. Paul's

---

[101]Paul's language here is terse and has been the subject of much debate. For a helpful discussion, see Harris, *Second Epistle to the Corinthians*, p. 431.

[102]Cousar notes, "The phrase 'new creation' recalls a promise which in various forms the prophets reiterated to Israel. God was to do a new thing for his people. Sometimes it is pictured as a new exodus from bondage (cf. Isa. 42:9; 43:18-19), at other times as a new heaven and a new earth (cf. Isa. 65:17; 66:22). God's action was to be decisive, ultimate, and final so that 'the former things' which had thus far sustained Israel could be forgotten. It would involve not merely a renewal or a restoration, but an altogether new creation. This, Paul says, is precisely what has happened in Christ. To participate in the death of Christ is to be brought into this new world" (Charles B. Cousar, "II Corinthians 5:17-21," *Int* 35 [1981]: 181).

[103]Campbell suggests that here Paul has the "realm of Christ" more in mind than union or participation (Campbell, *Paul and Union with Christ*, p. 117). Shillington suggests that union is the more appropriate category (V. G. Shillington, *2 Corinthians*, BCBC [Scottdale, PA: Herald, 1998], pp. 130-31).

[104]Campbell writes of 2 Cor 5:21, "Since Christ—who knew no sin—was made 'sin,' thus sharing in the plight of the sinful, so sinners are made righteous by sharing in his right standing" (Campbell, *Paul and Union with Christ*, p. 187). Likewise, Harris writes, "In a sense beyond human comprehension, God treated Christ as 'sin,' aligning him so totally with sin and its dire consequences that from God's viewpoint he became indistinguishable from sin itself" (Harris, *Second Epistle to the Corinthians*, p. 454).

[105]Belleville notes that the idea of identification with humanity is present here as well (Belleville, *Second Corinthians*, p. 159).

whole point is that this covenant faithfulness of the one God, having been *enacted* in the death of the Messiah, is now being *embodied* in his own representative, ambassadorial, apostolic ministry."[106] While scholars have debated Wright's interpretation of "righteousness of God" here and elsewhere,[107] in context his larger point rings true. Christ's death and resurrection fashioned the means by which humans may exchange death for life. God re-forms those who live for him—who live in Christ—to be representatives of the reconciling work that has already begun transforming them.

SUMMARY

We must remind ourselves that Paul was first a Jew, and a well-educated one. His Scriptures are our "Old Testament," and his "thought patterns" derive from his Jewish context. This does not mean, of course, that Paul must always and only think in ways identical with his Jewish world. The revelatory work of God in Christ transformed his thinking and his life. But neither does it mean, of course, that Paul's somehow completely disassociated his thinking from familiar Jewish categories. "Christianity" was not, for Paul or any other Christian then, as far as we can tell, a "new religion," separate from Judaism. Christianity grew out of Judaism. It was shaped by Jewish apostles and prophets. It displayed the outworking of God's plan for Israel and the world at large.

When Paul thinks about how individuals get wrapped up in this idea of election, his thought occurs along similar lines as other Jews who wrote before him. Identifying individuals (and sometimes groups) as "elect" frequently meant to recognize their "excellence" or their piety, as Paul seems to do with Rufus. In other cases, the emphasis lay with the vocation or role they were to play, as with Paul in Galatians 1. In other cases still, the dynamic between the representative individual and the group is in view. I would agree with Wright when he suggests that Paul

---

[106]N. T. Wright, *Paul and the Faithfulness of God* (Minneapolis: Fortress, 2013), p. 883. Likewise, see Hooker, "On Becoming the Righteousness of God," p. 368.

[107]For a discussion, see Michael F. Bird, "Incorporated Righteousness: A Response to the Recent Evangelical Discussion Concerning the Imputation of Christ's Righteousness in Justification," *JETS* 47, no. 2 (2004): 253-75.

did not go looking for these concepts and then relate them to Jesus, since I doubt Paul first thought about these incorporative ideas existing in Judaism and then figured out how he could reapply them.[108] The ideas certainly existed among Jews at the time, yet the significance of the work of Jesus recalibrates them. More than just emulating or associating with him, as we saw in the examples of Jacob, Levi, Judah and the Elect One, believers are dependent on him for their own standing before God. Paul sees Christ's activity and the believer's place "in him" as incorporative, representative and emulative. Jesus accomplished what no mere human could so humans could gain what only the incarnate Jesus secured. We will see next how Paul's emphasis on the "collective" of the elect likewise finds good grounding in the writings of Jews in the Second Temple period.

---

[108]Wright, *Paul and the Faithfulness of God*, p. 827.

Who Are the
People of God?

In the last chapter we saw that these texts of Judaism emphasized the character or purpose of individuals when employing "election language" or focused on the individual as a corporate representative. We also saw how certain Pauline texts indicate that the apostle was thinking along similar lines. We have much more to examine, of course, concerning Jewish understandings of election beyond how they relate to individuals, who are rarely the focus. More often, the texts from the period concentrate on the "collective" of the elect rather than individuals. Frequently this is seen in the form of corporate metaphors, or a general corporate/collective focus where the nation or its remnant takes center stage.

CORPORATE METAPHORS

One of the ways these texts shine a spotlight on the collective is in using corporate metaphors. The two employed most commonly are vine/plant imagery and the "remnant motif." In the Old Testament, in places like Isaiah 5, Jeremiah 2 and Ezekiel 15, the prophets describe Israel like a vine, plant or vineyard. This same imagery carries over in significant ways to the Jewish writers in the Second Temple period. Likewise, the emphasis of the prophets on the "remnant" of Israel seeing God's salvation (e.g., Ezra 9; Is 10–11; 37; Jer 23; 31; 44; Mic 5; Zeph 2; Zech 8) finds parallels in this body of literature. As we shall see, other images indicate a corporate focus as well.

Dead Sea Scrolls. Few discoveries have influenced biblical scholarship like the Dead Sea Scrolls (hereafter DSS). Textual, theological and archaeological studies have attempted to recover and reconstruct the community at Khirbet Qumran, which I will be assuming authored the sectarian literature discovered there. While some debate has persisted, the general consensus is now that the group in some sense reflected the Essenes mentioned by Josephus, though some differences between his descriptions and the theology found in the scrolls exist.[1] I will assume here, due to the large extent to which they agree, that the sectarian writings were the product of a single religious community of Essenes who separated themselves from Jerusalem. Though I assume interconnectedness, each text will be dealt with individually.[2]

The *Community Rule* (hereafter 1QS) served as the basis of the community's religious beliefs and observances. As Sarianna Metso summarizes, "The community that produced it is widely identified as belonging to the ancient Jewish movement of the Essenes, some members of which inhabited the site from about 150 BCE (or, as recently argued, ca. 100 BCE) to 68 CE."[3] Copies of the text survived in Caves 1, 4, 5 and 11, including a nearly perfectly preserved copy in Cave 1 (1QS).[4]

According to 1QS, those who enter into the covenant yet revert to idolatry will be destroyed forever and experience the covenant curses (1QS 2.11-18). There thus exists the possibility that those who have been enlightened may commit apostasy and abandon the covenant.[5]

---

[1]In comparing 1QS and *Ant.* 13.171-72, Emmanuel Tukasi concludes, "This ethical determinism of the Essenes as articulated in Josephus' passage is incompatible with the determinism of 1QS" (Emmanuel O. Tukasi, *Determinism and Petitionary Prayer in John and the Dead Sea Scrolls: An Ideological Reading of John and the Reading of the Community (1QS)* [New York: T&T Clark, 2008], p. 61). Concerning Josephus' Essenes, Paul Heger notes, "We should rely on the texts written by the members of the Community themselves, rather than on portrayals by outsiders" (Paul Heger, *Challenges to Conventional Opinions on Qumran and Enoch Issues* [Leiden: Brill, 2012], p. 325). For a comparison, see Kenneth Atkinson, "Josephus's Essenes and the Qumran Community," *JBL* 129, no. 2 (2010): 317-42. For a discussion on approaches to the possibility of doctrinal development evidenced in the scrolls, see Philip R. Davies, "Eschatology at Qumran," *JBL* 104, no. 1 (1985): 39-55.
[2]All translations taken from Florentino García Martínez and Eibert J. C. Tigchelaar, *The Dead Sea Scrolls: Study Edition* (Grand Rapids: Eerdmans, 1997), 2 vols., unless otherwise noted.
[3]Sarianna Metso, "Rule of the Community (1QS + fragments)," in *The Eerdmans Dictionary of Early Judaism*, ed. John J. Collins and Daniel C. Harlow (Grand Rapids: Eerdmans, 2010), p. 1169.
[4]Ibid.
[5]See Aharaon Shemesh, "Expulsion and Exclusion in the Community Rule and the Damascus Document," *DSD* 9, no. 1 (2002): 48.

Those who refuse to enter into the covenant[6] are wicked and forbidden from fellowship since they regard "darkness as paths of light" (1QS 2.26–3.3).[7] What divides God's people and outsiders is clear. As Alfred Leaney states, "Only members of the sect will in the final judgment of God be reckoned as Israelites."[8] God will not forgive those outside of the community since the Qumranites' atoning rituals only benefit themselves (1QS 3.4-7). Humans can find atonement only through the covenant, and outsiders must submit themselves to obeying its ordinances (1QS 3.7-12).[9]

1QS 6.1-23 also regulates the social interactions of community members as well as the "session of the Many" (6.8). Here 1QS requires examining "anyone from Israel who freely volunteers to enroll in the council of the Community," which includes subjecting themselves to the scrutiny of "the Many" and a two-year period of partial membership prior to full recognition (6.14-23). Additional guidelines regulating improper behavior are found in 1QS 6.24–7.16, which specifies the punishments for those who knowingly lie, utter "the Name," speak angrily against the priests, insult a fellow member, negligently handle shared property, are angry, use improper speech, sleep during meetings, display unnecessary nudity, spit and giggle. Questioning or speaking against "the Many," questioning "the foundation of the Community" or fraternizing

---

[6]Leaney states, "It seems natural to interpret this passage (2.25b-3.12) as a commination against those who, after their probation, refuse to enter the covenant, balancing the part of the scroll so far considered (1.1–2.24) which deals with those who enter" (Alfred R. C. Leaney, *The Rule of Qumran and Its Meaning: Introduction, Translation and Commentary* [Philadelphia: Westminster, 1966], p. 137).

[7]Timmer suggests "the non-covenantal form of the Priestly Blessing of Numbers 6 . . . meant that this modified blessing was perfectly suited for application to the community's members on the basis of their election *rather than* their covenantal fidelity" (Daniel C. Timmer, "Variegated Nomism Indeed: Multiphase Eschatology and Soteriology in the Qumranite *Community Rule* (1QS) and the New Perspective on Paul," *JETS* 52, no. 2 [2009]: 346). This appears, however, to create a false dichotomy. Clearly, adherence to the Torah as interpreted by the Teacher of Righteousness *and* belief in their election (however defined) were central tenants of the community. We should maintain neither at the expense of the other.

[8]Leaney, *Rule of Qumran*, p. 138.

[9]Ringgren writes, "This certainly implies that the hope is based on the work of God's spirit; but at the same time it becomes apparent that salvation presupposes a conversion and a new willingness to fulfill God's law" (Helmer Ringgren, *The Faith of Qumran: Theology of the Dead Sea Scrolls* [New York: Crossroad, 1995], p. 105).

with those who have been expelled: all could result in the expelling of the offender (1QS 7.16-25).[10]

The council of the community must ensure the faithfulness of the covenant members "in order to atone for sin by doing justice and undergoing trials, and to walk with everyone in the measure of the truth and the regulation of the time" (1QS 8.1-4). This atoning function, Mark Adam Elliott notes, "reflects the view that the sectarian cult intended, by means of a spiritual kind of worship, to replace the apostate priesthood and cult in Jerusalem."[11] The author of 1QS further states, "When these things exist in Israel the Community council shall be founded on truth, to be an everlasting plantation, a holy house for Israel and the foundation of the holy of holies for Aaron, true witnesses for the judgment and chosen by the will (of God) to atone for the land and to render the wicked their retribution" (1QS 8.5-7; also 9.3-6). Here again the group clearly envisages itself as the true Israel, the faithful remnant, which God has preserved in this period when Belial rules over most of the Jews. Their perfect obedience will "prepare the way of [YHWH]" and "open there His path" (1QS 8.13-14).[12] The images used (plantation, house and foundation) demonstrate the author has the collective in mind.

As the *Rule* closes, 1QS 9.12–11.22 records the regulations for the "Instructor" as well as a dedicatory prayer. In 1QS 11.7-8, the author writes, "To those who God has selected he has given them (wisdom, knowledge, and justice) as everlasting possession; and he has given them an inheritance in the lot of the holy ones. He unites their assembly to the sons of the heavens in order (to form) the council of the Community and a foundation of the building of holiness to be an everlasting plantation

---

[10]Of these regulations, Tukasi notes, "Another way by which the text articulates human responsibility is in its emphasis on the standard of living within the community. As a way of enforcing the standard, the text enumerates the punishment for every misdemeanour" (Tukasi, *Determinism and Petitionary Prayer*, p. 59).

[11]Mark Adam Elliott, *The Survivors of Israel: A Reconsideration of the Theology of Pre-Christian Judaism* (Grand Rapids: Eerdmans, 2000), p. 333.

[12]Tukasi again notes, "The text makes it clear that continuation of membership in the Community is guaranteed on the condition that one's actions befit the purpose which identified the group as a predestined Community" (Tukasi, *Determinism and Petitionary Prayer*, p. 58).

throughout all future ages."[13] The soteriology of 1QS, as we shall see later, does not necessarily support the idea that God selects here specific individuals for salvation.

1QS is primarily concerned with ordering the life of the sect. Life from the covenant belongs to them, the true Israel, alone. They constitute the remnant of Israel, and God has preserved them to fulfill his promises.[14] Only they experience the covenant blessings. The author emphasizes the collective by recognizing that the *community* maintains the covenant as well as by describing the group as a "plantation," a "foundation" and a "house." God chose this people as his remnant, and individuals become covenant members through submission to the rites and regulations of the group and its leaders.

The *War Scroll* (hereafter 1QM) dates to the first or second century B.C.E., and is preserved in manuscripts and fragments discovered in Caves 1, 4 and 11.[15] 1QM describes the battle to take place between the sons of light (also called "the sons of Levi, the sons of Judah and the sons of Benjamin," see 1QM 1.2) and the sons of darkness (Gentiles[16] and Jewish traitors to the true covenant alike[17]), led by Belial (1QM 1.1-3). According to E. P. Sanders, "In 1QM the enemies are always the Gentiles.

---

[13]Here Vermes states, "Their attitude in regard to the Covenant was that only the initiates of their own 'new Covenant' were to be reckoned among God's elect and, as such, united already on earth with the angels of heaven" (*The Dead Sea Scrolls: Qumran in Perspective* [Cleveland: William Collins & World, 1978], p. 170).

[14]See Preben Wernberg-Møller, *The Manual of Discipline: Translated and Annotated with an Introduction* (Grand Rapids: Eerdmans, 1957), pp. 13-14.

[15]Jean Duhaime, "War Scroll (1QM)," in Collins and Harlow, *Eerdmans Dictionary of Early Judaism*, p. 1329. For a detailed discussion of the relationship of the various scrolls copies and the compositional history of the *War Scroll*, see Brian Schultz, *Conquering the World: The War Scroll (1QM) Reconsidered* (Leiden: Brill, 2009).

[16]Flusser identifies the Kittim of the War Scroll as the Romans, and that "the scroll was composed some time after Pompey's entrance into Egypt, or perhaps Julius Caesar's" (David Flusser, *Judaism of the Second Temple Period* [Grand Rapids: Eerdmans, 2007], 1:141). See also Alexander Bolotnikov, "The Theme of Apocalyptic War in the Dead Sea Scrolls," *Andrews University Seminary Studies* 43, no. 2 (2005): 261-66. Treves, however, sees the mention of Assyria and Egypt as reference to the Macedonians of Syria and Egypt, and thus "in the period 167-69 B.C., when there were hostilities between the Jews and the Seleucids, and thus did not originate with the Qumranites" (Marco Treves, "The Date of the War of the Sons of Light," *VT* 8 [1958]: 420).

[17]Yigael Yadin notes that the language here "doubtlessly referred to those amongst the Jews whom the sect considered to be traitors and persecutors of the righteous" (Yigael Yadin, *The Scroll of the War of the Sons of Light Against the Sons of Darkness* [Oxford: Oxford University Press, 1962], p. 26).

The only reference to enemies within Israel is the phrase 'offenders against the covenant' in 1.2. These are said to assist the Gentile armies against whom the Sons of Light wage their first engagement."[18] The "violators of the covenant" can refer *only* to Jews who have abandoned the covenant as defined by the community. These apostates fight *alongside* of the Gentiles, and thus are numbered among the enemies of the sons of light. The sons of light are on the offensive in the conflict, bringing the battle to Jerusalem, and the event will be a "period of rule for all the men of [God's] lot, and of everlasting destruction for all the lot of Belial" (1QM 1.3-5). During the battle, both camps make advances, but ultimately God will assist the sons of light and he will defeat Belial, his angels and his armies (1QM 1.10-17).[19]

After their return from battle, the congregation will cleanse themselves and then say, "Blessed be the God of Israel, the one who keeps mercy for his covenant and pledges of deliverance for the people he has redeemed. He has called those who are tottering to wondrous [exploits], and has gathered the assembly of peoples for destruction with no remnant" (1QM 14.4-5). God will use the weak and poor, "the perfect ones of the path" (1QM 14.7), who are "the rem[nant of your people]" (14.8) to bring about the destruction of the wicked (14.6-8). Furthermore, God has "wondrously bestowed [his] mercies to the rem[nant of your inheritance] during the empire of Belial" (1QM 14.9), who has "not separated us from your covenant" (14.9-10). Ultimately Belial and his armies will be destroyed, and the priests and Levites and chiefs will bless God for his salvation and his faithfulness to his covenant with them (1QM 17.10–19.14).

The War Scroll serves as both a military plan and a theological encouragement. It assures the sect of their success. All who will side with them will likewise enjoy victory, while those who oppose them in reality oppose God, and God will destroy them for their failure to accept the true revelation he has given. The sect sees themselves as inheriting the

---

[18]E. P. Sanders, *Paul and Palestinian Judaism* (Minneapolis: Fortress, 1970), p. 248. Steudel likewise seems to hold that the Israel in 1QM is national Israel, and not the sectarians (Annette Steudel, "The Eternal Reign of the People of God—Collective Expectations in Qumran Texts (4Q246 and 1QM)," *RevQ* 17 [1996]: 507-25).

[19]Elliott, *Survivors of Israel*, p. 614.

promises given to Israel, for they alone stand in the line of the covenant. Here as elsewhere the text emphasizes their collective identity, and God's plans are collectively described. He has chosen the nation (i.e., the community), this remnant, the "sons of light," as his people. Jean Duhaime recognizes the rhetorical force of this emphasis in stating, "This powerful and encompassing vision certainly helped legitimize the decision of the sectarians to cut themselves off from a corrupted environment; it also provided them with a strong sense of identity as the true remnant of Israel and helped them consolidate their commitment to the Mosaic Law as interpreted and enforced in the community by its religious authorities."[20] As seen in 1QS, the Qumran sectarians understood themselves to be God's chosen people, the inheritors of God's promises to Israel, since they were the true remnant of Israel.

1 Enoch. The Book of Watchers also contributes to the collective emphasis seen in the Jewish literature concerning the elect. Much of the book concentrates on the antediluvian period and the intermingling of two hundred heavenly beings with the children of men, led by the wicked angel Semyaz (*1 En.* 7:1). These beings took wives from humanity and "taught them magical medicine, incantations, the cutting of roots, and taught them (about) plants. And the women became pregnant and gave birth to great giants" (*1 En.* 7:1-2), who then began to oppress the human race (7:3-6). The human race became corrupt (*1 En.* 8:1-3), and "(the people) cried and their voice reached unto heaven" (8:4).

Following a period of seventy generations, the author declares the "eternal judgment" will occur, and the wicked angels, and "those who collaborated with them, will be bound together" forever (*1 En.* 10:13-15). Then "every iniquitous deed will end, and the plant of righteousness and truth will appear forever and he will plant joy" (*1 En.* 10:16). This "plant of righteousness and truth" represents the community of the righteous described in the Watchers, and is a "corporate metaphor" for the "true Israel."[21] Likewise, the figure of Noah serves as a type of the

---

[20]Duhaime, "War Scroll (1QM)," p. 1329.

[21]Elliott, *Survivors of Israel*, p. 330. The terminology (both seed and plant imagery) occurs elsewhere in *1 Enoch* and will be addressed in those instances separately.

righteous ones who will escape the final judgment just as righteous Noah and his sons escaped the flood.[22] With all iniquity gone from the earth, "all the children of the people will become righteous, and all the nations shall worship and bless me," and the earth will be blessed forever (1 En. 10:21–11:2).

Book four, also known as the Book of Dreams,[23] recounts two visions Enoch received during two different periods of his life. The first vision is of the flood (1 En. 83–84), and the second, and longer, vision recounts the history of Israel, from Adam to the Maccabees (85–90). Mahalalel, Enoch's grandfather, interprets his vision of the flood as a vision of "all the sins of the whole world as it was sinking into the abyss and being destroyed with great destruction" (1 En. 83:7). He instructs Enoch to pray that "a remnant shall remain upon the earth and that the whole earth shall not be blotted out" (1 En. 83:8). Enoch asks that God would "save for me (a generation) that will succeed me in the earth; and do not destroy all the flesh of the people and empty the earth (so that) there shall be eternal destruction. Do now destroy, O my Lord, the flesh that has angered you from upon the earth, but sustain the flesh of righteousness and uprightness as a plant of eternal seed" (1 En. 84:5-6). Again, as in the Book of Watchers, the author likely views the flood as a paradigmatic judgment event, and sees his own community as the "remnant" that will survive in the last days.[24]

The second vision in the Book of Dreams is an extended metaphor,

---

[22]George W. E. Nickelsburg, 1 Enoch, Hermeneia (Minneapolis: Fortress, 2001), 1:226; Ryan E. Stokes, "Watchers, Book of the (1 Enoch 1–36)," in Collins and Harlow, Eerdmans Dictionary of Early Judaism, p. 1333. Elliott notes that, in light of the flood being a paradigmatic judgment, "the present-day Israel is thereby itself implicated and warned of the coming judgment when only the 'righteous ones will escape' (v. 17)" (Elliott, Survivors of Israel, pp. 430-31). See also ibid., p. 623. Even Sanders here recognizes that "the righteous must be those who obey the will of God, just as the unrighteous disobey" (Sanders, Paul and Palestinian Judaism, p. 350).

[23]The typically suggested date for the Book of Dreams is ca. 165 B.C.E. (especially for chaps. 85–90) (Daniel Assefa, "Dreams, Book of (1 Enoch 83–90)," in Collins and Harlow, Eerdmans Dictionary of Early Judaism, p. 552). For a detailed discussion, see Patrick A. Tiller, A Commentary on the Animal Apocalypse of I Enoch [Atlanta: Scholars Press, 1993], pp. 61-82).

[24]Nickelsburg perhaps hints at this in noting, "Enoch prays in v 6 that, as a true judge, God distinguish between sinful humanity, which has rightly aroused the divine wrath (v 4), and the righteous and true humanity, which should remain as a remnant that will bear seed for a new planting" (Nickelsburg, 1 Enoch, 1:353).

frequently referred to as the Animal Apocalypse, in which the characters and groups depicted by Enoch are animals. The account retells the biblical history from Adam (a cow) through Judas Maccabeus (a ram). Several interesting features stand out. In discussing Jacob and Esau, the author depicts Jacob as white sheep, the beginning of the line of sheep, while Esau is a black boar, an evil color and an unclean animal (*1 En.* 89:10-12).[25] While wandering in the wilderness, the sheep (i.e., Israel) "went astray from the path" that the Lord showed them, causing some to be killed while others returned to their folds (*1 En.* 89:28-35). The notion of blindness or dimness is essentially equated in the Animal Apocalypse with apostasy and disobedience.[26] The pattern of blindness/disobedience continues throughout the Apocalypse, and eventually lambs (i.e., the author's righteous community and/or the younger generation)[27] are born and cry aloud to the blind sheep, but the sheep "became exceedingly deafened, and their eyes became exceedingly dim-sighted" (*1 En.* 90:6-7). The call from the lambs is most likely to return to obedience to the law or pious living (see *1 En.* 90:7), but the sheep apparently ignore their appeal.[28]

---

[25] Tiller notes that "it may be that the colors here do not represent any specific characteristics of the three brothers but that taken together they serve to characterize the postdiluvian age as essentially the same as the antediluvian age—inhabited by both righteous and wicked, both perpetrators and victims of evil" (Tiller, *Animal Apocalypse*, p. 267). Black suggests, "The three colours here seem to have a different connotation from the 'red' and 'black' of Abel and Cain at v. 3. In this verse they symbolize three races, Semites (white), Japhethites (red) and Hamites (black)" (Matthew Black, *The Book of Enoch or I Enoch: A New English Edition* [Leiden: Brill, 1985], p. 264). Of Esau as a black boar, Tiller states, "The contrast between Jacob/Israel and Esau/Edom could hardly be greater" (Tiller, *Animal Apocalypse*, p. 275).

[26] So Tiller writes, "The implication of seeing, then seems to be possession of God's law and obedience to it. From this point on the ability of the sheep to see will represent Israel's obedience or disobedience to God. The metaphor of blindness is also frequently coupled with the metaphor of straying, both together representing apostasy (cf. 89.32, 54)" (*Animal apocalypse*, p. 293). See also George W. E. Nickelsburg, *Jewish Literature Between the Bible and the Mishnah* (Minneapolis: Fortress, 2005), p. 84; Nickelsburg, *1 Enoch*, 1:378.

[27] Compare Tiller, who notes, "These lambs no doubt represent one of the circles to which the author of the *An. Apoc.* belonged. If there is any social group that can be said to have produced the *An. Apoc.*, it is this group" (*Animal Apocalypse*, p. 350); and Nickelsburg, who suggests, "Here the younger generation has begun to see the error of the nation's ways and calls its elders to repentance" (Nickelsburg, *1 Enoch*, 1:398).

[28] As Tiller summarizes, the righteous community "is characterized by (1) a revival of correct obedience to the law (90.6, they could see); (2) an appeal to others to join them (90.6, they cried to the sheep); (3) lack of success and forcible opposition from other within Israel (90.7-8, the

After one of the sheep sprouts a horn, this ram (Judas Maccabeus) battles the wild animals while crying aloud "so that (God's) help should come" (*1 En.* 90:8-14). The sheep,[29] however, turn against the ram and come upon him with the wild animals (Gentiles), but the Lord of the sheep strikes the earth, giving victory to the ram and the sheep over the beasts (*1 En.* 90:15-19). Here, clearly, Israel stands divided as to their allegiances, with some supporting the Gentiles and others the Maccabees, a phenomenon likewise found in 1 and 2 Maccabees.[30] The people of God in the Book of Dreams are thus those who are faithfully obedient to God, and who possibly also supported the Maccabean revolt, over and against those Jews who were apostate and/or sided with the Gentile oppressors of the faithful of Israel.[31] The imagery, however, emphasizes the people as a collective based on the behavior, type and color of animal represented.

In chapter 93 of the Epistle of Enoch, Enoch recounts the seven weeks (i.e., periods) that precede the weeks of judgment outlined in *1 Enoch* 91.[32] Enoch lived during the first week, followed by a second week when evil grows on the earth. In the third week, a man "shall be elected as the plant of the righteous judgment, and after him one (other) shall emerge as the

---

[29]sheep failed to hear, afflicted them, and prevailed); (4) unsuccessful armed revolt (90.9, they grew horns which the ravens crushed); (5) later adherence to the Maccabees, both militarily and doctrinally (90.9-10, one sheep grew a great horn and mustered all the rams, and they could see). The Maccabees are viewed as being at least acceptably obedient to the law" (Tiller, *Animal Apocalypse*, p. 350).

[29]Tiller suggests that these are likely "Jews who were not only disobedient ('blind') but who had also become Hellenized or collaborators and thus joined the nations in the battles against Judas" (ibid., p. 363). Elliott likewise notes, "*In line with the symbolism of the work generally,* therefore 'sheep' remains a designation for *the whole population of Israelites,* not simply a specific group of opponents or the leaders of Israel. Thus v. 16 certainly intends *this* Israel when it says that '*all* the sheep of the field' conspire together with the Gentiles in one final mass confrontation with the horn" (Elliott, *Survivors of Israel,* p. 79 [emphasis original]).

[30]Elliott says, "What is especially important is how these groups are portrayed as being in *fundamental religious conflict*" (ibid., p. 77 [emphasis original]).

[31]Tiller suggests as much in stating, "The author of the *An. Apoc.* represents a militant, pro-independence, religious reform group. This group is politically quite close to what can be known about the Hasidim and its critique of the Second Temple is paralleled in the *Testament of the Twelve Patriarchs,* the *Testament of Moses,* and certain sectarian compositions from Qumran" (Tiller, *Animal Apocalypse,* p. 126).

[32]For a summary of the narrative in the weeks, Loren T. Stückenbruck, "Enoch, Epistle of (1 Enoch 91–108)," in Collins and Harlow, *Eerdmans Dictionary of Early Judaism,* p. 584.

eternal plant of righteousness" (*1 En.* 93:5). The author here first refer-ences Abraham, and second Jacob (or possibly Isaac), who stand as rep-resentatives of the nation that would be born from them. Here the author affirms both the eternality of this election and the characteristic of the "plant" as a righteous one. In the fourth week, the law is given "for all the generations," which Loren Stückenbruck notes constitutes the only ex-plicit reference to the law in all of the work,[33] and in the fifth week the temple and kingdom are established (*1 En.* 93:6-7). In the sixth week the people "forget wisdom," the kingdom burns and "the chosen root shall be dispersed" (*1 En.* 93:8).[34] Then, in the seventh week, "an apostate generation shall arise; its deeds shall be many, and all of them criminal" (*1 En.* 93:9). The author apparently suggests here that the entirety, or at least majority, of the nation was characterized by disobedience at this time.[35] At this week's completion God has "elected the elect ones of righteousness from the eternal plant of righteousness, to whom shall be given sevenfold instruction concerning all his flock" (*1 En.* 93:10),[36] who stand in the line of Abraham.[37] The fact that Enoch here identifies the elect as a subgroup of the plant indicates that they are a remnant of Israel, a "true Israel," who received a special wisdom that separates them from the apostates of Israel, which apparently includes all who are outside of

---

[33]Ibid., p. 107. Stückenbruck further notes that the law here "is closely bound up with both the former ('holy and righteous ones,' i.e. angels) and the latter ('the enclosure,' i.e. the tabernacle)" (ibid.).

[34]"The double emphasis on 'all' indicates how completely the sixth period is marked by an aban-donment from the unfolding plan of God through Israel's election (week 3), the giving of the Torah and the ark of the covenant (week 4), and the Temple cult (week 5). Withdrawal from these is tantamount to blindness that corresponds to a lack of insight into the divine purpose" (ibid., p. 113).

[35]Nickelsburg suggests, "This viewpoint constitutes a wholesale condemnation of the return, the restoration, the rebuilding of the temple, and the events of the Persian and Hellenistic periods" (Nickelsburg, *1 Enoch*, 1:447).

[36]Stückenbruck notes, "One would therefore be hard pressed to suppose that this is simply a reference to ethnic Israel in its entirety, which if anywhere has just been mentioned in relation to the figure of Abraham. It is, rather, none other than a designation for a select, collective off-spring of Abraham concerning which the *Apocalypse* has been authored . . . 'plant of righteous-ness/truth' denotes a group, a 'true Israel' selected from amongst Abraham's offspring, that provides a continuous link between biblical and eschatological time" (Loren T. Stückenbruck, *1 Enoch 91-108* [Berlin: de Gruyter, 2007], pp. 101-2).

[37]Nickelsburg, *1 Enoch*, 1:448.

the community.[38] Chapter 93 then closes with a reflection on the incomprehensibility of the heavenly realm and the Holy One.

First Enoch, as a whole, emphasizes the collective identity of the elect. This occurs through several images. We find the first in the paradigmatic depiction of the great flood. Noah represents the righteous whom God will save from the waters of judgment, subsequently resulting in God destroying the wicked sinners. The author implies that many ethnic Jews belonged among the "wicked" in their day. The same implication comes in the Animal Apocalypse, where the author focuses on the collective of God's people as represented through the animal imagery. Likewise, and more explicitly, the image of the true Israel as a "plant of righteousness" or a "seed" emphasizes the collective nature of God's people.

CORPORATE FOCUS

The above texts sketched out the collective nature of Israel's election through imagery like "the path of life," a plant, a house, a foundation, a plantation, a remnant, a possession or a seed. The texts surveyed below provide such an emphasis by discussing God's people in general, "corporate" terms. While some of this language was interspersed in the texts examined above, it is more concentrated and explicit in the examples shown below. These texts again show that election language for Second Temple Jews was focused on Israel as a nation, or its remnant, as the chosen people.

Wisdom of Ben Sira. Ben Sira recognizes God's choice of Israel. In Sirach 17, a chapter that describes the various capacities with which humanity has been endowed (e.g., authority over creation, the image of God and the ability to know and reason), Ben Sira assures the Lord appointed a leader over every nation,[39] "but Israel is the Lord's own portion"

---

[38]See Black, *Book of Enoch*, p. 291; Elliott, *Survivors of Israel*, p. 331; George W. E. Nickelsburg, "The Apocalyptic Message of *1 Enoch* 92–105," *CBQ* 39 (1977): 326; Nickelsburg, *1 Enoch*, 1:446; Chris VanLandingham, *Judgment and Justification in Early Judaism and the Apostle Paul* (Grand Rapids: Baker Academic, 2006), p. 93.

[39]There is some question here as to whether Ben Sira is speaking of a heavenly leader (see Deut 4:18; 32:8; Dan 10:13-21; see, e.g., Goering, *Wisdom's Root Revealed*, p. 99) or an earthly king (see, e.g., Michael E. Fuller, *The Restoration of Israel: Israel's Re-Gathering and the Fate of the Nations in Early Jewish Literature and Luke-Acts* [Berlin: de Gruyter, 2006], p. 41 n. 104). What is clear is the emphasis on YHWH's special relationship with Israel.

(Sir 17:17). As the passage continues, he focuses on the knowledge of the Lord of all "their" sins, though he does not specify the referent. He may have intended humans in general or Israel. Given the references to "almsgiving" (Sir 17:22), and "repentance" and "return" (17:23), he may have had Israel in mind, which would suggest that for Ben Sira only a portion of Israel (the remnant) were/would be faithful to Yнwн.[40]

Ben Sira also recognizes that God had preserved a remnant of Jacob and the line of David even when the kingdom itself became depraved. He first addresses this when recounting the division of the kingdom under Solomon. In the context, he asserts that the Lord will "never[41] blot out the descendants of his chosen one, or destroy the family line of him who loved him. So he gave a remnant to Jacob, and to David a root from his own family" (Sir 47:22), though the nation itself was exiled from the land for their ever-increasing sin (47:24-25). He again presents the remnant motif in discussing the exile in Sirach 48:15-16, where he asserts that because the people did not repent, "they were carried off as plunder" and "the people were left very few in number, but with a ruler from the house of David." The section of the hymn recounting biblical history ends, however, with little attention spent to the return from exile (Sir 49:12-13). Though not explicit, Ben Sira's allusions may recognize that God chose the nation through Abraham's line, but this did not entail a choice of every descendant. Rather those who remained in the covenant through keeping the law (an important theme in the book) were among God's chosen people.

1 Maccabees. The book of 1 Maccabees is a narrative description of the revolt of Judean Jews under the rule of the Seleucids during the mid-second century B.C.E. The book focuses on the exploits of the Maccabean brothers, led by Judas Maccabeus. The revolts were prompted by the

---

[40]Skehan and Di Lella seem to view the rest of the text as universal in scope, noting, "Because of human freedom, there is hope even for the sinner: he can repent" (Patrick W. Skehan and Alexander A. Di Lella, OFM, *The Wisdom of Ben Sira: A New Translation with Notes*, AB [New York: Doubleday, 1987], p. 83).

[41]The LXX uses a series of four emphatic negatives to assure that Israel, and specifically David's line, will never be totally wiped out of existence: ὁ δὲ κύριος οὐ μὴ καταλίπῃ τὸ ἔλεος αὐτοῦ; καὶ οὐ μὴ διαφθείρῃ ἀπὸ τῶν λόγων αὐτοῦ; οὐδὲ μὴ ἐξαλείψῃ ἐκλεκτοῦ αὐτοῦ ἔκγονα; and καὶ σπέρμα τοῦ ἀγαπήσαντος αὐτὸν οὐ μὴ ἐξάρῃ.

activities of Antiochus IV,[42] who desecrated the temple and forbade the exercise of the Jewish religious practices, greatly offending and outraging the Jews (1 Macc 1:20-50). The author upholds the Maccabees in the book as the heroes of the conflict, fighting against both their syncretistic brethren and against the tyrannies of Antiochus IV and subsequent rulers.[43] Consensus is that the book was authored prior to the end of the second century B.C.E., and thus near the occurrence of the events. Though historical in nature, the author blended a theological commentary on the events of the period, setting the conflict in a spiritual framework. This does not necessarily diminish the historical veracity of the events (this was commonplace of "historical narratives" in the ancient world), and Mary Chilton Callaway notes that scholars often consider the book to be "the most reliable historical resource for the study of the Maccabean revolt."[44]

In numerous examples throughout the book, Israel's dissenters (i.e., those who break the covenant and/or oppose the Maccabees) act lawlessly, while the Maccabees and their supporters[45] prove to be God's chosen agents and stand within the ranks of the great men of Israel's history.[46] Thus lawless renegades from within Israel convince the people

---

[42]Concerning the impetus for the persecution, Elliott summarizes, "The cause, and exact significance, of this event are widely debated. Antiochus's 'campaign against Judaism' has been interpreted, on the one hand, as an expression of a mad ruler's rigorous personal *Hellenizing program* (Antiochus assuming the weight of the 'blame'); but, from a completely opposite point of view, it has also been viewed as only the *result of the Jews' resistance to Hellenism*, which in turn enraged the ruler and further hardened him in his intentions (Jews assuming the weight of the 'blame'). . . . If psychological or ideological motivations fail to explain Antiochus's actions, some other explanation is required, and one solution has been offered by what might be called Jewish conspiracy theories. Such theories maintain that the events of persecution were catalyzed by a Hellenizing party *within* Judaism, an understanding that is strongly encouraged by the writer of 1 Maccabees (esp. 1:11-15)" (Elliott, *Survivors of Israel*, p. 192 [emphasis original]).

[43]See David A. deSilva, *Introducing the Apocrypha: Message, Context, and Significance* (Grand Rapids: Baker Academic, 2002), p. 250.

[44]Mary Chilton Callaway, "1 Maccabees," in *The New Oxford Annotated Apocrypha*, ed. Michael D. Coogan (New York: Oxford University Press, 2001), p. 201.

[45]Gathercole states, "During the crisis of the second century, Judas Maccabeus's army consisted of 'all who observe the Law' (1 Macc 2:67-68), and Simon later settled in Gazara 'those who observe the Law' (13:48)" (Simon J. Gathercole, *Where Is Boasting? Early Jewish Soteriology and Paul's Response in Romans 1-5* [Grand Rapids: Eerdmans, 2002], p. 186).

[46]Elsewhere, the author compares Judas's situation to that of Hezekiah and the Assyrians (1 Macc 7:39-42; cf. 1 Kings 19), and Jonathan may be viewed as a successor of Josiah (see Jonathan A. Goldstein, *I Maccabees: A New Translation with Introduction and Commentary*, AB [New York:

to forsake the covenant (1 Macc 1:11), oppose the Maccabees militarily (1 Macc 1:34), flee to the Gentiles in fear (1 Macc 2:44; 3:5-6), are equated with the Gentiles (1 Macc 3:20), bring false accusations against the Hasmoneans (1 Macc 7:5; 9:58; 11:25) and seek out the Maccabean sympathizers after the death of Judas (1 Macc 9:23).[47] The Maccabees, on the other hand, are lauded for their opposition to these lawless renegades (1 Macc 3:5-6; 9:69), and Simon is praised for doing "away with all the renegades and outlaws" (1 Macc 14:14).[48] As the Maccabees' reputation grows, they become allies with Gentile rulers, who laud their accomplishments. Jonathan is established as governor and high priest (1 Macc 10:18-20, 65), and thus the offices that had been separate prior to the revolt became combined in one ruler and would remain so for over a century. In Simon's plea to the people after the death of Jonathan, he reminds the people of the greatness of his deceased brothers and father, who faithfully kept the law, protected the sanctuary and died for the preservation of Israel (1 Macc 13:3-6). "All Israel" mourns Jonathan's death, which is clearly either an exaggeration or an assertion that those Jews who opposed the Hasmoneans or forsook the covenant have no place in the people of God (1 Macc 13:26).[49] While King Alexander, and later King Antiochus, appoints and publicly confirms Jonathan as high priest in Jerusalem (1 Macc 10:20; 11:26, 57), Simon is recognized as such by the people (1 Macc 13:42; 14:35, 41, 47), perhaps an attempt to legit-

---

Doubleday, 1976], p. 395). In addition, the campaigns against the "sons of Esau" may be construed as a fulfillment of Obad 15-21 as Goldstein has observed (ibid., p. 294). See also deSilva, *Introducing the Apocrypha*, p. 259.

[47]As Bickerman summarizes, "Again and again, their complaints cause the Syrians to march against Israel. These complaints are listed even in cases where the government would not have remained inactive anyway, such as during the siege of the citadel in Jerusalem by the Maccabees (1 Macc 6:21; 7:5, 25; 9:58; 11:21; cf. 6:19; 1:21). . . . The author wants to equate the Jewish opponents of the native dynasty with the pagan enemies of the people" (Elias Bickerman, *The God of the Maccabees: Studies on the Meaning and Origin of the Maccabean Revolt* [Leiden: Brill, 1979], p. 18).

[48]So while Harrington states that "[the author] . . . comes close to equating the Maccabees with the 'true Israel' and their Jewish opponents with 'lawless men'" (Daniel J. Harrington, *Invitation to the Apocrypha* [Grand Rapids: Eerdmans, 1999], p. 124), it seems likely that this is what he in actuality does.

[49]DeSilva affirms the latter in stating, "'All Israel' mourns Mattathias's passing (2:70), thus limiting 'Israel' narrowly to those sympathetic to the Hasmonean attacks on apostates and the Gentile occupying forces" (deSilva, *Introducing the Apocrypha*, p. 262).

imize the combination of the two offices for the author's intended audience and future generations.

While 1 Maccabees is widely recognized as the most historically accurate
account of the revolt available, its bias is clear. The author seeks to legitimize
the Hasmonean dynasty by portraying its opponents as lawless God-
forsakers and by showing the Maccabees to be the continuation of Israel's
history, God's chosen deliverers of his oppressed people. Here it is not just
disobedience to the law, but opposition to God's chosen rulers, that distinguishes outsiders.[50] The Hasmonean dynasty was not, however, without its
controversy.[51] First Maccabees itself indicates that the opposition posed by
the Hellenizers was a sizeable group,[52] though this could be due to their
alliances with the Gentiles. While the Hasmoneans were not outside of the
"mainline" of Judaism, many pious Jews opposed the regime, criticizing their
lax handling of the priesthood.[53] The author of 1 Maccabees, however, sees
the "true Israel" as those who both uphold the law's centrality for Jewish
identity and support, or at least do not oppose, the Hasmoneans and their
Maccabean predecessors. As such, the book affirms the notion of the
remnant motif since "all Israel" does not include every Israelite, thus emphasizing the collective of God's people as his chosen ones.

Psalms of Solomon. *Psalms of Solomon* 7 contains a plea for God to
remember his "holy inheritance" (*Pss. Sol.* 7:2) and not deliver them to

---

[50]See Goldstein, *I Maccabees*, p. 330.

[51]Josephus records the enmity between the Hasmoneans and the Pharisees (*Ant.* 13.10), and the
Qumran community had its issues with the Hasmonean priest-kings as well. (For discussions, see
John J. Collins, *The Apocalyptic Imagination* (Grand Rapids: Eerdmans, 1998), pp. 148-50; Edward
Dąbrowa, "The Hasmoneans in the Light of the Qumran Scrolls," in *The Dead Sea Scrolls in
Context: Integrating the Dead Sea Scrolls in the Study of Ancient Texts, Languages and Cultures*, ed.
Armin Lange, Emanuel Tov and Matthias Weigold (Leiden: Brill, 2011), pp. 501-10; Hanan
Eshel, *The Dead Sea Scrolls and the Hasmonean State* (Grand Rapids: Eerdmans, 2008), pp. 29-62;
Larry R. Helyer, *Exploring Jewish Literature of the Second Temple Period: A Guide for New Testa-
ment Students* (Downers Grove, IL: InterVarsity Press, 2002), pp. 226-75.

[52]See Joseph Hellerman, "Purity and Nationalism in Second Temple Literature: 1–2 Maccabees
and *Jubilees*," *JETS* 46, no. 3 (2003): 402.

[53]A large measure of the discontent associated with the Hasmoneans was due to their acceptance
or advocacy of the combination of the offices of high priest and king/governor and what was
viewed as their corruption of those offices. See Elliott, *Survivors of Israel*, p. 224; Harrington,
Invitation to the Apocrypha, p. 135. Schofield and VanderKam have, however, argued the Hasmoneans may not have actually been non-Zadokites, as many have assumed (Alison Schofield and
James C. VanderKam, "Were the Hasmoneans Zadokites?," *JBL* 124, no. 1 [2005]: 73-87).

the Gentiles (7:3). The psalmist has confidence that God will not destroy his people (*Pss. Sol.* 7:5), and that he "will have compassion on the people of Israel forever" (7:8). Sanders sees the confidence here as an assurance that God will forever remember the nation of Israel as a whole, with no particular emphasis on the remembrance of the obedient only.[54] As Chris VanLandingham notes, however, that statements like this "address only the nation as an entity. Statements such as *Pss. Sol.* 9:5, which have as their basis Lev 18:5; Deut 28–32 (especially Deut 30:15-20), address the individual."[55] Thus a nationalistic view here should not overturn the emphasis on the preservation of the devout alone, which occurs frequently throughout the collection.

We find a similar perspective in the closing verses of *Psalms of Solomon* 12. After the psalmist prays, "The salvation of the Lord be upon Israel his servant forever," he next prays that the wicked will perish and that the "Lord's devout inherit the Lord's promises" (*Pss. Sol.* 12:5-6). Here again the author qualifies the nationalistic language with specific mention of the devout, indicating that the nondevout, that is, the sinners, will not inherit these promises and, in keeping with the rest of the collection, will be judged and destroyed.[56] In *Psalms of Solomon* 15[57] the righteous are

---

[54]Sanders, *Paul and Palestinian Judaism*, p. 390.

[55]VanLandingham, *Judgment and Justification*, p. 145.

[56]This distinction is taken up in the psalm that follows, which affirms that the righteous are disciplined for their sin but not destroyed, and thus "the discipline of the righteous . . . is not the same as the destruction of the sinners," since "the Lord will spare his devout . . . [and] the life of the righteous (goes on) forever, but sinners shall be taken away to destruction, and no memory of them will ever be found" (*Pss. Sol.* 13:7, 10-11). Likewise in *Pss. Sol.* 14, the devout live by the law and are "firmly rooted forever . . . but not so are sinners and criminals," whose "inheritance is Hades, and darkness and destruction; and they will not be found on the day of mercy for the righteous. But the devout of the Lord will inherit life in happiness" (*Pss. Sol.* 14:4, 6, 9-10). Here the sinners who do not keep the law are destined for destruction. Grindheim thus notes, "In Psalm 14 the thought is not that Israel as such is rejected but that the sinners of Israel are" (Sigurd Grindheim, *The Crux of Election: Paul's Critique of the Jewish Confidence in the Election of Israel* [Tübingen: Mohr Siebeck, 2005], p. 50).

[57]Concerning *Pss. Sol.* 15, Atkinson suggests, "Because this psalm does not refer to Gentile intervention, it is possible that the author was describing an intra-Jewish conflict from which his community escaped. This particular *Ps. Sol.* may possibly refer to the civil warfare that erupted between Aristobulus II and Hyrcanus II, in part fueled by the ambitions of Antipater" (Kenneth Atkinson, "Toward a Redating of the Psalms of Solomon: Implications for Understanding the *Sitz im Leben* of an Unknown Jewish Sect," *JSP* 17 [1998]: 103-4). If true, this further illustrates the sectarian nature of the *Psalms*, drawing divisions between Jewish "saints" and "sinners."

further said to be marked with the mark of salvation, which ensures that they will not by harmed by the Lord's judgment and anger against sinners (*Pss. Sol.* 15:4-6), while sinners, marked with the mark of destruction, will not escape the judgment of God (15:8-9). As in *Psalms of Solomon* 14, the sinners inherit death, darkness and destruction (*Pss. Sol.* 15:10-12), but the righteous will find mercy in God (15:13).[58]

In *Psalms of Solomon* 17, God will separate the faithful Jews from the unfaithful (*Pss. Sol.* 17:27) by purging Jerusalem of all sinners (17:30). The psalmist notes that the people have been unfaithful and guilty of numerous sins, but as he closes, he notes, "Blessed are those born in those days to see the good fortune of Israel which God will bring to pass in the assembly of the tribes. May God dispatch his mercy to Israel; may he deliver us from the pollution of profane enemies" (*Pss. Sol.* 17:44-45). Here again, in light of the rest of the psalm, Israel must be seen as equivalent with the devout, as those Jews who are sinners, apparently the entirety of those in Jerusalem, are to be judged, destroyed and purged from the city and the devout currently in "exile" restored.[59] The collection thus emphasizes that God will remain faithful to his promises to Israel as a people, but the individuals who constitute that people are those who respond in faithful obedience.

Dead Sea Scrolls. The *Liturgical Prayers* (see 1QLitPr; 1Q34; 4Q508, 509) contain prayers for the various festivals observed at Qumran. Though fragmentary, the prayers offer a glimpse into the liturgical content of the community. In particular, 1Q34, frag. 3, 2.1-8 notes that humanity, in spite of God's revelation, does not obey God and is utterly wicked (2.3-4). The author notes, "This is why you reject them, because

---

[58]Likewise, in *Pss. Sol.* 16:15, the righteous are assured God's mercy by their victory over temptations, though this victory is one that is requested from God in prayer as the psalmist asks that he be protected from these evils.

[59]Embry agrees in stating, "*Pss. Sol.* 17 details the advent and origin, impetus and work of the Messiah. The end result of this work is the purification of the nation of Israel, so called precisely because they are now pure before the God of Abraham (*Pss. Sol.* 9.9; 18.3), not because they are genealogically Israelites. They are no longer Israelites simply because they were born Israelites (note John the Baptist in Mt. 3.9; Lk. 3.8)" (Brad Embry, "The *Psalms of Solomon* and the New Testament: Intertextuality and the Need for a Re-Evaluation," *JSP* 13, no. 2 [2002]: 121, 133). See also Mikael Winninge, *Sinners and the Righteous: A Comparative Study of the Psalms of Solomon and Paul's Letters* (Stockholm: Almqvist & Wiksell International, 1995), pp. 96, 98, 109.

you do not like s[i]n, and the wicked person will not endure before you"
(2.5). In spite of the existence of the wicked, God has

> chosen a people in the period of your favour, because you have remem-
> bered your covenant. You established them, isolating them for yourself in
> order to make them holy among all the nations. And you have renewed
> your covenant with them in the vision of glory, and in the words of your
> holy [spirit], by the works of your hand. Your right hand has written to let
> them know the regulations of glory and the everlasting deeds. (2.5-7)

The sect, as elsewhere in the Qumran writings, views themselves as those
who have inherited the covenant and its promises and are the chosen
remnant of Israel.

4Q Commentary on Genesis A (hereafter 4Q252) offers a brief
summary and commentary on various texts within Genesis 7:10–49:10,
focusing on Noah and the flood judgment (4Q252 1.1–2.7), the life of
Abraham (2.8–3.14, all quite fragmentary), and the descendants of
Jacob and Esau (4.1-7). In 4Q252 5.1-6, the author states that the descendants of Judah will receive the perpetual throne of David, "the
covenant of royalty," which will be renewed by the "messiah of righteousness" who is linked with the community and their obedience to
the covenant. Though fragmentary, the notion here is also likely that
the community represents a "true Israel" and is the sole inheritor of the
covenant promises.[60]

Pseudo-Philo. The *Biblical Antiquities* of pseudo-Philo (also known
as *Pseudo-Philo* or by its Latin title, *Liber Antiquitatum Biblicarum*) is a
first-century-C.E. work, likely written before 70 C.E., though the date is
disputed.[61] The author was most certainly not Philo but was likely a
well-educated Palestinian Jew. The book retells the Old Testament narratives, spanning from Adam to the death of Saul, and interweaves
quoted and summarized biblical material with unique additions.[62] The

---

[60]See George J. Brooke, "The Thematic Content of 4Q252," *JQR* 85, nos. 1/2 (1994): 55.

[61]For a discussion, see Frederick J. Murphy, "Biblical Antiquities (Pseudo-Philo)," in Collins and
Harlow, *Eerdmans Dictionary of Early Judaism*, p. 440; Howard Jacobson, *A Commentary on
Pseudo-Philo's* Liber Antiquitatum Biblicarum *with Latin Text and English Translation* (Leiden:
Brill, 1996), 1:208.

[62]For a study of Pseudo-Philo's compositional strategy, see Bruce Norman Fisk, *Do You Not Re-*

work survives only in medieval Latin manuscripts but is most likely a translation of a Greek translation of a Hebrew original.[63] My focus here is pseudo-Philo's additions to the Old Testament narratives, which best disclose his own theology.[64]

Following the 210 years in Egypt, the text picks up with Israel's enslavement. The Egyptians had decided to kill all the male Hebrews and keep the females as slaves. In response, the elders of Israel decided to forbid the people from procreating "lest the fruit of their wombs be defiled and our offspring serve idols" (*Bib. Ant.* 9.2). Amram, however, answered,

> It will sooner happen that this age will be ended forever or the world will sink into the immeasurable deep or the heart of the abyss will touch the stars than that the race of the sons of Israel will be ended. . . . For God will not abide in his anger, nor will he forget his people forever, nor will he cast forth the race of Israel in vain upon the earth; nor did he establish a covenant with our fathers in vain. (*Bib. Ant.* 9.3)

Pseudo-Philo here expresses his absolute confidence that God will preserve Israel in spite of the apparently insurmountable obstacle they faced. Amram resolves to procreate with his wife, an action that pleases God because "he has not put aside the covenant . . . so behold now he who will be born from him will serve me forever, and I will do marvelous things in the house of Jacob through him and I will work through him signs and wonders for my people that I have not done for anyone else. . . . And I will reveal to him my Law and statutes and judgments" (*Bib. Ant.* 9.7-8). The covenant here, and obedience to it/confidence in it, figures prominently in pseudo-Philo's mind, though he likewise affirms God's preservation of Israel seemingly unconditionally.

After the author recalls the giving of the law in chapter 11, the Israelites resume the pattern of idolatry in the golden calf episode. The sons of

---

member? *Scripture, Story and Exegesis in the Rewritten Bible of Pseudo-Philo* (Sheffield: Sheffield Academic, 2001).

[63]Murphy, "Biblical Antiquities (Pseudo-Philo)," p. 440.

[64]As guided by Harrington's translation. This is not to say that the way in which pseudo-Philo arranges the material is not important, as his theology is certainly seen in how the material is organized and shaped, as well as by what is omitted. The goal in isolating the material unique to the *Bib. Ant.* is to examine the material that most clearly represents the "voice" of the author.

Israel, growing impatient with Moses' absence, make the calf-god to be like "the other nations" (*Bib. Ant.* 12.2). This episode causes God to ask if the promises of the covenant are now "at an end" since the people have forsaken him before they even entered the land (*Bib. Ant.* 12.4). God states that he "will forsake them" but "will turn again and make peace with them so that a house may be built for me among them, a house that will be destroyed because they will sin against me" (*Bib. Ant.* 12.4). Thus, though God questions the continuation of the people,[65] he affirms it, acknowledging they will be wayward throughout their history.[66] Moses declares only the mercy of God will allow his "vine" to continue to flourish, since even if he plants another vine (i.e., chooses another people), they will not trust him because he destroyed the first people (*Bib. Ant.* 12.8-9). The issue of the continuation of the people is thus, for pseudo-Philo's Moses, an issue of the continued worship and service of God (*Bib. Ant.* 12.10).

Following the giving of festival instructions in chapter 13, God recalls Adam's disobedience and the intrusion of death into the world (*Bib. Ant.* 13.8). He then commands,

> If they will walk in my ways, I will not abandon them but will have mercy on them always and bless their seed. . . . But I know for sure that they will make their ways corrupt and I will abandon them, and they will forget the covenants that I have established with their fathers; but nevertheless I will not forget them forever. For they will know in the last days that on account of their own sins their seed has been abandoned, because I am faithful in my ways. (*Bib. Ant.* 13.10)[67]

---

[65]This questioning occurs in various places throughout the *Bib. Ant.* (e.g., *Bib. Ant.* 15:5-7; 20:4; 21:4; 22:2).

[66]Here Murphy says, "It is noteworthy that God passes from forsaking to peace without an intervening stage where the people repent. Although repentance is present in the *Biblical Antiquities* and although the author advocates the connection between sin and punishment, the full pattern of sin-punishment-repentance-forgiveness is not always present" (Frederick J. Murphy, *Pseudo-Philo: Rewriting the Bible* [Oxford: Oxford University Press, 1993], p. 71).

[67]In chap. 15, pseudo-Philo recounts the sending of the spies into Canaan. In addressing Israel's unbelief and unfaithfulness, God tells Moses that he will abandon them to the wilderness as they have abandoned him. Here again, Moses intercedes for the people, praying that God will sustain them with his mercy (*Bib. Ant.* 15.7).

Preston Sprinkle sees here an affirmation of the unconditional nature of God's faithfulness to Israel, noting, "There is evidence in *LAB* that the emphasis on God's unconditional covenant supplants any potential conditional elements."[68] The tension here, as in other writings of the period, is between the conditions established in the covenant, the unfaithfulness of Israel and the promises of God. However, it seems more likely that the book as a whole holds confidence that God will preserve Israel because it believes a remnant of faithful Jews exists on the earth, and not because God, who is "faithful in [his] ways" (*Bib. Ant.* 13.10), overrides the covenant stipulations and consequences with little or no consideration of Israel's, or humanity's, behavior.[69] Here God commands Israel to obey,[70] recognizing they will sin, and promising that he will abandon them for it, though not permanently. Though no explicit mention of repentance or renewed obedience occurs here,[71] this theme occurs throughout the book, with its emphasis on moral causality.[72] Nothing here requires that there not be repentance or renewed obedience prior to or coinciding with God's remembrance of them. In other words, Israel can break the covenant and God not abandon it, though those unfaithful Israelites will not experience the covenant blessings.

As Moses' death nears, he predicts the people's rebellion and God's punishing them by sending the nations to rule over them, "but not forever, because he will remember the covenant" (*Bib. Ant.* 19.2).[73] Moses foresees that Israel will "rise up . . . and lament the day of my death" and

---

[68]Preston M. Sprinkle, "The Hermeneutic of Grace: The Soteriology of Pseudo-Philo's *Biblical Antiquities*," in *This World and the World to Come: Soteriology in Early Judaism*, ed. Daniel M. Gurtner (New York: T&T Clark, 2011), p. 55.

[69]Jacobson agrees, stating, "I think it more likely that the words mean that God is faithful to his principles and therefore punishes when punishment is merited" (Jacobson, *A Commentary*, 1:525).

[70]So Murphy writes, "The lesson of moral causality is explicit in 13:10. Obedience brings God's merciful blessing" (Murphy, *Pseudo-Philo*, p. 75).

[71]It is mentioned explicitly elsewhere, such as in *Bib. Ant.* 21.6, where the people, "having repented of their deeds, will hope for the salvation that is to be born from them."

[72]See Murphy, *Pseudo-Philo*, pp. 247-48.

[73]Sprinkle here again sees an unconditional promise to Israel of their national salvation, noting, "If our author believed that God's mercy did have certain conditions, then he certainly does not state this clearly. In fact, he seems to alter the biblical text to convince his audience that God's mercy is unconditional" (Sprinkle, "Hermeneutic of Grace," p. 56).

long for a mediator to come (*Bib. Ant.* 19.3). The present generation, however, is in need of Moses' warning that if they "transgress and grow corrupt" God will cut them off (*Bib. Ant.* 19.4). Here again, conditions (i.e., obedience/disobedience) are intermingled with both God's cursings and blessings. The Deuteronomic formula persists in acknowledging that God will not forsake them forever. While not an unqualified recognition of repentance, by occurring after God's promise not to forsake them and the restatements of the Deuteronomic formula in *Biblical Antiquities* 19.2, 4 and 6, it suggests the conditionality of the covenant still continues as a reality in the mind of pseudo-Philo.[74] Israel's continued existence depends on God's mercy because of their current and coming rebellion (*Bib. Ant.* 19.8-9, 11), but this does not exclude the need for their future obedience in order to receive the covenant blessings. Their disobedience brings about God's punishment of their sins, and his mercy sustains their existence when they act unfaithfully, but their receipt of blessings and future life is dependent on their keeping the covenant.

Following the ascension of Phinehas (*Bib. Ant.* 48.1-3), pseudo-Philo again affirms that "each one did what was pleasing in his own eyes" due to the absence of leadership in Israel (48.4). The people cast lots to try to find a leader to deliver them, but are unable to do so, and conclude that God has hated them (*Bib. Ant.* 49.1-2), though they ironically recognize there are no worthy men among them (49.2). Nethez responds to this conclusion by declaring,

> He does not hate us, but we have made ourselves so hateful that God should abandon us. And so, even if we die, let us not abandon him, but let us flee to him. . . . For I know that God will not reject us forever, nor will he hate his people for all generations. And so strengthen yourselves, and let us pray again, and let us cast lots by cities. For even if our sins are many, nevertheless his long-suffering will not fail. (*Bib. Ant.* 49.3)

Here again the recognition both of their sin and of their need to live in faithfulness to God precedes Nethez's appeal. The lot falls on Elkanah,

---

[74]Pseudo-Philo, *Bib. Ant.* 20–21 reinforces the notion that their disobedience brings judgment but obedience brings blessings.

who is unwilling to lead the people because of the responsibility he would bear for their sins (*Bib. Ant.* 49.5).[75] The people blame God for the lot turning out as a failure (*Bib. Ant.* 49.6). God declares that if Israel was really getting what they deserved, they would be extinguished, and confirms that Elkanah's son (Samuel) will rule them, instilling hope in the people that they might be delivered from their enemies (*Bib. Ant.* 49.7-8).

From what we have surveyed above, several clear and consistent themes stand out. We frequently see the failures of Israel and her leaders and the faithfulness of God to the covenant in spite of them.[76] Pseudo-Philo also takes great care to ensure that every sin that gains attention in the work receives a punishment, either swiftly or eventually, in a retributive fashion.[77] God bases his judgment, both in the present and in the future, on the deeds of the individual. The righteous are rewarded with life and resurrection and the wicked with death and destruction.[78] So while God preserves the chosen people *as a whole*, each individual's fate is determined by their keeping or forsaking the covenant.

PAUL AND THE CHOSEN COLLECTIVE

We saw in what preceded that certain Second Temple texts frequently emphasize the corporate or collective nature of God's election of Israel. The themes became evident by examining corporate metaphors as well recognizing that these texts generally focus on the people as a whole in terms of election and covenant language, while individuals or even entire

---

[75]See Jacobson, *A Commentary*, 2:1076-77; Murphy, *Pseudo-Philo*, p. 187.

[76]So Murphy summarizes, "The most prominent theme is God's faithfulness to Israel. God continues to maintain a covenant relationship with Israel despite the repeated failures of the people and of some leaders. This theme is accompanied by a pessimistic picture of the people of Israel and indeed of all humans" (Murphy, "Biblical Antiquities (Pseudo-Philo)," p. 441). See also Harrington, "Pseudo-Philo," p. 865; Nickelsburg, *Jewish Literature*, p. 267.

[77]And so, again, Murphy summarizes, "Given the prevalence of human sin and failure, it is not surprising to find many instances of punishment in the *Biblical Antiquities*. This gives the author many opportunities to demonstrate that the punishment, which comes from God, fits the crime. Pseudo-Philo finds a fairly strict retributive scheme in Israel's history" (Murphy, "Biblical Antiquities (Pseudo-Philo)," p. 441). Nickelsburg likewise notes that Israel's affinity for the gods of the nations causes them to be "perennially" at their mercy (Nickelsburg, *Jewish Literature*, p. 267).

[78]And so Nickelsburg states, "What is clear about Pseudo-Philo's expectations about the future is the belief in the resurrection of the dead, a final judgment, and punishment for the wicked and eternal life for the righteous" (Nickelsburg, *Jewish Literature*, p. 269).

generations may or may not experience the blessings of the covenant depending on their own behavior. I now turn again to Paul. I would suggest with this background in mind Paul's emphasis on the elect as a collective becomes clearer.

2 Thessalonians 2:13-15. Scholars have historically accepted 2 Thessalonians as an authentic Pauline letter, though some have questioned its authenticity due to the issues involved in comparing it with 1 Thessalonians.[79] The questions have persisted mainly because of the literary issues seen when comparing the content of the two letters, which has also raised questions of the original order of writing.[80] Since the strength of the evidence favors Pauline authorship of the letter, I will assume the letter's authenticity.[81]

Because our passage begins with "but" (δὲ), we must examine the previous context before investigating Paul's election rhetoric. Second Thessalonians 1 begins with Paul thanking the Thessalonians for their faithfulness during persecution and affirming that those who have tormented this body of believers will be judged by God and "undergo the penalty of eternal destruction, away from the presence of the Lord and from the glory of his strength" (2 Thess 1:9 NET). Paul prays that God will make them "worthy of his calling" (2 Thess 1:11 NET), and then corrects the misunderstanding among them that the day of the Lord had already arrived (2 Thess 2:1-12). The passage presents interpretive difficulties since Paul is attempting to correct a misconception concerning the

---

[79]According to Foster, 57 percent of scholars surveyed at the 2011 British New Testament Conference affirmed Pauline authorship for 2 Thessalonians, 31 percent were uncertain, and only 12 percent believed Paul did not write the letter (Paul Foster, "Who Wrote 2 Thessalonians? A Fresh Look at an Old Problem," *JSNT* 35, no. 2 [2012]: 171). For a summary, see Gene L. Green, *The Letters to the Thessalonians,* Pillar New Testament Commentary (Grand Rapids: Eerdmans, 2002), pp. 59-64; Leon Morris, *The Epistles of Paul to the Thessalonians: An Introduction and Commentary,* TNTC (Grand Rapids: Eerdmans, 1984), pp. 26-36; Charles A. Wanamaker, *The Epistles to the Thessalonians: A Commentary on the Greek Text,* NIGTC (Grand Rapids: Eerdmans, 1990), pp. 17-28.

[80]For a summary, see Wanamaker, *Epistles to the Thessalonians,* pp. 29-37.

[81]As Jewett concludes in his review, "The evidence concerning the authenticity of 2 Thessalonians is equivocal, with the likelihood remaining fairly strongly on the side of Pauline authorship" (Robert Jewett, *The Thessalonian Correspondence: Pauline Rhetoric and Millenarian Piety* [Minneapolis: Fortress, 1986], p. 16).

parousia,[82] and yet does not reveal the exact nature of the issue, though the recipients of the letter would have been well aware of its substance.[83] Paul states that the rebellion[84] and the "man of lawlessness" (ὁ ἄνθρωπος τῆς ἀνομίας) must come first, and the lawless one will seat himself in God's temple and deceive all who do not possess the truth before the Lord destroys him.[85]

Though fraught with difficulties, the basic sense of the passage seems clear. Paul wrote to correct a misunderstanding among this church concerning the timing of the day of the Lord and the parousia of Christ. In Paul's eschatological framework, the rebellion and the revelation of the lawlessness one, events that had apparently not yet occurred, must happen first. Paul's intent here was to show the day of the Lord had not yet come, and those who reject the truth, who were deceived by the lawless one, will share in his punishment.[86] It seems significant that this section ends with a description of the deceived as being so because "because they did not receive the love of the truth for themselves so as to be saved," and so "all of them who did not believe the truth but delighted in evil will be condemned" (2 Thess 2:10, 12).[87]

---

[82]For a study of the text in its Jewish apocalyptic context, see J. Julius Scott Jr., "Paul and Late-Jewish Eschatology—A Case Study, I Thessalonians 4:13-18 and II Thessalonians 2:1-12," *JETS* 15, no. 3 (1972): 133-43.

[83]See Green, *Letters to the Thessalonians*, pp. 302-4; Wanamaker, *Epistles to the Thessalonians*, pp. 238-40; David J. Williams, *1 and 2 Thessalonians*, UBCS (Grand Rapids: Baker Books, 2011), p. 121. Elias suggests, following Jewett, that Paul is simply addressing their misinterpretation of his first letter, but disassociating himself from the way in which it was interpreted (Jacob W. Elias, *1 and 2 Thessalonians*, BCBC [Scottdale, PA: Herald, 1995], p. 276).

[84]See Williams, *1 and 2 Thessalonians*, p. 124.

[85]Williams notes that Gaius may be in mind here, or a prediction of the destruction of the temple under Titus in 70 C.E. (Williams, *1 and 2 Thessalonians*, p. 125). Elias notes that the impression made by Antiochus IV can still be seen here and elsewhere in the New Testament, along with the more recent invasions by Pompey (63 B.C.E.) and Gaius (ca. 40 C.E.) (Elias, *1 and 2 Thessalonians*, p. 279). If Paul had a single historical individual in mind, he does not make this clear in the letter. Part of the difficulty here as well is whether Paul is speaking in terms of a general eschatological framework, alluding to an event that he thinks imminent in his own time, or invokes some combination of the two.

[86]Wanamaker, *Epistles to the Thessalonians*, p. 264.

[87]Wanamaker notes that although the deceit portrayed "might be understood in terms of predestination, the next clause in v. 10 makes it clear that those who are perishing chose the path of destruction for themselves. Therefore the 'parousia' of the rebel will inevitably deceive them" (Wanamaker, *Epistles to the Thessalonians*, p. 260). See also Elias, *1 and 2 Thessalonians*, p. 287. Likewise, Marshall states, "Paul lays the final emphasis upon the human responsibility of those

It is with this background in mind that Paul again states his thankfulness for the Thessalonian believers:

> But we ought to be thanking God always for you, siblings who have been
> loved by the Lord, because God chose you as firstfruits for salvation in
> consecration of spirit and in faithfulness of truth, for which He called you
> through our good news for gaining glory from our Lord Jesus the
> Anointed One. So, as a result, siblings, be standing firm and holding fast
> to the traditions which you have been taught whether through word or
> through our letter. (2 Thess 2:13-15)

The δὲ here, then, likely serves to draw a contrast between those who delight in evil and do not accept the truth (2 Thess 2:10-12), and the Thessalonian believers who have received the gospel by faith.[88] The cause for Paul's thanks, as the ὅτι clause demonstrates, is God's choosing of them, which functions "to reassure the readers of their salvation in the face of the eschatological dangers discussed in vv. 3-12."[89]

Paul begins by stating God had chosen[90] the Thessalonians "for salvation," indicating that the selection here is soteriological. For this reason, many have taken the passage to refer to individual election unto salvation in terms of a double-predestinarian framework.[91] The interpretation arises, in part, from some disagreement concerning the proper rendering of the text. The textual issue here concerns whether Paul has described the selection as occurring "from the beginning." Some manuscript evidence[92] prefers the reading ἀπαρχὴν ("firstfruits") over and

---

[88]who are condemned" (I. Howard Marshall, *1 and 2 Thessalonians*, NCB [Grand Rapids: Eerdmans, 1983], p. 204).

[88]See Wanamaker, *Epistles to the Thessalonians*, p. 265. Green notes, "The author signals this contrast between the two groups in v. 13, which begins with the adversative 'but' (*de*). In fact, the apostle contrasts the action of God toward the two . . . the means used to bring about his purposes . . . and the ultimate destiny of both" (Green, *Letters to the Thessalonians*, p. 325).

[89]Wanamaker, *Epistles to the Thessalonians*, p. 265.

[90]Paul here employs εἵλατο, the aorist middle/passive form of the verb αἱρεω, which can mean either "to take, prefer or to choose" (BDAG 28). The word is also found in the LXX in Deut 26:18, where it is translated, "The LORD has today chosen you to be his people," where it is earlier said in Deut 26:17 that the people have "chosen" (εἵλου) God to be their God.

[91]Beale, for example, sees God's choice to limit his love to certain individuals and choose whom he plans to redeem (G. K. Beale, *1-2 Thessalonians*, IVP New Testament Commentary [Downers Grove, IL: InterVarsity Press, 2003], pp. 225-26).

[92]According to NA²⁷, the reading is attested in B; F; G⁹ʳ; P 075, 33, 81, 256, 365, 1573, 1739, 1881,

against the oft translated ἀπ᾽ ἀρχῆς ("from the beginning").[93] According
to Bruce Metzger, the former reading has greater support because ἀπ᾽
ἀρχῆς occurs nowhere else in Paul's writings, Paul typically uses ἀρχή to
mean "power" rather than "beginning,"[94] ἀπαρχη does occur elsewhere
in Paul's writings, and later copyists more likely altered the reading ἀπ᾽
ἀρχῆς.[95] Ἀπαρχη is also likely the harder reading, while ἀπ᾽ ἀρχῆς may
have been expected by a later copyist. In light of the text-critical evidence,
"God has chosen you [as] firstfruits[96] for salvation" seems the better rendering. Favoring this alternate reading, David Williams notes, "*Aparchēn*,
'first-fruits,' is as well if not better attested. On this reading, the most
likely meaning would be that Paul saw the Thessalonians as only the
beginning—an intimation—of a harvest which was yet to be gathered."[97]

Paul also describes God's selection of the Thessalonians as "firstfruits"
as coming "by consecration of spirit and faithfulness in truth" (ἐν ἁγιασμῷ
πνεύματος[98] καὶ πίστει ἀληθείας). Some, again, have seen here an *ordo*

1912, 2127, 2464; it[f]; vg; syr[h]; cop[bo]; Didymus[dub]; Theodore[lat1/2]; Ambrose[1/2]; Pelagius.

[93]Of the major translations examined, the ASV, CEB, HCSB, KJV, NASB, NET, NIV and NKJV chose
the reading "from the beginning," while only the ESV, NLT, NRSV and TNIV chose "firstfruits."

[94]As is in Rom 8:38; 1 Cor 15:24; Eph 1:21; 3:10; 6:12; Col 1:16, 18; 2:10, 15; Tit 3:1. The only
exception is Phil 4:15, in which ἐν ἀρχῇ is used for "at the beginning" with reference to Paul's
preaching of the gospel.

[95]Bruce M. Metzger, *A Textual Commentary on the Greek New Testament*, 2nd ed. (Stuttgart:
Deutsche Bibelgesellschaft, 2005), p. 568. Olson notes, "This is not some pre-temporal election
by God, but a historical event recorded in Acts 17. God's picking them as firstfruits alludes to the
fact that the Thessalonian church was one of the early churches planted by Paul and was the re-
cipient of his earliest epistles" (C. Gordon Olson, *Getting the Gospel Right: A Balanced View of
Calvinism and Arminianism* [Cedar Knolls: Global Gospel Publishers, 2001], p. 285). Contra
Wanamaker, who suggests that ἀπαρχὴν does not make good sense contextually (Wanamaker,
Epistles to the Thessalonians, p. 266). Also, contra Best, who prefers ἀπ᾽ ἀρχῆς here (Ernest Best,
1 and 2 Thessalonians, BNTC [Peabody, MA: Hendrickson, 2003], pp. 312-14).

[96]It is worth noting here that "firstfruits" is in the singular, and thus may be thought of as God
choosing "a firstfruit." This may indicate that the Thessalonians were simply among the earliest
recipients of Paul's gospel preaching, since they were not chronologically the earliest, either of
Paul's ministry or within their region. It may also serve to reinforce the collective sense in which
Paul presents this notion.

[97]Williams, *1 and 2 Thessalonians*, p. 134. See also Green, *Letters to the Thessalonians*, p. 326; and
Michael D. Martin, *1, 2 Thessalonians*, NAC (Nashville: Broadman & Holman, 1995), pp. 252-53,
who essentially agree with Williams.

[98]Though nearly all commentators take ἐν ἁγιασμῷ πνεύματος here as "in sanctification by the
Spirit," it is possible here that Paul is referring to their personal piety, as he does in Rom 6:19
and 1 Thess 4:3-7. Paul does not use ἁγιασμός anywhere else in his writings in connection with
πνεῦμα, but his use of ἁγιασμός elsewhere at least opens the possibility of the same emphasis
here. Martin suggests that since the use here of πνεύματος is singular and lacks a possessive

salutis, with Paul affirming that spiritual awakening through the gift of the Spirit comes first before the exercise of faith occurs.[99] G. K. Beale suggests that Paul mentions faith here after the Spirit because "faith arises as a gift from God. Not until our stone heart is taken out and a spiritual heart is put in can we exercise saving faith in Christ."[100] Exegetically, this seems to force quite a bit of weight on καὶ, which rather seems more likely a simple connector than indicating a sequence of soteriological events. In fact, one could argue the use of καὶ here actually affirms both the role of God and the role of the individual in the effecting of salvation.[101] Furthermore, it is not clear that Paul even refers to the "Holy Spirit" here, since πνεύματος lacks the article and the phrase is not a typical Pauline construction to refer to God's Spirit. In addition, the mention of their "faith in the truth" probably acts as a contrast with those who have *chosen* to ignore the truth (2 Thess 2:12). All this together makes it more likely that Paul is referring to the Thessalonians' commitment to the good news and their identity as early recipients of it rather than a pretemporal soteriological arrangement of those God would save.

As Paul continues, he states, "unto which [also] he called you through our gospel" (εἰς ὃ [καὶ] ἐκάλεσεν ὑμᾶς διὰ τοῦ εὐαγγελίου ἡμῶν). The neuter singular pronoun ὃ here likely functions as a summative pronoun,

---

pronoun, it is unlikely that this was Paul's intent (Martin, *1, 2 Thessalonians*, p. 253), though the same could be said of πίστει ἀληθείας, which follows and is connected to ἐν ἁγιασμῷ πνεύματος with καὶ. One could, then, understand the phrase as "God chose you for salvation as firstfruits by spiritual-sanctification and true-faith."

[99]So Williams states, "This verse summarizes the process by which we become Christians. There is the sovereign, gracious choice of God; there is the Spirit's action which makes effective to us the work of Christ; and there is our response of faith in welcoming that work and clearing the way for God's Spirit to act upon us" (Williams, *1 and 2 Thessalonians*, pp. 134-35). Beale interprets this as meaning that "God sends the Spirit to others to set them apart from falsehood so that they have faith *in the truth*" (Beale, *1–2 Thessalonians*, p. 228). He likewise connects this to God's irresistible call, which he sees described in 2:14 (ibid., p. 228), though this seems likely to be a reference to the preaching of the apostles.

[100]Beale, *1–2 Thessalonians*, p. 230.

[101]Wanamaker affirms this in stating, "Just as salvation has a divine dimension, so also it involves a human response in the form of faith" (Wanamaker, *Epistles to the Thessalonians*, p. 267). Elias agrees: "The ministry of the Spirit does not unilaterally bring *salvation*. A response is required from the human side: *and belief in the truth*. . . . The community of faith manifests *belief in the truth* when they respond in gratitude, trust, and obedience to God's love and call as supremely made known in Christ" (Elias, *1 and 2 Thessalonians*, p. 300, italics original).

referring to all that has preceded.[102] This would include, at least, their salvation through consecration of spirit and faith in the truth, and possibly also God's choice of them as firstfruits. Some see the call as describing a unilateral action of God given only to his elect.[103] The call here in context, however, is clearly the preaching of the good news about Jesus, which Paul and his companions delivered among the Thessalonians.[104] We see this even more clearly in what follows in 2 Thessalonians 2:15, where Paul gives the summative command (Ἄρα οὖν) to "stand firm and hold on to the traditions that we taught you." The double imperative clearly puts the impetus on the Thessalonians, in light of their response to God's calling, delivered through the preaching of the missionaries, to persevere in the truth. This, by Paul's own portrayal, is more than just a "sign" of their election.[105] Rather, it is what separates them from those who found no place for the truth in their hearts. Thus Charles Wanamaker states, "The fact that the command to keep these traditions represents an inference drawn from the discussion of salvation in vv. 13f. implies that nothing less than the salvation of the Thessalonians depended on their holding to these traditions."[106] It does not appear, then,

---

[102]It should be noted at this point that there is no grammatical break in the thought from what begins in 2 Thess 2:13. The punctuation breaks in English translations are for ease of reading, but are not original to the text.

[103]So Schreiner states that "God's call, which is exercised in history through the gospel, is closely conjoined with his choosing people for salvation. . . . Nor should we fail to see that the call guarantees the outcome. Those who are called through the gospel will possess eschatological glory (2 Thess 2:13). The one who called believers will see to it that they obtain the sanctification needed to stand before the Lord" (Thomas R. Schreiner, *Paul, Apostle of God's Glory in Christ: A Pauline Theology* [Downers Grove, IL: InterVarsity Press, 2001], p. 242). The "call," however, is sometimes described as universal and portrayed as rejected (see Matt 9:13; 22:3-9; Luke 5:32; Gal 1:6). Most instances of its use in Paul, however, are directed at believers who have already responded to it.

[104]So Elias states, "God calls people to experience salvation. Paul and his partners refer to their message as *our gospel*, since they have proclaimed and embodied God's gracious invitation to the people of Thessalonica" (Elias, *1 and 2 Thessalonians*, p. 300). Likewise, Wanamaker recognizes, "The Thessalonians were called by God (cf. 1 Thes. 2:12; 4:7; 5:23) to share in salvation when Paul and his missionary colleagues were visiting their city to preach the gospel. For this reason Paul can specify that his readers were called ('through our gospel')" (Wanamaker, *Epistles to the Thessalonians*, p. 267).

[105]Beale, *1–2 Thessalonians*, p. 231.

[106]Wanamaker, *Epistles to the Thessalonians*, p. 265. It is also reminiscent of the writings from Qumran where passages frequently interpreted as deterministic are followed by conditions or commands (e.g., 1QS cols. 1-5 and CD cols. 1-3).

that Paul affirms a form of double predestination. Rather, he draws a contrast between those who have rejected the truth of the missionaries' "traditions," and those who have committed themselves to them.[107] Those who had responded in faith are the "firstfruits" of the eschatological people of God, who through their spiritual sanctification and faith in the truth are assured eschatological salvation,[108] if they remain faithful to the truth they have received.[109]

I must address one final question within this text: How might we see a collective emphasis in this passage, which interpreters have more commonly understood as applying to individuals? Gary Shogren, for example, states, "It would be awkward to regard election as 'corporate.' It would involve Paul in a tautology (a statement that is true by necessity and thus not worth saying): that he was certain that God had chosen the Thessalonian church because that group received the gospel. It makes better sense if Paul is thinking of the faith that he detects in the believers as individuals."[110] In light of the backgrounds we have examined, however, it seems probable that this is Paul's framework. The terminology Paul employs was primarily applied to the collective of God's people. When applied to individuals, it focused on their character or role, not their soteriological status. In drawing a contrast between those who have accepted the truth and the Thessalonian believers, Paul filters both through the sieve of the gospel. The Thessalonians' response to the call of the gospel is the separating factor.[111] Furthermore, if Paul believed God had

---

[107]So Elias comments, "In the final judgment, God delivers what the people have ordered. Members of the Thessalonian Christian community likely recognize their persecutors in this description . . . those who acknowledge the lordship of Christ can therefore anticipate that, even though they suffer now, they will finally be vindicated by God" (Elias, *1 and 2 Thessalonians*, p. 288).

[108]Thus Shogren notes, "Salvation is to be understood, as it is in these two letters, as eschatological—the disciples are saved from God's wrath at Christ's return" (Gary S. Shogren, *1 and 2 Thessalonians*, Exegetical Commentary on the New Testament [Grand Rapids: Zondervan, 2012], p. 303).

[109]So Martin summarizes, "Paul both affirmed and reassured the church while at the same time reminding them of the vital importance they should attach to fidelity to the apostolic gospel. They must stand firm in the truth of the gospel, for confusion and deception are the tools of Satan, and those who succumb ultimately are destined for perdition" (Martin, *1, 2 Thessalonians*, p. 254).

[110]Shogren, *1 and 2 Thessalonians*, p. 310.

[111]Capes, Reeves and Richards state, "Paul always uses the term 'elect' to refer to those who are already members of God's people. He never uses it to prescribe who is going to be saved. Instead

unilaterally accomplished their salvation with no response on their part, not only in his work through Jesus but also in his guaranteeing a salvific response from the Thessalonians, what good would it do for him to command them to hold fast to what they had received? If Paul asserts that their fate was already determined, Paul's imperative here seems quite out of place.

By viewing Paul's language here as both conditional and emphasizing the collective, the activity of God (election and salvation) as well as the intended response (faith and endurance) may both be upheld. Ben Witherington's summary of this is worth repeating: "Election for Paul is corporate. It was in ethnic Israel and is now 'in Christ.' Paul carries over concepts of corporate election from early Judaism into his theologizing about the Christian assembly."[112] In sum, God has chosen the Thessalonians as "firstfruits" because they represent part of the first ingathering of the "good news" harvest. They are distinguished from those who stand condemned because they have believed and committed themselves to Jesus, which means they now stand within the collective of the people of God. The apostle commands them to continue in this truth lest they share in the fate of those who have rejected it, as those who delight in evil have done.

1 Corinthians 1:18-31. New Testament scholars widely accept Paul's first letter to the Corinthians as authentic. Most know the letter for the breadth of issues the apostle addresses in it. Paul's opening appeal in 1 Corinthians addresses the unity of the Corinthian church. Disunity apparently rose up from different allegiances among the believers to the ministers of the good news who had ministered among them or had become known by them, including Apollos, Cephas and Paul himself

---

he employs it to remind those who have answered God's call that they are members of God's covenant people" (David B. Capes, Rodney Reeves and E. Randolph Richards, *Rediscovering Paul: An Introduction to His World, Letters and Theology* [Downers Grove, IL: IVP Academic, 2007], p. 130).

[112]Ben Witherington III, *1 and 2 Thessalonians: A Socio-Rhetorical Commentary* (Grand Rapids: Eerdmans, 2006), p. 65. He continues, "Just as apostasy was and could be committed by individual Israelites, whom God then broke off from the people of God, at least temporarily (see Rom 11:11-24), so there was also the same danger for individual Christians, hence all the warnings about falling away in 1 and 2 Thessalonians" (ibid.).

(1 Cor 1:10-16).[113] In his argument, Paul contends that Jesus and his cross, not human wisdom or allegiances, should unite them (1 Cor 1:17-20).[114] For Paul the issue represents no petty disagreement, but has the potential to empty the cross of its meaning.[115] As Paul transitions from this earlier section (1 Cor 1:10-17) to what follows (1 Cor 1:18-31), his earlier "thesis statement" in 1 Corinthians 1:10 clues the reader in to the goal of the passage.[116] There Paul asserts that they should "all say the same thing and let there be no divisions among you, but that you might be restored in the same mind and in the same purpose" (1 Cor 1:10).

With the larger context in mind, we must see Paul's discussion in 1 Corinthians 1:18-31 as driving toward the stated goal. Paul begins by stating that the "word of the cross" is foolishness to "the ones who are being destroyed" but is the power of God to "the ones who are being saved." Paul does not, perhaps unexpectedly, draw his contrast here between foolishness and wisdom, but between foolishness and power. Paul will clarify how the cross is power, but here he affirms that one's attitude to the cross determines their present status with God. There are those

---

[113]Some have postulated that these were formal divisions or "parties" that had distinctive approaches to Christian doctrine and practice. While different models pursuing this thesis have been proposed, it seems more likely that the division was less formal and more orientated around preference of association resulting in "playing favorites" and sparking disunity. See Gordon D. Fee, *The First Epistle to the Corinthians*, NICNT (Grand Rapids: Eerdmans, 1987), pp. 52-59; Anthony C. Thiselton, *The First Epistle to the Corinthians: A Commentary on the Greek Text*, NIGTC (Grand Rapids: Eerdmans, 2000), pp. 123-33. Garland summarizes the problem well: "The slogans turn out to be put-downs rather than self-designations. It betrays the individualism that Paul finds so problematic in this community. The 'I' is repeated for emphasis to show that they suffer from an 'I' disease that is not physical. Why 'I' when they are all a part of Christ's body (3:22-23)? R. Collins . . . contends that 'the "I" points to the root of the problem at Corinth as located in a radical individuality rather than substantive theological differences'" (David E. Garland, *1 Corinthians*, BECNT [Grand Rapids: Baker Academic, 2003], p. 48).

[114]Paul states that he did not baptize many of the believers, indicating perhaps "baptism-based allegiance" was part of the problem in Corinth (see Maria Pascuzzi, "Baptism-Based Allegiance and the Divisions in Corinth: A Reexamination of 1 Corinthians 1:13-17," *CBQ* 71 [2009]: 813-29). As Hays has recognized, all of the individuals named by Paul as recipients of baptism from him were wealthy or prominent in the community (Richard B. Hays, *First Corinthians*, IBC [Louisville: Westminster John Knox, 1997], p. 24).

[115]See Joseph A. Fitzmyer, *First Corinthians*, AYB (New Haven, CT: Yale University Press, 2008), p. 138. Paul retorts by asking if Christ can be divided, unveiling the absurdity of the Corinthians' behavior. See Hays, *First Corinthians*, p. 23.

[116]What is known as the *propositio*. See Ben Witherington III, *Conflict and Community in Corinth: A Socio-Rhetorical Commentary on 1 and 2 Corinthians* (Grand Rapids: Eerdmans, 1995), pp. 94-95.

"being destroyed" and those "being saved," and apparently no "in between." Paul's verbs here are in the present passive, indicating that God is the one destroying and saving, and also indicating that judgment and salvation begin in the "now," though God has not yet handed down the final verdict.[117] What is startling about Paul's claim is that the cross, the ultimate sign of weakness and humiliation, contains a display of God's power.[118] The Corinthians, however, and this is key, continued holding on to human definitions of status rather than embracing the cross. Of this, Anthony Thiselton observes, "Many at Corinth seek the shortcut to 'power' without the cross, seeking to become 'already rich' (4:8) by a 'transeschatological' route which avoids the humiliation of the apostolic cruciform lifestyle (4:9–13). But this places *the gospel* at stake no less than it is in Galatians. By rejecting the cry 'I am for Paul' (1:12), Paul personally adopts a cruciform posture in relation to 'power.'"[119]

In order to reinforce his point, Paul calls on Jeremiah and Isaiah throughout the passage to argue that God's action was "unexpectedly expected." Paul's first quotation (1 Cor 1:19), from Isaiah 29:14, declares that God will destroy the wisdom of the wise. In the context of Isaiah, the prophet warns Judah that their plans to build an alliance with Egypt rather than trust God would short circuit. God would show Judah's "political wisdom" to be folly.[120] Though they might have developed a sound political strategy, this was not the plan of God and thus was senseless. Likewise, the Corinthians, likely by elevating Greek rhetorical style over the content of the good news, not realizing the gospel transcends human wisdom, were playing the part of Judah's fools, and Paul expected the same outcome for them. In his rhetorical questions, Paul likely refers to the σοφός, γραμματεύς and συζητητής as references to Greek "wise men,"

---

[117]Hays, *First Corinthians*, p. 28. See also Craig Blomberg, *1 Corinthians*, NIVAC (Grand Rapids: Zondervan, 1994), p. 52; Marion L. Soards, *1 Corinthians*, UBCS (Grand Rapids: Baker Books, 2011), pp. 39-40.

[118]See Hays, *First Corinthians*, p. 27. See also Raymond Collins, *First Corinthians*, Sacra Pagina (Collegeville, MN: Liturgical Press, 2007), pp. 91-92, 102-3; Witherington, *Conflict and Community*, p. 109.

[119]Thiselton, *First Epistle to the Corinthians*, p. 157.

[120]See Hays, *First Corinthians*, p. 29; Simon J. Kistemaker, *Exposition of the First Epistle to the Corinthians*, New Testament Commentary (Grand Rapids: Baker Books, 2001), p. 55.

Jewish experts in the law and seekers after truth, asserting that refined human means of truth are foolishness in comparison to the message of the cross (1 Cor 1:20).[121] Paul did not take issue with eloquence or human wisdom per se,[122] but rather with those forms of eloquence that overshadowed the cross,[123] since the proponents of those forms of wisdom viewed the cross as illogical and offensive.[124] In other words, the Corinthians cannot have it both ways, seeking the status that comes with worldly wisdom when those very forms reject the message of the cross.[125] God saves those who trust in Jesus, in the "foolish" message of a crucified Messiah (1 Cor 1:21).

Paul next explains why these "intellectuals" do not see the value of the message of the cross. As always, Paul's discussion of Jews and "Gentiles" (here, Greeks) begins with the Jews first, an important salvation-historical distinction.[126] Such a distinction, as is reiterated in 1 Corinthians 1:24, recognizes that Paul includes all humanity in his line of thinking.[127] For the Jews, who seek a sign, the cross is a "stumbling block," which may well have in mind the curse pronounced in Deuteronomy 21:23 (see 1 Cor 1:23). For the Greek, the cross is simply foolishness, since only criminals, not divine rescuers, were victims of crucifixion.[128] But to the "called," Jews and Greeks, Paul states, the message of the cross is God's power and wisdom displayed in Jesus, the anointed one (1 Cor 1:24).[129] Commen-

---

[121]See Fitzmyer, *First Corinthians*, p. 156.

[122]Fitzmyer observes, "Although Paul is inveighing against human eloquence, he employs many stylistic devices: rhetorical questions (v. 20), various kinds of parallelism (standard, antithetical) (v. 18, 22), anaphora (the threefold 'where?' v. 20), and developed contrasts" (Fitzmyer, *First Corinthians*, p. 152). See also Collins, *First Corinthians*, pp. 75-76.

[123]See Thiselton, *First Epistle to the Corinthians*, pp. 142-47, 165.

[124]See Witherington, *Conflict and Community*, p. 110.

[125]See Fitzmyer, *First Corinthians*, p. 160.

[126]See Collins, *First Corinthians*, p. 106. This is likely because the message came to the Jews first (chronologically speaking) and because they were the "first step" in God's plan for the world. In short, without Israel, there is not the Messiah-from-Israel-for-the-world.

[127]Thiselton, *First Epistle to the Corinthians*, p. 170. See also Collins, *First Corinthians*, p. 108.

[128]Soards writes, "They all understand the divine gift as something that provides them with a visible status and that gives them a visible advantage over against the non-elect. . . . His implicit message, however, is that the Corinthians, by demanding of their teachers that they display wisdom in the manner of the rhetoricians, run the risk of identifying themselves with the Greeks who are lost in their pursuit of wisdom" (Soards, *1 Corinthians*, p. 45).

[129]Mangan summarizes the OT and Second Temple conceptions of wisdom as practically oriented, associated with power, particularly with God's power, is linked with creation and Torah, and is at

tators commonly recognize that Paul uses "the called" (τοῖς κλητοῖς) as a term referring to believers (thus the same group mentioned in 1 Cor 1:22). Some see in this term the implication of a doctrine of individual election or double predestination.[130] As Herman Ridderbos recognizes, the term is rooted in the Old Testament as a designation for God's people and of his "calling" for Israel.[131] James Thompson likewise observes the connection and notes, "This terminology indicates the place of Paul's churches within Israel's narrative world. Paul's usage reflects the influence of Deuteronomy, according to which God's choice of Israel requires Israel's separation from the practices of the world around them. Just as God chose ancient Israel to be a holy people and called them to live a countercultural existence, God has called the gentile churches to holy living."[132] I assume Paul has this connotation in mind in his letters, which fits both with the Old Testament literature and the Second Temple context from which Paul wrote. Such a term emphasizes God's people as a *collective*, and reinforces the necessity of their right behavior, which is the central issue in this section of the letter. Here in particular it emphasizes the need for Christ followers to live distinctly from "the world," as was Israel's calling. It also emphasizes the *continuity* between Israel as God's chosen people and those who are his people through the Messiah-from-Israel.

In a biting line of irony, Paul then asserts that God's foolishness is wiser than humans, and God's weakness is stronger (1 Cor 1:25). This is not, of course, to suggest Paul believed God foolish or weak, but rather that what humans viewed as folly and impotence, namely the cross, God used to accomplish his plan through a power and wisdom transcending human categories. Paul returns to his "calling" terminology (here,

---

times connected with salvation (Celine Mangan, "Christ the Power and the Wisdom of God: The Semitic Background to 1 Cor 1:24," *PIBA* 4 [1980]: 21-34).

[130]Kistemaker, e.g., seems to view Paul's discussion here as relating to individual election and the "effectual call" (Kistemaker, *First Epistle to the Corinthians*, p. 58). See also Schreiner, *Paul*, pp. 241-42.

[131]Herman N. Ridderbos, *Paul: An Outline of His Theology* (Grand Rapids: Eerdmans, 1975), pp. 332-33.

[132]James W. Thompson, *Moral Formation According to Paul: The Context and Coherence of Pauline Ethics* (Grand Rapids: Baker Academic, 2011), p. 67.

κλῆσις), telling the Corinthians to "look at" their calling.[133] Paul intends here, as is clear in what follows, to overturn their expectations of what is important, and may well have Deuteronomy 7 echoing in the background, which declares that God did not choose Israel because they were mighty or important, but rather because of his promise to Abraham. God works in ways upside down from human intuitions.[134] The Corinthians, likewise, since they stand in the line of God's chosen people, which began as a counterintuitive decision and culminated in the embracing of the ultimate sign of shame and weakness, must readily accept an identity the world views as shameful (1 Cor 1:26-28).

Much has been made of Paul's statement that "there were not many wise according to the flesh, not many powerful, not many born with high status" in interpreting both the social makeup of the Corinthian assembly and of the early church in general. Some have suggested that Paul employs an interrogative here and actually affirms that there were many powerful, noble and strong among the Corinthian fellowship, which would sharpen the contrast that follows.[135] Others more commonly view Paul as stating that most of the Corinthians were not of such high social status.[136] In either case, the Corinthians must embrace the foolishness of the message and Messiah rather than hold on to or seek

---

[133]Witherington suggests that "calling" here refers to "life circumstances." While this is possible, it seems more profitable to interpret it in its Jewish context as outlined above (Witherington, *Conflict and Community*, p. 113). According to Demarest, Paul is here expounding the order of salvation as "election, calling, union with Christ ('in Christ Jesus'), justification, and sanctification" (Bruce Demarest, *The Cross and Salvation: The Doctrine of Salvation* [Wheaton, IL: Crossway, 1997], p. 40), which seems unlikely unless Paul views "redemption" as something that follows "sanctification" (v. 31). See Fee, *First Epistle to the Corinthians*, p. 86.

[134]As Garland states, "Throughout the biblical narrative God consistently chooses the most unlikely figures, and Paul maintains that God has continued this pattern in choosing the believers in Corinth" (Garland, *1 Corinthians*, p. 77).

[135]O'Day, following Wuellner, suggests that the verse is better understood as an interrogative, with Paul affirming the wise, strong and noble status of the Corinthian believers (or at least of many of them) (Gail R. O'Day, "Jeremiah 9:22-23 and 1 Corinthians 1:26-31: A Study in Intertextuality," *JBL* 109, no. 2 [1990]: 263-64; following Wilhelm Wuellner, "The Sociological Implications of 1 Corinthians 1:26-28 Reconsidered," in *Studia Evangelica* VI, ed. E. A. Livingstone [Berlin: Akademie, 1973], pp. 666-72). As such, then, "the Corinthian triad of wise/powerful/noble birth derives directly from the Jeremian triad of wise/strong/rich in Jer 9:22. The Pauline text replicates the three terms of the Jeremian triad, the exact order of the triad, and its function—to critique false sources of security" (ibid., p. 265).

[136]E.g., Hays, *First Corinthians*, p. 32.

to obtain a position of privilege, either within the Christian community or in the world at large.[137]

The purpose of God's choosing of the "foolish things," "the weak things" and "the insignificant things," "the things that have been despised" and "the things that are not," was so that no flesh would boast before God (1 Cor 1:27-29). It seems clear that boasting in status, whether based on wealth, lineage, power or one's spiritual mentor, was a problem among the Corinthians and was causing serious divisions in their midst. But God's purpose, Paul asserts, in using the cross as a central and symbolic action to move his plan forward was to eliminate such boasting, and thus eliminate division among his people. The Corinthian community needed to embrace God's upside-down plan rather than use it to gain worldly prominence.[138] Simply put, as Leander Keck states summarizing 1 Corinthians 1:30, "Christ functions soteriologically ('for us') as wisdom because God chose to use the foolishness of the cross-kerygma to save those who believe it."[139]

To summarize: God has chosen to form a people who, just as in Deuteronomy, defy the values and expectations of the world. In an ultimate and final sense, Paul's argument envisions the chosen people as united in the climactic action of God's anointed one, who embraced a form of public humiliation and execution. However, by being raised from the dead, Jesus was vindicated and exalted as God's wisdom, righteousness, consecration and redemption (1 Cor 1:30). Since God has expressed this transcendent identity in the Messiah, those who trust God must do so through his Messiah. In order to do that, they must embrace that "foolish" and "shameful" identity. If Paul sought to encourage unity, as I have argued, it seems to me that arguing that God predetermined Corinthian believers individually to obtain salvation would undermine that purpose. Neither does that view accord well with what the Old Testament and, more specifically, Jews in the Second Temple period,

---

[137]See Leander E. Keck, "God the Other Who Acts Otherwise: An Exegetical Essay on 1 Cor 1:26-31," *WW* 26, no. 4 (1996): 440.
[138]See C. K. Barrett, *The Epistle to the First Corinthians*, BNTC (Peabody, MA: Hendrickson, 1968), p. 57; Thiselton, *First Epistle to the Corinthians*, p. 184; Collins, *First Corinthians*, p. 110.
[139]Keck, "God the Other," p. 441.

understood "election" to mean and entail. Paul here argues that God has chosen to create a cruciform, upside-down people who must take the shape of their Savior. Those who trust in Jesus must adopt his identity in order to share in the wisdom, righteousness, consecration and redemption he embodies.[140]

Summary

I have attempted to outline here the way in which most Jews likely understood election. God's choice was to form a people who would represent him to the world. Paul does not explicitly re-create this framework, but in adopting the language and concepts of Israel's election, he builds on what his compatriots already understood, as is evidenced in Jewish literature. Just as those writings maintain a collective focus, either by recalling the promises to the patriarchs, by speaking of a "true Israel," by emphasizing the remnant motif or by using corporate metaphors like a "plant," "vineyard" or "foundation," so Paul likewise maintains such a focus. To state it bluntly, it seems to me difficult to make the case that Jews of the period held to any notion of our concept of individual election unto salvation. In 2 Thessalonians, by intermingling conditional elements with election language, Paul seems to consistently apply the logic we see in the Jewish literature. God has chosen a people who obligate themselves to live a certain way. Being a part of that people carries with it certain conditions or expectations. The whole discussion of "insiders" and "outsiders" we find throughout the literature of the period is concerned with just that: who are God's people, and how do we recognize them? That question is a collective one.

Likewise, in 1 Corinthians 1, a passage taken by some to teach individual election or double predestination, Paul argues for the importance of the unity of God's people. Paul expresses that unity as living after the pattern of Jesus, something that does not conform to what the world thinks to be wise or important. In fact, it means quite the opposite, since the humiliation of the Savior is a defining characteristic of Paul's good

---

[140]See Hays, *First Corinthians*, p. 35.

news. In recalling the terminology first used of national Israel, words like "called" and "elect" and "beloved," Paul indicates to his readers that he views them as God's people *if* they are defined by God's Messiah. Paul does not abandon the collective framework, but rather redefines it around Jesus. Paul thus, like other Jewish writers of his day, understands "election" to be about God's people *as a people*.

4

Who's In and Who's Out?

Election and "Conditions"

We perhaps have noticed that a debate existed among Jews of the Second Temple period as to how to identify God's people. Various groups contributed different, and sometimes contradictory, pictures of what defined God's people, though some common threads run throughout. In order to get a better sense of what beliefs and activities defined God's people, I now turn to explore the "conditions," implicit and explicit, that these texts offer us. This will inform our understanding of Paul's thinking concerning the identity of the people of God.

IMPLICIT CONDITIONS

I will shortly discuss those texts that explicitly define the "boundaries" of God's people. A number of texts, however, do not explicitly delineate which Jews are "in" and which are "out," or which Jews God judges or will judge versus those whom he blesses or will bless. In these texts, however, we find implicit clues pointing to an underlying assumption that these authors indeed made such a distinction.

Tobit. The book of Tobit tells the multifaceted and colorful tale of a suffering righteous man whose plight is resolved through the exploits of his son Tobias, and some angelic intervention.[1] The author likely intended, at least in part, to encourage faithfulness and piety among Di-

---

[1]Moore suggests that the characters in Tobit are representatives of the people of Israel: "There is also a heilsgeschichtlich ('salvation history') colorization to the book. For as God has looked out for these individuals, so, the author argues, God will respond to the present suffering of his dispersed people (Tobit 13–14)" (Carey A. Moore, *Tobit: A New Translation with Introduction and Commentary*, AB [New York: Doubleday, 1996], p. 32).

aspora Jews,[2] especially with his emphasis on almsgiving and pursuing righteousness in difficult circumstances.[3]

We find the only explicit election language in Tobit 8:15, where Raguel, Tobias' father-in-law, exhorts the saints, angels and "chosen ones" to praise God forever. The title here functions in connection with praising God and focuses on the whole of the people of God. In Tobit 13–14, the author records the prayers of Tobit in which he addresses the current plight of the people of "Israel." Tobit foresees God restoring those Jews who will return to him in faithful obedience, as well as the conversion of many nations (Tob 13:6-11).[4] He also foresees the coming fulfillment of the words of the prophets in which the Jewish people will be restored in their land and rebuild the temple (Tob 14:5).

The author does not depict the restoration, however, as universal, but inclusive only of the Israelites "who are spared and are truly loyal to God," while the ungodly "will vanish from the whole earth."[5] Tobit would have no doubt conveyed to those Jews in "exile" (i.e., under foreign authority and oppression) a message that there is a responsibility involved in their election.[6] They must remain faithful and obedient to God, even during difficult circumstances.[7]

---

[2]As Macatangay writes, "all that Tobit can do is maintain a sense of what defines him as a member of God's elect and foster cohesion and a sense of belonging among his fellow dispersed" (Francis M. Macatangay, *The Wisdom Instructions in the Book of Tobit* [Berlin: de Gruyter, 2011], p. 283).

[3]Or, as Griffin states, "The Book of Tobit is written for those under Hellenistic domination in Palestine and the Diaspora, the same principles advocated by the deuteronomistic historian may be applied to the situation of the author's own time: remain faithful to the Lord and to the Law" (Patrick J. Griffin, *The Theology and Function of Prayer in the Book of Tobit* [PhD diss., Catholic University of America, 1984], pp. 358-59).

[4]Nickelsburg states that this "mercy is predicated on Israel's repentance. When they 'turn' back to God, then God will 'turn' to them" (George W. E. Nickelsburg, "Tobit," in *The HarperCollins Bible Commentary*, ed. James L. Mays [New York: HarperCollins, 1988], p. 729).

[5]Moore, *Tobit*, p. 288.

[6]Though "divine providence" plays an important role in the book, Moore asserts correctly that, for Tobit, "God is not some heavenly chess master who skillfully (and willfully) moves the 'pieces' (i.e., the characters in the story) apart from their own will. In God's providence, a man's cooperation with God . . . can bring the entire matter to a successful resolution" (ibid., p. 32). On the corporate emphasis of the book, see Philip R. Davies, "Didactic Stories," in *Justification and Variegated Nomism*, vol. 1, *The Complexities of Second Temple Judaism*, ed. D. A. Carson, Peter T. O'Brien and Mark A. Seifrid (Grand Rapids: Baker Academic, 2001), p. 113.

[7]See Chris VanLandingham, *Judgment and Justification in Early Judaism and the Apostle Paul* (Grand Rapids: Baker Academic, 2006), p. 134.

Wisdom of Ben Sira. One of Ben Sira's most unique contributions concerning election in Jewish literature occurs in its connection with wisdom. In the beginning of the "Wisdom hymn," Ben Sira describes Wisdom's primordial journey from the presence of the Most High through the heavens and the abyss and through every nation, looking for an abode. God commands Wisdom to dwell "in Jacob, and in Israel receive your inheritance" (Sir 24:8 NRSV). Wisdom rooted herself in "an honored people, in the portion of the Lord, his heritage" (Sir 24:12 NRSV). Ben Sira later equates the giving of Wisdom with the giving of the Torah as an inheritance for Israel (Sir 24:23).[8] Central, then, to Ben Sira's understanding of Israel's election is their receipt of, and living in accordance with, Torah. As Greg Goering explains, "The association of Wisdom with Israel results from YHWH's election of Israel as the place where Wisdom dwells most fully on earth."[9] God's choosing Israel is, for Ben Sira, fundamentally rooted in his giving Wisdom/Torah to them.[10]

In Sirach 36:1-22, Ben Sira discusses YHWH's relationship to the nations. A tension persists between Ben Sira's apparent desire for the nations to know YHWH (Sir 36:1-7) and for him to judge and destroy them (Sir 36:8-12).[11] E. P. Sanders sees here an affirmation of the nationalistic view of election in which "God will, on that day, save all the tribes of Jacob."[12] This stands in tension, however, with Sanders's statement that

---

[8]Thus Grindheim affirms in stating, "The giving of wisdom is to be identified with the giving of the Torah and the temple service. To be elect is thereby defined as to be given the Torah" (Sigurd Grindheim, *The Crux of Election: Paul's Critique of the Jewish Confidence in the Election of Israel* [Tübingen: Mohr Siebeck, 2005], p. 35).

[9]Greg S. Goering, *Wisdom's Root Revealed: Ben Sira and the Election of Israel*, JSJSup 139 (Leiden: Brill, 2009), p. 179.

[10]Collins affirms this connection in stating, YFF "exercise[s] the election of Israel through Wisdom" (John J. Collins, *Jewish Wisdom in the Hellenistic Age* [Louisville: Westminster John Knox, 1997], p. 51).

[11]The judgmental nature of the text has led some to suggest that it was not original to Ben Sira and was added later. Collins, for example, notes, "This prayer in chapter 36 is remote in spirit from the rest of the teaching of Sirach, and was most probably inserted into the book at the time of the Maccabean crisis. Sirach's own view of history has no eschatological urgency" (Collins, *Jewish Wisdom*, p. 111).

[12]E. P. Sanders, *Paul and Palestinian Judaism* (Minneapolis: Fortress, 1970), p. 333. He also argues that, in chap. 36, "he calls upon God to hasten the day when he will destroy the Gentile nations, gather again *all* the tribes of Jacob, and establish the Israelite theocracy throughout the earth. Thus it is clear that Ben Sirach had a firm view of the election of Israel and of the ultimate fulfillment of God's covenant to establish the chosen people" (ibid., p. 331).

Ben Sira's view of the individual's fate "does not depend on whether or not the individual is elect . . . but on whether or not he is counted among the wicked or the righteous."[13] The statement prompts the question as to how the fate of the wicked and righteous relates to the fate of the elect.[14] It seems from the outset that the two views cannot stand together. Unless Ben Sira holds that all Israel will in fact be righteous (which does not appear possible, especially in light of Sir 44–51), it cannot be that all of Israel is a part of the elect. According to Jason Maston, "When not overlaid [as per Sanders] with supposed rabbinical understandings of how one comes to be in a covenantal relationship with God (by grace), Ben Sira's own perspective about how one enters into a covenantal relationship with God appears differently. He gives priority to the human act of obedience."[15] Ben Sira asserts the election of Israel, and the special connection between wisdom, Torah and Israel's election, but does not speak in explicit soteriological/eschatological terms.[16]

Ben Sira develops the remnant motif explicitly in Sirach 44–50, though dealing primarily with Israel's past rather than its future. One may, however, in light of Ben Sira's emphasis on the correspondence between deeds and judgment, see it as necessitating a conditional view of Israel's election in which only the faithful remain among the people of God and do not receive a dishonorable death/punishment.[17] This is

---

[13]Ibid., p. 333.

[14]Sanders notes the inherently corporate or collective nature of Ben Sira's view and states that the question of how the individual relates to election and soteriology cannot be answered from Ben Sira's work (ibid.).

[15]Jason Maston, *Divine and Human Agency in Second Temple Judaism and Paul* (Tübingen: Mohr Siebeck, 2010), p. 37.

[16]It should be noted, however, as Di Lella states, that the "possibility of rewards or punishments in some sort of afterlife receives no mention at all in the original Hebrew text of Ben Sira. But the Greek translation does make definite allusions to retribution in the hereafter" (Patrick W. Skehan and Alexander A. Di Lella, OFM, *The Wisdom of Ben Sira: A New Translation with Notes*, AB [New York: Doubleday, 1987], p. 86). For example, the Greek text of Sir 7:17 adds "fire" to the judgment received by the ungodly, whereas the Hebrew text states only that their punishment will be "worms" (i.e., death).

[17]Or, as Maston summarizes, "In Ben Sira's view, each individual must reconfirm the covenant, and God's goodness to previous generations is the result of their obedience and does not carry over to later generations" (Maston, *Divine and Human Agency*, pp. 42-43). Grindheim acknowledges the preservation of a remnant as indicating both judgment and salvation (see Sir 44:17; Grindheim, *Crux of Election*, p. 150), and he in turn suggests, "To speak of a remnant implies judgment on the majority of Israel, while the minority will be saved" (ibid., 150). Though the

also in keeping with Ben Sira's asserting human freedom to choose life or death (i.e., obedience or disobedience) in Sirach 15:15-17, as well as his acknowledging God's judgment being consistent with human choice in Sirach 33:11-15. The general emphasis, however, on the nature of election connects it with the behavior of the elect. Ben Sira makes clear the correlation of Wisdom and election in the giving of the Torah, God's special relationship with Israel, and the ability of humanity to choose obedience or disobedience (life or death). It thus is likely that Ben Sira's recognition of the remnant motif and emphasis on human choice and faithfulness would favor a conditional view of election. A faithful remnant maintains this elect identity, and the primary description of the elect is their faithfulness to keeping the Torah (piety) and living under the guidance of Wisdom.

Baruch. Baruch represents the Second Temple genre of "rewritten Bible," in which the author compiled and expanded on existing biblical traditions. Though the author sets the book near the time of the exile in the sixth century B.C.E., he likely wrote after Ben Sira, given the presence of allusions to Sirach 24 and dependence on Isaiah, Ezekiel and Daniel.[18] The book's emphasis on the importance of faithfulness to the Torah, repentance and the future restoration of Israel in the land makes it a fitting contribution to the theology of Diaspora Judaism.[19]

The author affirms the special relationship between Yhwh and Israel in Baruch 2:34-35, where God promises the restoration of the land. Here the author invokes Jeremiah 32:38-40 and Ezekiel 36:28, stating, "I will make an everlasting covenant with them to be their God and they shall be my people; and I will never again remove my people Israel from the land that I have given them" (nrsv). Like Ben Sira before him, Baruch

---

theme may not be explicit, it seems logical to view Ben Sira's perspective in this light given the tension that would result from viewing election both as conditional and national.

[18]Mark E. Biddle, "Baruch," in *The New Oxford Annotate Apocrypha*, ed. Michael D. Coogan, 3rd ed. (New York: Oxford University Press, 2001), p. 176. Osterley notes, "It is obvious that the purported historical background of our book is merely a literary device adopted for the purposes of disguising the actual historical background" (W. O. E. Osterley, *An Introduction to the Books of the Apocrypha* [New York: MacMillan, 1935], p. 259).

[19]See also David A. deSilva, *Introducing the Apocrypha: Message, Context, and Significance* (Grand Rapids: Baker Academic, 2002), p. 205.

(likely influenced by him) also connects Wisdom and Torah with Israel's election.[20] Wisdom is "the book of the commandments of God," and

> all who hold her fast will live,
>   and those who forsake her will die. (Bar 4:1-2 NRSV)

Here Israel's elect status is portrayed as contingent on her living faithfully to the terms of the covenant outlined in the Torah.[21] Baruch 4:12-35 foresees Israel's restoration as coming through God destroying those who have oppressed her, though the exile is also viewed as God punishing Israel for their unfaithfulness and idolatry (Bar 4:5-16). The author grounds the appeal for restoration in God's mercy alone (Bar 2:19), and not in any meritorious deeds of Israel's ancestors, though this does not eliminate Israel's responsibility. The book makes brief mention of the remnant motif in Baruch 2:13, where the people are now "few in number, among the nations where you have scattered us" (NRSV). Carey Moore notes that this is curious given the widespread dispersion of the Jews, who were large in number, during the Diaspora.[22] This text may, then, harken back to the notion of the number of *faithful* Jews being few rather than there being few Jews from an ethnic perspective.

As reflected throughout the letter (and especially in Bar 2:19), Israel willfully disobeyed and possessed no merits to which they could appeal for restoration.[23] Only YHWH's mercy allowed them to hope for salvation and restoration. Though their repentance and adherence to the Torah were expected, they needed to appeal to God's gracious response because

---

[20]Grindheim also affirms this, noting, "The striking connection between election and wisdom comes to expression also in Baruch. . . . Jacob being given wisdom from God is indicative of his election" (Grindheim, *Crux of Election*, p. 40).

[21]Hogan notes that the allusion in Bar 4:1 to Israelites forsaking the law is consistent with the sections that follow, which emphasize Israel's failures, though in sharp contrast with the triumphant tone that ends the poem (Karina Martin Hogan, *Theologies in Conflict in 4 Ezra: Wisdom, Debate, and Apocalyptic Solution* [Leiden: Brill, 2008], p. 85). This is also seen, for example, in Bar 1:18-22, where Israel's punishment is seen as being consistent with what YHWH proclaimed in Deut 28 in that the people would be blessed for faithfulness and cut off and cursed for disobedience and idolatry.

[22]See Carey A. Moore, *Daniel, Esther, and Jeremiah: The Additions*, AB (New York: Doubleday, 1977), p. 287.

[23]There is also an appeal to the preservation of God's reputation as seen in his relationship with Israel. So deSilva concludes, "God must not abandon Israel to perdition, if for no other reason than to preserve God's own honor in the world" (deSilva, *Introducing the Apocrypha*, p. 211).

they had broken the covenant.[24] Baruch also seems to share Ben Sira's this-worldly outlook on Israel's salvation.[25] This is seen especially in Baruch 2:17, where he states, "The dead who are in Hades, whose spirit has been taken from their bodies, will not ascribe glory or justice to the Lord" (NRSV). Though this does not eliminate, for example, a hope for future eschatological resurrection, the author expresses no such hope and couches Israel's salvation primarily in terms of a physical return to the land and the destruction of those who oppose them. Thus we may see their receipt of the covenant blessings as conditioned on their response to the Torah of YHWH, and subsequently Baruch envisions only a portion of Israel truly repenting, though we find this more implicitly than explicitly.

Wisdom of Solomon. The Wisdom of Solomon stands as a unique entry in the collection known as the Apocrypha. Written either shortly before or shortly after the beginning of the common era, probably in Alexandria,[26] scholars typically classify the work as Jewish Wisdom literature. It—perhaps more than any other work of the period, outside of Philo—demonstrates an intentional integration with Greek philosophical thought to defend the superiority of the Jewish wisdom and legal traditions,[27] though it includes only a few vague references to the Torah itself. Thus, as Daniel Harrington has stated, "It is more a book about wisdom—its benefits, nature, and role in history—than a wisdom book giving practical advice (like Proverbs and Sirach)."[28] The work is not purely descriptive, however, in that it no doubt expects certain behavioral responses of its readers who have accepted its teachings.[29] Of its

---

[24]DeSilva summarizes quite aptly, "The confession of the Judean remnant and the exiles allows the participant to remove from himself or herself the cause of displacement and thus remove the obstacle to the hoped-for future. By naming the cause of the disruptive circumstances 'sin,' the circumstances are tamed, in effect, since individual Jews (and their community) have the resources to deal with 'sin,' even if they do not have the resources to fight for political liberation for all their coreligionists" (ibid., p. 206).

[25]See Simon J. Gathercole, *Where Is Boasting? Early Jewish Soteriology and Paul's Response in Romans 1–5* (Grand Rapids: Eerdmans, 2002), p. 41.

[26]See Collins, *Jewish Wisdom*, pp. 178-79.

[27]See George W. E. Nickelsburg, *Jewish Literature Between the Bible and the Mishnah* (Minneapolis: Fortress, 2005), p. 205.

[28]Daniel J. Harrington, *Invitation to the Apocrypha* (Grand Rapids: Eerdmans, 1999), p. 55.

[29]Collins, *Jewish Wisdom*, p. 182.

audience, David deSilva says, "Wisdom is thus surely written to encourage continued adherence to the Jewish way of life in a setting where the enticements of Hellenization and the ability of apostates to reject their heritage as of little value weigh heavily upon the Jewish consciousness."[30] Most divide the work into three sections: Wisdom of Solomon 1–6 contrasts the righteous and the wicked; Wisdom of Solomon 7–10 offers praise of Lady Wisdom; and Wisdom of Solomon 11–19 gives a series of contrasts based on the Exodus narratives.

As the author concludes the first section, he affirms that Wisdom, the mediator of God's salvation,

> is easily discerned by those who love her,
> and is found by those who seek her.
> She hastens to make herself known to those who desire her. . . .
> Love of her is the keeping of her laws,
> and giving heed to her laws is assurance of immortality,
> and immortality brings one near to God;
> so the desire for wisdom leads to a kingdom. (Wis 6:12-20 NRSV)

Here Wisdom comes to those who seek her, and those who keep her laws (i.e., are faithful to the stipulations of the covenant)[31] will inherit eternal life and rewards. As Ernest Clarke observes, one must avoid seeing here "works-righteousness" in which the faithful earn eternal life. God alone grants eternal life, and if it (as mediated through Wisdom and the Torah) is rejected through unfaithfulness or ignorant self-absorption, then humans will not enter into a covenant with God, but with death.[32]

---

[30]David A. deSilva, "Wisdom of Solomon," in *Dictionary of New Testament Background*, ed. Craig A. Evans and Stanley E. Porter (Downers Grove, IL: InterVarsity Press, 2000), p. 1271. See also Daniel J. Harrington, "'Saved by Wisdom' (Wis 9.18): Soteriology in the Wisdom of Solomon," in *This World and the World to Come: Soteriology in Early Judaism*, ed. Daniel M. Gurtner (New York: T&T Clark, 2011), p. 182; deSilva, *Introducing the Apocrypha*, p. 136. The work also contains numerous points of overlap with the New Testament (see Nickelsburg, *Jewish Literature*, p. 212).

[31]DeSilva notes, "While she is not here identified with the Torah as in Ben Sira, she does teach what pleases God, and this involves keeping the commandments (Wis 6:18; 9:9)" (deSilva, "Wisdom of Solomon," p. 1272). While less overt than in Ben Sira, the book does still connect wisdom and Torah, and thus salvation with the covenant.

[32]See Ernest G. Clarke, *The Wisdom of Solomon* (Cambridge: Cambridge University Press, 1973), p. 12. See also Maurice Gilbert, "Wisdom Literature," in *Jewish Writings of the Second Temple Period*, ed. Michael E. Stone (Philadelphia: Fortress, 1984), 2:310.

The book, in affirming the afterlife, dispels the idea that the righteous will always experience blessing in the present and the wicked will always face punishment.[33] As in many other texts of the period, true justice will come in the eschaton or the afterlife,[34] when the just receive rewards for their faithfulness and the wicked receive destruction. The author identifies the righteous as those who live according to the law and wisdom (Wis 12:21; 16:6, 26; 18:4, 22), which is imparted to those who seek her through prayer.[35] The wicked, however, mock the righteous and, more specifically, practice adultery, violence, dishonesty, theft and sexually immorality.[36] The wicked undoubtedly include certain Jews who reject the law and are unrepentant.[37] As Karina Martin Hogan describes, they "forfeit immortality through their sinful lives, so for them, physical death does amount to annihilation."[38] Thus again, though more implicitly described, God's choice of Israel is best thought of in conditional terms since only those faithful to the covenant will partake of its blessings.

Sibylline Oracles. The *Sibylline Oracles* are a collection of Jewish and Christian apocalyptic writings[39] derived from the "Sibyl," an elderly woman who predicts future disasters. In summarizing the *Oracles*, John Collins states, "The content shows at least the same basic pattern of di-

---

[33]Collins, *Jewish Wisdom*, pp. 183-84.

[34]For Wisdom, it seems likely that a disembodied eternal existence of the soul is expected by the author. So Collins states, "There can be little doubt, however, that the immortality envisaged is immortality of the soul, as in Philo. There is never any suggestion of resurrection of the body, nor indeed of resurrection of the spirit. . . . The author does not, however, speak of immortality as a natural property of the soul. Rather it is the fruit of righteousness and wisdom" (Collins, *Jewish Wisdom*, p. 186).

[35]Donald E. Gowan, "Wisdom," in Carson, O'Brien and Seifrid, *Complexities of Second Temple Judaism*, p. 229.

[36]Collins, *Jewish Wisdom*, pp. 191-92.

[37]See Mark Adam Elliott, *The Survivors of Israel: A Reconsideration of the Theology of Pre-Christian Judaism* (Grand Rapids: Eerdmans, 2000), p. 73.

[38]Karina Martin Hogan, "The Exegetical Background of the 'Ambiguity of Death' in the Wisdom of Solomon," *JSJ* 30, no. 1 (1991): 2. See also Harrington, "Saved by Wisdom," p. 190.

[39]Concerning their relevance, Collins notes, "They are an important source for early Judaism and for the thought of the early Church. Yet they have only rarely been studied in modern times" (John J. Collins, *The Sibylline Oracles of Egyptian Judaism* [Missoula: University of Montana Press, 1972], p. xiii). Lightfoot agrees with this sentiment (J. L. Lightfoot, *The Sibylline Oracles: With Introduction, Translation, and Commentary on the First and Second Books* [Oxford: Oxford University Press, 2007], p. vii). As these texts are examined, Christian interpolations, as much as is possible, will be excluded from this study.

saster followed by a transformation of the world, often accompanied by the establishment of a new kingdom."[40] The books date from the second century B.C.E. to the seventh century C.E., and originated primarily in Egypt.[41] Books one, two and three are all Jewish in origin and came about before the destruction of the temple.[42] The oracles promote moral purity and the rejection of idolatry.[43] Books one and two constitute a single unit. Most scholars see them as a part of a Jewish work later edited and expanded by a Christian redactor. In the second book, it is difficult to determine the extent of the Christian redaction. Collins suggests that several sections (*Sib. Or.* 2.45-55, 177-83, 190-92, 238-51, 311-47) likely have Christian origins, while the remainder (*Sib. Or.* 2.39-44, 149-53, 184-89, 193-237, 252-310) could be either Jewish or Christian in origin.[44]

In the *Oracles*, the author thinks of Israel in collective terms throughout. They are God's chosen people, the pious ones and the righteous. However, unlike the previous literature examined, the book seems to look toward a national restoration of Israel, with no explicit indications that a "true Israel," a group of faithful Jews amid a largely unfaithful populace, exists. However, several themes recur in the *Oracles* that suggest the subtle presence of the idea. First, the book clearly emphasizes the importance of obedience, with eschatological salvation belonging *solely* to the pious/righteous (*Sib. Or.* 1.128-36; 2.27-28; 3.283-85, 573-83).[45] The *Oracles* also

---

[40]Collins, *Sibylline Oracles*, p. 19.

[41]John J. Collins, "Sibylline Oracles," in Evans and Porter, *Dictionary of New Testament Background*, p. 322. According to Collins, books 4, 6 and 7 probably originated in Syria; books 1 and 2 in Asia Minor; and book 8 outside of Egypt in an undeterminable region. Buitenwerf argues for an Asian provenance of the third book (Rieuwerd Buitenwerf, *Book III of the Sibylline Oracles and Its Social Setting* [Leiden: Brill, 2003], pp. 130-33).

[42]See Collins, "Sibylline Oracles," p. 1108; Collins, "Sibylline Oracles," in *The Eerdmans Dictionary of Early Judaism*, ed. John J. Collins and Daniel C. Harlow (Grand Rapids: Eerdmans, 2010), p. 1227. These texts have a complex compositional history, making the Jewish and Christian layers of the text sometimes difficult to separate. See Lightfoot, *Sibylline Oracles*, p. viii.

[43]Collins, "Sibylline Oracles," in Collins and Harlow, *Eerdmans Dictionary of Early Judaism*, p. 1226.

[44]Though disagreements exist, suggested redaction divisions are taken from Collins. Collins also notes that *Sib. Or.* 2.56-148 contains a lengthy excerpt from pseudo-Phocylides (Collins, "Sibylline Oracles," in *The Old Testament Pseudepigrapha*, vol. 1, *Apocalyptic Literature and Testaments*, ed. James H. Charlesworth [1983; repr., Peabody, MA: Hendrickson, 2011], p. 330).

[45]See Collins, "The Sibylline Oracles," in Stone, *Jewish Writings*, 2:368; Buitenwerf, *Book III*, p. 336.

recognize (particularly in *Sib. Or.* 1.155-79; 3.265-81, 594-600, 601-18, 741-61, and possibly in 2.168-79) that Israel has committed certain sins, or is susceptible to them, namely, idolatry, violence, deceit, adultery and sexual sins.[46] The author promotes obedience and sacrifice in book three, though elsewhere (particularly in *Sib. Or.* 1.167-69) repentance is expected. Rieuwerd Buitenwerf affirms the author of *Oracle* 3 (along with books 1 and 2) wrote to his Jewish audience both to praise their pious lifestyle and "to admonish them to persevere in this way of living."[47] The risk exists for the Sibyl's audience to commit apostasy or sin, and thus they must guard themselves against it. And so, Buitenwerf writes, "Throughout the book, the author has the Sibyl confront a possibly disobedient audience with the threat of divine punishment. Only those who live according to the divine principles may expect to share in a happy future and to enjoy God's protection during his future intervention in world history."[48] If apostates exist within the audience, the warnings of judgment and promises of salvation to the righteous point them to the danger of their choice. Thus, though not as explicit as in other writings of the period, the Sibyl suggests the possibility or reality of disobedience among the Jews, and the inevitability of God's judgment to follow.

Pseudo-Philo. The *Biblical Antiquities* begins with a summary of the genealogies from Adam to Lamech (*Bib. Ant.* 1.1–2.10). Here the author reveals that "in that time, when those inhabiting the earth began to do evil deeds (each one with his neighbor's wife) and they defiled them, God was angry . . . and those inhabiting the earth began to make statues and to adore them" (*Bib. Ant.* 2.8-9). The author here reveals two of the

---

[46]So Donaldson notes, "But in describing this law, the author does not mention at all those aspects of the Torah that separate Israel from the nations (circumcision, dietary regulations, etc.). The law is presented instead as a basic moral code, accessible, and hence applicable, to all. . . . The essence of the Torah for the Sibyl, therefore, is to be found in the avoidance of idolatry, the worship of the one true God in the Jerusalem temple, and adherence to a basic code of morality" (Terence L. Donaldson, "Proselytes or 'Righteous Gentiles'? The Status of Gentiles in Eschatological Pilgrimage Patterns of Thought," *JSP* 7 [1990]: 18-19).

[47]Buitenwerf, *Book III*, pp. 384-85.

[48]Ibid., p. 335. He later notes, "The main function of the prediction of divine intervention in world history, and a judgement in which evil people will be punished and the pious rewarded, is to emphasize the importance of the author's warning to live piously and righteously" (ibid., p. 364).

prominent sins of the book, which are improper sexual relations, often in the form of intermarriage with Gentiles, and idolatry.[49] The whole earth is here implicated in these sins, thus explaining the author's affirmation of God's anger against humanity.[50] In *Biblical Antiquities* 3.9-10, the author adds, following God's affirmation that he would never again flood the earth,

> but when those inhabiting the earth sin, I will judge them by famine or by sword or by fire or by death; and there will be earthquakes, and they will be scattered to uninhabited places. . . . But when the years appointed for the world have been fulfilled, then the light will cease and the darkness will fade away. And I will bring the dead to life and raise up those who are sleeping from the earth. And hell will pay back its debt, and the place of perdition will return its deposit so that I may render to each according to his works and according to the fruits of his own devices, until I judge between soul and flesh. And the world will cease, and death will be abolished, and hell will shut its mouth.

The author clearly expects a general resurrection followed by a judgment of all humanity. Pseudo-Philo also affirms here that the final judgment of individuals will be according to their works (*Bib. Ant.* 3.10). Here Murphy comments, "the principle for the rest of the book is clearly delineated: Sin will inevitably result in punishment in this life, the life hereafter, or both."[51]

As the book transitions to the arrival of Abraham, pseudo-Philo writes of Abraham's ancestor Serug, "From him there will be born in the fourth generation one who will set his dwelling on high and will be called perfect and blameless; and he will be the father of nations, and his covenant will not be broken, and his seed will be multiplied forever" (*Bib. Ant.* 4.11). While humanity at the time was idolatrous, the author says, "Serug and his sons did not act as these did" (*Bib. Ant.* 4.16). The text in

---

[49]See Frederick J. Murphy, "Biblical Antiquities (Pseudo-Philo)," in Collins and Harlow, *Eerdmans Dictionary of Early Judaism*, p. 441.

[50]See Frederick J. Murphy, "Retelling the Bible: Idolatry in Pseudo-Philo," *JBL* 107, no. 2 (1988): 276.

[51]Frederick J. Murphy, *Pseudo-Philo: Rewriting the Bible* (Oxford: Oxford University Press, 1993), p. 34.

4.11 does not make explicit how Abraham will be found blameless, but the note in 4.16 suggests that it is the resistance to idolatry that establishes him as such.[52] This also establishes the intended pattern for Israel, as Frederick Murphy describes, "Israel begins with Abraham's rejection of idolatry and choice to serve God. Such service separates Israel from the rest of humanity. This alerts us to the converse, viz., mixing with the nations leads to disloyalty to God."[53]

Pseudo-Philo introduces Abraham by name ("Abram") in chapter six, as he, with a handful of others, resists participation in the Babel project, citing their worship of Yhwh as reason for their resistance (*Bib. Ant.* 6.3-5). Throughout the ordeal, Abraham remains confident that God will protect him (*Bib. Ant.* 6.11). The author thus places on Abraham an unwavering confidence in God along with a blameless character. Following these events, God selects Abraham as his "child" with whom to make a covenant in order to "bless his seed and be lord for him as God forever" (*Bib. Ant.* 7.4), a covenant that is established in *Biblical Antiquities* 8.3, generally in keeping with its presentation in Genesis 13 and Genesis 17.

In chapter twenty-five, the author expands on the biblical figure of Kenaz as the tribes prepare to battle the Philistines. After God has judged the sinners among them, the author recounts a vision in which Israel forsakes God and is corrupted, prompting Kenaz to question Israel's future (*Bib. Ant.* 28.3-5).[54] Kenaz then receives his own ecstatic vision (*Bib. Ant.* 28.6-9). As Murphy summarizes, he sees "the sweep of creation and the beginning and end of humanity. He shares the fruit of that experience with the people. . . . Since they know such things, their behavior should reflect that. Subsequent chapters show that the essence of Kenaz's vision is lost on them."[55]

---

[52]Murphy writes, "Abraham comes from a family which alone, of *all* the inhabitants of the earth, distinguishes itself by its rejection of idolatry" (Murphy, "Retelling the Bible," p. 276).

[53]Ibid.

[54]Murphy notes, "Whether or not God's commitment to Israel is unconditional is a point of tension throughout the *Biblical Antiquities*. In the course of the work, humans both presume on the indestructibility of the covenant and assume that it is destructible. God is often on the brink of annulling the covenant because of Israel's unfaithfulness, but the narrative shows that God cannot annul it" (Murphy, *Pseudo-Philo*, p. 131).

[55]Ibid., p. 133.

After the passing of Zebul, Israel's continual disobedience finally arouses God's judgment as he sends their enemies to "rule over them" (*Bib. Ant.* 30.2). This prompts the people to recognize their sins (30.2-4). As a result, the people fast, hoping to renew God's favor toward them, an action that prompts God to send Deborah to "take pity" on them "because of his covenant that he established with your fathers and the oath that he has sworn not to abandon you forever" (*Bib. Ant.* 30.7). Rather than forsake the people, God is faithful to the covenant, though the people were not.[56] We should acknowledge here, however, as often throughout the work, that this response of mercy comes after the people have recognized their sin.[57]

After God delivers Israel from Sisera (*Bib. Ant.* 31), Deborah affirms that God has been faithful to the covenant, and is worthy of praise because of this (*Bib. Ant.* 32.11-17). In her farewell speech, she tells Israel to "direct your heart to the LORD your God during the time of your life, because after your death you cannot repent of those things in which you live. . . . Do not hope in your fathers. For they will not profit you at all unless you be found like them. But then you will be like the stars of the heaven, which now have been revealed among you" (*Bib. Ant.* 33.2-5). As Murphy recognizes, death seals the fate of the dead, for "only decisions made in this life matter."[58] The people are instructed that, in order to receive eternal blessing and life, they must "be found like" their ancestors, meaning that they must be faithful to God. Here again, Murphy recognizes that the eternality of the covenant does not guarantee "any individual Israelite or a specific Israelite generation will be in God's graces. . . . Individual Israelites and even whole generations can be punished, but that will never mean the end of Israel."[59]

Further episodes (Gideon, Samson, Micah, the concubine of Gibeah,

---

[56]See Howard Jacobson, *A Commentary on Pseudo-Philo's* Liber Antiquitatum Biblicarum *with Latin Text and English Translation* (Leiden: Brill, 1996), 2:841.

[57]See VanLandingham, *Judgment and Justification*, p. 31.

[58]Murphy, *Pseudo-Philo*, p. 151. Or, as Jacobson summarizes, "Be faithful to God now, for after you die, you will be unable to repent [even if you want to]. But if [rather than desiring to repent] you will want to continue acting badly, you won't be able to do that either" (Jacobson, *A Commentary*, 2:901-2).

[59]Murphy, *Pseudo-Philo*, p. 152.

Eli's sons and Saul) demonstrate the author's commitment to a retributive view of divine punishment. Throughout, pseudo-Philo holds together both the eternality and surety of God's commitment to the covenant and the real danger for Israel to violate it and for God to cut them off. Frequently sins of immorality, mixing with Gentiles and idolatry ensnare the Israelites. Since the final judgment will be over the deeds of each individual, and examples of immediate and eventual retribution abound through the book, the author communicates that though the covenant is eternal because of God's faithfulness, each generation must respond in faithfulness in order to receive its blessings and, ultimately, eternal life with God.

EXPLICIT CONDITIONS

Our next group of texts more explicitly identifies certain Jews, along with Gentiles, as being under God's judgment. We do not find total agreement among these texts about how to identify God's people, though there are some rough commonalities. The respective authors of each of these documents quite adamantly assert that certain Jews, by their beliefs and/or behaviors, stand under God's judgment. This clearly defines the "boundaries" of God's people, and delineates those who do not live up to those expectations as outsiders and sinners.

Jubilees. We find the same tension observed in pseudo-Philo between promise and condition present in *Jubilees.* While some (e.g., E. P. Sanders[60]) have argued that *Jubilees* more or less sees election as unconditional, based especially on the first chapter of the work,[61] others emphasize the conditional nature of what the author develops in chapter one as being more consistent with the overall tone of the book apart from the statements of restoration found in *Jubilees* 1:15-18 and 1:22-29. Chris VanLandingham notes of this chapter, "God does forsake the people when they sin, but remembers them when they repent, even though they *had previously* sinned."[62] For VanLandingham, God's action depends on

---

[60]Sanders, *Paul and Palestinian Judaism*, p. 371.
[61]See previous discussions of *Jubilees* in chap. 2.
[62]VanLandingham, *Judgment and Justification*, p. 75 (emphasis original).

Israel's response. Elliott also sees a more negative,[63] even sectarian outlook in the book.[64] Though the first chapter includes two detailed references to the future restoration of Israel, the rest of the book calls this hope into question since the author makes clear that many Israelites were not faithful to the covenant.

Jubilees grounds a number of the Torah commands in the actions of the patriarchs, extending even back before Adam. In *Jubilees* 2:17-33 the author presents the Sabbath as a part of the created order, something observed by the angels in heaven as well as by those on earth. Before humanity's creation, Yhwh had purposed to set apart a people for himself to keep the Sabbath (*Jub.* 2:19).[65] Michael Segal suggests that the passage's significance lies in the way it expands on the biblical account:

> In the Torah, the election of Israel as a special nation is understood as recompense for their acceptance of God's commandments: "Now then, if you will obey me faithfully and keep my covenant, you shall be my treasured possession among all the peoples, for the earth is all mine. And you shall be to me a kingdom of priests and a holy nation . . ." (Exod 19:5-6). But in the view of *Jubilees*, Israel was already awarded this special status from the time of creation.[66]

For the recipients and readers of the book, this presents the Sabbath not only as an ordinance in the Mosaic law to which Israel is expected to adhere but also as a fundamental part of the created order and as a reflection of the order of heaven. Thus to transgress the Sabbath ordinance is not only to break the law and betray the covenant but also to fall out of step with the workings of the heavenly hosts themselves.

This notion of the pre-Mosaic nature of the Torah occurs throughout

---

[63]Elliott notes, "The constant and repeated reminder of Israel's sin in the passage, in other words, hardly adds up to a good case for Israel's forgiveness" (Elliott, *Survivors of Israel*, pp. 180-82). See also Jeffrey R. Wisdom, *Blessing for the Nations and the Curse of the Law: Paul's Citation of Genesis and Deuteronomy in Gal 3.8-10* (Tübingen: Mohr Siebeck, 2001), p. 98.

[64]Thus he notes, "It would appear that *the basic condition for the salvation of the nation is accepting the foundational beliefs of the righteous community*" (Elliott, *Survivors of Israel*, p. 537 [emphasis original]).

[65]Goering, *Wisdom's Root Revealed*, p. 242.

[66]Michael Segal, *The Book of Jubilees: Rewritten Bible, Redaction, Ideology, and Theology* (Leiden: Brill, 2007), p. 6.

the book. In 3:8-14, the author portrays Adam and Eve as observing the purity laws related to childbirth; in 4:31-32 the law of retaliation is invoked in connection with Cain's murder of Abel, Noah's sacrifice after the flood is described in keeping with the Mosaic ordinances (*Jub.* 6:1-3; cf. Gen 8:20; Exod 29:40; Lev 2:2-5; 18:26-28; Num 35:33-34) and the feast of Shebuot (weeks/firstfruits) was instituted after his sacrifice (*Jub.* 6:17-31), and the law of the tithe is delivered to Abram (13:26-27). Thus, as Elliott notes, "Moses' covenant is understood in *Jubilees* as little more than a *renewal* of the ancient laws and covenants (everywhere Mosaic legislation is introduced by reference to former patriarchs)."[67]

The Abraham narratives in *Jubilees* also contribute significantly to the book's purpose and theme. As the author introduces Abraham, he states that a young Abraham began to understand the evils of idolatry and separated himself from his father to avoid transgression. Thus Abraham "began to pray to the Creator of all so that he might save him from the straying of the sons of men, and so that his portion might not fall into straying after the pollution and scorn" (*Jub.* 12:17). The expansions in *Jubilees* clearly put the impetus of faithfulness on Abraham rather than YHWH, showing, even in his ignorance, that he faithfully sought after God. Abraham even goes so far as to burn the house of idols, an action that prompts Terah to take his family and head toward Canaan (see *Jub.* 12:1-15). Only after Abraham's prayer of commitment, in which he confesses his allegiance to the Most High God and prays for deliverance from evil spirits, does God call him and give him the promises of blessing (*Jub.* 12:19-31).

Jubilees also offers expanded details concerning the law of circumcision (15:25-34). Here the author affirms that anyone who is not circumcised on the eighth day "is not from the sons of the covenant which the LORD made for Abraham since (he is) from the children of destruction . . . (he is) destined to be destroyed and annihilated from the earth and to be

---

[67]Elliott, *Survivors of Israel*, p. 251. This was not, however, entirely imaginative on the part of the author. As Segal points out, mentioning specifically the giving of circumcision (Gen 17), prohibition of eating blood (Gen 9) and Noah's following proper sacrificial guidelines (Gen 7-8) were already present in the Pentateuch (Segal, *Book of Jubilees*, p. 276). *Jubilees* expands on the concept in order to reinforce the interests important to the author/redactor.

uprooted from the earth because he has broken the covenant" (*Jub.* 15:26). This absolute language concerning a prerequisite for covenant membership is apparently intended as a polemic against "Ishmael and his sons and his brothers and Esau" (*Jub.* 15:30), who likely stand for both the Gentiles and the compromising Jews.[68]

In *Jub.* 23:8-32 the author again emphasizes the coming failures of many of Jacob's descendants, which is likely a projection of what he sees as the unfaithfulness among the people of his own day.[69] After the death of Abraham, the author notes that all generations that follow Abraham will not have prolonged life (*Jub.* 23:8-13), and the "evil generation" to come will contaminate the land with their sins and forsake the covenant, leading to war and oppression (*Jub.* 23:14-21). This disobedience will lead to "judgment and to captivity and pillage and destruction" (*Jub.* 23:22). Furthermore, the people will find no reprieve from this oppression, for Israel will pray for salvation, "but there will be none who will be saved" (*Jub.* 23:24).[70] This state of affairs will continue until the people return to the ways of the covenant and righteously adhere to the law and commandments (*Jub.* 23:26),[71] ushering in an era of restoration, peace and blessing for Israel and judgment and annihilation for their enemies (*Jub.* 23:27-31).

A. Andrew Das suggests the books display that God "intended the law to be obeyed *without transgression*."[72] Echoing Sanders's view, Das further explains, "'All Israelites have a share in the world to come' (*m. Sanh.* 10:1). . . . According to *Jubilees* and the rabbis, only the most egregious sinners who had turned their backs on God's relationship with the people would be excluded."[73] This view, however, overlooks the overall

---

[68]See Elliott, *Survivors of Israel*, p. 93.

[69]Ibid., p. 89. See also Timothy Wardle, *The Jerusalem Temple and Early Christian Identity* (Tübingen: Mohr Siebeck, 2010), pp. 61-62.

[70]Sanders here simply notes, "Thus Israel when attacked by 'the sinners of the Gentiles' will pray to be saved from 'the sinners, the Gentiles' (23.23f.)" (Sanders, *Paul and Palestinian Judaism*, p. 374). Sanders does not appear to recognize, however, that this prayer is not answered until Israel repents and returns to the Torah. It is not simply an appeal to God's grace as his extension of mercy to Israel is conditioned on their return to covenant faithfulness.

[71]See VanLandingham, *Judgment and Justification*, pp. 79-80; Elliott, *Survivors of Israel*, p. 539.

[72]A. Andrew Das, *Paul, the Law, and the Covenant* (Peabody, MA: Hendrickson, 2001), pp. 14-17.

[73]Ibid., p. 95.

emphasis in the book that obedience correlates with election. To be in the elect, for *Jubilees*, is to be in right standing in the covenant. To be in the unelect is to transgress it, something that it appears the author believes many Israelites in his own generation have done. Sigurd Grindheim affirms this: "The logical causal relationship is from righteousness to election [which] is seen in the re-writing of the history of Abraham's departure from Ur of Chaldea. God is no longer the initiator; Abraham is."[74] We should thus recognize *Jubilees'* emphasis on the conditionality of the covenant and on the causal relationship between covenant obedience and election.[75]

The emphasis on covenant obedience in the book thus strongly favors a conditional understanding of election, which the author applies to a faithful group of Jews who, at his time, seems small in number though a revival of sorts is anticipated.[76] In addition, the requirement for the proper circumcision of males at birth and abstaining from certain sins, which were "unatonable," emphasize conditionality. We should not understand this as "good works" outweighing "bad works," or even as "perfect obedience," since some sins can be atoned for, but rather as faithfulness to the covenant obligations and *especially* to those obligations that the book describes as affecting the exclusion of the offender from the covenant community and blessings.

Testaments of the Twelve Patriarchs. We find a more explicit conditional view in the sin-exile-return (S-E-R) passages of the *Testaments*.[77] The sin and exile aspects of the pattern show up in nine of the

---

[74]Grindheim, *Crux of Election*, p. 45.

[75]Thus Elliott, who states, "Every indication is that restoration was *conditional* upon repentance. Israel will first conform to the righteousness demanded of God (i.e., demanded by the community) and *then* they will be restored" (Elliott, *Survivors of Israel*, p. 538); and, "There is little indication that the author thought the faithfulness of God would cover for the disobedient (*contra* Sanders)" (ibid., p. 125). See also VanLandingham, *Judgment and Justification*, p. 80.

[76]Enns supports this notion: "The point is that the author of *Jubilees*, from first to last, is concerned to emphasize God's promise never to forsake his *people*. *Israel as a people* will always remain because God is faithful. Transgression of eternal commands, however, will result in individual punishment and forfeiture of one's individual covenant status. The fact of Israel's election, however, remains sure" (Peter Enns, "Expansions of Scripture," in Carson, O'Brien and Seifrid, *Complexities of Second Temple Judaism*, p. 97).

[77]*T. Levi* 14:4–19:3; *T. Jud.* 23:1–26:4; *T. Iss.* 6:1-4; *T. Zeb.* 9:1–10:6; *T. Dan* 5:1–6:11; *T. Naph.* 4:1-5; *T. Gad* 8:1-3; *T. Ash.* 7:1-7; *T. Benj.* 9:1–11:5.

Testaments, while return occurs in eight. While all of the *Testaments* contain warnings against sin and disobedience, those that contain the S-E-R passages make specific predictions about the future (though likely present to the author's time)[78] apostasy of a given tribe. The author often generically describes the sins of Israel as wicked deeds or disobedience to the ordinances of God. The author also mentions specific sins, including sexual immorality and infidelity (*T. Levi* 14:6; *T. Jud.* 23:2; *T. Dan* 5:6-7; *T. Benj.* 8:1–9:1), intermarriage with Gentiles (*T. Levi* 14:7; *T. Dan* 5:5), profaning the temple (*T. Levi* 16:1), witchcraft and idolatry (*T. Jud.* 23:1) and rebellion against Levi and Judah (*T. Dan* 5:4; *T. Gad* 8:1-3).

In the S-E-R pattern, the author frequently mentions the restoration of the people. Here we should note that repentance is required for the people *before* God restores and/or blesses.[79] In the *Testament of Simeon* 6:1-7 the people must first divest themselves "of envy and every hardness of heart" before restoration comes. The *Testament of Judah* 23:5 attests that the people will be oppressed and in exile "until you return to the Lord in integrity of heart, penitent and living according to all the Lord's commands. Then the Lord will be concerned for you in mercy and will free you from captivity under your enemies." Likewise, the *Testament of Issachar* 6:3-4 states, "Tell these things to your children, therefore, so that even though they might sin, they may speedily return to the Lord, because he is merciful: He will set them free and take them back to their land." The *Testament of Zebulun* 9:7 declares, "You will remember the Lord and repent, and he will turn you around because he is merciful and compassionate." In all of these cases, repentance precedes restoration and blessing.

While scholars debate the origin and purpose of the work,[80] the Jewishness of the document persists in its attention to key figures in Israel's history, concern with keeping the Torah (though often generically de-

---

[78]See Elliott, *Survivors of Israel*, p. 389.

[79]*T. Sim.* 6:1-7; *T. Levi* 13:1-9; 14:4–19:3; *T. Jud.* 23:1–26:4; *T. Iss.* 6:1-4; *T. Zeb.* 9:1–10:6; *T. Dan* 5:1–6:11; *T. Naph.* 4:1-5; *T. Ash.* 7:1-7; *T. Benj.* 9:1–11:5.

[80]See Robert A. Kugler, "Testaments," in Collins and Harlow, *Eerdmans Dictionary of Early Judaism*, p. 1297.

scribed) and the future of Israel, which is at times intermingled with that of the Gentiles.[81] In light of this, Elliott has commented,

> It is accordingly not difficult to discern the function of the testamentary form in these passages in condemning present-day Israel by means of the *combination of ethical and future material*. But this combination also offers the opportunity for the author to *define who he does think belongs to the righteous community*. . . . One can discern a double function for the testament form in the *Testaments of the Twelve Patriarchs*: to warn Israel regarding their apostasy, on the one hand, and to establish a standard of righteous behavior, on the other.[82]

The *Testaments*, when read by their authoring community or by Jews in general during the period, accomplished both an ethical and a theological purpose. We again find "election" depicted in the *Testaments* as being contingent either on faithfulness or repentance.[83] The identity stands available to the whole of Israel, though it applies only to the obedient who may be represented by the Levi-Judah motif.[84] The S-E-R texts best evidence the presence of the theme of election in the work. While the *Testaments* lack explicit language concerning the ultimate exclusion of unfaithful Jews, they uphold the rather consistent message that the faithful and penitent alone belong to the people of God. They condemn "present" Israel for its apostasy and demonstrate that the

---

[81]Here de Jonge has aptly pointed out that in some cases only the future of Israel is mentioned (*T. Levi* 16:5; *T. Iss.* 6:4; *T. Ash.* 7:7; cf. *T. Zeb.* 10:2 after 9:9), in other places the Gentiles are mentioned alongside Israel as their enemies and oppressors (*T. Lev.* 10:4; 15:1-3; 16:5; *T. Jud.* 23:3; *T. Iss.* 6:2; *T. Zeb.* 9:6; *T. Dan* 5:8; *T. Naph.* 4:2; *T. Ash.* 7:2), and in other places the Gentiles are mentioned as recipients of salvation alongside Israel or as humanity in general (*T. Reu.* 6:11; *T. Sim.* 6:5-7; 7:2; *T. Lev.* 2:11; 4:4; 5:7; 10:2; 14:2; 17:2; *T. Jud.* 22:2; 24:6; 25:5; *T. Zeb.* 9:8; *T. Dan* 5:11; 6:7; *T. Naph.* 4:5; 8:3; *T. Ash.* 7:3; *T. Jos.* 19:4-6; *T. Benj.* 3:8; 9:2; 10:5) (Marinus de Jonge, "The Future of Israel in the Testaments of the Twelve Patriarchs," *JSJ* 17, no. 2 [1986]: 196-97).

[82]Elliott, *Survivors of Israel*, p. 391 (emphasis original).

[83]Thus Grindheim states, "The continued elect status of the people is thus understood as contingent upon their righteousness" (Grindheim, *Crux of Election*, p. 54). Elliott likewise, commenting on *T. Ash.* 1, states, "The idea of 'pairs' seems to perpetuate the notion, inherent in the 'two ways' as well, that there is choice or decision involved in everything, especially the covenant" (Elliott, *Survivors of Israel*, p. 281).

[84]Thus contra Hollander and de Jonge, who seem to suggest that all of Israel, regardless of their response, will receive compassion because of their ethnic standing (Harm W. Hollander and Marinus de Jonge, *The Testaments of the Twelve Patriarchs: A Commentary* [Leiden: Brill, 1985], pp. 51-52, 55).

means by which God will accept individual Jews (in the view of the author/defining community) comes through repentance and obedience to the Torah and the leadership of Levi/Judah.

1 Maccabees. Much of 1 Maccabees serves as a polemic (as well as an apologetic for the Hasmonean rulers) against both the regime of Antiochus and the Hellenized Jews who, at least in the view of the Maccabees and their sympathizers, refused to stand against pressure posed by outsiders. This is first seen in 1 Maccabees 1:11-15, when "certain renegades" came and deceived Israel into making a covenant with the Gentiles, resulting in their removing the marks of circumcision and forsaking their covenant with YHWH.[85] Shortly after, Antiochus raided the city, overtook it by force and then demanded that all of the conquered peoples give up their customs to be united (1 Macc 1:20-41). The author notes that "many even from Israel gladly adopted his [Antiochus's] religion; they sacrificed to idols and profaned the sabbath" (1 Macc 1:43 NRSV). Antiochus also forbade the Jews from offering sacrifices, observing festivals and practicing circumcision (1 Macc 1:45-48). Those Jews who forsook the law even went so far as to betray their Torah-abiding kinsmen, forcing them into hiding (1 Macc 1:51-53). The temple was desecrated, the books of the law burned and those faithful to the law condemned to death (1 Macc 1:54-61). In spite of this intense oppression, many in Israel remained faithful (1 Macc 1:62-64).

When Mattathias, a descendent of the priestly line of Yehoyarib/Joarib (see 1 Macc 2:1),[86] and his sons were rounded up with the rest of the Jews and asked to sacrifice to the king, Mattathias killed a Jew who stepped forward to sacrifice and killed the king's soldiers along with him, an act compared to the righteous anger of Phinehas (1 Macc 2:15-26; cf. Num. 25:6-15).[87] Mattathias and his followers agreed to fight against the Gen-

---

[85]Goldstein notes, "The language of vs. 11 is a deliberate imitation of Deut 13:7-8 and 31:17; the author intends to show how close those who propose violation of the separation required by Deut 7:2 are to those who propose idol worship" (Jonathan A. Goldstein, *I Maccabees: A New Translation with Introduction and Commentary*, AB [New York: Doubleday, 1976], p. 200).

[86]See ibid., p. 8.

[87]It was not simply the Gentiles but also the Hellenistic Jews whom the Maccabees opposed. See Elliott, *Survivors of Israel*, p. 221; Uriel Rappaport, "Maccabees, First Book of," in Collins and Harlow, *Eerdmans Dictionary of Early Judaism*, p. 904.

tiles, even on the Sabbath, in order to stand against the enemies of God and the apostates in Israel (1 Macc 2:39-48).[88]

On Mattathias's deathbed, he admonished his sons to be faithful to and zealous for the covenant and to remember the great ancestors of Israel. Here Abraham, Joseph, Phinehas, Joshua, Caleb, David, Elijah, Hananiah, Azariah, Mishael and Daniel are pointed out as examples of those who were faithful in times of testing and were rewarded as a result of their faithfulness.[89] Of particular significance is the nature of the examples selected by the author. Abraham is venerated throughout Second Temple literature as a model of faithfulness to the Torah. Joseph, Joshua, Caleb, Hananiah, Azariah, Mishael and Daniel are all variously oppressed by foreigners. Phinehas and Elijah both encountered opposition in the form of apostasy within Israel. David faced pressures from within and outside of Israel and is praised by the author for his "mercy." While some of these men of Israel's history dealt with their trials through nonviolent obedience or protest (Abraham, Joseph, Elijah, Hananiah, Azariah, Mishael and Daniel), others required retaliation to protect the interests of God's people (Phinehas, Joshua, Caleb and David). In selecting these examples, the author has not ostracized the passive dissenters in Israel (i.e., the faithful who have not responded with physical violence but do not oppose the Maccabees), though clearly his favor lies with the military offensives launched by the Maccabees.

Recalling the deeds of the ancestors of Israel inspires the Maccabees (and the reader) with zeal for the law and unwavering faithfulness to God. The result will be the receipt of "great honor and an everlasting name" (1 Macc 2:51, 64 NRSV), not an eternal existence, but an eternal influence on future generations. The final admonition of Mattathias is

---

[88] As Goldstein notes, "The Hasmonaean position allowing defensive warfare on the Sabbath was inacceptable to many Pietists" (Goldstein, *I Maccabees*, p. 237).

[89] Abraham is faithful in testing and it is reckoned unto him as righteousness (ἐλογίσθη αὐτῷ εἰς δικαιοσύνην), Joseph is faithful and becomes a ruler in Egypt, Phineas's zeal is rewarded with the covenant of everlasting priesthood (ἔλαβεν διαθήκην ἱερωσύνης αἰωνίας), Joshua was obedient and became a judge over Israel, Caleb testified in the assembly and received an inheritance in the Promised Land, David's mercy is rewarded with an everlasting kingdom, Elijah's zeal is rewarded with being taken up to heaven, the three faithful Jews are saved from fire, and Daniel's innocence is rewarded with deliverance from the lions.

for his sons to heed the counsel and leadership of Simeon and Judas, that they might "rally around you all who observe the law, and avenge the wrong done to your people" (1 Macc 2:67 NRSV).

Throughout the book, there are numerous examples illustrating the author's belief that the faithful are those who (1) keep the law and (2) support the Maccabean revolt.[90] Those who fail to meet these "requirements" are outside of the people of God and opposed to God's purposes. In the encounter with Apollonius, it is the "lawless" and "godless" Gentiles who oppose the Maccabees and thus incur the wrath of God (1 Macc 3:10-22). Judas's army, however, shows their piety through fasting, mourning, prayer and reading the Book of the Law (1 Macc 3:46-57).[91] In addition, those who were occupied with other affairs were allowed to go home, all done in accordance with the law (1 Macc 3:54-60; cf. Deut 20:5-9). Furthermore, after the temple sanctuary was reclaimed, Judas made sure to select "devoted" priests to cleanse it, and directed the building of a new altar and restoration of the temple vessels according to the specifications of the law (1 Macc 4:41-51; cf. Exod 20:25; 25:27; 30:7-8; Deut 27:5-6). The Hasmoneans, for the author, clearly have the favor of God as his chosen instrument of deliverance for the Jews.

The depiction, then, of the "elect" in 1 Maccabees is limited to the family of the Maccabees (and the subsequent Hasmonean rulers) and those who follow the Torah and the leadership of these chosen rulers. The author identifies only a subset of the Jews, socially and religiously defined rather than ethnically so, as the true chosen Israel of God.[92]

---

[90]See ibid., p. 12.

[91]To further illustrate that God had anointed the Maccabees as Israel's deliverers, when a group of Jews, inspired by the deeds of the Maccabees, goes to battle with the Gentile forces in Jamnia, Gorgias and his army kill two thousand of the Jewish army because "they did not listen to Judas and his brothers" and "did not belong to the family of those men through whom deliverance was given to Israel" (1 Macc 5:55-62). Goldstein notes, "Just as the author of the book of Samuel proved that God had chosen David and his dynasty to rule by exhibiting the failure of the house of Saul and the superiority of the house of David over all competitors, so our author proves the divine election of the Hasmonaean dynasty" (ibid., p. 304). See also Harrington, *Invitation to the Apocrypha*, p. 122.

[92]See Elliott, *Survivors of Israel*, p. 223. Hellerman has noted the similarities between 1 and 2 Maccabees and *Jubilees* in that these books "draw implicit and explicit connections between Jewish purity practices, on the one hand, and the election and preservation of national Israel as the people of Yahweh, on the other" (Joseph Hellerman, "Purity and Nationalism in Second

While the whole Torah is assumed as binding by the author, circumcision, Sabbath, dietary regulations and the purity of the temple and priests are elevated by the author.[93] This is not to the exclusion of the other commands, but the emphasis intends to demarcate the "outsiders" and lift up the Maccabees as the leaders of the faithful Jews, the "true Israel."[94] Those Jews who are marked as outsiders have forsaken the covenant of God through their disobedience and/or their rejection of God's appointed rulers.

2 Maccabees. The book of 2 Maccabees, like its counterpart discussed above, addresses the events surrounding the Maccabean revolt. Unlike 1 Maccabees, however, the book focuses primarily on Judas Maccabeus, and the restoration of the temple provides the end of the story. The author, more so than that of 1 Maccabees, emphasizes the Deuteronomic view of retribution, wherein the judgment of the Jews is a result of their disobeying and their blessing a result of their following God, much like the sin-exile-return (S-E-R) cycles found in the Old Testament and in many postbiblical works.

In the past, scholars derided the work as rather unhistorical in comparison to 1 Maccabees, but this opinion has changed more recently. Though 2 Maccabees utilizes more obvious theological interpretations of events and contains historical inaccuracies (such as the attempted conversion of Antiochus IV to Judaism), the book in places offers a more accurate account than its Judean counterpart.[95] The book has a complex compositional history since it incorporates two letters and is an abridgement, with theological reflections, of the work of Jason. The work

---

Temple Literature: 1–2 Maccabees and *Jubilees*," *JETS* 46, no. 3 [2003]: 421). Here again "national" Israel, however, must be defined as those who adhere to the standards of inclusion expressed by the various authors represented.

[93]See Rappaport, "Maccabees, First Book of," p. 904.

[94]This is, again, as Hellerman notes, to identify "Israel's 'otherness,' vis-à-vis the Gentiles, as the chosen people of God" (Hellerman, "Purity and Nationalism," p. 402) as well as to identify those Jews who truly belong to God's people versus those who do not.

[95]See David S. Williams, "Recent Research in 2 Maccabees," *Currents in Biblical Research* 2, no. 1 (2003): 69-83. Schwartz argues, "If we avoid the psychological fallacy, revise the chronology, and bear in mind that even a religious author may tell the historical truth, even if he or she packages it in religious interpretation and decorates it with religious motifs, there is room to reopen the discussion of our book's historical worth" (Daniel R. Schwartz, *2 Maccabees* [New York: de Gruyter, 2008], p. 39).

also has a thoroughly Hellenistic style and vocabulary,[96] which presents a bit of an irony considering its message of the danger Hellenism poses to the Jewish people.[97] The book emphasizes God's role in delivering Israel from their oppressors.[98] The compiler forms this emphasis through the lens of Deuteronomy 32, paying close attention to the role of foreigners in the punishment of Israel for their sin and their deliverance arising only after God has meted out their punishment.[99]

The purpose of the book was, in part, to justify and encourage the participation of Egyptian Jews in the observance of Hanukkah.[100] Following the introductory letters, the book begins with an idyllic description of the state of Jerusalem. The city was "in unbroken peace and the laws were strictly observed" (2 Macc 3:1 NRSV). Trouble arises throughout the book, however, because of certain instigators who bring turmoil upon the city and its inhabitants. The trouble begins with a certain Simon,[101] who, in opposition to the pious Onias, reports to the governor of the region that the temple held a great treasury that could come under the king's possession (2 Macc 3:2-6). When a certain Heliodorus is sent by the governor, Apollonius, to inspect the temple (2 Macc 3:7-14), a heavenly manifestation appears, which strikes Heliodorus

---

[96]See Daniel R. Schwartz, "Maccabees, Second Book of," in Collins and Harlow, *Eerdmans Dictionary of Early Judaism*, p. 905.

[97]See Martha Himmelfarb, "Judaism and Hellenism in 2 Maccabees," *Poetics Today* 19, no. 1 (1998): 19-40. Schwartz, however, has also noted that though 1 Maccabees is stylistically more similar to Jewish canonical works and 2 Maccabees to Greek works, the core of 2 Maccabees "is informed by a central biblical chapter, Deut. 32. Add to this the oft-noted fact that God, as in biblical historiography, is very obviously and even sensationally involved in the story of 2 Maccabees, in contrast to that of 1 Maccabees" (Daniel R. Schwartz, "On Something Biblical about 2 Maccabees," in *Biblical Perspectives: Early Use and Interpretation of the Bible in Light of the Dead Sea Scrolls*, ed. Michael E. Stone and Esther G. Chazon [Leiden: Brill, 1998], p. 232).

[98]See Schwartz, "Maccabees, Second Book of," p. 906.

[99]See George W. E. Nickelsburg, "1 and 2 Maccabees—Same Story, Different Meaning," *CTM* 42 (1971): 52.

[100]See Schwartz, "Maccabees, Second Book of," pp. 906-7. Schwartz argues that it may also have encouraged the observance of "Nicanor's Day," which is mentioned more often in the narrative of the book than Hanukkah (Schwartz, *2 Maccabees*, pp. 8, 168). Other purposes, such as "temple propaganda" (Robert Doran, *Temple Propaganda: The Purpose and Character of 2 Maccabees* [Washington, DC: Catholic Biblical Association of America, 1981]) and anti-Hasmonean response to 1 Maccabees (Jonathan A. Goldstein, *II Maccabees*, AB [New York: Doubleday, 1983]) have also been suggested. See also Nickelsburg, *Jewish Literature*, p. 108.

[101]Or, as Schwartz states, "Our problems began because some nincompoop started a feud with such a wonderful high priest" (Schwartz, *2 Maccabees*, p. 189).

down on the ground (2 Macc 3:15-28). Heliodorus is spared through the intercession of Onias, and he recognizes and declares that the power of God is the protector of the city (2 Macc 3:29-40).

The narrative changes, however, in 2 Maccabees 4. While the sovereign God previously came to the aid of the temple, the troubles of 2 Maccabees 4 bring God's judgment on Jerusalem. Since his first scheme fails, Simon turns to slandering Onias and accuses him of treason (2 Macc 4:1-6). After Onias gets ousted from the priesthood by Jason, who had bought it with a significant sum, Jason begins to shift "his compatriots over to the Greek way of life" (2 Macc 4:11). Though the author does not specify how,[102] he comments that Jason established customs contrary to the laws of Jerusalem.[103] The extreme Hellenism led even to the priests being "no longer intent upon their service at the altar" (2 Macc 4:14). The trouble coming on Jerusalem was justified in the author's mind because of their wickedness and irreverence for the divine laws (2 Macc 4:18-20). The treachery continues as the priesthood changes hands from one unqualified bidder to another (2 Macc 4:25).[104] The continued turmoil surrounding the priesthood reaches Antiochus, who believed the region is in revolt, prompting a massacre of the people and the profaning of the temple (2 Macc 5:11-15). The author here reveals that God allowed this punishment to come upon the people because of their many sins (2 Macc 5:17-18). Since God had chosen the temple for the sake of the people, it shared in their judgment.[105]

---

[102]Schwartz states, "The issue was a more general one of introducing 'Greek style' (v. 10), which competed with an marginalized Jewish practices" (Schwartz, *2 Maccabees*, p. 222). DeSilva agrees that this was likely either outright apostasy or dangerous syncretism (deSilva, *Introducing the Apocrypha*, p. 275).

[103]Though Jason held the office of priest, he was, as Elliott observes, "backed by a group of Hellenists (1 Macc 4:14; cf. 1:11). Cf. also 2 Macc 4:9, where these are given the name 'Antiochenes'" (Elliott, *Survivors of Israel*, p. 215 n. 96).

[104]As Himmelfarb, however, explains, "For 2 Maccabees, gentiles are not the enemy. It assumes, for example, that most gentiles were horrified by the murder of Onias III (4:35). Rather, the Greek way of life is the enemy because it is the agent of a dangerous transformation of values that can occur without actual idolatry, as the description of the priests who prefer exercise to sacrifice recognizes" (Himmelfarb, "Judaism and Hellenism," p. 29). See also Schwartz, "Maccabees, Second Book of," p. 905.

[105]And so Schwartz states, "Our book clearly views the Temple as of only secondary importance. This is explicit at 5:19, where the author pedantically explains that God's choice of the Temple is secondary to his choice of the people" (Schwartz, "Maccabees, Second Book of," p. 906).

The complete "Hellenization" of the Jews was attempted shortly after these events, and the Jews were told to abandon "their ancestors and no longer to live by the laws of God; also to pollute the temple in Jerusalem and to call it the temple of Olympian Zeus" (2 Macc 6:1-2 NRSV). Cultic prostitution infiltrated the temple, the altar was defiled and the people were unable to observe the Sabbath and festivals (2 Macc 6:3-6). The author illustrates the dire nature of the situation with several stories of martyrdom:[106] the two mothers and their circumcised babies (2 Macc 6:10), those who left the city to observe the Sabbath (2 Macc 6:11), righteous Eleazar (2 Macc 6:18-31), and the seven brothers and their mother (2 Macc 7:1-42). The author prefaces the most intense of the stories with the disclaimer that these acts of judgment were deserved and show God's mercy toward Israel since he does not allow their sins to reach full measure as he does with the nations (2 Macc 6:12-17).[107]

Several important issues surface in the martyrdom tales. First, as noted by Jonathan Goldstein, the martyrs "are classified according to the principles for which they give up their lives: circumcision (vs. 10 and I 1:60-61), the Sabbath (vs. 11 and I 2:29-38), and the dietary laws, including the prohibition on eating the meat of a pagan sacrifice (vss. 18-31 and 7:1-41; I 1:62-63)."[108] It is specifically because of their faithfulness to these laws (all of which would have resonated strongly with Diaspora Jews) that these martyrs die. The martyrs will be rewarded for their faithfulness (see 2 Macc 7:9, 11, 14, 23, 29) and their deaths bring about Israel's restoration to God and his judgment on Antiochus (see 2 Macc 7:14, 17-19, 31-38).

For the author, Israel as a nation deserved its punishment, and in spite of their faithfulness, the pious were not exempt from suffering. As Daniel Harrington observes, the author "interprets their martyrdoms as atoning

---

[106]Goldstein notes here that anti-Hasmonean sentiments may have been responsible for the composition or inclusion of the story of the seven sons and mother who were martyred (Goldstein, *II Maccabees*, pp. 299-303). Unlike in 1 Maccabees, however, here those who do not fight against the Seleucids are not disparaged because of it.

[107]Harrington, *Invitation to the Apocrypha*, p. 149; VanLandingham, *Judgment and Justification*, p. 137.

[108]Goldstein, *II Maccabees*, p. 278.

for the people's sin and so making it possible for Judas to reclaim the temple and restore it to its rightful place in Israel."[109] The author sees the death of the martyrs as bringing to an end God's judgment on Israel, and in 2 Maccabees 8, the restoration of Israel begins through the efforts of Judas and his men.[110] Second Maccabees sees obedience to the law, and specifically to certain key commands like circumcision and the Sabbath, which set Israel apart from the Gentiles, as the definitive marker of God's people.[111] Those who keep the law as envisioned in the book, and especially in spite of persecution, are the true people of God, while those who reject it or are ashamed of it will not share in the glory of the resurrection the pious anticipate.

Psalms of Solomon. I will say more about the *Psalms of Solomon* in the next chapter, but here a representative view of its depiction of the conditionality of the covenant will suffice. In *Psalms of Solomon* 3:3, the righteous acknowledge the judgments of God as being "just" and accept discipline from him for their own sins. Unlike the sinners, the righteous constantly search out their sins and atone for them through fasting and

---

[109]Harrington, *Invitation to the Apocrypha*, p. 138. See also Mary Chilton Callaway, "Introduction to 2 Maccabees," in *The New Oxford Annotated Apocrypha*, ed. Michael D. Coogan (Oxford: Oxford University Press, 2001), p. 246; Lester L. Grabbe, "1 and 2 Maccabees," in Evans and Porter, *Dictionary of New Testament Background*, p. 669; Nickelsburg, "1 and 2 Maccabees," p. 525; Nickelsburg, *Jewish Literature*, p. 108; Schwartz, *2 Maccabees*, pp. 299, 323; VanLandingham, *Judgment and Justification*, p. 136. See also John R. Bartlett, *The First and Second Books of the Maccabees* (Cambridge: Cambridge University Press, 1973), p. 276. Contrary to the depiction in 1 Maccabees, van Henten affirms, "The depiction of the Maccabean martyrs does not at all result in an image of wallowing in passivity, resignation or even acceptance of oppression and discrimination. On the contrary. The Maccabean martyrs are presented as heroes whose behavior has led, directly or indirectly, to the defeat of the Seleucid enemy" (Jan Willem van Henten, *The Maccabean Martyrs as Saviours of the Jewish People: A Study of 2 and 4 Maccabees* [Leiden: Brill, 1997], p. 303).

[110]So deSilva notes, "Just as the sin of individuals brought collective punishment, so the covenant loyalty of individuals can effect reversal. . . . The martyrs take their place alongside Judas and his warriors as heroes of the Jewish people, whose courage and dedication contributed something essential to the reestablishment of religious and political independence" (deSilva, *Introducing the Apocrypha*, p. 275).

[111]See Schwartz, "Maccabees, Second Book of," p. 906; Schwartz, *2 Maccabees*, p. 282. Faithfulness to the Sabbath, for example, is emphasized over and above its function in 1 Maccabees, where those who fight see no option but to fight on the Sabbath. DeSilva writes, "The epitomator has preserved those portions of the history that elevate Sabbath observance, circumcision, dietary regulations, and the like as inviolable tenets of the covenant, to be kept even under pain of death rather than violated" (deSilva, *Introducing the Apocrypha*, p. 271).

humility (*Pss. Sol.* 3:5-8), and thus "the Lord will cleanse every devout person and his house" (*Pss. Sol.* 3:8).[112] Instead of accepting discipline and atoning for their sins, the sinners, by contrast, curse their life, multiply their sins and are destroyed forever. The devout, however, will "rise up to eternal life" (*Pss. Sol.* 3:12).[113] Again, what separates God's people from those who will receive judgment is their inner disposition *and* outward behavior.

Likewise, *Psalms of Solomon* 9 affirms God's rightness in judging Israel, here with the exile, which was brought on them because of their "lawless actions" (*Pss. Sol.* 9:2). In Deuteronomic language reminiscent of Deuteronomy 28, the psalmist declares that the choice of right/ blessing/life and wrong/curse/death is within the "power of our souls" (*Pss. Sol.* 9:4-5). Those who "call upon the Lord" are cleansed from their sins and blessed when they repent (*Pss. Sol.* 9:6-7). Such mercy is not extended to sinners. As the psalmist concludes, he affirms:

> We [the devout] are the people whom you have loved; look and be compassionate, O God of Israel . . . for you chose the descendants of Abraham above all the nations, and you put your name upon us, Lord, and it will not cease forever. You made a covenant with our ancestors concerning us, and we hope in you when we turn our souls toward you. May the mercy of the Lord be upon the house of Israel forevermore. (*Pss. Sol.* 9:9-11)

Here again, though "Israel" is affirmed as God's people, the author clearly has in mind the devout alone, since only they are forgiven of their sins when they repent (*Pss. Sol.* 9:7), and only they have hope because their souls are turned to God (9:10). Much disagreement has occurred over how to understand this part of the collection. Grindheim, along the lines of Sanders's covenant nomism, sees all Israel as elect, but the unrighteous

---

[112]So Atkinson writes, "The psalmist recognizes that the righteous, including his own community, is not perfect. The devout, as the author of *Psalm of Solomon* 3 makes clear, are not those who are free from sin, but those who confess their transgressions and justify God (*Pss. Sol.* 3.3)" (Kenneth Atkinson, "Enduring the Lord's Discipline: Soteriology in the *Psalms of Solomon*," in Gurtner, *This World and the World to Come*, p. 152).

[113]Winninge sees in the *Pss. Sol.* the resurrection of the body, stating, "Thus the ultimate perspective is eschatological, and the belief in the resurrection of the dead is at hand" (Mikael Winninge, *Sinners and the Righteous: A Comparative Study of the Psalms of Solomon and Paul's Letters* [Stockholm: Almqvist & Wiksell International, 1995], p. 41).

as forfeiting the covenant benefits.[114] Grindheim recognizes, however, that it is the free choice of the individual as to whether they are obedient, and thus righteous according to the covenant/Torah.[115] Mikael Winninge sees here a broader affirmation of the election of Israel, noting that the designations in *Psalms of Solomon* 9:9 and 11 indicate that the psalmist sees that "Israel as a whole is involved."[116]

The psalmist has couched this section, however, by noting that it is those who repent, not Israel as a whole, who are forgiven and blessed (*Pss. Sol.* 9:7), and that only those who turn to God who have hope (*Pss. Sol.* 9:10). While the psalmist may hope for a full national restoration, clearly here the devout are those who are enjoying the blessings of the covenant. Kenneth Atkinson has recognized the tension here in noting that the author believes God is obligated to protect Israel,[117] though only the pious will enjoy the covenant blessings,[118] and thus, "the community of the *Psalms of Solomon* believes that it constitutes the true Israel because its members live in accordance with the covenant, and are therefore assured salvation."[119] So while the author uses terms that appear to refer to all of Israel, clearly the intent is to equate Israel with the righteous Jews who faithfully observe the Torah and repent when they violate it, and not with all Jews from an ethnic/national perspective.[120]

Dead Sea Scrolls. The *Damascus Document* (hereafter CD) dates to the first century B.C.E., and contains a more complex compositional

---

[114]Grindheim, *Crux of Election*, p. 49.

[115]Ibid., p. 52. See also Robert B. Wright, "Psalms of Solomon," in *The Old Testament Pseudepigrapha*, vol. 2, *Expansions of the "Old Testament" and Legends, Wisdom and Philosophical Literature, Prayers, Psalms, and Odes, Fragments of Lost Judeo-Hellenistic Works*, ed. James H. Charlesworth (1985; repr., Peabody, MA: Hendrickson, 2011), p. 645.

[116]Winninge, *Sinners and the Righteous*, p. 72.

[117]Atkinson, "Enduring the Lord's Discipline," pp. 151, 155.

[118]Ibid., pp. 151, 155, 158.

[119]Ibid., p. 159.

[120]This limited perspective on the "true Israel" appears to be repeated in *Pss. Sol.* 10, where again it is the devout who love God and whom God cleanses from sin (*Pss. Sol.* 10:1-3). While "Israel shall praise the Lord's name in joy," it is the devout who give thanks, the poor who receive mercy and the synagogues of Israel (not the temple or Jerusalem) who glorify God's name (*Pss. Sol.* 10:5-8). *Pss. Sol.* 11, perhaps more than any other psalm in the book, echoes a nationalistic hope, though as VanLandingham has noted, the national imagery here need not obscure the clear and numerous references to the separation between the devout and the sinners that occurs throughout the book (VanLandingham, *Judgment and Justification*, p. 145).

history than many of the other scrolls.[121] Much of the debate over the contents of the document has centered on the origins of the community, which CD alludes to within its contents.[122] The document contains theological material intermingled with detailed precepts for the community and moral exhortations.[123]

In the opening chapters, CD recounts the rebellion of the Watchers and the subsequent corruption of humanity (CD 2.17–3.1). During this ordeal, Abraham "was counted as a friend for keeping God's precepts and not following the desire of his spirit" (CD 3.2). Isaac and Jacob followed Abraham's example, but "Jacob's sons strayed because of them and were punished in accordance with their mistakes" (CD 3.3-5). Their punishment here results from their disobedience to the commandments. The author acknowledges the disobedience of Israel (which the sons of Jacob are likely intended to have foreshadowed), which caused many to be forsaken from the covenant, while those "who remained steadfast" received the covenant (CD 3.5-17). These too, however, sinned, and God graciously pardoned them and built them a safe city (CD 3.17-20).[124]

The author defines the "sons of Zadok" as "the chosen of Israel, the men of renown, who stand (to serve) at the end of days" (CD 4.3).[125] Belial encroaches on the rest of Israel, who stand outside of the covenant, and whom Belial has caught in his "three nets": fornication, wealth and defilement of the temple (CD 4.13-21).[126] In CD 5.1-21 the author

---

[121]For a brief summary, see Charlotte Hempel, "Damascus Document," in Collins and Harlow, *Eerdmans Dictionary of Early Judaism*, p. 511.

[122]Ibid., p. 511.

[123]The document shares a number of similarities, though differences are also present, with 1QS. See Preben Wernberg-Møller, *The Manual of Discipline: Translated and Annotated with an Introduction* (Grand Rapids: Eerdmans, 1957), p. 15. For a comparison and discussion, see Hilary Evans Kapfer, "The Relationship Between the Damascus Document and the Community Rule: Attitudes Toward the Temple as a Test Case," *DSD* 14, no. 2 (2007): 152-77.

[124]Nickelsburg writes, "This remnant has been built as 'a sure house in Israel' (cf. 1 Sam 2:35). Others may still join them, but the end of the age is near, and soon the wall of that house will be complete and outsiders will be excluded" (Nickelsburg, *Jewish Literature*, p. 124). See also Michael A. Knibb, *The Qumran Community* (Cambridge: Cambridge University Press, 1987), pp. 35-38.

[125]So Vermes states, "The Essenes not only considered themselves to be the 'remnant' of their time, but the 'remnant' of all time, the final 'remnant'" (Geza Vermes, *The Dead Sea Scrolls: Qumran in Perspective* [Cleveland: William Collins & World, 1978], p. 165).

[126]Stokes rightly notes, "The *Damascus Document*'s teaching deals with the sins of Jews outside

condemns the Jerusalem priests for committing sins of a sexual nature. In spite of these abominations, God remembered the covenant and "raised from Aaron men of knowledge and from Israel wise men" (CD 6.2-3) who established the law in Damascus to guide the faithful through the present age of wickedness (CD 6.3-11). The author forbids those who stand within God's covenant (i.e., the Qumran sectarians) from entering the temple, which he views as corrupt. They, instead, must keep separate from the wicked and wealthy, and must observe the law exactly, including keeping the feasts, loving one another, helping the poor and deprived, refraining from fornication and avoiding defilement (CD 6.12–7.4).[127] The covenant provides "a guarantee for them that they shall live a thousand generations" (CD 7.5-6).

All members must strive to follow the precepts of the law perfectly, with specific instructions being provided as relating to public sins, oaths, purity issues and the Sabbath (CD 8.21–13.23).[128] There exists the possibility for banishment from the community if disobedience occurs, though they resolve most offenses through a period of temporary punishment.[129] The author then declares, "(to) all those who walk in them, the covenant of God is faithful to save them from all the nets of the pit, but 'the ignorant walk on' (Prov 27:12) and are punished" (CD 14.1-2). CD thus contains a very limited view of who is in God's covenant, though not too far removed from other texts I have already surveyed.

---

the sect, those who do not interpret the law according to sectarian standards" (Ryan E. Stokes, "The Origin of Sin in the Dead Sea Scrolls," *SwJT* 53, no. 1 [Fall 2010]: 63).

[127]On the community's separation from the temple cult, see Ben Zion Wacholder, *The New Damascus Document: The Midrash on the Eschatological Torah of the Dead Sea Scrolls (Reconstruction, Translation and Commentary)* (Leiden: Brill, 2007), p. 224.

[128]The instructions are given "to keep the unclean apart from the clean, and distinguish between holy and profane. And these are the ordinance for the Instructor, so that he walks in them with every living thing, according to the regulation for every time. And in accordance with this regulation shall the seed of Israel walk and it will not be cursed" (CD 12.19-22).

[129]Shemesh has linked this practice to the community's identification with the exile. "Exclusion, like exile, was temporary removal; after a process of repentance, the offender was allowed to return to his original status" (Aharaon Shemesh, "Expulsion and Exclusion in the Community Rule and the Damascus Document," *DSD* 9, no. 1 [2002]: 58). Furthermore, the "idea that the temporary exclusion of an unfitting offender from the Community is a substitute for ritual expiation through sacrifice is based on the paradigm of Israel's exile; and according to the sectarian conception of history that was the punishment for unintentional offenses" (ibid., p. 62).

1 Enoch. In the Book of Luminaries (*1 En.* 72-82), Enoch is instructed
to share all of his knowledge with his son Methuselah, and is consoled
with the fact that "the sinners shall die together with the sinners; and the
apostate shall sink together with the apostate. But those who do right shall
not die on account of the (evil) deeds of the people" (*1 En.* 81:7-9). Enoch
follows the orders given to him and again affirms to his son, "Blessed are
all the righteous ones; blessed are those who walk in the street of righteousness and have no sin like the sinners in the computation of the days
in which the sun goes its course in the sky" (*1 En.* 82:4). In part, at least,
the guilt of the sinners in the Book of Luminaries stems from their failing
to observe the proper calendrical cycles. As Elliott asserts, the gravity of
this sin lies in the connection between the calendar and the covenant, and
those who fail to observe the correct calendar fall out of synch with creation and into disobedience of the cycles established by God himself.[130] As
Elliott notes, this is a distinctly *Jewish* issue,[131] and thus those sinners tar-
geted for their "computation of days" by the sun are Jews. Though we do
not find the explicit language of a "true Israel" present, the author makes
such an identification by assuring the righteous that their rewards will
await them, and warning the sinners, primarily Jewish sinners, they will
face God's judgment if they do not change their ways. The Book of Luminaries thus evidences an emphasis on the importance of righteous behavior in faithfulness to the covenant with the King of Glory.

The Epistle of Enoch (*1 En.* 91–108) begins with Enoch dispensing
advice to his children, admonishing them to love righteousness and
resist wickedness, for the judgment of the wicked will soon commence
(*1 En.* 94:1-3). They must, instead, "choose righteousness and the elect
life!" (*1 En.* 94:4). Clearly the author of the Epistle views election here as
conditional,[132] and by choosing the elect life he no doubt intends that

---

[130]Elliott, *Survivors of Israel*, p. 147. See also Collins, *Apocalyptic Imagination*, p. 62.

[131]Elliott, *Survivors of Israel*, p. 82.

[132]Grindheim notes, "That which is 'elect' is now a quality that may or may not be the object of
someone's choice. The connotations of the term are that which is ethically and religiously good,
and that which is worthy of being elected, that which is choice (cf. also 93:10)" (Grindheim, *Crux
of Election*, p. 42). See also Sanders, *Paul and Palestinian Judaism*, pp. 355-56; VanLandingham,
Judgment and Justification, p. 93.

this choice entails a righteous and upright lifestyle. Following these instructions begin seven sections of woes/judgment pronouncements against the wicked (*1 En.* 94:6–95:2; 95:4-7; 96:4-8; 97:3-10; 98:4-8; 98:9–99:2, 6-9; 99:11-16; 100:1-4; 100:7–102:3), with messages of encouragement to the righteous interspersed among them (*1 En.* 95:3; 96:1-3; 97:1-2; 99:3-5; 99:10; 100:5-6). The author charges the wicked throughout these woes with oppression and injustice (*1 En.* 94:6, 9; 95:6-7; 96:5, 7-8; 97:6, 8; 98:13-14; 99:13, 15; 100:7), deceit (94:6; 95:6; 96:7; 97:10; 98:15–99:1; 99:12), trust in and flaunting of their riches (94:8; 96:4-5; 97:8), dependence on self rather than God (94:8; 96:6; 97:8), hatred (95:2), pronouncing curses (95:4), rewarding of evildoers (95:5; 99:11), lack of repentance (96:4), blasphemy (96:7), foolishness (98:9-10), stubbornness (90:11; 100:8), distortion and rejection of the law (99:2; 99:14), and idolatry (99:6-9, 14). The sins of the wicked have all been recorded against them, and they will not escape in the day of judgment (*1 En.* 97:3-7; 98:4-8; 100:1-6, 10-13; 104:7).

The sinners no doubt include, perhaps predominantly, Jewish apostates, especially as their sin relates to their distortion of the law.[133] They also include, at least in part if not predominantly, the ruling class, which holds social power and thus oppresses the impoverished righteous community.[134] The righteous will eventually judge the wicked (*1 En.* 95:3; 96:1; 99:3-5) and will flourish in the absence of their oppressors (96:2-3; 97:1-2; 99:10; 100:5-6). The sinners have not feared God in spite of his sovereignty over creation (*1 En.* 101:1-9). God will judge, destroy and accurse them forever (*1 En.* 102:1-3), and they will experience "evil and great tribulation" in Sheol (103:7). The righteous, in contrast, though they died in sorrow and because of oppression (102:4-11), will "live and rejoice; their spirits shall not perish" (103:4), and they will "shine like the lights of heaven" (104:2).[135]

---

[133]See George W. E. Nickelsburg, *1 Enoch*, Hermeneia (Minneapolis: Fortress, 2001), 1:51; Sanders, *Paul and Palestinian Judaism*, pp. 353-54.

[134]See George W. E. Nickelsburg, *Resurrection, Immortality, and Eternal Life in Intertestamental Judaism and Early Christianity* (Cambridge, MA: Harvard University Press, 2006), pp. 143, 156.

[135]As Nickelsburg summarizes, "In 1 Enoch, the function of the resurrection of the righteous has broadened in two respects. First, God raises the righteous not because they have suffered unjustly

As the Epistle closes, it, as seen elsewhere in *1 Enoch*, recalls the story of Noah, which the author views as paradigmatic of the salvation and judgment of the righteous and wicked. Here Enoch has foreseen the coming cataclysm, in which God "will surely make new things upon the earth" (*1 En.* 106:13). Humanity has lived disobediently by bearing children with the Watchers (*1 En.* 106:14).[136] Enoch declares Noah "shall be the remnant for you; and he and his sons shall be saved from the corruption which shall come upon the earth on account of all the sin and oppression that existed" (*1 En.* 106:18). Enoch himself indicates that this judgment comes as a foreshadowing of a future judgment when an even more wicked generation will rise up on the earth (*1 En.* 106:19–107:1). It is not until a "generation of righteous ones" comes that God removes wickedness and sin from the earth (*1 En.* 107:1).[137] In this final judgment, the names of the sinners "shall be blotted out from the Book of Life and the books of the Holy One; their seeds shall be destroyed forever and their spirits shall perish and die" (*1 En.* 108:3).[138] The ungodly, whose sins include blasphemy, altering the words of the Lord, defiling their bodies and accruing wealth, will be taken into a dark cloud of burning fire while the righteous will be summoned to God and seated on a throne and honored forever (*1 En.* 108:4-15). The description of these fates no doubt serves to spur on the righteous to continued faithfulness and the wicked

---

for his sake, but simply because they have suffered unjustly. Secondly, resurrection to life is not an answer to an unjust and violent *death*. . . . In 1 Enoch, God vindicates the behavior of the righteous vis-à-vis those who have claimed that such conduct goes unrewarded" (ibid., p. 156).

[136]The language here is more generic than elsewhere in the book in that the Watchers are not specifically identified. It may be that the author views the sin of intermarriage in his day as a catalyst for judgment just as the sin of the Watchers brought about the flood of Noah.

[137]So Elliott comments, "The significance of the flood typology for the writer's own community is accordingly caught up with the idea of a remnant: as there was a remnant in Noah's day, so there will be a remnant *after* the coming judgment" (Elliott, *Survivors of Israel*, p. 625).

[138]The fact that these heavenly books can be altered speaks against the notion that whenever heavenly books or tablets are present, they indicate an assumption or promotion of determinism or fatalism. As Elliott comments, "The idea of the full number of the righteous is directly associated in this passage with the 'books of the living' and may suggest a suitable provenance for what has conventionally—but quite wrongly—been taken as a deterministic teaching. In this passage the 'number' of the righteous follows naturally from the idea of a set number of names listed in the book of the living and may actually have little to do with abstract determinism *per se*" (ibid., p. 290). This is contra Nickelsburg, who writes, "In any case, the notion [of names being blotted out] is odd, because the idea of heavenly books suggests a determinism that seems to preclude later exclusion from them" (Nickelsburg, *1 Enoch*, 1:555).

to repentance.[139] The author describes their inclusion in the "elect body" as conditional throughout the work, as apostates are on the outside, and the elect live uprightly by choosing "an elect life." The group is thus limited to the Enochic community, who are the recipients of the special revelation given to them.[140]

THE CONDITIONS OF PAUL'S GOSPEL

The limited, non-nationalistic[141] understanding of election permeated much of Jewish thought during this period. By and large, Jews did not assume that being Jewish meant one belonged among the people of God. Rather, these authors asserted different and competing conditions or markers by which an individual could know they were within God's people. These conditions vary from receiving special knowledge, observing certain rites (Sabbath, circumcision, food laws, etc.), keeping the proper calendar, observing the festivals correctly, resisting Hellenism and idolatry, supporting or opposing the Jerusalem establishment and correctly interpreting and following the Torah. With this backdrop in mind, it seems to me that Paul joins in this same theological soiree as he lays out his own understanding of what defines the people of God, though he obviously diverges significantly from his contemporaries.

Galatians 2:15–3:14. We could go to many texts to examine what Paul views as the proper defining marker(s) of the people of God, but few would offer as much richness (and controversy!) as Galatians 2–3.[142] Though we do not find election language present in the passage, the delineation of "insiders" and "outsiders" places the discussion squarely

---

[139]See Elliott, *Survivors of Israel*, p. 362.

[140]See Andreas Bedenbender, "The Place of the Torah in the Early Enoch Literature," in *The Early Enoch Literature*, ed. Gabriele Boccaccini and John J. Collins (Leiden: Brill, 2007), p. 79; George W. E. Nickelsburg, "Enochic Wisdom: An Alternative to the Mosaic Torah?," in *Hesed Ve-Emet: Studies in Honor of Ernest S. Frerichs*, ed. Jodi Magness and Seymour Gitin (Atlanta: Scholars Press, 1998), pp. 123-32; Nickelsburg, *1 Enoch*, 1:5; Patrick Tiller, "The Sociological Settings of the Components of *1 Enoch*," in Boccaccini and Collins, *Early Enoch Literature*, p. 253.

[141]By this, again, I do not mean they did not think of themselves in a nationalistic sense, for some or many Jews certainly did, but rather that they did not view all ethnic Jews as a part of God's people.

[142]This section is taken in part from my article "'Spheres of Influence' in the Epistle to the Galatians," *HBT* 36, no. 1 (2014): 21-41.

within the intra-Jewish debate about what defined God's chosen people. Questions persist as to the exact audience and context of Paul's discussion in this section.[143] Regardless, a clear problem developed among the Galatians, in part either caused or escalated by the actions of Peter, which drove a wedge between the Jews and the Gentiles. Writers frequently overlook Paul's "spherical" language in this passage, wherein he speaks more in terms of "identity" than "modality."[144] This is due, at least in part, to the choices most of our translations make regarding the prepositions in the passage (primarily ἐν and ἐκ). In addition to these prepositions, we must pay attention to which audiences Paul has in mind in his argument.

This section of Galatians no doubt follows logically from what Paul has developed in Galatians 1:6–2:10. He primarily intended to show that the Jerusalem apostles validated his gospel proclamation. These apostles "added nothing" to Paul's kerygma (Gal 2:6). In context, Paul carefully notes his concern to demonstrate that they did not affirm the teachings (especially as relating to circumcision) of the Judaizers (see Gal 2:3-9). This is important because Peter's actions in 2:11-14 contradict this previous validation. Paul disputes the validity of any Jewish separation from the Gentiles, a mentality to which Peter and Barnabas had succumbed (Gal 2:11-14).[145] As with the schisms seen in 1 Corinthians 1–2,

---

[143]There is a long history of debate concerning the exact nature of the problem, if the issue occurred before or after the Jerusalem council recorded in the book of Acts, and what Paul's phrases "works of the law" and "faith(fulness) of Christ" refer to. While these issues are important, space does not permit a discussion here. For a summary of the issues from both a traditional and "new perspective" author, see Douglas J. Moo, *Galatians*, BECNT (Grand Rapids: Baker Academic, 2013), pp. 156-63; and Don Garlington, *An Exposition of Galatians: A Reading from the New Perspective* (Eugene, OR: Wipf & Stock, 2007), pp. 141-61.

[144]Wright supports this in principle, noting that the central question is "about which community, which table-fellowship, you belong to" (N. T. Wright, *Paul and the Faithfulness of God* [Minneapolis: Fortress, 2013], p. 856). Grindheim has offered a similar argument concerning the "domain" language present here and Paul's central concern of the identity of God's people (Sigurd Grindheim, "Not Salvation History, but Salvation Territory: The Main Subject Matter of Galatians," *NTS* 59 [2013]: 93).

[145]As Wright summarizes, "Up to that point, Peter had been ignoring the normal Jewish taboo according to which Jews and Gentiles would not eat together. . . . He is putting apparent moral pressure on the gentile Messiah-believers to 'live like Jews,' in other words, to join the company of Torah-keeping Abraham-children, the elect people of God" (Wright, *Paul and the Faithfulness of God*, p. 855). "The issue at stake in Antioch consisted, quite simply, in the question: were Jewish Messiah-believers allowed to sit and eat at the same table as non-Jewish Messiah-believers?" (ibid., p. 854).

the action of these Jewish believers was not a peripheral issue, but a gospel-centered issue.

Paul's prepositions in Galatians contain great significance. He first speaks in Galatians 2:12 of those to whom Peter succumbed: τοὺς ἐκ περιτομῆς, literally "those from the circumcision." Here Don Garlington offers an important observation. As he suggests, ἐκ as the genitive of "'origin' can entail the notion of *position within* or *participation*; that is, to be 'from' (ἐκ) a realm means to 'belong' to it. Such being the case, ἐκ is not so far removed from ἐν in its locative sense."[146] "Those from the circumcision"[147] contains participatory language since it identifies a group that was quite concerned with enforcing the observance of the law.

Paul transitions in Galatians 2:15 to the first-person plural ("we"), likely indicating that he now focuses on something that he and his Jewish Christ-following brethren agreed on concerning the identity of God's people. "We," he says in 2:15, "are Jews by nature and not sinners from [ἐξ ἐθνῶν ἁμαρτωλοί] among the Gentiles." Garlington sees Paul's first significant use of ἐκ as occurring in Galatians 2:15, which "sets up the antithesis of justification ἐξ ἔργων νόμου versus one ἐκ πίστεως Χριστοῦ,"[148] but we should note the contrast begins in Galatians 2:12. Dunn has suggested that this identification of the "sinners from among the Gentiles" represents a typical way to designate "outsiders" who transgressed the law and were unacceptable by God. As he notes, Paul has likely adopted the rhetoric of "those from the circumcision" since his

---

[146]Don Garlington, "Paul's 'Partisan ἐκ' and the Question of Justification in Galatians," *JBL* 127, no. 3 (2008): 567.

[147]Witherington notes that these may be "zealotic Jews or zealotic Jewish Christians, or zealotic Jewish Christians who had raised the spectre of angry Jews causing major trouble for the assembly of Christians in Jerusalem" (Ben Witherington III, *Grace in Galatia: A Commentary on Paul's Letter to the Galatians* [Grand Rapids: Eerdmans, 1998], p. 156). The important thing to note is that Paul identifies them as belonging to and participating in a group whose primary feature was their emphasis on circumcision.

[148]Garlington rightly notes of this phrase "that justification is διὰ πίστεως Ἰησοῦ Χριστοῦ is straightforward enough: it comes through the instrumentality of faith. The disputed component in this phrase and in ἐκ πίστεως Χριστοῦ pertains to the hotly debated question of how the genitive case is to be understood" (Garlington, "Paul's 'Partisan ἐκ,'" p. 573). It is not possible here to adequately address the contentious issue of Paul's intended use of the genitive. The phrase has here been rendered in its subjective sense, which seems to me the more straightforward reading.

pro-Gentile calling would likely not have permitted such characterization.[149] It seems that Paul's "we" was directed toward his Jewish-Christian
brethren since they understood Jesus' work as the realm in which they
are made right with God.

Paul has thus contrasted "those from the circumcision" (τοὺς ἐκ
περιτομῆς; 2:12) with the "sinners from among the Gentiles" (ἐξ ἐθνῶν
ἁμαρτωλοί; 2:15). Paul does not accept the designation, which may come
from the mouths of τοὺς ἐκ περιτομῆς themselves (though it no doubt at
least represents their attitude). His statement in Galatians 2:16 clearly
shows this since, unlike "those from the circumcision," Paul and his
Jewish-Christian brethren know (or should) works of the law are not the
realm of "justification," but rather this comes "through the faith(fulness)
of Jesus Christ." Scholars often see Paul's uses of ἐξ ἔργων νόμου and διὰ
πίστεως Ἰησοῦ Χριστοῦ as parallel, both indicating agency or
instrumentality and translated as "by."[150] We must inquire why, if Paul
intended their equivalency, he did not simply use διὰ in both phrases.[151]

---

[149]James D. G. Dunn, *The New Perspective on Paul* (Grand Rapids: Eerdmans, 2005), pp. 230-33.

[150]Schreiner, for example, appeals to Rom 3:30 and Rom 5:1 as evidence that ἐκ should be taken
as indicating means or instrumentality in Galatians, suggesting that it is essentially synonymous with Paul's use of διὰ, and that Paul's use of prepositions are imprecise and nontechnical
(Thomas R. Schreiner, *Galatians*, Exegetical Commentary on the New Testament [Grand Rapids: Zondervan, 2010], p. 158). I think Paul's use is more than a stylistic accident. Rom 3:30 is
more difficult to explain in terms of a normative use of the prepositions. It seems, though, that
Paul there contrasts the starting point of the Jews (ἐκ) with the means through which the
Gentiles are declared righteous (διὰ). The distinction is that the Jews are declared righteous
"from faith(fulness)" rather than "through faith(fulness)." Stowers has argued that "Paul consistently applies διὰ τῆς πίστεως to the redemption of the Gentiles. The case is different for ἐκ
πίστεως, which can refer to both Jews and Gentiles" (Stanley K. Stowers, "*Ek pisteos* and *dia tes
pisteos* in Romans 3:30,*" JBL* 108, no. 4 [1989]: 672). Stowers concludes, "The phrase διὰ πίστεως
refers very specifically to Jesus' atoning life and death for the redemption of the Gentiles. Paul
elsewhere writes of this as Jesus' 'obedience unto death' (Phil 2:8). . . . Both Jews and Gentiles
share in blessings ἐκ πίστεως of Abraham and Jesus, although not in identical ways. Thus Paul
can apply ἐκ πίστεως to Jews in 3:30 but not διὰ πίστεως" (ibid., p. 674). Without belaboring
the exact distinctions intended in Rom 3:30, it seems more likely, at least in Rom 3:30, that Paul
makes a distinction between Jews and Gentiles by his use of different prepositions rather than
that his language is accidental, and no less repeated again elsewhere. Paul does not argue that
there is absolutely no distinction between Jew and Gentile, but rather that there is no exclusion
of the Gentiles. Wright comments along similar lines that Paul differentiates between the two
paths by which Jews and Gentiles "came in" to the new covenant. The Jews were already on the
right track, so to speak, while the Gentiles were outsiders who had to be brought in (Wright,
Paul and the Faithfulness of God, p. 864).

[151]Lambrecht has argued that the spherical understanding, even of ἐν Χριστῷ (!) in Gal 2.17, is

To solve the dilemma, we can examine uses of ἐκ and διά with a passive verb[152] in other contexts. In Ephesians 2:8, the author clearly intends διά to mark the agent or instrument, while ἐκ should be taken as a phrase of origin. This is also demonstrated by the construction of Philippians 3:9 ("from the law" and "through the faith(fulness) of Christ"), which contrasts the law and faith in a similar fashion as Galatians 2:16. Though Paul uses ἐκ here with a passive verb, this is atypical of his usage in the letter (occurring only in Gal 2:16 and Gal 3:24). In the numerous other instances, he does not employ the passive, and we should not read the idea of agency into those separate uses if it is not necessary. Further, Paul could have used διά or ὑπό had he wished to express agency or instrumentality more clearly. Taking Paul's formulations here at face value, we must recognize his spherical language. As such, we may render Galatians 2:16 (and the subsequent uses of ἐκ that relate to it) as follows:

> We are Jews by birth, and not sinners from among the Gentiles, who know that a person is not declared "right" from [within the realm of] the works of the law but through the faith(fulness) of Jesus Christ, and we believed in Christ Jesus, so that we might be declared right from [within the realm of] the faith(fulnesss) of Christ and not from [within the realm of] the works of the law, because no flesh will be justified from [within the realm of] the works of the law.

Paul's issue lies with those Gentiles who are "seeking to be part of the community that relates to God on the basis of the Mosaic covenant."[153] He deemed his statement so important that it bore the need for repetition. The statement here is chiastic, and emphatic.

---

incorrect. The function of ἐκ should be understood throughout the passage as equal to διά, indicating means. Lambrecht thus derives the meaning of the subsequent uses of ἐκ from this first use. As has been seen, however, Paul's use, beginning in Rom 2:12, starts as spherical, and this would thus be an interruption of its former function. As Lambrecht states, "Over against faith in Christ stand works done in obedience to the law" (Jan Lambrecht, "Critical Reflections on Paul's Partisan 'ἐκ' as Recently Presented by Don Garlington," *ETL* 85, no. 1 [2009]: 138). This is no doubt a stretching of Paul's phrase (ἐξ ἔργων νόμου), from which Lambrecht eventually extrapolates that Paul's case is against the failure of the Jews to do the law and their attempt at self-salvation.

[152]Particular to this construction and also in Rom 3:24 is the use of these prepositional phrases with a passive-voice verb

[153]Witherington, *Grace in Galatia*, p. 172.

A—a person is not declared righteous from [the realm of] the works of
the law

  B—but through the faith(fulness) of Jesus Christ

    C—and we believed in Christ Jesus

  B'—so that we might be declared righteous from [within the realm
  of] the faith(fulness) of Christ

A'—and not from [within the realm of] the works of the law (because no
flesh will be justified from [within the realm of] the works of the law).

For Paul, returning to the law as the realm through which he relates to
God would result in his breaking the very law he sought to keep (Gal
2:18). He has died to the law and been transferred to the new realm of
life.[154] Being "in Christ" (Gal 2:17) is what counts, and returning to this
other realm would result in nullifying God's grace and denigrating the
cross (Gal 2:20-21).[155]

    In Galatians 2:17-20, Paul affirms that right-standing happens for
those in Christ (ἐν Χριστῷ; Gal 2:17).[156] Accordingly, he asserts that
those who seek justification in Christ cannot relate to God within the
sphere of the law and outside of Christ, without violating God's purposes
and thus being found as sinners, something of which they would quickly
accuse Gentiles! The "I" Paul introduces here probably represents himself
and his fellow Jewish Christ followers, since Gentiles never lived "under
the law."[157] Moreover, the death and resurrection (surely what Paul summarizes by his reference to the cross in Gal 2:19) of Christ has ushered in

---

[154]Garlington asserts, in operating in the realm of the law rather than the realm of the faith(fulness)
of Christ, the Galatians' "quest for perfection is anachronistic: they are going in the wrong
direction; they want to reverse the plan of the ages" (Garlington, "Paul's 'Partisan ἐκ,'" p. 578).

[155]Cosgrave supports such an interpretation in noting that Paul's question, as evidenced by his
prepositional phrases, is not "whether one can be justified on the basis of the law or works but
remains always whether one can be justified in the sphere of the law" (Charles H. Cosgrove,
"Justification in Paul: A Linguistic and Theological Reflection," *JBL* 106 [1987]: 662).

[156]As Witherington affirms, "It is true that Paul could be using ἐν to mean 'by' here, but the ἐν
Χριστῷ formula normally carries a locative sense, and Paul is here contrasting life within two
spheres—the sphere of the Law and the sphere of Christ" (Witherington, *Grace in Galatia*, p. 185).

[157]Contra Fung, among others (Ronald Y. K. Fung, *The Epistle to the Galatians*, NICNT [Grand
Rapids: Eerdmans, 1988], pp. 122-23).

a new era, and has brought with it a new covenant.[158] To live "in Christ" as one would have lived "in law" was to live as if the work of God in Christ was invalid (Gal 2:21).[159] Here Paul has identified the chief marker of God's people. So N. T. Wright states, "The 'elect,' in other words, consist primarily of the Messiah himself, and secondarily of all those who belong to him."[160]

Having established the likelihood of Paul's "spherical" connotation for ἐκ, we see that Galatians 3:2-24 also fits well within this paradigm. In Galatians 3:2, Paul inquires of the Galatians ("you") if they received the Spirit from the works of the law (ἐξ ἔργων νόμου) or from the hearing of faith (ἐξ ἀκοῆς πίστεως).[161] Paul does not here contrast "works" and "faith"; rather "works" against "hearing" and "law" against "faith."[162] Paul does not denigrate obedience, especially since hearing frequently carries that connotation,[163] as does also "faith" (πίστις).[164] He reiterates his point again in Galatians 3:5, where he asks, "Therefore does he [God] supply the Spirit to you and work powerful deeds in you from the works of the law or from the hearing of faith?" Paul puts the basic identity of these

---

[158]See also Wright, *Paul and the Faithfulness of God*, pp. 856-57.

[159]Of this verse, Wright comments, "Indeed, that mention of 'love' ought to have told us, with its echoes of Deuteronomy and elsewhere, that this was all about the divine purpose in election" (ibid., p. 860).

[160]Ibid., p. 856.

[161]Garlington is correct to note, "These respective phrases, 'from works of the law' and 'from the hearing of faith,' have frequently been understood as though they were in the dative (instrumental) case; that is, 'by works of the law' and 'by the hearing of faith.' However, the preposition again is ἐκ, with stress placed on the origin but also embracing its 'partisan' sense" (Garlington, "Paul's 'Partisan ἐκ,'" p. 579).

[162]Contra, e.g., F. F. Bruce, *The Epistle to the Galatians*, NIGTC (Grand Rapids: Eerdmans, 1988), p. 151. Though Paul contrasts works and faith in Gal 2, the more important point of delineation is between law and Christ, which are the defining modifiers of works and faith.

[163]Thus Kittel can state, "NT hearing as reception of the declared will of God always implies affirmation of this will as the willing of salvation and repentance by the man who believes and acts. There thus arises, as the crowning concept of the obedience which consists in faith and the faith which consists in obedience" (Gerhard Kittel, "Ἀκούω, ἀκοή, εἰσ-, ἐπ-, παρακούω, παρακοή, ὑπακούω, ὑπακοή, ὑπήκοος," in *Theological Dictionary of the New Testament*, ed. Gerhard Kittel and Gerhard Friedrich, trans. Geoffrey W. Bromiley [Grand Rapids: Eerdmans, 1964], 1:220). Garlington here suggests a possible connection with Paul's "obedience of faith" in Rom 2:16 (Garlington, "Paul's 'Partisan ἐκ,'" p. 580).

[164]As McKnight defines it, faith is *"the initial and continual response of trust in, and obedience to, Christ by a person for the purpose of acceptance with God"* (Scot McKnight, *Galatians*, NIVAC [Grand Rapids: Zondervan, 1995], p. 121 [emphasis original]).

Christians in Galatia at stake. Because they have already received the Spirit of God apart from works of the law, Paul adamantly contends that their being "in Christ" is sufficient for right-standing with God.

Paul then brings Abraham to bear on the Galatians' current dilemma. He asserts that God declared Abraham "right" because of his πίστις. As such, "those who are *from* [the realm of] faith" (οἱ ἐκ πίστεως),[165] those who stand in the Messiah's faithful obedience and resurrection, belong to Abraham's family (Gal 3:6-8).[166] Being "from faith" would mean the Gentiles would be declared right (Gal 3:8), because "those who are from faith" (οἱ ἐκ πίστεως) are blessed along with the faithful man Abraham (Gal 3:9).[167] Many translations, as we have seen above, muddy the meaning of Galatians 3:10 in rendering it as something along the lines of "For all who rely on observing the law are under a curse" (Gal 3:10 NIV). The NASB comes closest in translating, "For as many as are of the works of the Law are under a curse."[168] The Greek here says nothing of "observing" (NIV), "depending" (NLT, ISV) or "relying" (ESV, GWT, NRSV, NET). The confusion has come from assuming either the necessity of the instrumentality or agency of the phrase, or assuming the presence in Second Temple Judaism of "works righteousness." Paul says nothing of the sort. The ones under a curse are "as many as are from the works of the law" (Ὅσοι γὰρ ἐξ ἔργων νόμου εἰσίν). Paul again speaks in terms of spheres of existence. Those who operate within the Christ-realm alone stand "right" before God. The Torah does not accomplish this for either Jew or Gentile.[169]

---

[165]Harris notes that the phrase here "has a *neutral* sense, with ἐκ simply signifying 'belonging to, connected with' or 'member(s) of'" (Murray J. Harris, *Prepositions and Theology in the Greek New Testament: An Essential Reference Resource for Exegesis* [Grand Rapids: Zondervan, 2012], p. 109).

[166]Wright states, "If the family is redefined by the Messiah's *pistis*, then those who themselves have *pistis* are clearly the members of this family" (Wright, *Paul and the Faithfulness of God*, p. 859).

[167]For Paul, πίστις is connected with Jesus (see Gal 2:16, 20; 3:22, 26). It is not a matter of doing versus trusting, but the law versus Christ as the fundamental marker or means of definition for God's people.

[168]The KJV is quite good as well, translating, "For as many as are of the works of the law are under the curse."

[169]As we will discuss later, Paul never commands Jewish Christ followers to stop following the law. His issue is always with their attempting to force Gentile Christ followers to keep it. Wright suggests that the narrative Paul develops is "(a) that the Torah was a necessary, God-given thing, with its own proper role within that story, and (b) that the God-given role of Torah has now come

Many take Paul's quotation of Deuteronomy 27:26 to suggest the Jews have failed to keep the law and thus are guilty because they could not obtain works-based righteousness.[170] How can Paul say those ἐξ ἔργων νόμου stand under a curse? As Garlington suggests, "The logic behind Paul's words is simply that exclusion from blessing equals curse."[171] If we trace Paul's argument syllogistically we can better identify his designation of spheres.

1. Those who are "from faith" (ἐκ πίστεως) are blessed.

2. Abraham/the sons of Abraham are "from faith" (ἐκ πίστεως).

3. Therefore, Abraham/the sons of Abraham are blessed.

By substituting ἐξ ἔργων νόμου for ἐκ πίστεως, cursing for blessing, and Paul's opponents for Abraham/the sons of Abraham, the contrast emerges. Abraham, and all who exist ἐκ πίστεως, obtains the blessing. Paul's opponents, who exist ἐξ ἔργων νόμου, suffer the curse. The Judaizers themselves may have appealed to these passages to persuade Gentile believers to adhere to the Torah.[172] According to Grindheim, Paul's reversal here, moving along the trajectory of the prophets, has loyalty to God primarily in view, and thus the curse falls on those who are disloyal because they have rejected God's Messiah.[173]

In contrast, Thomas Schreiner suggests the alternative sequence for understanding Galatians 3:10-11.

---

to a proper and honourable end—not that there was anything 'wrong' with it, but that it was never designed to be permanent" (ibid., p. 862). But though the law had an "end" or "goal" that had been accomplished, what ended was its functioning as a defining marker of the people of God, but Paul apparently continued to keep it and likely assumed his Jewish brethren would too.

[170]Timothy George, for example, states, "The Bible says that those who do not perfectly obey the law are cursed, and in fact those who seek to be justified by works really are under such a curse because no one (except Jesus) ever has or indeed can fulfill the entire law" (Timothy George, *Galatians*, NAC [Nashville: Broadman & Holman, 2001], p. 230). Of Paul's use of the OT here, Grindheim summarizes well, "The quotations from Scripture do not appear to be proving Paul's point. While Paul's argument is directed against those who keep the law, his quotation from Deut 27.26 curses those who break it. What is more, far from condemning law observers, the quotation from Lev 18.5 promises life to law keepers" (Sigurd Grindheim, "Apostate Turned Prophet: Paul's Prophetic Self-Understanding and Prophetic Hermeneutic with Special Reference to Galatians 3:10-12," *NTS* 53 [2007]: 20, www.sigurdgrindheim.com/Prophet.pdf).

[171]Garlington, "Paul's 'Partisan ἐκ,'" p. 581.

[172]Don Garlington, "Role Reversal and Paul's Use of Scripture in Galatians 3.10-13," *JSNT* 65 (1997): 107.

[173]Grindheim, "Apostate Turned Prophet," p. 26.

1. Those who do not keep everything in the law are cursed.

2. No one keeps everything in the law (implicit premise).

3. Therefore, those who rely on the works of the law for salvation are cursed.[174]

The problem here is that the second premise is neither implicit nor obtains. It does not accord with what we have seen of the majority of Second Temple Jewish beliefs, and neither do Paul's statements necessitate it. Paul already provided the better implicit premise in Galatians 2:15-21, where he asserts, as one who is ἐκ πίστεως and ἐν Χριστῷ, to seek to orient himself to God by being ἐξ ἔργων νόμου would actually result in his breaking of the law! We can correct the syllogism as follows:

1. Those who do not persevere in keeping everything written in the law are cursed.

2. Living ἐξ ἔργων νόμου when one is ἐκ πίστεως results in breaking the law (explicit premise via Gal 2:18).

3. Therefore, those who live ἐξ ἔργων νόμου when they are ἐκ πίστεως break the law and are cursed.

We must make one final note on Galatians 3:12. Here Paul states that the law is not ἐκ πίστεως, but those who keep it will live by it. This no doubt seems a strange contrast. The law gives life, but is not ἐκ πίστεως, and Paul has just argued that those who live ἐξ ἔργων νόμου are under a curse! Many identify the referent of αὐτὰ here as ἔργων νόμου.[175] While that is, especially in light of Galatians 3:10, a possible reading, Paul may well be referring back to Galatians 3:11[176] and arguing something along the lines of, "The righteous will live from [within the realm of] faith," and "those who do these things [i.e., related to life ἐκ πίστεως] will live by them." This makes sense of (or attempts to) the sharp antithesis between Galatians 3:12a and Galatians 3:12b. Garlington agrees

---

[174]Thomas R. Schreiner, *The Law and Its Fulfillment: A Pauline Theology of the Law* (Grand Rapids: Baker Books, 1993), p. 44.

[175]E.g., Bruce, *Galatians*, p. 162.

[176]This is made possible by the parallels between Gal 3:11 and Gal 3:12: ὁ δίκαιος ἐκ πίστεως ζήσεται and ὁ ποιήσας αὐτὰ ζήσεται ἐν αὐτοῖς.

in principle with such an interpretation in noting the role reversals Paul employs in Galatians 3. As it relates to Galatians 3:12, he states, "Now, however, the call for faithfulness has been projected into the present eschatological context, whereby 'doing the law' [or "doing these things"] is redefined as faith(fulness) directed to *the Christ of Paul's gospel*."[177]

There is (much!) more I could say about this section in Galatians and what follows. Central to the argument, however, is that a reversal of sorts has come about because of what God has done through Jesus. The resurrection of Jesus, combined with the experience of the Spirit given to Gentile believers, indicated God had done something "new" and he was bringing his promises to fruition.[178] But since experience dictated operating within the "faith realm," which means both to trust in what the Messiah faithfully accomplished and to live in faithfulness to him, was sufficient for Gentile believers, Torah-works (and here specifically purity regulations and circumcision) became not only unnecessary for Gentiles but also destructive since they overlooked these two realities.[179] God redefined what demarcated his people, and Paul had confidence that the redefinition had indeed taken place because of the resurrection of Jesus and the outpouring of the Spirit. Thus the "outsiders" included not those Gentiles who did not define their identity by works of the law, but rather those Jews who insisted on living as if the work of the Messiah had not occurred by pushing these "works" upon Gentile believers.

---

[177]Garlington, "Role Reversal," p. 108 (emphasis original). Grindheim is also helpful in stating, "This contrast between being in Christ and being without him does not correspond precisely to being without and with the law. Even though they are free from the law, those in Christ are expected to hear the law (4.21) and to fulfill it. 'The whole law is fulfilled in one word: "love your neighbor as yourself"' (5.14), and love describes the life of the believer (5.6, 13, 22). However, those in Christ do not seek to be justified in the law (2.16, 21; 5.4), they are not under the law (3.23, 25; 4.5, 21; 5.18), and they are not enslaved by it (4.3, 9, 24-25, 31; 5.1)" (Grindheim, "Not Salvation History," p. 97).

[178]As Garlington notes, this is part and parcel of God's "righteousness" wherein God is "doing the right thing" in fulfilling his promises even though Israel had been unfaithful to their end of the bargain (Garlington, *An Exposition of Galatians*, pp. 143-49).

[179]Garlington states well, "If fidelity and infidelity have been redefined eschatologically with respect to God's purposes in Christ, ministerial role reversal has *ipso facto* occurred. Now that 'the faith' has come (Gal 3.23), it is Paul who promotes genuine fidelity to God's (new) covenant, not the Judaizers. The latter actually foster unfaithfulness, because although they champion Jesus as Israel's messiah, the Torah for them remains indispensable as the Jewish gateway to salvation" (Garlington, "Role Reversal," p. 90).

SUMMARY

The Jewish discussion about what "conditions" were necessary to be in the people of God or what markers distinguished them took various twists and turns. Some of the expectations in the literature surveyed above contradicted other writings, illustrating that no single, clear-cut criterion existed by which all Jews agreed God's people could be recognized. All of these texts recognize certain aspects, such as the centrality of the Torah, but debate occurred regarding other aspects, like what calendar to follow, whether to participate in the temple establishment, whether to support the Hasmoneans or how to interact with Gentiles.

Paul's discussion of what condition or marker defines God's people did not take place in a vacuum. Since his discussion in Galatians 2 occurs in the context of separation between Jews and Gentiles, and the way he frames his discussion bears striking similarities to the Jewish debate, we can conclude with confidence that Paul entered into that same discussion. But what shaped Paul's convictions was what God had accomplished in Jesus through his death and resurrection and what he had done in the lives of the Galatian believers and other Gentile converts. Because God had acted, imparting his Spirit apart from the observation of purity regulations or circumcision, Paul took these events as being indicative of what defined God's new-covenant people. Gentiles need not adopt Jewish identity marks to be considered a part of God's people. As Wright asserts, "*The boundaries of God's people now consist of the Messiah and his death and resurrection.*"[180] Only those "in Christ," operating within the realm of "faith," could be considered a part of God's chosen people. All other proposals fall flat as they disparage the decisive act of God in Christ.

---

[180]Wright, *Paul and the Faithfulness of God*, p. 858 (emphasis original).

5

How Big a Tent?

We have seen that many Jews, if not perhaps most, at least as is evidenced from the extant literature, did not believe that all Jews belonged to God's people. This became evident through implicit and explicit "markers" or "conditions," which differing authors used to define who belonged to the people of God and who did not. As such, these writers and communities believed a portion of ethnic Jews were not a part of the people of God. But some writings also speak of the inclusion of Gentiles in the people of God, usually in subtle, but sometimes in alarming ways. In this chapter, we will look more closely at Jewish inclusion and exclusion as well as Gentile inclusion and exclusion in the writings of the Second Temple period.

JEWISH INCLUSION AND EXCLUSION

We've seen already that many texts of the period view at least some Jews as outside of the covenant because they understood covenant membership as requiring certain marks or conditions. When lacking those conditions, those Jews were viewed as outside of the covenant and thus under the judgment of God. In the text surveyed below, I will attempt to identify the extent to which this exclusion of Jews from the covenant community persisted. As we shall see, this too varied among the different authors of the period.

2 Maccabees. As I noted earlier, the trouble in 2 Maccabees occurs because of the actions of certain instigators seeking to advance the Hellenistic agenda among the Jews, though the extent to which this movement grew among the Jews is unclear.[1] These "wicked" Jews initially bear the blame for Israel's troubles, and the author viewed the ensuing judgment as deserved (see 2 Macc 5:17-20; 6:1-17). Though the entire nation presently shared in the same fate of judgment, regardless of their personal piety, the faithful who died had a hope in resurrection that the unfaithful, Jews and Gentiles alike, did not.[2] As Solomon Zeitlin suggests, this point is illustrated by "the fourth victim [who] told Antiochus that he himself would be resurrected by God but not Antiochus; only pious people would be resurrected, not sinners."[3] While in some cases (Heliodorus, Lysimachus, Antiochus, Menelaus and Nicanor), justice comes swiftly, the book deals only implicitly with the judgment of the wicked, and does not indicate that the unfaithful outnumber the faithful.[4] This contrasts not only the view of 1 Maccabees, where the faithful are limited to the Hasmonean supporters,[5] but also most of the literature of the

---

[1]John R. Bartlett, *The First and Second Books of the Maccabees* (Cambridge: Cambridge University Press, 1973), p. 265. Schwartz suggests that "whether or not he was aware of it, our author has suppressed evidence both for Jewish traitors and for fighting among Jews—which fits the diasporan tendency . . . to limit the number of Jewish villains as much as possible" (Daniel R. Schwartz, *2 Maccabees* [New York: de Gruyter, 2008], p. 325). Zeitlin suggests, for example, that the Jews "compelled" to join Nicanor may have actually done so voluntarily in opposition to the Hasmonean agenda (Solomon Zeitlin, *The Second Book of Maccabees* [New York: Harper & Brothers, 1954], p. 239). Schwartz, however, disagrees, noting that such a view "runs counter to the plain wording of the text, and also requires us to assume that loyalist Jews who willingly supported the Seleucid cause nevertheless took the Sabbath so seriously that they would allow it to interfere with military operations" (Schwartz, *2 Maccabees*, p. 497).

[2]See Chris VanLandingham, *Judgment and Justification in Early Judaism and the Apostle Paul* (Grand Rapids: Baker Academic, 2006), p. 136. See also David A. deSilva, *Introducing the Apocrypha: Message, Context, and Significance* (Grand Rapids: Baker Academic, 2002), p. 275; Bartlett, *Books of the Maccabees*, pp. 265, 273.

[3]Zeitlin, *Second Book of Maccabees*, pp. 162-63. See also Jonathan A. Goldstein, *II Maccabees*, AB (New York: Doubleday, 1983), p. 355.

[4]Goldstein notes, "The author of First Maccabees was glad to tell how the Hasmonaeans fought against such wicked persons. Jason or the abridger seems to have preferred to focus on the righteous martyrs at this point, leaving the presence of the wicked to be inferred from 8:6-7, 33, and 10:15 (cf. 2:21)" (Goldstein, *II Maccabees*, p. 270).

[5]While 2 Maccabees is decidedly not pro-Hasmonean as is 1 Maccabees, whether or not it was intended as an anti-Hasmonean work is unclear. DeSilva states, "The book's emphasis falls on God's deliverance through any and all agents God chooses, rather than on the contribution of a particular family to the well-being of Israel" (deSilva, *Introducing the Apocrypha*, p. 274). Nickelsburg suggests that the author's "silence about Jonathan and Simon may well indicate that he was opposed to the Hasmonean high priesthood. This need not mean that his version of the story was intended to set straight what he considered to be the distortions of the account related in 1 Maccabees. . . . The Deuteronomic scheme provides the framework within which to see how this piety and God's reward of it are played out. The anti-Hasmonean tone of the work and its favorable view toward the Romans suggest that it was likely composed during the reign of Alexander

period. As Chris VanLandingham surmises, 2 Maccabees 4:10-16 and 2 Maccabees 5:17-18 present an exception to the normal pattern of Second Temple literature, which is that the

> preponderance of these texts surveyed state or strongly imply that most Jews would be damned at the Last Judgment. Many texts are explicit that the Last Judgment is the time when the wicked element is removed from Israel and the world. Those righteous enough to merit survival or resurrection into the next age will be cleansed, purified, and forgiven.[6]

For the author of 2 Maccabees, there is no indication as to the number of faithful and unfaithful Jews, and even the Gentiles are often portrayed favorably, with only certain individuals and groups from among the Jews and Gentiles identified as sinners. What is clear, however, is that the uncompromising Jew safely belongs among God's people. Though this does not exempt them from physical suffering now, they will enjoy resurrection and restoration in the future.[7]

In 2 Maccabees 1:25 the author notes that it was God who made the ancestors his chosen people (ὁ ποιήσας τοὺς πατέρας ἐκλεκτοὺς). Those Jews who abandoned the laws of the ancestors (μεταβαίνειν ἀπὸ τῶν πατρίων νόμων) have forfeited the covenant, the God of the covenant and the blessings of the covenant. The point is illustrated further in 2 Maccabees 12:40-45, where Judas makes supplication and sacrifice for the fallen Jews who were found with the idols of Jamnia beneath their tunics. As Jonathan Goldstein writes, Judas "was looking to the splendid reward that is laid up for those who fall asleep in godliness.... Therefore he made atonement for the dead, so that they might be delivered from their sin" (2 Macc 12:45).[8] Resurrection, reward and piety here go hand in

---

Janneus" (George W. E. Nickelsburg, *Jewish Literature Between the Bible and the Mishnah* [Minneapolis: Fortress, 2005], p. 108).

[6]VanLandingham, *Judgment and Justification*, p. 172.

[7]See VanLandingham, *Judgment and Justification*, p. 137. Gathercole seems to agree with the sentiment in noting, "First, resurrection comes to those who are faithful to Torah.... Second, the reward comes in the form of 'poetic justice': that God will give life back to the martyrs because they were willing to give it up for him" (Simon J. Gathercole, *Where Is Boasting? Early Jewish Soteriology and Paul's Response in Romans 1–5* [Grand Rapids: Eerdmans, 2002], p. 54).

[8]The author's depiction of Judas's sacrifice is particularly interesting considering the Hasmoneans were known for their opposition to such views. See Goldstein, *II Maccabees*, p. 450.

hand. Those who sin and forsake the covenant without making resti-
tution will not enjoy the rewards of the resurrection life. David deSilva
summarizes aptly: "Fidelity to the covenant ensures peace, sin against
the covenant brings punishment, and repentance and the renewal of obedience leads to restoration."[9] The fathers of Israel, and thus Israel, are
God's chosen people, but only faithful Israelites definitively remain in the
covenant through their obedience to God.

Psalms of Solomon. *Psalms of Solomon* 1 serves as a brief introduction
to the collection, though it introduces a theme prevalent throughout.
Here Jerusalem cries out to God for deliverance from foreign invaders.
She is sure God will hear her, for she believes she "was full of righteousness"
because she had flourished (*Pss. Sol.* 1:3). Her abundance, however, had
led to her children becoming arrogant and failing to present to God the
tribute he deserved (*Pss. Sol.* 1:6). Jerusalem was unaware of the secret sins
of her inhabitants, which were lawless (ἀνομίαι) in nature, and the extent
of which were even beyond the Gentiles in that they profaned the holy
place of the Lord (*Pss. Sol.* 1:7-8). Here clearly the Jews of Jerusalem are in
rebellion against God, and hold a false confidence that he will continue
to deliver them from their enemies in spite of their sin.

The result of the sin of the Jerusalem Jews is the invasion of the city by
the Gentile sinners. God declares, "Remove them far from me; I do not
take pleasure in them" (*Pss. Sol.* 2:4), judging the young and old alike (*Pss.
Sol.* 2:8). Throughout this psalm, the sins of the people justify God's
handing them over to the Gentiles (*Pss. Sol.* 2:3-5, 7-9, 16-17, 34), and thus
God is righteous in his judgment of them (*Pss. Sol.* 2:10, 15, 18, 32).[10] Specific sins mentioned here are typical of the collection, and include defiling the sanctuary and the offerings (*Pss. Sol.* 2:3) and sexual impurity

---

[9]DeSilva, *Introducing the Apocrypha*, p. 273.

[10]The psalmist, in fact, states that they will "justify" God for his right judgments. Winninge notes,
"It is remarkable that the verb δικαιοῦν is used with the devout as subject, as it is something new
in comparison with the Hebrew Bible. God is never declared righteous by those he created in the
Hebrew Bible, the Apocrypha, and the Greek OT Pseudepigrapha. In the PssSol the devout declare
God righteous thrice in a direct way (2:15; 3:5; 8:7). It is significant that the psalmist proves God
right with reverence to God's activity as a judge (v 15)" (Mikael Winninge, *Sinners and the Right-
eous: A Comparative Study of the Psalms of Solomon and Paul's Letters* [Stockholm: Almqvist &
Wiksell International, 1995], p. 35).

(*Pss. Sol.* 2:11-13), the extent of which was so offensive that it was ridiculed by the Gentiles (*Pss. Sol.* 2:12). Though judgment was deserved, the psalmist prays for God to deliver Jerusalem (*Pss. Sol.* 2:22-25), a prayer that is answered, at least in part, by the dishonorable death of the "dragon," likely intended to represent the emperor Pompey (*Pss. Sol.* 2:25-30). As the psalmist concludes, he affirms that God is merciful to those who fear him, judging between the righteous and sinners, and raising the righteous to glory (*Pss. Sol.* 2:31-37).[11] The sinners here clearly include Jews first and Gentiles secondarily.

Psalms of Solomon 4 offers another indictment against the unrighteous, with the offenders including at least some members of the Sanhedrin.[12] The offenses of the guilty here are their transgression of the Torah (*Pss. Sol.* 4:1, 12), harshness (4:2), lust (4:4), deceit (4:4, 10-11) and covetousness (4:9). The psalmist prays for these hypocrites to be exposed (*Pss. Sol.* 4:7), expelled (4:6, 24), afflicted (4:16-18) and punished with a humiliating death (4:6, 19-20). In contrast, the righteous will prove God to be in the right when the eventual expulsion of these men who "deceitfully quote the Law" takes place (*Pss. Sol.* 4:8). The psalm ends with a prayer that God would show mercy to "all those who love you" (*Pss. Sol.* 4:25). Not only are the unrighteous here Jews, but they are also influential religious leaders among the Jews.[13] Mikael Winninge notes, "Clearly enough the sinners are the majority here, which is why the main interest has to be focused on them."[14]

---

[11]Of this, Wright comments, "Life after death is concentrated entirely in the hope for bodily resurrection (viz. 2:31; 3:12)" (Robert B. Wright, "Psalms of Solomon," in *The Old Testament Pseudepigrapha*, vol. 2, *Expansions of the "Old Testament" and Legends, Wisdom and Philosophical Literature, Prayers, Psalms, and Odes, Fragments of Lost Judeo-Hellenistic Works*, ed. James H. Charlesworth [1985; repr., Peabody, MA: Hendrickson, 2011], p. 645).

[12]As Wright notes, those "sitting in the council of the devout" (*Pss. Sol.* 4:1) is likely a reference "to the supreme council, *the* Sanhedrin" (ibid., p. 655).

[13]See also Kenneth Atkinson, "Toward a Redating of the Psalms of Solomon: Implications for Understanding the *Sitz im Leben* of an Unknown Jewish Sect," *JSP* 17 (1998): 102; Winninge, *Sinners and the Righteous*, p. 55. Winninge suggests that the leaders here may include the Hasmoneans as well as the members of the Sanhedrin, whom he identifies as only the Sadducees since he holds to a Pharisee origin of the collection. See also Wright, "Psalms of Solomon," p. 642.

[14]Winninge, *Sinners and the Righteous*, p. 47. Of 5:1, Winninge further observes that the "we/Israel-group is called ἐπιστάμενοι τὰ κρίματά σου (v 1), perhaps implying that the community alone has real knowledge and a true theology" (ibid., p. 111).

Psalms of Solomon 8 records the sieging of Jerusalem and, as in *Psalms of Solomon* 4, the psalmist shows God to be just in his judgments (*Pss. Sol.* 8:7), since the people of the city had been involved in secret sexual deviances (8:8-10), thefts from the temple (8:11) and the desecration of the temple site (8:12). Their sins here, again, have surpassed even the sins of the Gentiles (*Pss. Sol.* 8:13). The instrument of God's judgment was "someone from the end of the earth, one who attacks in strength" (Pompey, cf. *Pss. Sol.* 8:14-21). With the judgment complete, the psalmist hopes God will restore his people to the city (*Pss. Sol.* 8:27-28), and Israel will be forever faithful to their God (*Pss. Sol.* 8:33-34). While the hope for restoration seems to be inclusive of all Israel, the psalmist also suggests that the devout alone will enjoy this blessing (*Pss. Sol.* 8:23, 34). Thus Mark Adam Elliott notes, "The devout here cannot be Israel as a whole . . . but only the righteous community, always carefully distinguished from the apostates."[15] Thus the sin of the city appears to have been widespread,[16] the judgment deserved and the devout, "like innocent lambs" (*Pss. Sol.* 8:23), collateral damage, caught up with the judgment of the sinners. The "sinners" constitute a majority of Jerusalem Jews, while the righteous community and all like them will alone experience God's blessing.

Dead Sea Scrolls. We find a similar picture in the writings of the Qumran community. The *Pesher on Habakkuk* (hereafter 1QpHab)[17] dates to the second half of the first century B.C.E., and was likely written after 63 B.C.E., the year Pompey overtook Jerusalem.[18] The text describes a specific conflict between the righteous of the community and their leader, the Teacher of Righteousness, the wicked of the Jerusalem temple cult, led by the Wicked Priest, and the Kittim, foreign oppressors who bring judgment on Jerusalem, who are likely the Romans.[19]

---

[15]Mark Adam Elliott, *The Survivors of Israel: A Reconsideration of the Theology of Pre-Christian Judaism* (Grand Rapids: Eerdmans, 2000), p. 95.

[16]Ibid., p. 94.

[17]For a discussion on the identification of the genre of the text, see William H. Brownlee, *The Midrash Pesher of Habakkuk* (Missoula, MT: Scholars Press, 1979), pp. 23-35.

[18]Ibid., p. 23. See also Kathleen M. Tyrer Atkinson, "The Historical Setting of the Habakkuk Commentary," *JSS* 4, no. 3 (1959): 238-63.

[19]Brownlee, *Midrash Pesher of Habakkuk*, p. 22; Maurya P. Horgan, *Pesharim: Qumran Interpretations of Biblical Books* (Washington, DC: Catholic Biblical Association of America, 1979), p. 26.

1QpHab interprets the text of Habakkuk in light of the community's situation. In 1QpHab 1.11-17, interpreting Habakkuk 1:4-5, the author compares those outside the community with those who have rejected the law of God, and identifies "the evildoer" as "the Wicked Priest" and the "upright man" as "the Teacher of Righteousness." William Brownlee suggests the Wicked Priest is likely a chief priest, with attention throughout on "his wicked deeds."[20] The outsiders are those who do not heed the instruction of the Teacher of Righteousness and the new/true covenant (1QpHab 2.1-4).[21] Defectors from the community also join these outsiders.[22] The revelation of the Teacher of Righteousness is ignored by these violators of the covenant, who do not heed his warnings of the judgment to come on disobedient Israel at the hands of the Kittim (1QpHab 2.5–4.17).[23]

In the face of this destruction, however, "God is not to destroy his people at the hand of the nations, but in the hand of his chosen ones God will place the judgment over all the nations; and by their reproof all the evildoers of this people will be pronounced guilty, (by the reproof) of those who kept his commandments in their hardship" (1QpHab 5.3-6).[24] The "chosen ones" here, Brownlee notes, is ambiguous, and

---

[20]Brownlee, *Midrash Pesher of Habakkuk*, pp. 46-47. Brownlee notes there has been debate as to whether the Teacher of Righteousness was a single individual or was viewed as an enlightened line of teachers ever present within the community (ibid., pp. 48-49). For a discussion of the identity of the Man of Lies, the Wicked Priest and the Teacher of Righteousness, see ibid., pp. 95-98, 204-5; James H. Charlesworth, *The Pesharim and Qumran History: Chaos or Consensus?* (Grand Rapids: Eerdmans, 2002); Horgan, *Pesharim*, pp. 6-8; Timothy H. Lim, "The Wicked Priests of the Groningen Hypothesis," *JBL* 112, no. 3 (1993): 415-25; Arthur E. Palumbo, "A New Interpretation of the Nahum Commentary," *FO* 29 (1992–1993): 153-62; H. H. Rowley, "The Kittim and the Dead Sea Scrolls," *PEQ* 88 (1956): 92-109; A. S. van der Woude, "Once Again: The Wicked Priests in the *Habakkuk Pesher* from Cave 1 of Qumran," *RevQ* 17, nos. 1-4 (1996): 375-84.

[21]So Brownlee writes that "they never had 'believed in the words of the Teacher of Right'; but such unbelief constituted defection from true Israel" (Brownlee, *Midrash Pesher of Habakkuk*, p. 54).

[22]See ibid., p. 55.

[23]As Elliott points out, 1QpHab 2.14 contains the interesting statement that the followers of the Teacher of Righteousness (and his teachings) "will be saved 'by their works and by their faith in the *moreh ṣedeq*'" (Elliott, *Survivors of Israel*, p. 136).

[24]Elliott notes, "It is the elect, not the nations, who will be the *final* dispensers of judgment in the last days. This passage does not, as might appear on the surface of things, contrast two completely opposite *views* of judgment . . . so much as it contrasts two *agents* of judgment—the nations and the *elect* from Israel" (ibid., p. 71).

could refer either to the Teacher of Righteousness or the future Messiah, or to the community as a collective, which is the more likely option given the interchange in the passage between the nations and the community.[25] The wrath of the Kittim will bring death to many (1QpHab 6.1-12), but the "men of truth" will remain faithful through the calamity,[26] and "God will come at the right time" and "will free" those who are faithful to the Teacher of Righteousness (1QpHab 7.7-8.3).[27] So, "all observing the Law in the House of Judah" are freed "on account of their toil and of their loyalty to the Teacher of Righteousness" (1QpHab 8.1-3). Here the author contrasts the "House of Judah," as the faithful of the community, with Jewish outsiders, who are likened to the wicked northern kingdom of Israel.[28]

Brownlee suggests the purpose of 1QpHab was to vindicate the Teacher of Righteousness and the community against opponents, strengthen the faith of the community, warn against apostasy and prepare the way for the coming judgment against sinners.[29] The author views the collective of the community as the elect, the "true Israel." Those outside of the community, both Jews led astray by the Wicked Priest and the Man of Lies, and Gentile sinners, will face God's judgment for their rejection of his

---

[25]Brownlee, *Midrash Pesher of Habakkuk*, pp. 86-87. See also Horgan, *Pesharim*, p. 32; Nickelsburg, *Jewish Literature*, p. 129. For a discussion of the figure of the "Chosen One" in *1 Enoch*, 1QpHab and the New Testament, see Joseph Coppens, "L'Elu et les élus dans les Ecritures Saintes et les écrits de Qumrân," *ETL* 57, no. 1 (1981): 120-24.

[26]Brownlee notes correctly, "'good works' as such do not enter the picture at all, but only a steadfast faith which makes possible the endurance of suffering. . . . Such faith in any case would involve faithfulness to the law as the Teacher expounded it; for it is precisely the 'doers of the Law' who are the righteous" (Brownlee, *Midrash Pesher of Habakkuk*, p. 130).

[27]The exclusivity of the attitude of the author concerning the community's status before God is noted by Horgan, who writes, "Considering themselves to be the people of the New Covenant, the true remnant of Israel living in the end-time, the members of the Qumran community believed that they were the guardians of the purity and authenticity of the true priesthood and of the correct interpretation of Scripture, an interpretation revealed to the Teacher of Righteousness" (Horgan, *Pesharim*, p. 2).

[28]See Brownlee, *Midrash Pesher of Habakkuk*, p. 126. Horgan notes likewise that Judah is a self-designation for the community in 4QNah, where "Ephraim = the Pharisees, Manasseh = the Sadducees, and Judah = the Essenes" (Horgan, *Pesharim*, p. 210). John S. Bergsma has argued that the community never used Judah as a designation for the community itself. While this may describe the Essenes, he suggests that the community itself did not use the designation, though they may have still identified themselves with the larger Essenic movement (John S. Bergsma, "Qumran Self-Identity: 'Israel' or 'Judah'?," *DSD* 15 [2008]: 172-89).

[29]Brownlee, *Midrash Pesher of Habakkuk*, pp. 35-36.

covenant. E. P. Sanders suggests that this text, along with 1QM and 1QSa, promotes the final judgment of Gentiles only, "while the elect are the Israelites—apparently all of Israel which survives, not just the present sectarians."[30] This, however, runs against the emphasis of the text itself, which views the community as decidedly exclusive. In referring to itself as the congregation of Israel or the House of Judah,[31] the community depicts itself as the only genuine expression of the covenant community. *All* outsiders in 1QpHab, and especially the Wicked Priest and his followers (i.e., Jews), will be judged, and the faithful of the community will be delivered. So, commenting on 1QpHab 5.3-5, Elliott summarizes rightly that "the scrolls *never* teach that the righteous in this way atone for the *wicked* in Israel; atonement is only efficacious for the individual *if he joins the community.* Whatever the salvific purpose of the existence of the community, in other words, it was certainly not a question of saving all Israel, especially apart from prior repentance and conformity to the community's teachings."[32] So a majority of Jews are thought to stand under the judgment of God.

Further evidence of this very restricted view of God's chosen people is found in the *Community Rule* (1QS). Here, the community of the sons of light "refine their knowledge in the truth of God's decrees" and obey all of his precepts as he has intended (1QS 1.14-18). The Levites of the community are responsible for reciting "the iniquities of the children of Israel . . . during the dominion of Belial," and the people respond by confessing the sins of Israel (1QS 1.21-26). As a result, the priests may intercede for the congregation to be blessed, protected and illumined and the "lot of Belial" (all outsiders) to be cursed, terrorized, destroyed and

---

[30]E. P. Sanders, *Paul and Palestinian Judaism* (Minneapolis: Fortress, 1970), p. 247.

[31]Harvey notes, "'Judah' is a self-designation indicating the group's origins within a region and a wider community. 'Judah' is not a 'pure community' but one which has faced, and will face, judgment" (Graham Harvey, *The True Israel: Uses of the Names Jew, Hebrew, and Israel in Ancient Jewish and Early Christian Literature* [Leiden: Brill, 1996], p. 33), and, "'Judah' is applied to both 'good' and 'bad' in Qumran Literature. Reflecting the contemporary situation of a plurality of Judaisms, it is applied to both the producers of Qumran Literature and their opponents in other groups" (ibid., p. 41).

[32]Elliott, *Survivors of Israel*, pp. 69-70 (emphasis original). See also David Flusser, *Judaism of the Second Temple Period* (Grand Rapids: Eerdmans, 2007), 1:10, also p. 17.

ignored by God when they petition him (1QS 2.1-10).[33] It is the community, however, and not national Israel that receives blessings.

The *Rule of the Congregation* (also known as the *Messianic Rule*, hereafter 1QSa) is appended to 1QS, where it is best preserved, though a number of fragments have been identified from Cave 4.[34] The text dates to around 100 B.C.E., though it may be dated earlier than that, depending on its relationship to the aforementioned fragments of Cave 4.[35] 1QSa is a guiding document for the community "in accordance with the regulation of the sons of Zadok, the priests, and the men of their covenant who have turn[ed away from the] path of the nation" (1QSa 1.1-2).[36] The obedience of the community to the covenant is performed "to ato[ne for the ear]th" (1QSa 1.3). Here, as Lawrence Schiffman describes, "We are told that through its adherence to its covenant with God, the sect had atoned for the land. . . . The sect's observance of the law prevented the destruction of the Jewish people who were otherwise deserving of so grievous a penalty."[37] So the community, as the remnant of Israel, prevents the complete destruction of Israel, while the nation on the whole stands under condemnation. The author refers to the community as "native Israelites" (1QSa 1.6), "Israel" (1QSa 1.14; 2.2, 14, 15, 20) and "the congregation of Israel" (1QSa 1.20; 2.12), indicating clearly that he viewed them as the true Israel. They no doubt saw their commitment to purity and obedience in the present as a reflection of what the community would look like in the eschaton, when the messiahs were present in their midst.[38]

The majority of Israel in the "now" stood outside of the covenant, and

---

[33]Timmer notes that even in its reformation of the priestly blessing of the OT in 1QS 2, the Qumran community identified itself as the recipients of the blessings and outsiders as under the covenant curses (Daniel C. Timmer, "Sectarianism and Soteriology: The Priestly Blessing (Numbers 6,24-26) in the Qumranite *Community Rule* (1QS)," *Biblica* 89 [2008]: 389-96).

[34]Géza G. Xeravits, "Rule of the Congregation (1Q28a)," in *The Eerdmans Dictionary of Early Judaism*, ed. John J. Collins and Daniel C. Harlow (Grand Rapids: Eerdmans, 2010), p. 1171.

[35]Ibid., p. 1172.

[36]For a discussion of the function of the leaders of the community, see Lawrence H. Schiffman, *The Eschatological Community of the Dead Sea Scrolls* (Atlanta: Society of Biblical Literature, 1989), pp. 28-36.

[37]Ibid., pp. 12-13.

[38]Ibid., pp. 68-71.

many Israelites would no doubt be excluded in the future as well, though it appears that the community expected their numbers to increase through the events of the last days, since the "th[ousands of Israel]" would be gathered at the messianic banquet (1QSa 2.15). Though there may be a future ingathering of Israelites into the community, nothing in the text indicates God would save "all of Israel" in the last days. Likewise, the emphasis on following the precise prescriptions of the new covenant indicates that inclusion in the community required adherence to the precepts given to them by God, the sons of Zadok and his messiahs.[39]

The *Rule of Blessings* (hereafter 1QSb), written around 100 B.C.E., is a partially preserved appendix to 1QS and 1QSa, which "apparently pertains to life in the messianic age following the eschatological restoration."[40] 1QSb offers a prayer of blessing for the community, which is composed of those who "keep his commandments, remaining constant in his holy co[ven]ant and walk with perfection [on all the paths of] his [tru]th, those he has chosen for an eternal covenant wh[ich] endures for ever" (1QSb 1.1-3). Though fragmentary, 1QSb draws a clear distinction between the community, on which the blessings of God are prayed, and those outside, who apparently are to be destroyed with no remnant because they are corrupt (1QSb 1.7; 3.7). The community receives these blessings because the sons of Zadok "have established [his covenant] in truth and have examined all his precepts in justice, and they have walked in accordance with wha[t] he chooses" (1QSb 3.24).

The *Pesher on Nahum* (hereafter 4QpNah) again predicts a coming judgment at the hands of the Kittim (4QpNah frags. 1 + 2, 1-9). Here the antagonist is "the Angry Lion," an allusion to Alexander Jannaeus,[41] who

---

[39]Elliott summarizes, "Even if, however, these columns from 1QSa allow an interpretation that relates them to a future gathering of *others* from Israel, it is crucial to note that this belief still does not entirely conflict with notions of judgment and exclusivity, inasmuch as *throughout the work the converts from Israel are said to join the community and to obey the ordinances taught by its members*. There is no such thing as a general restoration that does not have at its center the teaching and community organization already known by the sect" (Elliott, *Survivors of Israel*, p. 550 [emphasis original]).

[40]Daniel K. Falk, "Rule of Blessings (1QSb)," in Collins and Harlow, *Eerdmans Dictionary of Early Judaism*, p. 1168.

[41]See Horgan, *Pesharim*, p. 175.

struck "the simple folk of Ephraim" and took revenge against "those looking for easy interpretations" by hanging "living men [from the tree, committing an atrocity which had not been committed] in Israel since ancient times, for it is [hor]rible for the one hanged alive from the tree" (4QpNah frags. 3 + 4, 1.5-8).[42] Those who are "looking for easy interpretations" (the Pharisees)[43] are accused of walking "in treachery and lie[s]," thereby bringing judgment on the people through their "fraudulent teaching and lying tongue" (frags. 3 + 4, 2.1-8). Their evil deeds, however, "will be exposed to all Israel in the final time; many will fathom their sin, they will hate them and loathes them for their reprehensible arrogance," abandoning their teachings and joining instead "the [majori]ty [of I]srael" (frags. 3 + 4, 3.1-8). Though its ending is fragmentary, fragments 3 + 4, 4.1-8, also appears to predict the end of the influence of Manasseh (the Sadducees) and Ephraim (the Pharisees) over the people of Israel. The wicked Pharisees, Sadducees and temple cult, along with the Hasmonean king, clearly stood outside of the covenant community and thus would face judgment, along with those whom they led astray.

Though Gentiles (primarily the Romans) are identified as enemies of the community, it is primarily the apostates Jews, identified as the temple leadership, Pharisees, Sadducees and possibly even non-Qumranite Essenes,[44] along with all those whom they have led astray, who are outside of the covenant, and thus under the judgment of God.[45] While

---

[42]Yadin has suggested that 4QpNah approved of the crucifixion of the Pharisees, and thus Jannaeus was enacting God's judgment on the Pharisees, which was deserved because of their treachery (Yigael Yadin, "Pesher Nahum (4QpNahum) Reconsidered," *IEJ* 21 [1971]: 3-12). Martínez, among others, has argued against this hypothesis, noting that the strong language of the pesher and the quotation of Deut 21 seems to clearly condemn the action (Florentino García Martínez, "1QpNah y la Crucifixión: Nueva hipótesis de reconstrucción de 4Q 169 3-4 I, 4-8," *Estudios bíblicos* 38 [1979]: 221-35).

[43]See Horgan, *Pesharim*, p. 173.

[44]Even Sanders recognizes that "a study of the extant literature reveals that three different groups are considered outside the covenant: Gentiles, non-Essene Jews and apostate Essenes" (Sanders, *Paul and Palestinian Judaism*, p. 243). He maintains, however, that the sect did not view itself as the "true Israel," but rather as a "specially chosen part of Israel" (ibid., p. 247).

[45]Elliott summarizes, "The scroll writers were also well aware of the view that others in Israel were not believed to share in this corporeity, and so they could express their view of the community in a negative way also, that the rest of Israel would be judged according to their relationship to that community—namely, according to their treatment of it and their acceptance or nonacceptance of its revelation. It is almost as if the center of salvation had become the *yaḥad*

there exists now an opportunity for repentance, God's wrath will come against all who forsake the new covenant, including members of the community who commit apostasy. Israel remains as God's chosen people, but they now are identified as the remnant community. All who commit themselves to the community and its teachings may enjoy the blessings of the covenant and thus stand within the number of the elect.

Wisdom of Solomon. As the book opens, the Wisdom of Solomon assures that those who seek God will find him, while those who love folly and perversion will be exposed (Wis 1:1-3). Wisdom separates the righteous who possess her and the wicked who do not (Wis 1:4-5).[46] The lawless deeds (ἀνομημάτων αὐτοῦ) of the ungodly bring their conviction, and their folly opens an invitation to death (Wis 1:10-12). In language reminiscent of Isaiah 28, the ungodly, by their words and deeds, made a covenant with death, while the fate of the righteous is immortality (Wis 1:14-16).

Given that the offenses of the unrighteous are "lawlessness" and "against the law" (ἁμαρτήματα νόμου), it is reasonable to assume that apostate Jews who have forsaken their heritage and adopted pagan beliefs and behaviors are included in the number of the ungodly.[47] The

---

itself, leading to the conclusion that soteriology was to a point *defined* in terms of corporate identity" (Elliott, *Survivors of Israel*, p. 347 [emphasis original]).

[46]Harrington affirms, "'There can be no coexistence between God's wisdom and sin. On the one hand, wisdom refuses to 'enter a deceitful soul' or to 'dwell in a body enslaved to sin' (1:4). On the other hand, 'a holy and disciplined spirit' will have nothing to do with unrighteousness (1:5)" (Daniel J. Harrington, *Invitation to the Apocrypha* [Grand Rapids: Eerdmans, 1999], p. 58). See also Nickelsburg, *Jewish Literature*, p. 205. Pseudo-Solomon here goes on to note that while wisdom is a kind spirit, it does not free the guilty from their offenses (Wis 1:6).

[47]John J. Collins, *Jewish Wisdom in the Hellenistic Age* (Louisville: Westminster John Knox, 1997), p. 194; David A. deSilva, "Wisdom of Solomon," in *Dictionary of New Testament Background*, ed. Craig A. Evans and Stanley E. Porter (Downers Grove, IL: InterVarsity Press, 2000), p. 1271; Donald E. Gowan, "Wisdom," in *Justification and Variegated Nomism*, vol. 1, *The Complexities of Second Temple Judaism*, ed. D. A. Carson, Peter T. O'Brien and Mark A. Seifrid (Grand Rapids: Baker Academic, 2001), p. 226; Harrington, *Invitation to the Apocrypha*, pp. 59-60. Grabbe is particularly insightful in stating, "The righteous are never directly identified with the Jews, nor the wicked with the Gentiles. Since righteousness is closely associated with obedience to the law and knowledge of God (2.12), one would expect the righteous to be confined mostly to the Jewish people, but whether the author might have conceived of a 'righteous Gentile' is difficult to know. Similarly, to what extent the company of the wicked was thought to include Jews is unclear, though no doubt apostates (however defined) would have been included" (Lester Grabbe, *Wisdom of Solomon* [New York: T&T Clark, 1997], p. 51).

righteous, however, have assurance God will ultimately vindicate them
and reward them with immortality (Wis 3:1-6). Faithfulness is the condition for enjoying the presence of God, since

> grace and mercy are upon his holy ones,
> and he watches over his elect. (Wis 3:9; 4:15 NRSV)[48]

While James Crenshaw sees here, and in Wisdom 15:1-2, an affirmation of
the national and unconditional election of Israel,[49] this ignores the real,
and even likely, possibility that apostate Jews are a part of, or even are
primarily in view as, the wicked who will be judged because of their lawlessness. These unrighteous scoffers will be condemned by the righteous
(Wis 4:16),[50] and then will shamefully take their place among the dead,
coming to a fearful realization of their error (Wis 5:1-14). Again in Wisdom
5:15 and Wisdom 6:10, the faithful are rewarded with eternal fellowship
and life with God and made holy. The failure of the ungodly, Jews and
Gentiles, to honor Wisdom and faithfully follow God will result in their
destruction. Though not as explicit as texts like *Jubilees* or the Dead Sea
Scrolls, the Wisdom of Solomon subtly indicates that only a portion, even
if perhaps a majority, of Jews will receive the gift of immortality from God
as a reward for their faithful obedience to his commands.

Sibylline Oracles. Book three of the *Oracles*[51] has received the most
attention of the collection, and is more explicit in addressing the theme
of election, though it also raises several difficulties. It, like books one
and two, is also early in its original composition, and Rieuwerd Buitenwerf, for example, concludes the earliest portions of the third book
were "written by a Jew sometime between 80 and 40 BCE."[52] Specialists

---

[48]Here, Wright notes, "Lack of faith characterizes those whose membership in Israel is called into
question, whereas the true Israel have faith" (N. T. Wright, *Jesus and the Victory of God* [Min-
neapolis: Fortress, 1996], p. 260).

[49]James L. Crenshaw, *Old Testament Wisdom: An Introduction* (Louisville: Westminster John
Knox, 1998), p. 166.

[50]See Nickelsburg, *Jewish Literature*, p. 206.

[51]Collins states of this part of the collection, "It is generally agreed that the third book of sibylline
oracles is the oldest part of the Jewish and Christian corpus (John J. Collins, *The Sibylline Oracles
of Egyptian Judaism* [Missoula: University of Montana Press, 1972], p. 21).

[52]Rieuwerd Buitenwerf, *Book III of the Sibylline Oracles and Its Social Setting* (Leiden: Brill, 2003),
p. 130.

recognize the work as a composite, and John Collins suggests the original portion of the corpus includes 97-161; 162-195; 196-294; 545-656; 657-808.[53]

Sibylline Oracles 3.218-93 follows a series of prophecies against the nations and contains lofty praise of the Jews.[54] Within this praise of the Jews, the Sibyl states that they are "a race of most righteous men" (*Sib. Or.* 3.219), "always concerned with good counsel and noble works" (3.220), "care for righteousness and virtue and not love of money" (3.234-35). They furthermore do not practice astronomy or sorcery, do not steal from their neighbors and act generously toward the poor (*Sib. Or.* 3.225-47). The setting of these praises given by the oracle is apparently of the people ("in the land of Ur of the Chaldeans"; *Sib. Or.* 3.218) prior to the exodus, as the exit from Egypt and appointment of Moses is yet "future" (3.248-54). They will not escape, however, the aforementioned evil, which will come upon them in the form of the Assyrian captivity, an event prompted by their idolatry and general disobedience of the law of God (*Sib. Or.* 3.265-81).[55] Awaiting them on the other side of this period of judgment is "a good end and very great glory" in the form of a messianic king who will restore the people, punish their enemies and effect the building of a new temple of God (*Sib. Or.* 3.282-94). Throughout this section, there is no recognition on the part of the Sibyl of a "true Israel" or faithful remnant who receive the promised blessings as a result of their perseverance. While the perseverance of the people is expected (*Sib. Or.* 3.283-85), there is no explicit indication that an eschatological judgment awaits a portion of the Jewish people who are unfaithful.

The next section (*Sib. Or.* 3.573-808) follows after the pronouncement of oracles against the nations. The Sibyl here calls the Jews the "pious men" who keep the commands of God and honor the temple (*Sib. Or.* 3.573-83). They alone receive wisdom, faith and

---

[53]John J. Collins, "The Sibylline Oracles," in *Jewish Writings of the Second Temple Period*, ed. Michael E. Stone (Philadelphia: Fortress, 1984), 2:366.

[54]Buitenwerf notes the implicit tension here in stating, "On the one hand the Sibyl announces that she will describe the evil that will come upon the people living around the Jerusalem temple, on the other hand she states that she will praise them and their ancestors" (*Book III*, p. 197).

[55]Ibid., pp. 203-6.

knowledge (*Sib. Or.* 3.584-85), and they alone do not engage in sexually immoral behavior (3.594-600).[56] After a declaration of judgment against idolaters in *Sibylline Oracles* 3.601-18, the Sibyl calls for mortal men not to "tarry in hesitation but turn back, converted, and propitiate God." The call here for repentance and sacrifice is not directed specifically at Israel, but given as a general plea, though from the perspective of the Sibyl in book three, Israel alone honors God with sacrifices at the temple. This creates the possibility that those in need of repentance and sacrifice are apostate Jews, or those among the Jews who have neglected to uphold the law and are thus in need of God's mercy (*Sib. Or.* 3.628). Overall, however, the *Oracles* do not give much indication that Israel's election is limited to a remnant, the faithful, or a "true Israel," and thus largely stands outside of the majority of the literature of the period.

Testament of Moses. The *Testament of Moses* is another text of the period that frequently escapes attention. This may be due, perhaps in large part, to its uncertain textual history. As Kenneth Atkinson points out, "The *Testament of Moses* is a prophecy attributed to Moses that survives in a single, incomplete, partly illegible sixth-century C.E. Latin palimpsest in the Bibliotheca Ambrosiana in Milan, Italy."[57] We find the text listed, along with the *Assumption of Moses*, in several ancient apocryphal book lists,[58] but with no preserved ending it is impossible to identify the surviving manuscript with either title. Though the work survives in only a single manuscript, most scholars hold that the Latin text

---

[56]And so Buitenwerf states, "Although the author is not entirely consistent in treating this theme, the result is always the same: only the Jews serve the true God properly" (ibid., p. 261). Elsewhere, however, he notes, "According to the third Sibylline book, God will destroy the sinners and exalt the pious and righteous. The Jews are the only people who will all be saved because they are the only ones to live piously and virtuously (III 702-709). . . . This is not to say, however, that no pagan will be saved. By nature, every human being has knowledge of the divine principles of piety and righteousness. According to III 710-731, some pagans will acknowledge their mistakes in time and share in the glorious future" (ibid., p. 346).

[57]Kenneth Atkinson, "Taxo's Martyrdom and the Role of the *Nuntius* in the *Testament of Moses*: Implications for Understanding the Role of Other Intermediary Figures," *JBL* 125, no. 3 (2006): 454.

[58]See ibid., p. 454. For a discussion of the *Testament of Moses* and *Assumption of Moses*, and their possible distinctness and identification with known materials, see Fiona Grierson, "The Testament of Moses," *JSP* 17, no. 4 (2008): 265-80.

is a translation of a Greek translation of a Hebrew original,[59] originally predating 70 C.E.[60]

Moses' farewell message to Joshua begins with a recounting of the basic Deuteronomic formula: God has given the land to Israel, and they are to live in it under their appointed rulers and follow the law in order to receive God's blessing (*T. Mos.* 2:1-2). The specific sins mentioned are the violation of the covenant, sacrificing their children to other gods and making and worshiping idols in the temple (*T. Mos.* 2:7-9). The people will be exiled because of their disobedience, causing them to cry out and plead with God to remember the covenant (*T. Mos.* 3:1-9). Moses then predicts that, because of the intercession of the "one who is over them" (*T. Mos.* 4:1) and the invoking of the covenant, the people will be sent back to the land. Here Moses apparently alludes to the partial restoration of the people and the presence of a faithful remnant (*T. Mos.* 4:5-10). The author affirms Israel's election throughout chapter four as the intercessor recognizes the sin of the people and pleas for their deliverance.[61]

The emphasis on the partial faithfulness of Israel is again upheld in chapter five, when Moses states that kings will rise up to punish the people, causing them to "be divided as to the truth" (*T. Mos.* 5:1). The litany of the sins of the people include their lack of justice, pollution of the temple and idolatry (*T. Mos.* 5:3-4). The priests, leader and teachers (of the law) all stand guilty since they act corruptly, accept bribes and dishonor the law (*T. Mos.* 5:5). The author links these corrupt and malicious religious leaders with the Hasmoneans. The corruption of the city will bring judgment in the form of two powerful kings (Herod and Varus), who will persecute the people by killing the Jewish leaders

---

[59]See Craig A. Evans, *Ancient Texts for New Testament Studies: A Guide to the Background Literature* (Peabody, MA: Hendrickson, 2005), p. 43.

[60]Atkinson, "Taxo's Martyrdom," pp. 458-67. Regardless of its compositional history, Collins suggests, "in its present form the *Testament of Moses* must be dated around the turn of the era, since there is a clear allusion to the partial destruction of the temple in the campaign of Varus in 4 BCE (see 6:8-9)" (John J. Collins, "Testaments," in Stone, *Jewish Writings*, 2:347).

[61]And so Tromp notes, "It must be stressed that the people's restoration, which results from God's remembering them, is not presented as some kind of reward for their repentance; it is based solely on the covenant with the fathers. . . . The reason is to be found in God's autonomous promise to restore the covenant when the people repent" (Johannes Tromp, *The Assumption of Moses: A Critical Edition with Commentary* [Leiden: Brill, 1993], p. 178).

(Herod; see *Ant.* 17.8.1) and by destroying a portion of the temple and crucifying some of the Jews (Varus) (*T. Mos.* 6:1-9). Moses notes that these events will be like the period when the Hebrews were slaves in Egypt, likening their current plight to their situation prior to the exodus.[62] Moses foresees that after this time, the end of the age will come (*T. Mos.* 7:1). Johannes Tromp observes, "To him, the eschatological times are near. But the eschatological times will not start with the advent of God's kingdom (10:1-2). Unparalleled sinfulness and great woe will first come over the world,"[63] events that are described in *Testament of Moses* 7:1–8:5 and are characterized by the forced denouncement of Judaism.[64]

The apocalyptic tide turns, however, when the author introduces the figure of Taxo and his seven sons, from the tribe of Levi. Taxo laments the punishment of Israel but reminds his sons, "never did (our) fathers nor their ancestors tempt God by transgressing the commandments" (*T. Mos.* 9:4). Taxo here surely speaks of his ancestors in the sense of his family line, and not of Israel in general, as the book has indicted the nation on numerous occasions for its sins. Taxo thus can stand as a mediator for the nation, as he and his sons remained within the faithful remnant of Israel. Tromp and Atkinson note the contrast here between the Levitical line of Taxo and the priests serving in the temple who have profaned it.[65] Taxo vows, along with his sons, to flee rather than be forced to sin against God, expecting that God will avenge their deaths should they indeed perish (*T. Mos.* 10:6-7). Thus the author suggests that only a portion of his Jewish contemporaries actually belong to the people of God, something he deems true both for his time and for Israel's history.

Pseudo-Philo. I previously examined the conditional nature of

---

[62]See Tromp, *Assumption of Moses*, p. 202; Atkinson, "Taxo's Martyrdom," pp. 454, 476.

[63]Tromp, *Assumption of Moses*, p. 205. Kugler refers to this cycle of apostasy as "a catalogue of priestly sins (7:1-10) punished by a cornucopia of sufferings (7:1-8:5)" (Kugler, "Testaments," p. 1295).

[64]Priest notes, "This has been variously interpreted as an allusion to the fall of Jerusalem in 587 B.C., the Antiochan persecution, the capture of Jerusalem by Pompey in 63 B.C. or to some otherwise unknown historical event. It seems better to assume that the author has put together many past events that he believes are about to be replicated in the end-time" (John Priest, "Testament of Moses," in *The Old Testament Pseudepigrapha*, vol. 1, *Apocalyptic Literature and Testaments*, ed. James H. Charlesworth [1983; repr., Peabody, MA: Hendrickson, 2011], p. 931).

[65]Tromp, *Assumption of Moses*, p. 226; Atkinson, "Taxo's Martyrdom," p. 471.

election and covenant in pseudo-Philo, noting that the eternality of
God's commitment to the covenant did not entail that all Jews would be
among God's people. Preston Sprinkle, though recognizing that God
judges apostate Israelites,[66] suggests that the "most frequent tendency in
LAB is to affirm that all Israel will be rewarded with resurrection,"[67] and
"Individual Israelites are encouraged to repent from sin and obey the
Torah, but if they do not, God will save them nonetheless."[68] Frederick
Murphy likewise, though recognizing conditional elements in Israel's
receipt of covenant blessings,[69] states, "Pseudo-Philo conceives of the
covenant as unconditional. This is especially striking in that Pseudo-
Philo does not emphasize the notion of repentance found in Judges."[70]
Howard Jacobson has rightly critiqued this conclusion:

> LAB is generally strict on the matter of the responsibility of an individual
> (or a people) for his (its) own fate. Although God is merciful (e.g. 19.9), a
> sinner is obligated to repent his ways and in his lifetime (F.J. Murphy, *JSP*
> 1988, 43-57 seriously underestimates the role of repentance [= return to God:
> *Teshuva*] in LAB and fails to appreciate its relationship to God's mercy.
> There will be no ultimate salvation without repentance. See e.g. 21.6).[71]

In light of (1) the emphasis in the book on the retributive nature of
God's justice, (2) the affirmation, in the most explicitly eschatological
section of the book, that judgment is "according to [man's] works and
according to the fruits of his own devices" (*Bib. Ant.* 3.10), (3) the fact that
no sinner goes unpunished, and (4) the examples of the sinners of the
tribes of Israel in the days of Kenaz and Saul hoping for mercy in the afterlife instead of expecting it, it seems unnecessary to view God's faith-

---

[66]Preston M. Sprinkle, "The Hermeneutic of Grace: The Soteriology of Pseudo-Philo's *Biblical Antiquities*," in *This World and the World to Come: Soteriology in Early Judaism*, ed. Daniel M. Gurtner (New York: T&T Clark, 2011), p. 53.

[67]Ibid., p. 58. Sprinkle recognizes "two possible exceptions" to the expectation of national resurrection, even of the disobedient, in *Bib. Ant.* 3.10 and *Bib. Ant.* 64.7 (ibid., pp. 59-60).

[68]Ibid., p. 66.

[69]"God has chosen Israel and remains eternally faithful to the covenant. However, every sin will receive its recompense, and membership in the chosen people does not guarantee salvation, either in this world or the next" (Frederick J. Murphy, *Pseudo-Philo: Rewriting the Bible* [Oxford: Oxford University Press, 1993], p. 233).

[70]Ibid., p. 246.

[71]Howard Jacobson, *A Commentary on Pseudo-Philo's* Liber Antiquitatum Biblicarum *with Latin Text and English Translation* (Leiden: Brill, 1996), 1:246.

fulness and the conditionality present throughout the work as mutually exclusive concepts. Here, as has been seen in various other places, we should understand the covenant as eternal even if the people are not eternally obedient. In pseudo-Philo, God can remain faithful to the covenant by not casting off Israel, even if every member of the current generation is utterly wicked and punished. The covenant will not perish because God swore to the fathers that he would uphold it, because he knows some Israelites will keep it and because he will raise up godly leaders, like Kenaz, Samuel and David, to constantly remind the people of their need to keep it. To ignore the conditional elements and the importance of the law in the work is ultimately to reject its purpose for its readers.[72] If the purpose of the work is to call Jews at the present to obedience to the law and to warn them of the results of disobedience, it would do little good to affirm that their eternal status is in no way affected by their present life. It seems that the author's contemporaries were living like Gentiles and abandoning their religious identity.[73] If one sees the conditionality of the covenant as still present, as the work seems to indicate, this can function alongside God's unwavering commitment to Israel. It need not be that every Israelite, including apostates, sinners and the wicked, receive the reward of resurrection and eternal life. Rather, God is faithful to the covenant by not forsaking Israel, even when he should, and is true to his word to bless and save those who remain faithful to his prescripts.[74] So again, for pseudo-Philo, many Jews stand outside of the people of God.

GENTILE INCLUSION AND EXCLUSION

Most texts of the Second Temple period preoccupy themselves with the

---

[72]See Eckart Reinmuth, "'Nicht Vergeblich' Bei Paulus und Pseudo-Philo, Liber Antiquitatum Biblicarum," *NovT* 33, no. 2 (1991): 122; Michael Tilly, "Die Sünden Israels und der Heiden Beobachtungen Zu *L.A.B.* 25:9-13," *JSJ* 37, no. 2 (2006): 211.

[73]Murphy remarks, "Pseudo-Philo's choice of Israel's premonarchic period as his subject is significant. He chose a period when Israel was living in the land but was dominated by foreigners. Such contact led to impurities in Israel's religion, as Judges makes clear. . . . Skepticism about the divine status of the law, about the holiness of God's Temple, about God's ability to punish evildoers and those who oppress Israel may be things that he observes in his own community" (Frederick J. Murphy, "Retelling the Bible: Idolatry in Pseudo-Philo," *JBL* 107, no. 2 [1988]: 286).

[74]See VanLandingham, *Judgment and Justification*, p. 32.

election of Israel and the identity of the "true Israel," which thereby relates to the fate of individual Israelites depending on whether they possess the right "markers." Some texts also, however, deal with Gentile "outsiders." This attention usually comes in one of several different schemes. For some authors, Gentiles are outsiders and have no hope for becoming a part of God's people. Others preoccupy themselves with the fate of the Jewish people and pay little attention to Gentile outsiders. Others still express a hope for the inclusion of the nations in the people of God, a hope usually reserved for the eschaton.

Tobit. In its closing chapters the book of Tobit makes a brief mention of the fate of the nations. At the time when God will restore the faithful of Israel, the author states that the nations too will fear God and will put away their idols (Tob 13:11-13; 14:6-7). They will do so with all who love God "in truth and justice" (Tob 14:7). For Tobit, then, like the hopes of the Old Testament prophets, Israel's restoration will result in the drawing of the nations to God through their upright behavior. The author leaves the details of this inclusion unknown but does affirm that the nations will have some share in the future with the chosen people of God.

Sibylline Oracles. In book one, the author offers a summary of Noah and the flood (*Sib. Or.* 1.125-306). The human race had fallen into a deplorable state, and judgment was imminent. As Collins notes, the world was guilty of sins of violence, deceit, adultery, slander and irreverence for God. Following the fifth generation of insolent men, God tells Noah to "proclaim repentance to all the peoples, so that all may be saved. But if they do not heed, since they have a shameless spirit, I will destroy the entire race with great floods of waters," though Noah "and as many as live with [him] will be saved" (*Sib. Or.* 1.128-36). Here God extends the offer of salvation from the flood to the entire race, conditioned on the repentance of the people and their avoidance of the aforementioned sins.

In book three, following a prediction of a "King from the sun who will stop the entire earth from evil war" (3.652-53), the gathering of the kings of the earth to siege the temple (3.657-68) and the judgment of God over "all the impious" (3.669-701), the Sibyl declares, "the sons of the great God will all live peacefully around the Temple" (*Sib. Or.* 3.702-3),[75] for God "will shield them" (3.705) and "will be fighting for them" (3.709). This will prompt "all islands and cities" to recognize the greatness of the Most High God, renounce their idolatry and to ponder the law (*Sib. Or.* 3.710-23). The author gives a final moral exhortation in *Sibylline Oracles* 3.762-66, where the Sibyl urges the people to worship only the living God, avoid adultery and sexual sins, and to not sacrifice their children, "for the Immortal is angry at whoever commits these sins" (*Sib. Or.* 7.766). The book ends with a summary of the peace and prosperity of the eschatological kingdom, to which "every land will bring incense and gifts" (*Sib. Or.* 3.772), and which is given "to faithful men" (3.775).

While the fate of the Gentiles is uncertain in book two, book three indicates that, at the eschaton, the nations will recognize the God of Israel for who he is and begin to worship him. The *Sibylline Oracles* thus offer hope, at least eschatologically and possibly in the "now," for Gentiles to come to worship the God of the Jews.

Testament of Moses. The *Testament* begins with an introduction of Moses and Joshua, setting the words that follow in the form of a dialogue between Israel's leaders, as Moses commissions Joshua to lead the people after Moses' death (*T. Mos.* 1:1-9). Moses states here that God has decreed that "He created the world on behalf of his people, but he did not make this purpose of creation openly known from the beginning of the world so that the nations might be found guilty, indeed that they might abjectly declare themselves guilty by their own (mistaken) discussions (of creation's purpose)" (*T. Mos.* 1:12-13).[76] For the author of the *Testament*, God's purpose in calling a people to himself was not to bless the nations through them, but rather to preserve a people for himself while allowing the nations to continue in ignorance.

---

[75]Buitenwerf states, "In line 702 the phrase 'sons of (the great) God' is used. In Jewish literature of the period, it is sometimes used to distinguish between righteous and wicked people. Although this usage may have occasioned the author to use the phrase, its primary function here is to distinguish between Jews and non-Jews" (Buitenwerf, *Book III*, p. 280).

[76]Tromp suggests that "this concept should not be taken as some kind of metaphysical conviction about the reasons and motifs for creation, but rather as a strong expression of the idea of Israel's election" (Tromp, *Assumption of Moses*, p. 141).

While the nations will face judgment, God will ultimately preserve his people, which is composed of faithful Jews. Thus, unlike some texts of the period, the author gives no suggestion of hope for the Gentiles here. Their fate is to face the destruction God planned for them from the beginning of the world.

1 Enoch. In the Book of Dreams, following the deliverance of the sheep (Israel) from the animals (Gentiles) through the ram (Judas Maccabeus), the people erect a throne in the land, and the Lord comes to judge (*1 En.* 90:20-21). God judges the disobedient stars and shepherds (angels) first and casts them into the fiery abyss, followed by the blinded sheep (apostate Jews), who meet a similar fate (*1 En.* 90:22-27). Thus, here, the disobedient Jews, along with the fallen angels, all face eschatological judgment for their sin.[77] The Lord of the sheep then brings forth a new house, and he gives the snow-white sheep who had survived authority over the animals of the earth (*1 En.* 90:28-36). Then a snow-white bull with large horns (Messiah) is born, and all of the animals of the earth make petition to him. These all become snow-white cows, indicating a return to the original state of the earth, with all the animals (Jews and Gentiles!)[78] transformed into the original glory of the first snow-white cow (Adam) (*1 En.* 90:37-39). With this, Enoch's visions are completed (*1 En.* 90:40-42). The passage uniquely presents the large-scale inclusion of Gentiles, likely those who had not oppressed Israel,[79] in the eschatological people of God, resulting in one, righteous humanity,[80] now united in their worship of the one true God. The author thus seems to eliminate all distinctions between Jews and Gentiles.

---

[77]So Elliott suggests, "It is difficult to avoid the conclusion, given this colorful description of *Israel's* judgment, that the author was so completely at odds with the present situation in his homeland that he was unhindered by nationalistic doctrines from pronouncing on an apostate nation its judgment in the most extreme terms" (Elliott, *Survivors of Israel*, p. 80).

[78]Tiller notes, "The theological implications of this situation are quite surprising. The existence of the separate nations, one of which is Israel, is apparently seen as one of the negative effects of human history that the ideal future will undo" (Patrick A. Tiller, *A Commentary on the Animal Apocalypse of* I Enoch [Atlanta: Scholars Press, 1993], p. 20).

[79]See Matthew Black, *The Book of Enoch or I Enoch: A New English Edition* (Leiden: Brill, 1985), p. 279.

[80]George W. E. Nickelsburg, *1 Enoch*, Hermeneia (Minneapolis: Fortress, 2001), 1:407.

PAUL AND EXTENT

We have again observed some unevenness on our topic in the Jewish literature of the Second Temple Period. Most writings view only a portion, whether a majority or a minority, of Jews as being the "true Israel" who are faithful to God. With rare exceptions (*Sibylline Oracles*), the dominant paradigm is that God's choice of Israel clearly does not entail the salvation of every individual Jew, and often (especially in *Psalms of Solomon*, Dead Sea Scrolls, *Testament of Moses* and pseudo-Philo) a majority of Jews appear to be under God's judgment. We also observed this unevenness concerning the fate of the Gentiles. Most texts either do not hold out any explicit hope for the Gentiles (Baruch, *Sibylline Oracles*, pseudo-Philo) or deny even the possibility (*Testament of Moses*). Some, however, view the conversion of the Gentiles as an event reserved for the eschaton, when Israel is restored and the nations come to know YHWH (Tobit, Wisdom of Ben Sira, *Sibylline Oracles*, *1 Enoch*). It is in this context that we find Paul's somewhat (though not completely!) startling discussion of the place of Jews and Gentiles in the people of God.

Romans 3:21–4:17. The issue of the place of Jews and Gentiles in the people of God is a frequent topic of discussion in Paul, dominating the book of Romans, but also spilling over into several other Pauline epistles. I will limit my discussion here to two passages: Romans 3:21–4:17 and Ephesians 2:11-22. Here in Romans, Paul has been building up an argument prior to this section to show that Jewish privilege does not guarantee the salvation of the Jew since both Jews and Gentiles are under sin (Rom 3:9). The Jews certainly did have advantages as stewards of the message of God, but the nation was not faithful to its calling (Rom 3:1-8).[81] Paul's point largely seems to be that God does not show partiality in

---

[81]I do think N. T. Wright has a point that there are at least undertones of that being the Jewish privilege in mind by Paul. Paul's questioning here obviously concerns who is πίστις. Wright contends that Israel was entrusted with a commission to declare the "good news," as it were, to the Gentiles so that God would accomplish his purposes in the world, a commission they failed to fulfill. As he summarizes, "*The faithfulness of God* at the end of verse 3 is then, still, the determination of the covenant God to do what he has promised, even if the people through whom the promised blessings were to be delivered seem to have let him down through their own 'faithlessness'" (N. T. Wright, *Paul and the Faithfulness of God* [Minneapolis: Fortress, 2013], pp. 837-38).

judgment, but rather judges each based on the life lived (Rom 2:1-11).[82] Part of the tension, as becomes evident in our section, Paul seeks to resolve concerns whether God has done something wrong in this "new" arrangement.[83] Paul must bring, of course, more into the discussion than "living a good life," so to speak.[84] In the immediate context, however, that is not Paul's primary concern.

In Romans 3:21–4:17 Paul's discussion comes to the very narrow point of what it means for Gentiles to be included in the people of God.[85] Paul discloses that now God has revealed his "rightness" apart from the Law (Rom 3:21). This means, more specifically, God's rightness displayed in the faithfulness of Jesus (Rom 3:22).[86] Scholars have debated few passages as heavily and heatedly as this section of Paul's argument, which includes both the contested ideas of the "righteousness of God" and the

---

[82]This section of Romans has been particularly controversial since Paul suggests what amounts to a judgment based on works. Many solutions have been proposed from the statement representing the thoughts of Paul's interlocutor or a "typical" Jew, to Paul setting up a straw man or false view that he will proceed to tear down. From my vantage point, nothing in the passage suggests Paul is doing anything other than speaking his own view, but that it is in the context of the "new" covenant (see Rom 2:15), and the details of this tension (merit-based judgment and "human works" versus the grace and sovereignty of God) will be worked out throughout the letter. We will return to this point in later chapters.

[83]As Hays nicely puts it, "If Paul's gospel now somehow invalidates the special relationship established through these past events, it means that God's past dealing with his people was false dealing, that he made promises on which he is now backing out. Paul, however, is committed to the affirmation that the God who raised Jesus from the dead is the same God who gave the promises to Israel; consequently, the trustworthiness of the God who made these promises must be affirmed. This issue is, at bottom, the question of God's integrity" (Richard B. Hays, "Psalm 143 and the Logic of Romans 3," *JBL* 99, no. 1 [1980]: 109).

[84]For Paul "right living" before God for Paul only comes through the empowerment of God's Spirit. Likewise, the impartation of the Spirit only comes to those "in Christ."

[85]Hays argues convincingly that Paul is dealing with the same subject in this section as what has preceded it, showing that Paul's use of Ps 143 in Rom 3:20 follows the trajectory of the Jew-Gentile issue rather than as an abstract theological principle (Hays, "Logic of Romans 3," pp. 107-15). Campbell has argued that the chapter is integral to the development of further themes throughout the letter, and rightly notes that central to all of it is the relationship of Jews and Gentiles in the family of God (W. S. Campbell, "Romans III as a Key to the Structure and Thought of the Letter," *NovT* 23, no. 1 [1981]: 22-40).

[86]As Wright says in connection with Rom 3:3, "By speaking of the Messiah's 'faithfulness,' Paul clearly intends to relate the action (or passion) of the Messiah to the purpose of God to which Israel had been *un*faithful. . . . By speaking of the Messiah's death as an act of 'faithfulness' Paul makes it clear that what is accomplished through the Messiah (through the-Messiah-as-Israel-in-person) is the fulfilment of the active will and purpose of the covenant God" (Wright, *Paul and the Faithfulness of God*, p. 842).

"faithfulness of Jesus Christ."[87] While both of these issues have vital importance for understanding this passage, space does not permit a full discussion.[88] In my view, Paul clarifies in Romans 3:25-26 that God maintained his "rightness" through the public execution of Jesus.[89] In other words, as N. T. Wright, Richard Hays and others have argued, God did the right thing even when Israel, and humans in general, did not do right by God. God displayed his rightness through the faithful obedience of Jesus, even to the point of death.[90] This stands in contrast to humans, both Jews and Gentiles as indicated by πάντες in Romans 3:23, who universally are guilty of sin and thus have become subject to the power of death.[91] Paul's point here, however, does not involve so much proving that each individual person is a sinner but rather both of these groups, Jews and Gentiles, stand at God's mercy because of their sins and failures.[92]

Paul stands convinced that God's action through Jesus brought a sig-

---

[87]A work largely credited with accelerating the discussion is Richard B. Hays, *The Faith of Jesus Christ: The Narrative Substructure of Galatians 3:1–4:11*, SBLDS 56 (Chico: Scholars Press, 1983). See also George Howard, "Romans 3:21-31 and the Inclusion of the Gentiles," *HTR* 63 (1970): 223-33; Bruce W. Longenecker, "ΠΙΣΤΙΣ in Romans 3.25: Neglected Evidence for the 'Faithfulness of Christ'?" *NTS* 39 (1993): 478-80; Luke Timothy Johnson, "Rom 3:21-26 and the Faith of Jesus," *CBQ* 44 (1982): 77-90. For a structural argument against the so-called subjective genitive view, see R. Barry Matlock, "The Rhetoric of πίστις in Paul: Galatians 2.16, 3.22, Romans 3.22, and Philippians 3.9," *JSNT* 30, no. 2 (2007): 173-203.

[88]Though note the helpful discussions in the secondary literature mentioned throughout.

[89]On Jesus as ἱλαστήριον, Dunn suggests, "Properly speaking, in the Israelite cult, God is never 'propitiated' or 'appeased.' The objective of the atoning act is rather the removal of *sin*—that is, either by purifying the person or object, or wiping out the sin. . . . The atoning act thus removes the sin which provoked God's wrath, but it does so by acting on the sin rather than on God" (James D. G. Dunn, *The Theology of Paul the Apostle* [Grand Rapids: Eerdmans, 1998], p. 214).

[90]I take this, then, to refer more directly to what God has done in Christ than "how a person gets saved." For discussions of the various interpretations of justification in this passage, see Walter A. Maier, "Paul's Concept of Justification, and Some Recent Interpretations of Romans 3:21-31," *Springfielder* 37 (1974): 248-64; Thomas D. Stegman, SJ, "Paul's Use of *dikaio*- Terminology: Moving Beyond N. T. Wright's Forensic Interpretation," *TS* 72 (2011): 496-524.

[91]Blackwell rightly argues that "lacking glory" in Rom 3:23 most likely refers to corruptibility and death, which is the result of sin. As he states, "If the human experience of 'the glory of God' is a participation in divine incorruption, the lack of glory signifies the condition of corruption and mortality. Thus, in 3.23 Paul associates universal sin with universal mortality" (Ben C. Blackwell, "Immortal Glory and the Problem of Death in Romans 3.23," *JSNT* 32, no. 3 [2010]: 300).

[92]See J. William Johnston, "Which 'All' Sinned? Rom 3:23-24 Reconsidered," *NovT* 53 (2011): 153-64.

nificant shift in the unfolding plan of God for humanity. While the law for a time functioned to mark off the people of God, something both Paul and his Jewish contemporaries would have accepted, now union with the anointed one, Jesus, alone constituted the defining marker of God's people. Jesus' obedience[93] brought the means by which God might declare all people right with him and impart eschatological life to them. Both Jews and Gentiles with no distinction. Paul states that the "works of the law" no longer constitute the fundamental identification of God's people.[94] Paul likely does not mean by this phrase that the law required perfect obedience, something no person could accomplish, or that only certain commands were the essential markers.[95] While circumcision and separation from Gentiles were elevated in the Second Temple period, we have seen that a debate persisted among the various Jewish authors as to what conditions or markers defined God's people. "Works of the law" may have meant different things to different Jews and, like in Galatians, Paul probably more has in mind law keeping as a fundamental form of identity-definition versus participation in Jesus' faithfulness as the central, and indeed only, means of identification with God. The larger point Paul makes throughout Romans, though especially here in Romans 3 and Romans 4, affirms that Gentiles need not do what the Jewish law expected (e.g., circumcision) in order for God to declare them "in the right," or otherwise Gentiles would remain as outsiders.[96] As Wright summarizes this section, he suggests (and I think rightly, no pun intended),

---

[93]I take this to be the basic idea of the "faithfulness of Jesus Christ." For a helpful discussion of the theological implications of the view, see David L. Stubbs, "The Shape of Soteriology and the *Pistis Christou Debate*," *SJT* 61, no. 2 (2008): 137-57.

[94]It is certainly possible Paul would admit that they once did. If we get past the idea that Paul is discussing right and wrong ways to be saved (works or faith), and place this argument in a salvation-historical lens, that possibility becomes far less controversial. Suggesting that Jews were right with God by keeping the "old" covenant does not, of course, diminish God's grace or sovereignty. This was simply the arrangement God had designed, and the Jewish people were obligated to follow it as he intended. There are far more parallels here between the structuring of the "new" covenant and the "old" than are often admitted.

[95]This, of course, is a central interpretive tenet of Dunn and Wright. It seems to me that the diverse nature of Judaism would prevent us from being too decisive about what made up the "works of the law," but that it serves as a way of understanding God's people as marked out by the centrality of the Torah seems certain.

[96]See Wright, *Paul and the Faithfulness of God*, p. 1001.

Paul is thus taking themes to do with the establishment and renewal of the covenant *with* Israel and using them, completely consistently with his vision of the covenant purpose *through* Israel, to explain what the covenant God, who is also the creator God, has now done for all people, Jew and Gentile alike. This is all part of his redefinition of election.[97]

This brings us, then, to Romans 3:30, where Paul states that God "will declare right the circumcision from faith and the uncircumcision through faith." Stanley Stowers has noted that commentators of this verse in the history of interpretation have frequently overlooked or attributed Paul's different prepositions describing how God declares Jews (ἐκ) and Gentiles (διά) right as it relates to faith(fulness) to stylistic variation.[98] Citing Origen and Theodore of Mopsuestia, Stowers notes that a minority of interpreters have recognized that Paul is making some sort of distinction between the two, though disagreements about what constitutes the distinction exist. While Stowers opts for a sort of "two ways" conclusion where Paul does not see the atonement of Jesus as decisive for Jews but only Gentiles (which seems unlikely given the train of thought begun in Rom 3:9), it seems Paul does make some sort of distinction here. In my mind, Paul continues his understanding of Jewish advantage whereby the Jews already had a position "from within" (ἐκ) the covenant while Gentiles came in as outsiders "through" (διά) Jesus' faithfulness. We might say for the Jews this was a covenant re(new)al (i.e., the long-awaited renewal of the covenant that would take the form of Jeremiah and Ezekiel's "new covenant," though obviously in ways departing from Jewish expectations), while for the Gentiles this covenant relationship was now newly extended to them, as outsiders, as well. Departing from Stowers, I would argue that for Paul, Jesus' faithfulness serves as the decisive factor for both Jews and Gentiles, though their historic positions up to that point stood in stark contrast.[99]

---

[97]Ibid., p. 998.

[98]Stanley K. Stowers, "*Ek pisteos* and *dia es pisteos* in Romans 3:30," *JBL* 108, no. 4 (1989): 665-74.

[99]As Wright summarizes, "One is reckoned to be within the justified people, those whom this God has declared 'righteous,' 'forgiven,' 'members of the covenant,' on the basis of *pistis* and that alone. That—the Messiah's faithfulness, in which his people share through their own *pistis* as in (my reading of) 3.26, and also in 4.24-25—is the basic sign of membership" (*Paul and the Faithfulness of God*, p. 847).

In Romans 4, Paul turns again to Abraham to defend the case he has laid out.[100] As usual, Paul ventures into a dense discussion of the issue, and I cannot tease out every important aspect of it here. Paul's purpose here is more or less to support his argument against works of the law being a decisive factor, or a factor at all, in how God now declares people right with him.[101] Paul's assertion in Romans 3:21-31 declaring that God had done the right thing by the work of Jesus now finds its historical and theological footing in the case of Abraham. Paul does not contrast, as I have already suggested, works and faith as two ways (one right and one wrong) of trying to find salvation, but rather argues decisively that "works of the law" do not serve as a permanent and universal marker of the people of God.[102]

Paul offers, of course, a competing narrative against at least some of his Jewish contemporaries who elevated the behavior of Abraham and even saw him as a faithful keeper of the Torah.[103] Though chronologically we might call this anachronistic, it posed no problem for at least some Jews of the period to imagine that Abraham could live faithfully, even blamelessly, according to the Torah, in part since they viewed the Torah as eternal. Paul inquires in Romans 4:1 if we have "found Abraham to be our forefather according to the flesh?"[104] For Paul, God inaugurated the

---

[100]For a summary of interpretive approaches, see N. T. Wright, "Paul and the Patriarch: The Role of Abraham in Romans 4," *JSNT* 35, no. 3 (2013): 207-9. On connections between Romans 1 and 4, see Edward Adams, "Abraham's Faith and Gentile Disobedience: Textual Links Between Romans 1 and 4," *JSNT* 65 (1997): 47-66.

[101]Or "liberates" them, as Campbell argues should be the basic meaning of much of the δικαι-language through Paul's letters (Douglas A. Campbell, *The Deliverance of God: An Apocalyptic Re-Reading of Justification in Paul* [Grand Rapids: Eerdmans, 2013]).

[102]See Michael Cranford, "Abraham in Romans 4: The Father of All Who Believe," *HTR* 41 (1995): 72-73. "The 'works' in view here should not be lifted out of context and imbued with significance arising from the theological concerns of the Reformation; the works in view are clearly those which are of the law (3.20, 28) and which function primarily to designate who is and who is not a Jew (3.22, 29-30)" (ibid., p. 77). Both Sprinkle and Schreiner contest this interpretation, largely on the basis of Romans 9, which I will address in a later chapter (Preston M. Sprinkle, *Paul and Judaism Revisited: A Study of Divine and Human Agency in Salvation* [Downers Grove, IL: IVP Academic, 2013], pp. 148-60; Thomas R. Schreiner, *Paul, Apostle of God's Glory in Christ: A Pauline Theology* [Downers Grove, IL: InterVarsity Press, 2001], pp. 112-15).

[103]E.g., Sir 44:20; 1 Macc 2:52; *Jub* 15:1-2; 16:20-21. See also Adams, "Abraham's Faith," pp. 47-66; Francis Watson, *Paul, Judaism and the Gentiles: A Sociological Approach* (Cambridge: Cambridge University Press, 1986), pp. 136-37.

[104]"If we understand Ἀβραάμ not as the subject but as the direct object of the infinitive εὑρηκέναι,

covenant (which is of course the context of Genesis 15)[105] apart from Abraham yet following the Torah, since he was not yet circumcised when God made the covenant with him (Rom 4:10-11),[106] something the Torah itself bears witness to.[107] Abraham was not simply an example of one whom God declared right apart from following Torah, but rather Abraham first received the covenant and became the father of the whole family of God.[108] If God declared Abraham right apart from Torah, how much more would he for those in Christ, regardless of ethnicity! As Hays puts it, "The crucial issue in the chapter is not how Abraham got himself justified but rather whose father he is and in what way his children are related to him."[109] Paul's argument here inverts the typical Jewish opinion of Abraham as the father of Israel and makes Abraham the first Gentile convert whom God declared "right" apart from keeping the law.[110] Paul here likely even alludes to Abraham as the "ungodly" one whom God declares "in the right" through faith.[111] If God could declare "ungodly"

---

whose subject would then be understood as the 'we' of the immediately preceding ἐρουμεν, we could translate the verse in the following way: 'What then shall we say? Have we found Abraham (to be) our forefather according to the flesh?'" (Richard B. Hays, "Have We Found Abraham to Be Our Forefather According to the Flesh?," *NovT* 28, no. 1 [1985]: 81. See also Wright, "Paul and the Patriarch," pp. 226-29).

[105]See Wright, "Paul and the Patriarch," p. 210.

[106]Adams argues that Paul's allusions to Romans 1 and his allusions to Jewish traditions concerning Abraham reinforce his point that Abraham is not only a model for Jews but as a converted Gentile is a model for Gentiles as well (Adams, "Abraham's Faith," p. 62).

[107]Hays writes, "Interpreters of Romans have long recognized that the discussion of Abraham in Chap. 4 is an attempt to give some exegetical grounding to this provocative claim that the gospel confirms rather than overturns the Law by showing that the Law already teaches that Abraham was justified by faith" (Hays, "Have We Found," p. 86).

[108]See Cranford, "Abraham in Romans 4," p. 87. Wright has argued that the "reward" (μισθὸς) Paul has in mind has nothing to do with meriting salvation and everything to do with Gen 15:1, which is likely an echo to God's plan to have an innumerable people through Abraham (Wright, "Paul and the Patriarch," pp. 210-15).

[109]Hays, "Have We Found," p. 97. See also Ambrosiaster, *Commentary on Paul's Epistles*, in *Romans*, ed. Gerald Bray, Ancient Christian Commentary on Scripture, New Testament 6 (Downers Grove, IL: InterVarsity Press, 1998), p. 109.

[110]As Adams states well, "Rather, the case of Abraham indicates how God justifies Gentiles *while they remain Gentiles*. Three times over in vv. 11-12, it is emphasized that Abraham was in a state of uncircumcision—ἐν (τῇ) ἀκροβυστίᾳ—when he was accepted by God. While this means that Abraham was justified before he had submitted to the *rite* of circumcision, ἀκροβυστίᾳ is probably also intended to signify Abraham's *ethnic status* at the time (4.9; cf. 2.26-27)" (Adams, "Abraham's Faith," p. 62).

[111]See Cranford, "Abraham in Romans 4," p. 82.

(i.e., uncircumcised) Abraham right with him, could he not do so for Gentiles by the same means and in the same respect? Or, to invert the question, if God only declares people right with him through the works of the law, this excludes Abraham himself![112]

The fact that Paul works toward this point in the whole of the passage finds confirmation in his conclusion.[113] In the conclusion, he asserts,

> Therefore "it was credited to him for rightness" [Gen 15:6]. Now this was not written because of him alone, that "it was credited to him" but also because of us, to whom it is going to be credited, to those who are trusting upon the one who raised Jesus our Lord from among the dead ones, who was handed over because of our trespasses and was raised because of our acquittal. (Rom 4:22-25)

Abraham's trust in God provided the inaugural grounds by which God would declare "in the right" all those who trust the work of God's Messiah Jesus. His receipt of "rightness" with God came while he was still uncircumcised (Rom 4:10-11), allowing him to become the father of many nations (Rom 4:17-18; i.e., not just Israel),[114] circumcised and uncircumcised (Rom 4:12). And all of this took place prior to the giving of the law (Rom 4:13),[115] thereby serving as the basis by which God would unite Jews and Gentiles in one people through the covenant with Abraham, brought to completion in the resurrection of Jesus Christ.[116] Paul thus counters a prevalent Jewish narrative con-

---

[112]As Hays notes, the law itself is what confirms that Paul's argument is correct (Hays, "Have We Found," p. 88).

[113]Jipp notes the importance of keeping Paul's conclusion (Rom 4:23-25) in mind in examining this section, as many commentators seem to force Paul to go in a direction that his conclusion does not support (Joshua W. Jipp, "Rereading the Story of Abraham, Isaac, and 'Us' in Romans 4," *JSNT* 32, no. 2 [2009]: 228-29).

[114]Forman argues that Paul includes echoes of Isaiah 54 in this section and thereby connects the Abrahamic covenant and inheritance of land with the prophetic expectation and the future inheritance of those in Christ (Mark Forman, "The Politics of Promise: Echoes of Isaiah 54 in Romans 4.19-21," *JSNT* 31, no. 3 [2009]: 301-24).

[115]As we noted in Galatians 2, Snodgrass says of our passage here, "If the law is viewed as a sphere in keeping with Paul's participationist language, the statements in Rom. 4.13-16 become clearer. Paul's point here is that law is not the sphere from which the promise and salvation come. In 4.16 the promise does not belong only to those in the sphere of the law. It is also addressed to those having faith" (Klyne Snodgrass, "Spheres of Influence: A Possible Solution to the Problem of Paul and the Law," *JSNT* 32 [1988]: 103).

[116]"Paul sees the fulfillment of God's promise to give Abraham a son as something which was

cerning the place (or lack thereof) of Gentiles in the people of God.[117] It is "from faith" (i.e., prior to the law) so the promise could come to all descendants. If it came "from within the law" the promise would have validity only for the Jews (Rom 4:16). It is in this sense, then, that the promise to inherit the world (Rom 4:13) becomes nullified if God sets people right only through the works of the law, because then the world (i.e., Gentiles) are actually excluded (4:16-17).[118]

The point repeated throughout Romans 4 emphasizes that the unity of God's people could only come to completion outside of the law, not within it—Jews and Gentiles united in God's Messiah and his resurrection. We would do well to repeat, then, that the point Paul presents does not concern right and wrong ways of approaching God (works versus faith), but rather the covenant with Abraham coming to fruition apart from the law, just as God had inaugurated it in the first place.[119] And just as God maintained his promise in spite of "the deadness" (τὴν νέκρωσιν) of Sarah's womb (Rom 4:19), so he fulfilled it in spite of the deadness of the Messiah by raising him from among the dead (ἐκ νεκρῶν; Rom 4:24). As God began the promise, so he also completed it, apart from the law and through the demonstration of his power over death. So too those who trust in God's Messiah, like Abraham, who believed God would bring life from the dead, hope in their own future resurrection. God has publicly demonstrated his rightness through Jesus' faithfulness to death, raising him from the dead so that all who share in his faithfulness, from all the nations, might equally join in God's family and ultimately share in his vindication. Jesus thus fulfills the covenant program begun with Abraham so it might accomplish its divinely intended goal of creating a family from all the nations, who can equally call Abraham their father.

---

mediated not through circumcision, but through Abraham's own faithfulness in and toward the God who gives life to the dead" (Jipp, "Rereading the Story," p. 239).

[117] Cranford, "Abraham in Romans 4," p. 86.

[118] Thus we might suggest that the reason the law brings about wrath (Rom 4:15) is because the Gentiles would stand under God's wrath if the people of God were restricted by the law.

[119] And so Cranford writes, "Abraham is not functioning simply as an individual who was saved by grace through faith, but as a representative figure who established the boundaries of covenant membership through his decisive intervention on the part of his descendants" (Cranford, "Abraham in Romans 4," p. 86).

Ephesians 2:11-22. Scholars frequently question the authenticity of Ephesians. Though I believe there are good reasons to hold to the letter's authenticity, those who question it need not dismiss the text as irrelevant if we find the discussion of election consistent with the other Pauline texts.[120] Two issues in the opening of the letter are worth mentioning. First, the location of the recipients ("in Ephesus") is missing from the earliest manuscripts, and thus is probably not original, having been added by a later scribe to clarify the audience.[121] Second, though typically translated to indicate that a single group is in mind in the introduction (see NIV, NLT, NET, ESV, HCSB; the NASB comes close to indicating this in translating "To the saints who are at Ephesus and who are faithful in Christ Jesus"), the text may actually imply that two groups are in mind. Only the KJV and the ASB allow for this understanding: "to the saints which are at Ephesus, and to the faithful in Christ Jesus." The author may be differentiating here between the "saints" and the "faithful," a distinction he makes again in Ephesians 1:13, 15, 18, and Ephesians 2:19, where the author refers to Jewish Christians as "saints," and thus distinct from the Gentile believers who are the primary audience in the letter.[122] Paul maintains the distinction be-

---

[120]Fowl takes a similar approach in his commentary, noting, "I think the historical evidence leads one to conclude that either Paul wrote Ephesians or someone close to him wrote Ephesians within a decade or two after his death. Theologically and interpretively, it does not make much difference whether Paul or this close follower wrote the text" (Stephen A. Fowl, *Ephesians*, NTL [Louisville: Westminster John Knox, 2012], p. 28). For discussions on the relationship between Colossians and Ephesians, see Ernest Best, "Who Used Whom? The Relationship of Ephesians and Colossians," *NTS* 43 (1997): 72-96; Stanley E. Porter and Kent D. Clarke, "Canonical-Critical Perspective and the Relationship of Colossians and Ephesians," *Biblica* 78 (1997): 57-86; Friedrich Bießer, "Wann und von wem könnte der Epheserbrief verfasst worden sein?," *KD* 52 (2006): 151-64.

[121]So Martin writes, "Most scholars conclude that no name stood in the original text. If the document was composed as a circular letter, intended to be passed around to a group of churches, there is no reason why such geographical place(s) should have been left out. . . . So Ephesians may well have been composed more as a homily than as a pastoral letter addressed to a local congregation" (Ralph P. Martin, *Ephesians, Colossians, and Philemon*, IBC [Louisville: John Knox, 1991], pp. 3-4).

[122]The terms may collapse after the unification of Jews and Gentiles at the end of Eph 2, though it is possible to still maintain a distinction. Weedman maintains that the "saints" is used throughout the letter to refer to Jewish believers (Gary E. Weedman, "Reading Ephesians from the New Perspective on Paul," *Leaven* 14, no. 2 [2006]: 84). For others who have argued for such an interpretation, see J. C. Kirby, *Ephesians: Baptism and Pentecost* (London: SPCK, 1968), p. 170; Ben Witherington III, *The Problem with Evangelical Theology: Testing the Exegetical Foundations of Calvinism, Dispensationalism and Wesleyanism* (Waco: Baylor University Press, 2005),

tween Jews and Gentiles throughout Ephesians 1, as shall be seen, in the pronouns used. Beginning in Ephesians 1:3, the author uses the first-person-plural pronoun exclusively, aside from third-person pronouns referring to God and Jesus,[123] a total of eight times in Ephesians 1:3-12.[124] In addition, the verbal forms in Ephesians 1:3-12 are never in the second-person plural, with four first-person-plural verbs occurring. All in all, there are twelve references to a first-person-plural group in the span of these ten verses. In Ephesians 1:13, the author then states, Ἐν ᾧ καὶ ὑμεῖς ἀκούσαντες τὸν λόγον τῆς ἀληθείας ("in whom also *you*, having heard the word of truth . . ."). It seems more than coincidental that the author here has maintained such a distinction between the two groups. Again, in Ephesians 1:15, the author notes that he has heard of "your love for all the saints," possibly indicating that the saints are to be distinguished from these Ephesian believers. In Ephesians 2:11, the author makes explicit the distinction that has been developed, identifying the "you" of Ephesians 1 and Ephesians 2 with the Gentiles (τὰ ἔθνη).[125] Thus we must set Ephesians 1–2 in its proper context. Paul is here describing God's gifts to Israel, specifically now to Jewish believers, who are the heirs of God's promises through Israel's Messiah.

I will save a fuller account of Ephesians 1–2 for our next chapter, where

---

p. 199. O'Brien seems open to the possibility (Peter Thomas O'Brien, *The Letter to the Ephesians*, Pillar New Testament Commentary [Grand Rapids: Eerdmans, 1999] p. 128). Eph 2:19 makes it clear this is likely the distinction in mind, which can be supported then throughout the first two chapters. Even if this distinction is not present in the term "saints," however, it is clear enough that Paul is here addressing Gentile dependence on Israel in the first two chapters.

[123]Hoehner is right to recognize that the plural pronoun alone does not serve as a sufficient ground to see election here as corporate (Harold W. Hoehner, *Ephesians: An Exegetical Commentary* [Grand Rapids: Baker Academic, 2002], p. 176). Paul does not seem to have in mind, however, that God has chosen specific individuals for salvation and others for reprobation (ibid., p. 193). His discussion is more concerned with salvation history than a doctrine of individual predestination.

[124]This section is noted for being a notoriously long, complex sentence in Greek, which most translations break into many smaller sentences. For a detailed discussion of the form and structure, see Hoehner, *Ephesians*, pp. 153-61.

[125]Such a distinction is in keeping with Martin's description of the purpose of the letter. He suggests that the letter, penned by a disciple of Paul, was written "to show the nature of the church and the Christian life to those who came to Christ from a pagan heritage and environment and to remind the Gentile Christians that Paul's theology of salvation history never disowned the Jewish background out of which the (now predominantly) Gentile church came" (Martin, *Ephesians, Colossians, and Philemon*, p. 4). See also Jack Haberer, "Ephesians 1:15-23," *Int* 62, no. 3 (2008): 313.

I will discuss divine and human agency. While Paul makes a demarcation in Ephesians 1 between Jewish and Gentile believers in order to show the Gentiles that they stand on the historic promises to Israel and are indebted to their heritage, he seeks in Ephesians 2 to demonstrate that Jewish and Gentile believers stand on equal ground in Christ. In the final section of Ephesians 2, Paul makes explicit what he presented implicitly in Ephesians 1:3–2:10, namely, that the Jews had temporal priority in salvation history, but now, in Christ, all the fullness of God's blessings to Israel have opened to Gentiles in the same way they are to the Jews.

Paul begins with an explicit contrast between the Jews and Gentiles, reminding the Gentiles of their past status with six descriptors: "uncircumcision"[126] (as they are called by the "so-called circumcision"), "apart from Christ,"[127] "alienated from the citizenship of Israel," "strangers to the covenants of promise," "without hope" and "without God."[128] As Gentiles, outside of Christ, these Ephesian believers did not know the true God and his Messiah,[129] and all the benefits that commitment to them entailed.[130] The divisions between the two groups were pervasive and extensive,[131] based primarily on the hallmarks of Israel's unique

---

[126]Lit. "foreskins." It is worth noting that Paul never commanded Jews not to be circumcised, but only Gentiles. He did insist, however, that circumcision is useless for Jews as well if they are apart from Christ. As Weedman notes, "circumcision was still 'there' and practiced by Jews, at least as a reminder to them, and here to Gentiles, that it was Israel who was the original 'elect,' the recipients of God's grace. The 'circumcision' that Gentiles now enjoyed, one experienced by being 'in Christ,' was prefigured by the physical circumcision that Israel had observed. The subtle message is that these Gentiles are to recognize and appreciate that history" (Weedman, "Reading Ephesians," p. 87).

[127]Neufeld notes, "Here *without Christ* is part of the inventory of what it means for gentiles not to have been Jewish: they were excluded from the community *from whom* and *for whom* the Messiah would come" (Thomas R. Yoder Neufeld, *Ephesians*, BCBC [Scottdale, PA: Herald, 2001], p. 109).

[128]Lit. "atheist," though Paul probably means that they did not worship the true God, not that they denied the existence of any god, which was rare in the ancient world (Andrew T. Lincoln, *Ephesians*, WBC [Dallas: Word, 1990], p. 138; Arthur G. Patzia, *Ephesians, Colossians, Philemon*, UBCS [Grand Rapids: Baker Books, 2011], p. 191).

[129]Lincoln suggests, "Christ is thought of as the messiah belonging to Israel and in retrospect as present to Israel through the promise" (Andrew T. Lincoln, "The Church and Israel in Ephesians 2," *CBQ* 49 [1987]: 610). See also Fowl, who sees the messianic emphasis here as primary (Fowl, *Ephesians*, p. 87). Martin likewise recognizes the messianic importance here (Martin, *Ephesians, Colossians, and Philemon*, p. 33).

[130]See O'Brien, *Letter to the Ephesians*, p. 187.

[131]See Timothy G. Gombis, "Ephesians 2 as a Narrative of Divine Warfare," *JSNT* 26, no. 4 (2004): 403-18.

identity: the covenants, the law and the Messiah.[132] Now, however, Gentiles can come to God through Jesus the Messiah, being brought "near,"[133] with Christ having made the two groups one (Eph 2:13-14). He accomplished this, at least in part, by destroying the hostile wall[134] that divided them, nullifying "the law of commandments in ordinances" (Eph 2:15).[135] What exactly Paul meant by this phrase is unclear, but it seems unlikely he means that the law was completely done away with, as this would contradict his writings in other places.[136] What seems likely, and would better parallel his argument in Romans and Galatians, is that Paul understands that the people of God are no longer marked off by the law, but rather by their incorporation in Christ.[137] While the Torah itself contained no commandments forbidding Gentiles from becoming covenant members, Gentile conversion previously came only through their sub-

---

[132]As Lincoln notes, "The laws which forbade eating or intermarrying with Gentiles often led Jews to have a contempt for Gentiles which could regard Gentiles as less than human. In response, Gentiles would often regard Jews with great suspicion, considering them inhospitable and hateful to non-Jews, and indulge in anti-Jewish prejudice" (Lincoln, *Ephesians*, p. 142). See also Martin, *Ephesians, Colossians, and Philemon*, pp. 35-36.

[133]Lincoln and O'Brien recognize that this is the traditional language used in Judaism to speak of proselytization (Lincoln, *Ephesians*, p. 139; O'Brien, *Letter to the Ephesians*, p. 191).

[134]Gombis, following Best (Best, *Ephesians*, pp. 256-57) and Hoehner (Hoehner, *Ephesians*, p. 371), takes this as a general reference to the division between Jews and Gentiles (Gombis, "Ephesians 2," p. 414). But clearly what created this division was the Torah.

[135]The dividing wall is sometimes thought to be the outer court of the temple (Peter S. Williamson, *Ephesians*, Catholic Commentary on Sacred Scripture [Grand Rapids: Baker Academic, 2009], pp. 71-72). Martin hints at this (Martin, *Ephesians, Colossians, and Philemon*, p. 35). Paul's syntax here, however, seems to indicate that the "dividing wall," "hostility" and "the law of commandments in ordinances" are one and the same. This would also fit with what was above, where the covenants and circumcision were part of what in Paul's view separated Gentiles from the Jews. Others have taken this to be a reference to a certain portion of the law, such as the ceremonial or cultic aspects (e.g., Patzia, *Ephesians, Colossians, Philemon*, p. 195). However, nothing in the text indicates that this is a reference to the ceremonial laws, and it is unlikely that Jews ever saw such divisions to the law.

[136]Weedman notes that Paul does not think of the law as being completely done away with, and in using the phrase ἐν δόγμασιν, "he is qualifying law in a quite restrictive sense" (Weedman, "Reading Ephesians," p. 90).

[137]O'Brien suggests this is best viewed in terms of nullifying the old covenant (O'Brien, *Letter to the Ephesians*, p. 199). Weedman interprets this primarily in terms of boundary markers (Weedman, "Reading Ephesians," p. 91), and Capes seems to take a similar view (David B. Capes, "Interpreting Ephesians 1–3: 'God's People in the Mystery of His Will,'" *SwJT* 39 [1996]: 27). Neufeld notes that this Jewish author (be it Paul or another) generally views the law positively throughout the letter, and it seems unlikely that he would speak of the law's destruction (Neufeld, *Ephesians*, pp. 115-16). Lincoln creates too much of an antithesis between Israel and the Gentiles as it relates to the "abolishment" of the law (Lincoln, "Church and Israel," pp. 605-24).

mission to circumcision and keeping of the Torah. God removed this separation through the death and resurrection of Jesus, affecting the unification of Jews and Gentiles in the people of God.

Finally, in light of their incorporation into the covenant community "in Christ Jesus," Paul affirms that God has made Gentiles "no longer strangers or foreigners"[138] but "fellow citizens with the saints and members of the household of God" (Eph 2:19).[139] Paul views Jewish and Gentile believers as one corporate body in Christ.[140] Paul does not say Gentile believers are now Israelites,[141] and his declaration that they are fellow citizens probably has the "heavenly kingdom" in mind (see Eph 1:3, 20; 2:6; Phil 3:20; 2 Tim 4:18). Regardless, he makes clear that God has united Jews and Gentiles in Christ, who alone provides access to God. Christ, through the Spirit, has made access to God equally available to both, and no longer primarily to the Jew.[142] In this way, God made the election that first came to Israel universally accessible to Jew and Gentile alike through his work in Christ.

What Paul presents, then, in Ephesians 1–2 is far more than an affirmation of individual election unto salvation and double predestination. Paul is chiefly concerned with the relationship of Jews and Gentiles in

---

[138]Neufeld notes this designation was equally applied at times to Israel, particularly in Egypt and Babylon (see Ps 39:12; 1 Pet 1:1; 5:13), and thus "the ground for treating the outsider well is that Israel too was once *paroikos*, away from home" (Neufeld, *Ephesians*, pp. 124-25).

[139]See Lincoln, *Ephesians*, p. 150.

[140]As stated above, it is likely here that "saints" refers to Jewish believers. So Weedman states, "Again, the subtext is the same as before; the Gentile believers have come lately to the table; the 'saints,' that is, Israel, were already at the meal" (Weedman, "Reading Ephesians," p. 85). Lincoln identifies five approaches that have been taken concerning the "holy ones" in this verse: (1) Israel or the Jews, (2) Jewish Christians, (3) the first Christians, (4) all believers or (5) the angels (Lincoln, *Ephesians*, p. 150). Of these options, however, that this refers to Jewish Christians has the best contextual support.

[141]And so, contra Markus Barth, who suggests that all Jews, regardless of their acceptance of Christ, are a part of the people of God and that Gentile believers are incorporated into national Israel (Markus Barth, *Israel and the Church: Contribution to a Dialogue for Peace* [Eugene, OR: Wipf & Stock, 2005], p. 95).

[142]Neufeld states, "*Access* then has to do with special status of those who can enter into the innermost dwelling place of the sovereign God. This privilege was much more understandable for first-century readers of this text than for modern heirs to a piety that understands relationship to God in casual or even cozy terms. Both errant Jewish believers and unclean, sinful Gentiles can now, as a result of Christ's work, walk *together* as one humanity into the very presence of God" (Neufeld, *Ephesians*, p. 123).

Christ. So it seems in Ephesians that Paul's concern is with Gentile believers who have neglected to appreciate their dependence on Israel.[143]
The privileges of election belonged first to Israel, and the first believers
in Jesus the Messiah were Jews, who had temporal priority in the hearing
of the gospel. This privilege came secondarily, temporally speaking, to
the Gentiles through the work of Christ, who removed the obstacle of
the law as the marker of the people of God. Gentiles must remember,
however, they have become partakers of the inheritance that first came
to Israel and that God granted to them through Israel's Messiah.[144] Christ
alone now stands as that which identifies the true people of God, and
those who are "in him," who have heard the gospel and committed themselves to him, who are the elect of God, Jews and Gentiles, and who are
both inheritors of God's covenant promises.

SUMMARY

We have seen a mix of opinions concerning the composition of the
people of God. The Jewish literature shows strong inclinations toward
seeing only a portion of the Jewish people being included in the people
of God. As we saw in the previous chapter, the reasons for inclusion and
exclusion varied somewhat, but quite often a majority of Jews, or at least
a sizeable portion, were viewed as outsiders. Likewise, there were uneven
opinions concerning the fate of the Gentiles. While most saw no hope
for the Gentiles, others viewed them as coming to worship Israel's God
in the eschaton. Paul certainly shared similarities with his contempo-

---

[143]So, as Haberer states, "When the two chapters, 1:3 through 2:22, are read as a continuous dialogue between these two groups, we hear the writer introducing these Gentile upstarts to their
Jewish forebears, teaching them about the central importance of the church's foundation, which
includes not only Christ Jesus but also the prophets and apostles—armed with law and gospel"
(Haberer, "Ephesians 1:15-23," p. 313). See also Harvey, *True Israel*, p. 232.

[144]So Fowl states, "It appears that whether or not the Christians in Ephesus or elsewhere are
subject to Judaizing pressures, they must understand themselves as Christians in relation to
Israel and Israel's God. They must understand their past as a Gentile past because that is God's
understanding of their past. Moreover, this understanding makes sense only in the light of
God's call of Israel; if there are no Jews, then there are no Gentiles. Christian identity requires
the taking on or remembering of Gentile identity because Christian identity is always tied to
Israel. This is not to say that Jewish identity is untouched by the life, death, and resurrection of
Christ. Far from it. Jewish identity is also radically reconceived in the light of Christ" (Fowl,
Ephesians, p. 101).

raries since he viewed the "elect" as limited to a specific group. He refused, however, to define the boundaries of this group by differing interpretations or practices surrounding the Torah because this would exclude Gentiles. The death and resurrection of Jesus brought about the realization of God's covenant with Abraham, resulting in the exoneration of all who trust in God's Messiah. For Paul, defining the people of God any other way ultimately undermined God's purpose to bless the nations and bring the resurrection life of his son to humanity.

Whose Turn Is It?

Election and Responsibility

What we have explored raises some obvious questions about the nature of salvation and where the initiative and responsibility lies. Some interpretations in the past have understood this in two extremes, one favoring divine determinism and more or less eliminating human responsibility, and one favoring human responsibility at the expense of divine sovereignty. This chapter will explore this tension in Paul's Jewish thought world before examining two key passages where Paul addresses, though somewhat indirectly, this tension between divine and human agency.

THE INITIATIVE OF GOD

Some texts emphasize divine activity in ways that are often interpreted as favoring some form of divine determinism. Various authors present these deterministic leanings in different ways, through descriptions of the divine "books," through depictions of God's choices or through a divine perspective concerning history. We shall see in these texts, however, certain indications causing us to inquire whether these authors intended divine determinism as the necessary conclusion. Often these texts, sometimes in the same breath, lay out the necessity of human obedience within the very context in which deterministic ideas are present.

Jubilees. One final, and heavily debated, aspect of *Jubilees* concerns the role of the heavenly tablets and books in the work.[1] Some have seen

---

[1]The tablets are referenced in *Jub.* 3:10, 31; 4:32; 5:13; 6:17-38; 15:25; 16:3-9; 18:19; 19:9; 23:32;

the tablets as evidencing the presence of a deterministic outlook in *Jubilees*,[2] while others have viewed them as a heavenly record-keeping system or a ledger of good and evil works.[3] Many references to the tablets are rather innocuous, simply noting that certain actions and events have been recorded in the heavenly records.[4] Other references, however, require more careful attention (namely, *Jub.* 5:13; 16:3, 9; 19:9; 23:32; 24:33; 30:19-26; 31:32; 36:10).

In *Jubilees* 5:13, it is said that

> the judgment of all of them [apparently of the evil angels and their off-spring, though perhaps also including humanity in general (see 5:8-12)] has been ordained and written in the heavenly tablets without injustice. And (if) any of them transgress from their way with respect to what was ordained for them to walk in, or if they do not walk in it, the judgment for every (sort of) nature and every kind has been written.

Apparently, in light of *Jubilees* 5:13b, what is "ordained" here is not what must happen (i.e., a predetermined future), but rather the consequences to follow if a certain course of action (i.e., disobedience to the way ordained for each kind) is taken.[5] This seems to fall in line with the function of the heavenly tablets noted above, in which the items recorded

---

24:33; 28:6; 30:9-22; 31:32; 32:10-29; 33:10; 49:8; 50:13. As Christiansen summarizes, "The heavenly tablets in Jubilees contain all the liturgical and ethical commands to Israel given from creation, including the plan or creation revealed to Moses (cf. 4:21). Thus, the Old Testament laws that have a special significance for the readers at the time when Jubilees was written, are given a special prominence. . . . Another set of tablets contain the human behavior, kept until the day of judgment. . . . In one specific case, they are said to reveal future events to Jacob (32:31). The content of the tablets is not identical to the law" (Ellen Juhl Christiansen, *The Covenant in Judaism and Paul: A Study of Ritual Boundaries as Identity Markers* [Leiden: Brill, 1995], p. 71 n. 16).

[2] E.g., E. P. Sanders, *Paul and Palestinian Judaism* (Minneapolis: Fortress, 1970), pp. 366-67; Simon J. Gathercole, *Where Is Boasting? Early Jewish Soteriology and Paul's Response in Romans 1–5* (Grand Rapids: Eerdmans, 2002), p. 62; Sigurd Grindheim, *The Crux of Election: Paul's Critique of the Jewish Confidence in the Election of Israel* (Tübingen: Mohr Siebeck, 2005), p. 45.

[3] E.g., Chris VanLandingham, *Judgment and Justification in Early Judaism and the Apostle Paul* (Grand Rapids: Baker Academic, 2006), pp. 71-74; Mark Adam Elliott, *The Survivors of Israel: A Reconsideration of the Theology of Pre-Christian Judaism* (Grand Rapids: Eerdmans, 2000), pp. 121-29.

[4] In a number of places, it is simply the commandments that are written in the heavenly tablets (E.g., *Jub.* 3:10, 31; 4:32; 6:17, 29-30, 35; 15:25; 16:28; 18:18-19; 28:6; 30:9; 32:10-15, 28; 33:10; 39:6; 49:8; 50:13).

[5] See Hindy Najman, *Past Renewals: Interpretive Authority, Renewed Revelation, and the Quest for Perfection in Jewish Antiquity* (Leiden: Brill, 2010), p. 59.

therein serve as an eternal law and specify both the stipulations of the laws and the consequences for departing from them.[6] Likewise, in *Jubilees* 16:9, where it is said that Lot's seed will be uprooted and judged because of his sin with his daughters, the action is apparently described as conforming to the standards outlined in the eternal laws of the tablets, though it is apparently Lot's sin and not that of his descendants that has caused this judgment.[7]

In other references to the tablets, their function seems to act as a register or list of the faithful/good in contrast to the disobedient/evil.[8] Thus, for example, *Jubilees* states of Abraham and Levi that they, because of their faithfulness and righteousness, were written down as "a friend of God" (*Jub.* 19:9)[9] and "a friend and a righteous one" (30:20) in the heavenly tablets. Likewise, Esau's betrayal (see *Jub.* 37:20-23) results in not being "written (on high) in The Book of Life for (he is written) in the one which will be destroyed and pass on to eternal execration so that their judgment will always be renewed with eternal reproach" (36:10).

Jubilees does not make clear how the heavenly tablets and the books of life and destruction are related. An indication of their function emerges in *Jubilees* 30. Here the author states that, in the heavenly tablets,

---

[6]Thus, contra Elliott, who suggests that this is a list of individuals who break the covenant (Elliott, *Survivors of Israel*, p. 265), it seems instead that this is a record of the "laws" ordained for each kind and the punishments associated with breaking them. Martínez, in his taxonomical study of the function of the tablets, refers to this particular function as "the divine, pre-existing archetype of the Torah" (Florentino García Martínez, "The Heavenly Tablets in the Book of Jubilees," in *Studies in the Book of Jubilees*, ed. Matthias Albani, Jörg Frey and Armin Lange [Tübingen: Mohr Siebeck, 1997], p. 243).

[7]See Martínez, "Heavenly Tablets," p. 248.

[8]This function seems similar to the role of Enoch described in the book. According to *Jub.* 4:23-24, Enoch was placed in Eden to write the "condemnation and judgment of the world, and all of the evils of the children of men . . . so that he might bear witness against all of the children of men so that he might relate all of the deeds of the generations until the day of judgment." Enoch's role thus seems a clerical one in that he is recording evil deeds so that there is a record on the day of judgment. Thus, in *Jubilees*, final judgment is apparently based on one's deeds, though given the prominence of the Torah in the book, it seems that this is not best understood simply as "good works" but rather as faithfulness to the laws of God.

[9]Here Martínez notes that it seems correct "to view the inscription as a consequence of 'he was found faithful' and to consider Abraham's inscription in the HT as a registering of that fidelity" (Martínez, "Heavenly Tablets," p. 247). Martínez categorizes this under records of "good and evil," though it seems in Abraham's case, as in Levi's, in *Jubilees* that author has taken steps to demonstrate this "goodness" occurred in light of his obedience to the "proto-Torah" of the heavenly tablets.

the faithful are recorded as friends while the unfaithful are recorded as enemies (*Jub.* 30:21-22). The unfaithful are "blotted out of the book of life and written down in the book of those who will be destroyed." Thus an apparent correspondence arises since what is written in the heavenly tablets becomes reflected in the books of life and destruction, through either the blotting out of one's name from the book of life and/or its entry into the book of destruction. That the books have some fluidity indicates that a form of determinism is unlikely.

Finally, the heavenly tablets record in some instances events clearly yet future. In *Jubilees* 16:3, Isaac's name is revealed to Sarah "just as his name was ordained and written in the heavenly tablets." This reference to the tablets may be no more than a way to emphasize the surety by which the birth of Isaac would occur. If his name exists in the records of heaven, then surely his birth must come about. It seems unwarranted to read into this reference some suggestion of exhaustive predeterminism.[10]

Later we find Moses about to write concerning the judgment coming on the wicked in Israel "as a testimony for eternal generations" (*Jub.* 23:32). We find this function specified elsewhere when the blessings for Levi and Judah are affirmed and preserved "as an eternal testimony in the heavenly tablets" (*Jub.* 31:32).[11] In 23:32, however, the instance is different since it records both previous events and events yet to come (the completion of the apostasy and the future restoration). Florentino García Martínez has suggested that "this revelation contains a simple, but comprehensive, vision of history. . . . The whole of human destiny is written down in the HT."[12] The tablets elsewhere record information concerning

---

[10]Contra von Rad, who states, "Thus we learn, even with regard to details, that these have happened exactly as has been described in advance on the heavenly tablets, like, for example, the giving of the name of Isaac (16.3). . . . The concept of divine determination has taken complete control of all historical traditional material" (Gerhard von Rad, *Wisdom in Israel* [Harrisburg, PA: Trinity Press International, 1993], p. 271).

[11]Martínez suggests this is more than a blessing on Levi and Judah, but also "that the blessings predestine their future and the future of their descendants" (Martínez, "Heavenly Tablets," p. 250). The prayers of blessing that are affirmed to be recorded in the heavenly tablets seem, however, to again be an assurance of the future faithfulness of the lines of Levi and Judah. The text does not specify whether this should be viewed in light of foreknowledge or of predetermined activity. Again, the emphasis in the book on the established nature of the laws and their consequences (good or bad) seems to favor the former rather than the latter.

[12]Ibid., p. 249.

events yet future. In *Jubilees* 24:27-33, Isaac curses the Philistines. His curse, which proclaims their destruction from the earth and eternal state of disfavor, is "written and engraved concerning him in the heavenly tablets to be done to him in the day of judgment so that they might be uprooted from the earth."[13]

We thus find competing interpretations of the nature and function of the tablets. E. P. Sanders suggests that the tablets "are not actually account ledgers with debits and credits beside each name. They are the 'book of life' (30.22; 36.10) and the 'book of those who will be destroyed' (30.22)."[14] He thus collapses the two functions of recording the deeds/status of an individual and their status in the book of life/destruction into a single function. Simon Gathercole, agreeing in principle with Sanders, states, "To be written in the Book of Life appears to be the default position," though, contra Sanders, he continues, "However, the category of 'the righteous' whose destiny is spiritual resurrection is not merely a matter of being elect; it is inseparable from the concrete acts that are commended in the book. . . . Thus, in this important sense, there is a future dimension of Israel's relationship with God (*amicitia*) that is contingent upon obedience."[15]

In my view, it seems best to allow the book as a whole to interpret the function of the heavenly tablets in *Jubilees*. Thus, though elements on the timeline of history are clearly foreordained, this does not seem to include all of the actions of individuals as those actions relate to their obedience to or rebellion against God. Since the books of life and death may be changed to correspond to an individual's behavior, this seems to point away from some exhaustive form of determinism.

---

[13]Here again Martínez concludes, "The curse is effective because it already existed in the HT: the destruction of the Philistine progeny is predestined and will be accomplished on the Day of Judgment" (ibid.). Martínez sees a similar instance in 32:21-22, where Jacob is handed seven tablets, which foretell the future of his descendants. Though the Ethiopic text does not specify these as "heavenly" tablets, Martínez suggests that this is likely the meaning intended.

[14]Sanders, *Paul and Palestinian Judaism*, p. 366.

[15]Gathercole, *Where Is Boasting*, p. 62. Gathercole goes on to note, "The covenant, then, opens up the possibility for Israelites to be either obedient or disobedient. . . . *This points to an understanding of the relationship with God that is promised in the future and that depends upon (of course, covenantal) obedience to the Law*" (ibid. [emphasis original]). See also VanLandingham, *Judgment and Justification*, pp. 71-73.

Dead Sea Scrolls. The *Thanksgiving Hymns* (hereafter 1QH) is a large collection of hymns clearly authored by the Qumran community.[16] Much debate has taken place over the relationship of 1QH and 1QS, specifically in the "treatise" of the two spirits and the dualistic and deterministic language found therein, and the at times conflicting verbiage in the *Hymns*. 1QH, like 1QS, contains a number of statements seemingly indicating absolute determinism alongside other statements emphasizing human response and obedience. As such, some have come to interpret the collection as evidencing absolute determinism,[17] while others have found a coexistence (however resolved) between the sovereignty of God and human response.[18] As in previous texts, we must examine the context and intent of these statements to gain a sense of their meaning and function.

In 1QH 4.17-25, the author gives thanks "for the spirits which you placed in me" (4.17). He also acknowledges that God "[smoothen[s]] the path of the one whom you choose and by the insight [of your knowledge you pre]vent him from sinning against you" (1QH 4.22). He then prays that God would "[prevent] your servant from sinning against you, from tripping over all the things of your will" (1QH 4.23). Here the combination of an affirmation of the workings of God to keep the psalmist from sin with a petition to keep him from sinning should alert us to the issues present within the genre. Since hymns focus on praise to God for his grace and goodness, we should not be surprised to find a denigrating

---

[16]For a discussion of the authorship, form and function of the *Hymns*, see Denise Dombkowski Hopkins, "The Qumran Community and 1 Q Hodayot: A Reassessment," *RevQ* 10, no. 3 (1981): 323-64. Likewise, for an examination of the poetic structure of the *Hymns*, see Bonnie Kittel, *The Hymns of Qumran* (Atlanta: Scholars Press, 1981).

[17]Grindheim, for example, states, "It is therefore correct to speak of a broad concept of predestination in 1QH. Everything is predestined by God. Not only the salvation or damnation of the individual, but everything that takes place is predestined (1QHa 4:21; 5:13-14, 16-19; 6:11-12; 9:14-20, 23-31; 12:13)" (Grindheim, *Crux of Election*, p. 58). See also Menahem Mansoor, "Studies in the New *Hodayot* (Thanksgiving Hymns)—V: Some Theological Doctrines," *BR* 5 (1960): 1-21; Eugene H. Merrill, *Qumran and Predestination: A Theological Study of the Thanksgiving Hymns* (Leiden: Brill, 1975), pp. 19-28.

[18]See, e.g., Elliott, *Survivors of Israel*, p. 347; Paul Heger, *Challenges to Conventional Opinions on Qumran and Enoch Issues* (Leiden: Brill, 2012), p. 335; Eileen Schuller, "Petitionary Prayer and the Religion of Qumran," in *Religion in the Dead Sea Scrolls*, ed. John J. Collins and Robert A. Kugler (Grand Rapids: Eerdmans, 2000), pp. 29-45; VanLandingham, *Judgment and Justification*, p. 135.

view of humanity and an all-encompassing attribution of sovereignty to God.[19] We might not expect, however, the theology of the hymns to contradict what we see in the didactic and theological works at Qumran. This is not to say that the hymns contain false depictions of the beliefs of the sect, but rather that the nature of the genre results in some unbalance.[20] Even still, we must note that the impetus for humans to be obedient to God and to obey the covenant remains.[21]

In 1QH 7.11–7.28, the author acknowledges the complete sovereignty of God. He affirms:

> I know, thanks to your intellect, that [. . .] is not by the hand of flesh, and that a man [cannot choose] his way, nor can a human being establish his steps. I know that the impulse of every spirit is in your hand, [and all] its [task] you have established even before creating him. . . . You, you alone, have [created] the just man, and from the womb you determined him for the period of approval, to keep your covenant, and to walk on all (your paths), and to . . . on him with the abundance of your compassion, to open all the narrowness of his soul to eternal salvation and endless peace, without want. (1QH 7.15-19)[22]

Likewise,

> the wicked you have created for [the time] of your wrath, from the womb you have predestined them for the day of slaughter. For they walk on a path that is not good, they reject your covenant, their soul loathes your [. . .], and they take no pleasure in what you command, but choose what you hate. You have established all those [who . . .] your [. . .] to carry out

---

[19]Grindheim, for example, notes, "Hymns will typically stress the reasons for giving praise to God, whereas rules will typically stress that elect status is demonstrated by obedience" (Grindheim, *Crux of Election*, p. 64).

[20]VanLandingham suggests, "In comparing 1QS and 1QH, the differences or contradictions . . . between them are real, including the internal contradictions of 1QHᵃ. The differences, at least on the issues of a pessimistic anthropology and *sola gratia* soteriology, can be attributed to the same internal differences in the texts noted above. The reason derives from the genre, not Qumran theology. . . . There are not different or opposing views on how one joins the Community (i.e., by human obedience or God's grace) or how one survives the final judgment" (VanLandingham, *Judgment and Justification*, p. 135).

[21]In this passage in particular, Grindheim notes, "To be elect means to be given the discernment so as not to sin against God (4:22; cf. 6:17). Law observance is therefore the sign that one is elect" (*Crux of Election*, p. 59).

[22]A similar line of thought is expressed in 1QH 15.34-36; 18.1-13; and 20.4-36.

great judgments against them before the eyes of all your creatures, so they will be a sign and a por[tent for] eternal [generations] so that all will know your glory and your great might. (1QH 7.20-23)

The psalmist herein has attributed all of the ways of the just man, including his keeping of the covenant, to the workings of God. We seem to find in 1QH 7.15-23 no room for human response or initiative for either the righteous or the wicked.[23] In the preceding lines (1QH 7.11-14), however, the psalmist says he has loved God, purified his soul, committed himself to the commandments and joined the many, all apparently of his own volition. Furthermore, as quoted above, the psalmist says that the wicked choose what God hates and "walk on a path that is not good" (1QH 7.21-22).[24] Here, in the same psalm and context, the author affirms both the initiative and volition of humanity and what appears to be an exhaustive form of determinism.

Again in 1QH 11.19-36,[25] the hymnist offers assurance of God's sovereignty. He states, "The depraved spirit you have purified from great offense so that he can take a place with the host of the holy ones, and can enter in communion with the congregation of the sons of heaven. You cast eternal destiny for man with the spirits of knowledge, so that he praises your name in the community of jubilation, and tells of your wonders before all your creation" (1QH 11.21-23). The psalmist then states that he shares in "the lot of the scoundrels" because the "soul of a poor

---

[23]This is how Hopkins, Mansoor and Merrill interpret the hymn (Hopkins, "Qumran Community," p. 350; Mansoor, "Studies in the New *Hodayot*," p. 4; Merrill, *Qumran and Predestination*, p. 29).

[24]So Heger suggests, "These verses demonstrate explicitly that the wicked will be punished because they chose, by their own will, to act against the divine rules, not because they were damned to behave wickedly. God predestined that all who act likewise, who choose the bad way, will be severely punished, in order to serve as a sign and a premonition of his boundless might to castigate those who disobey him" (Heger, *Challenges*, p. 337). See also Helmer Ringgren, *The Faith of Qumran: Theology of the Dead Sea Scrolls* (New York: Crossroad, 1995), p. 107.

[25]1QH 11.19 is sometimes understood as a reference to eschatological salvation. In the context, however, and with the use of the past combined with the OT notion of Sheol as the underworld/grave, it seems likely here that the psalmist is simply noting when he was rescued by God from physical death. See, e.g., George W. E. Nickelsburg, *Resurrection, Immortality, and Eternal Life in Intertestamental Judaism and Early Christianity* (Cambridge, MA: Harvard University Press, 2006), p. 190. For a discussion on immortality in 1QH, see Robert B. Laurin, "The Question of Immorality in the Qumran 'Hodayot,'" *JSS* 3, no. 4 (1958): 344-55.

person lives amongst great turmoil" (1QH 11.25) and awaits for the "tor-
rents of Belial" to break loose (11.29), yet God will be "a massive rampart
for me" (11.37) and will set his "feet upon a rock . . . and /on/ the tracks
which you have chosen" (12.3-4). It seems here that his lot in life has
changed, and God indeed has rescued him from the trouble he faced and
will also rescue him from the advances of Belial.

1QH 12, in contrast, asserts that the wicked (12.1-18), who are full of
deceit, oppress the righteous, alter the law, are hypocrites, stubborn and
idolaters, "have not chosen the path of your [heart] nor have they listened to your word" (12.17). Because of their decision, God will anni-
hilate them in the day of judgment (1QH 12.18-21). The righteous will, in
contrast, stand in the presence of God, and he will sustain them in every
difficulty and forgive their sins (1QH 12.21-40). The righteous "walk on
the path of [God's] heart" (1QH 12.21) and have listened to the psalmist
(12.24), who himself had been barred from the covenant (12.35) and had
gained readmittance only because he humbled himself and recommitted
himself to the covenant (12.36-40). While the previous hymns have focused on the sovereignty of God, to the near (though not total) exclusion
of any recognition of the responsibility of humans, this hymn focuses
almost exclusively on the responsibility of humanity and the consequences for disobedience, to the near (though not total) exclusion of
God's sovereignty.[26]

1QH thus, like 1QS, affirms both human and divine activity concerning entrance into and obedience to the community. While 1QS emphasized the human aspect, though with several strong statements of
divine activity, in 1QH we find the reverse. Divine activity receives the
focus, and the activity of the psalmist and his community are minimized.
As was stated at the outset, we might largely attribute this to the genre of
the hymns, which focus on the greatness of God and the unworthiness

---

[26]In spite of this emphasis, Flusser sees here that man's election is due to preordained divine
grace, and the community is the sum total of the individual elect (David Flusser, *Judaism of the
Second Temple Period* [Grand Rapids: Eerdmans, 2007], 1:23). It seems, instead, that this hymn
focuses on the consequences of the behavior of individuals, which ultimately determines
whether they walk the path of God's heart or choose their own path instead. For more collective
rather than individual emphases in the *Hymns*, see 1QH 14 and 19.

of humanity, while legal, eschatological or historical texts maintain a different focus. God's enabling spirit and his gifting of truth to the community takes center stage in 1QH. While some have postulated ways we might reconcile free will under the umbrella of absolute determinism,[27] this is both unnecessary and inconsistent with the rest of the writings from Qumran. Several elements in 1QH create problems with this approach. As noted above, we cannot easily reconcile the petitionary[28] and volitional elements in the *Hymns* with a deterministic interpretation.[29] For the author, salvation belongs to the community alone since in it possesses the truth of God as delivered through the Teacher of Righteousness. The *Hymns* do not in general go so far to make the evil within these groups determined by God. The resolution here, as elsewhere in the scrolls, seems best found in recognizing certain actions do indeed come from the impetus of individuals.[30] We should not absolutize the presence of determinism, either in light of the genre or in light of the overall theology of the scrolls.

The *Damascus Document* (CD) opens with the declaration that God will judge those who "spurn him. For when they were unfaithful in forsaking him, he hid his face from Israel and from his sanctuary and de-

---

[27]Hopkins suggests that the dilemma between free will and election is resolved by positing that there is an "area of intersection [between] those outside of the community who are potentially saved but who have not yet heard the word as well as those inside the community who do not really belong there or who are not sure that they belong there" (Hopkins, "Qumran Community," p. 363). Merrill has suggested that the presence of "voluntarism" and "determinism" in 1QH are both under the umbrella of determinism, and the presence of free will is one that is simply mysterious or that free will only operates within the parameters of the sphere to which an individual is assigned (Merrill, *Qumran and Predestination*, pp. 39-45).

[28]See Schuller, "Petitionary Prayer," pp. 29-45.

[29]So Heger inquires if the author believes "in individual determinism at birth, or is he using a common manner of expressing divine omnipotence and generosity in contrast to human degradation and ineptitude? On the basis of the intertextual approach, as I will argue, I believe that the latter is correct" (Heger, *Challenges*, p. 335).

[30]Dimant states, "The total dependence of man on God, inherent in the fundamental laws of creation, implies that man's salvation, if possible, depends on God too. So it is expressed in the *Hodayot* and elsewhere. Yet such salvation demands a corresponding attitude of man. In fact, by truly repenting and by following God's true ways, i.e. the Law of Moses (1QH 10:30), man distinguishes himself as one who merits and is capable of receiving the divine grace" (Devorah Dimant, "Qumran Sectarian Literature," in *Jewish Writings of the Second Temple Period*, ed. Michael E. Stone [Philadelphia: Fortress, 1984], 2:537). See also Sanders, *Paul and Palestinian Judaism*, pp. 261, 265.

livered them up to the sword. But when he remembered the covenant with the forefathers, he saved a remnant for Israel and did not deliver them up to destruction" (CD 1.2-5). The remnant consisted of men who "realized their iniquity and knew that they were guilty," but "because they sought him with an undivided heart" God raised up a Teacher of Righteousness to lead them in truth and faithfulness (CD 1.8-11).[31] The author sees this as the time foretold by Hosea, when Israel would stray from God and invoke the covenant curses by following "easy interpretations" promoting injustice, and persecuting those who properly observed the law (CD 1.13-21).[32]

The author acknowledges that the penitent may find atonement, but those who turn aside from the path find complete destruction (CD 2.3-6), "for God did not choose them at the beginning of the world, and before they were established he knew their deeds, and abominated the generations on account of blood and hid his face from the land, from <Israel>, until their extinction" (CD 2.7-9). Some, for obvious reasons, have interpreted CD's view of foreknowledge and foreordination as an absolute arrangement. Philip Alexander, for example, states, "There is, it seems, a fixed, predetermined list of the righteous, and through 'those anointed in His holy spirit and who view His truth' God has made known to the elect the names of those who are to be saved."[33] Here, as in 1QS, the text does not postulate a complete determinism; rather the author indicates that God has rejected evil and all those associated with it ("he knew their deeds"). His foreknowledge may mean that he knows who will be in the lot of the wicked, but this is not the same as determining their identities. Indeed, following the statement, the author then

---

[31]It is of no doubt, as Elliott writes, that the "community believed itself to represent the *continuation* of the former remnant, indeed, but they were not only the descendants of this remnant but were, in some sense, a *new remnant* who found themselves in need of surviving the present times of trouble, and who hoped to survive the future judgment as well" (Elliott, *Survivors of Israel*, p. 627).

[32]Wacholder notes that the "Just Teacher's opponent could conceivably be understood as a reference to the leader of the Pharisees, a group whom the author labels as the מסיני (ה)נבול" (Ben Zion Wacholder, *The New Damascus Document: The Midrash on the Eschatological Torah of the Dead Sea Scrolls (Reconstruction, Translation and Commentary)* [Leiden: Brill, 2007], p. 151).

[33]Philip S. Alexander, "Predestination and Free Will in the Theology of the Dead Sea Scrolls," in *Divine and Human Agency in Paul and His Cultural Environment*, ed. John M. Barclay and Simon J. Gathercole (New York: T&T Clark, 2006), p. 43.

admonishes his "sons" to "choose what he is pleased with and repudiate what he hates, so that you can walk perfectly on all his paths and not allow yourselves to be attracted by the thoughts of a guilty inclination and lascivious eyes" (CD 2.15-16). God has established goodness and truth, and those who align themselves with the way of truth will receive the blessings he has predetermined, just as those who align themselves with evil will receive the curses.

The author also reveals God's judgment will come on "all those entering his covenant but who do not remain steadfast in them; they shall be visited for destruction at the hand of Belial" (CD 8.2). The author makes Jews who have rejected the covenant the "target" of these warnings of judgment.[34] The wicked person has "chosen the stubbornness of his heart. They did not keep apart from the people and have rebelled with insolence, walking on the path of the wicked ones" (CD 8.8-9). God loves those who follow in obedience as the fathers of Israel did, but has "hatred for the builders of the wall" (CD 8.17-18). Thus God will judge all who reject his commands (CD 8.18-19).

As was seen in its sister document, 1QS, though containing deterministic language, CD does not nullify the importance of human freedom and response.[35] The God who controls history has also chosen Israel, or specifically "true Israel," the remnant of Israel,[36] as his people. He has also determined "right and wrong," so to speak, and the rewards and consequences for behavior that fall into those categories.[37] Membership in the community rests on one's acceptance of and obedience to the covenant terms, which come through the authoritative interpretation of the Teacher of Righteousness.[38] Sigurd Grindheim suggests that the remnant

---

[34]See Elliott, *Survivors of Israel*, p. 61; Aharaon Shemesh, "Expulsion and Exclusion in the Community Rule and the Damascus Document," *DSD* 9, no. 1 (2002): 57.

[35]See Daniel R. Schwartz, "'To Join Oneself to the House of Judah' (Damascus Document IV, 11)," *RevQ* 10, no. 39 (1981): 445.

[36]See Grindheim, *Crux of Election*, p. 65.

[37]Schwartz's suggestion is helpful in stating, "In *Dam. Doc.* [predestination] controls only the framework of human history, the succession of epochs.... Any penitent outsider can join them, but they must hurry, for a time will come when people who are essentially no worse than the sectarians will be denied the opportunity to take shelter in their 'sure house'" (Schwartz, "To Join Oneself," p. 446).

[38]So Dimant writes, "Thus the sect's point of departure appears to have been a double awareness:

idea was individualized at Qumran,[39] but it is clear that the *community* is Israel. They have received the covenant, and only they have been faithful to it.[40] The concept of election here, as seen elsewhere, was non-national and against any purely ethnic notion, though still framed in a covenantal manner. And though the authors of the Scrolls identify their community as the elect, this does not eliminate the necessity of both receiving and obeying the covenant as they interpreted it.

Wisdom of Solomon. The final section of Wisdom (Wis 11–19, with a much-discussed excursus on ungodliness and idolatry in Wis 11:15–15:19) offers a series of seven contrasts, which Daniel Harrington summarizes as follows: "The basic principle operative in all seven contrasts is stated in 11.5: 'For through the very things by which their enemies [the Egyptians] were punished, they [Israel in the exodus] received benefit in their need.'"[41] Here the notion of retributive justice comes to the fore in the author's discussion. This final section has as its focus God's blessing of his people and cursing of the ungodly, who, though they mock the plight of his people, come to realize his power through the deliverance of the righteous (e.g., Wis 11:5-14). Though the ungodly worship false gods and creatures, God is still

> merciful to all, for you can do all things,
> and you overlook people's sins, so that they may repent.
> For you love all things that exist,
> and detest none of the things that you have made,
> for you would not have made anything if you had hated it. (Wis 11:23-24
>   NRSV; also Wis 12:1-2)[42]

---

on the one hand the recognition of their own sinfulness and the need to repent; on the other, the conviction that they possessed the true teaching and revelation through the Teacher of Righteousness. This explains why the sectaries call themselves both 'the Repenters of Israel' and 'the comers into the New Covenant'" (Dimant, "Qumran Sectarian Literature," p. 492).

[39]Grindheim, *Crux of Election*, p. 69.

[40]Dimant, again, is helpful in stating, "All these teachings were divulged to the community in a divine revelation and thus render the community elect and just by its very nature" (Dimant, "Qumran Sectarian Literature," p. 492).

[41]Daniel J. Harrington, "'Saved by Wisdom' (Wis 9.18): Soteriology in the Wisdom of Solomon," in *This World and the World to Come: Soteriology in Early Judaism*, ed. Daniel M. Gurtner (New York: T&T Clark, 2011), p. 188.

[42]Thus deSilva disputes, "It is not simply that 'sinning Jews are freed from punishment, but God hates the sinning Canaanites and exterminates them for their sins' (Reider 1957: 41). Rather,

Though God waits patiently for their repentance,[43] the author also notes that

> you were not unaware that their origin was evil
> and their wickedness inborn,
> and that their way of thinking would never change.
> For they were an accursed race from the beginning. (Wis 12:10-11 NRSV)

In spite of the strength of the rhetoric here, Lester Grabbe notes correctly that though "there are statements suggesting a strong view about determinism [Wis 3:10-12; 12:3-11] . . . the universal predestination of Gentiles to damnation is probably not envisaged by the book."[44] Rather, these stand together with commands to obey the law and polemics against idolatry. The judgment of the wicked thus came only after persistent wicked acts and warnings through "prior signs" (Wis 19:13-16).

As David Winston summarizes the issue, "What baffles the reader of ancient literature, however, is the easy coexistence in it of two apparently contradictory strands of thought, namely, an emphasis on God's ultimate determination of all human action coupled with an equally emphatic conviction that the human will is the arbiter of its own moral destiny."[45] On some level, though, it seems that most Jewish texts, the Wisdom of Solomon included, do not go so far as to explicitly argue that God determines "all human action." These statements may lead to determinism, but in most cases, as in the case of Wisdom, the author makes no such claim explicitly. Winston postulates, "Man's freedom is only relative, and that from the higher perspective, it is God who in reality makes certain individuals worthy of Wisdom, and destines others for 'Death.'"[46] The author, however, allows, for example, that death came as an intrusion

---

the author argues that God in fact loves all that God has created and detests none of God's works, infused with God's 'immortal spirit' as they are (Wis 11:23-12:1)" (David A. deSilva, *Introducing the Apocrypha: Message, Context, and Significance* [Grand Rapids: Baker Academic, 2002], p. 147). The author may primarily have Gentiles in mind, but sinning Jews are not exempt from God's judgment, nor are Gentiles excluded from the possibility of salvation if they were to repent, though this is not likely in the author's view. See also, John J. Collins, *Jewish Wisdom in the Hellenistic Age* (Louisville: Westminster John Knox, 1997), p. 220.

[43]See also Wis 12:12-22.

[44]Lester Grabbe, *Wisdom of Solomon* (New York: T&T Clark, 1997), p. 63.

[45]David Winston, *The Wisdom of Solomon: A New Translation with Introduction and Commentary*, AB (New York: Doubleday, 1979), p. 48. See also deSilva, *Introducing the Apocrypha*, p. 148.

[46]Winston, *Wisdom of Solomon*, p. 58.

into God's creation, which would certainly undermine the notion of absolute determinism.[47] So while the author upholds the traditional belief in God's choosing of Israel, and does not extend much, if any, hope to Israel's enemies,[48] the overall picture of the book is that God desires all people to repent and seek Wisdom, and the gift of Wisdom will be afforded to all who ask for her.[49]

1 Enoch. The Book of Luminaries[50] primarily recounts a summary of the workings of the heavenly bodies. Within the book, Enoch sees the heavenly tablets and "all the deeds of humanity and all the children of the flesh upon the earth for all the generations of the world" (*1 En.* 81:2). Nickelsburg suggests, "Divine foreknowledge implies a deterministic view of human history. Events and actions *must* happen because the omniscient God knows that they will happen and has revealed them to Enoch already in primordial times."[51] He also recognizes, however, that the function of the tablets is to comfort "the reader with the assurance that the sovereign God controls history and will execute righteous judgment in spite of present inequities."[52] As in *Jubilees,* though the tablets function differently, we need not see determinism in the thought of the author. The tablets function to assure the righteous of their rewards. Upon reading these accounts, Enoch declares, "Blessed is the man who dies righteous and upright, against whom no record of op-

---

[47]So Collins notes, "The primary point that Wis Sol. makes about the origin of death is that it was not from God. The same presumably holds true of sin. The author expends little effort in clarifying whence these evils arose" (Collins, *Jewish Wisdom,* p. 190).

[48]See John J. Collins, *Encounters with Biblical Theology* (Minneapolis: Fortress, 2005), p. 126; Harrington, *Invitation to the Apocrypha,* p. 75; Harrington, "Saved by Wisdom," p. 190.

[49]See Harrington, "Saved by Wisdom," p. 184.

[50]The Book of Luminaries is generally given a second-century-B.C.E. date (James C. VanderKam, "Enoch, Astronomical Book of (1 Enoch 72-82)," in *The Eerdmans Dictionary of Early Judaism,* ed. John J. Collins and Daniel C. Harlow [Grand Rapids: Eerdmans, 2010], pp. 582-83). See also George W. E. Nickelsburg, *Jewish Literature Between the Bible and the Mishnah* (Minneapolis: Fortress, 2005), p. 44.

[51]George W. E. Nickelsburg, *1 Enoch,* Hermeneia (Minneapolis: Fortress, 2001), 1:339. He reaffirms this notion in vol. 2, stating that "the notion of heavenly tablets inscribed with the deeds and fates of people gives expression to a belief regarding foreknowledge.... While they do record the actions of people, those actions are predetermined" (ibid., 2:537).

[52]Ibid., 1:339. Stückenbruck likewise notes, "Presumably the tablets record the rewards due to the righteous, and thus reassure the intended readers that such rewards are not in doubt" (Loren T. Stückenbruck, *1 Enoch 91–108* [Berlin: de Gruyter, 2007], p. 85).

pression has been written, and who received no judgment on that day"
(*1 En.* 81:4). There is no indication that God has determined the choices
of humans, but rather the author details the future fates of the righteous
and the wicked. In his critique of Gerhard von Rad's view of the relationship between prophecy and apocalypticism, Richard Bauckham
helpfully states,

> So the determinism of apocalyptic must be judged not as an abstract phi-
> losophy, but by its function within its context, which is precisely to counter
> fatalistic despair, to lay open to men the eschatological future, and call
> men to appropriate action. In terms of that function the gulf between the
> prophetic and apocalyptic concepts of history is by no means so un-
> bridgeable as von Rad assumes.[53]

Since the text does not require such a deterministic view, we should not read
one into it when the text functions to encourage right action. If the author
intended a fatalistic perspective, then there would be no reason for the sinner
to change their course, since their course had already been arranged.

Testament of Moses. Toward the end of the *Testament of Moses*, the
author resumes the dialogue between Moses and Joshua (*T. Mos.* 10:11).
Moses tells Joshua to keep the book of prophecy he has been given and
be ready to succeed Moses as Israel's mediator (*T. Mos.* 10:11-15). Joshua,
distraught over the revelation, doubts his ability to fulfill this role and
fears Israel's enemies will overtake them after Moses departs (*T. Mos.*
11:1-19). Moses replies by stating that God has foreseen all that will
happen in human history and remains in control of the course of history
(*T. Mos.* 12:4-7). Moses then states,

> those who truly fulfill the commandments of God will flourish and will
> finish the good way, but those who sin by disregarding the command-
> ments will deprive themselves of the good things which were declared
> before. They, indeed, will be punished by the nations with many tortures.
> But it is not possible for the nations to drive them out or extinguish them
> completely. (*T. Mos.* 12:10-12)

---

[53]Richard Bauckham, *The Jewish World Around the New Testament* (Tübingen: Mohr Siebeck, 2008),
p. 63.

Moses feels confident that Israel will continue because of the covenant God established with them (*T. Mos.* 12:13). Though some within Israel will become unfaithful, a faithful remnant will continue, and thus God's people will continue.

Regarding this preservation of Israel, Robert Kugler states that "all of Israel" will continue because of God's promises and covenants,[54] and God's control of history, and not individual mediation or righteous deeds, will assure Israel of this fate.[55] The text, however, in making distinction between the righteous and sinners *within* Israel throughout, both in the recounting of Israel's history,[56] and in its predictions for the future, seems to expect that certain Jews will face judgment because of their disobedience to the law. The text no doubt affirms that God rules over history, but nonetheless describes the future of individual Jews as conditioned on their obedience or disobedience to the law. We find here, as throughout much of the literature of the period, an affirmation both of God's sovereignty and foreknowledge, and of the responsibility of the Jews to remain faithful to the covenant. The covenant assures that Israel will continue, but this text, as do many others, only expects a remnant to enjoy this preservation.[57]

We should ask here, as elsewhere, if the occasional statements that seem to promote determinism override the persistent and consistent theme throughout the book of the need for the people's obedience and the conditionality of the covenant blessings.[58] John Priest similarly sees

---

[54]Robert A. Kugler, "Testaments," in Collins and Harlow, *Eerdmans Dictionary of Early Judaism*, p. 1295.

[55]Ibid.

[56]See John J. Collins, "Testaments," in Stone, *Jewish Writings*, 2:347.

[57]Tromp notes, "Having elaborated on the predetermined plan underlying creation, which ensures the safety of the people, the author of As. Mos. makes plain that the Lord's protection is no licence to neglect his commandments. Only some of the people will fulfil his commandments (*facientes . . . et consummantes mandata*) they will grow and prosper," and "The concluding verses exhort faithfulness to the commandments, promising good to those who fulfill them and evil to those who disregard them (12:10-11), and affirm that, in spite of all hazards, a nucleus of God's people will survive in accord with the covenant promises made long ago (12:12-13)" (Johannes Tromp, *The Assumption of Moses: A Critical Edition with Commentary* [Leiden: Brill, 1993], p. 268).

[58]On the tension, see Kugler, "Testaments," p. 1295.

the deterministic theme of the book as a dominant one.[59] As suggested previously, the deterministic outlook need not nullify the frequently repeated condemnations of disobedience and exhortations to obedience,[60] the conditional language found throughout the book and the explicit indications in chapters four, five, nine and twelve that only a remnant of Israel will remain faithful and receive the covenant blessings.[61] The author nowhere states that God will act unilaterally to restore and rescue all of Israel, and we should not understand the mention of covenant or election terminology as sustaining this view, especially when the covenant language is frequently couched in conditional terms.[62] Thus Mark Adam Elliott surmises, "The writer is not delineating 'exceptions' to the salvation of all Israel. There would be little purpose for such an abstract and detached theological concern in the midst of an emotive work like the *Assumption*. . . . We are probably witness here to one common method of combining two irreconcilable aspects of the covenant—promise (gift) and demand—in terms of the salvation of a *representative* segment of God's people."[63]

The Responsibility of Humans

In the previous section we saw instances where some have suggested that divine determinism underlies or results from various statements and images concerning historical events, the heavenly books or the final judgment. I suggested, though recognizing that these authors highlight the sovereignty of God, that none of these statements necessitate divine determinism, and actually, counter to the suggestion, most seem to require a form of human freedom in order to fulfill the authors'

---

[59]John Priest, "Testament of Moses," in *The Old Testament Pseudepigrapha*, vol. 1, *Apocalyptic Literature and Testaments*, ed. James H. Charlesworth (1983; repr., Peabody, MA: Hendrickson, 2011), p. 922.

[60]Gathercole states, "The *Assumption of Moses* is predicated on a very strong theology of election. So we can again see concepts of election and works leading to glory or resurrection running parallel with one another in the same texts" (Gathercole, *Where Is Boasting?*, p. 58).

[61]VanLandingham suggests that *T. Mos.* 2:4-9; 3:5; 5:2-6; 6:2; 7:3-10; 8:3, 5, all express a "pessimistic anthropology in which the majority of Jews 'will be damned'" (VanLandingham, *Judgment and Justification*, p. 173).

[62]See Collins, "Testaments," p. 347.

[63]Elliott, *Survivors of Israel*, p. 270.

purposes. In this section, I will look at those authors who highlight human responsibility as central to keeping the covenant and receiving eternal life or blessedness.

Wisdom of Ben Sira. Ben Sira emphasizes the correlation between behavior and consequences to encourage ethical and obedient behavior.[64] In the same vein, the author also assures those who depart from the way of obedience to pursue wickedness do so of their own volition (Sir 15:11-20). He admonishes those who turn away that they cannot place the blame on the Lord or accuse him of leading them astray. Rather, when he created humankind, he "left him in the hand of his counsel."[65] The individual must decide whether they will faithfully keep the Torah or reject it, and the consequence of the decision is framed in the classic Deuteronomic equation of choosing life or death (Sir 15:15-17; cf. Deut 30:19). The implications here appear to be universal, since the Lord watches both "the ones who fear him" and "every human work" (Sir 15:19).[66]

While Ben Sira seemingly affirms the "free will" of humanity to obey or disobey the Lord in Sirach 15, in Sirach 33 he creates a tension with those previous statements. Here he affirms that the Lord has chosen to bless some and curse others

---

[64]Sir 2:7-11, for example, admonishes that those who are faithful to YHWH will be rewarded, can hope for joy and mercy, and will not be neglected in times of distress (see also Sir 11:26). Witherington thus recognizes that "Ben Sira is very firm in asserting that the wicked and the righteous both get their just due (cf. Sir. 2:7-11; 7:1; 27:26-27). Sometimes he even affirms that retribution does not delay (Sir. 7:16). However, Ben Sira is well aware that just recompense is not always immediate and sometimes not apparent at all." Witherington continues that for Ben Sira, the way in which one dies—whether peacefully or tortuously—constitutes the ultimate judgment concerning a person's life (Ben Witherington III, *Jesus the Sage: The Pilgrimage of Wisdom* [Minneapolis: Fortress, 1994], p. 87). Collins affirms that Ben Sira "is at least clear that individuals can make atonement, whether by sacrifices or by good works, and can appeal to the mercy of God (Cf. also 2:7-11; 5:5-7; 18:1-15; 21:1-3)" (Collins, *Jewish Wisdom*, p. 91).

[65]Of this section, Maston remarks, Ben Sira "argues strongly for the individual's freedom to determine his or her own destiny through obedience to the Torah. Against the view that God dictates what humans will do (vv. 11-12), Ben Sira claims that after creating the human agent God 'has given him into the hand of his inclination'" (Jason Maston, *Divine and Human Agency in Second Temple Judaism and Paul* [Tübingen: Mohr Siebeck, 2010], p. 28).

[66]There is some question as to whether the Hebrew text reads "The eyes of God behold his works" or "His eyes are upon the ones who fear him." The LXX supports the latter reading, though it may not be original. For a discussion, see Greg S. Goering, *Wisdom's Root Revealed: Ben Sira and the Election of Israel*, JSJSup 139 (Leiden: Brill, 2009), pp. 135-36.

> like clay in the hand of the potter
>> to be molded as he pleases . . .
>> to be given whatever he decides. (Sir 33:13 NRSV)[67]

Both Greg Goering and Alexander Di Lella acknowledge, though recognizing the tension, that Ben Sira stops short of determinism. Di Lella writes,

> This texts seems to say that God has decreed for each person either a blessed or a cursed destiny, independent of the person's free choice. But Ben Sira stops far short of attributing human sin to God and of saying that divine predestination destroys human freedom to choose between good and evil. In fact, the most likely meaning of 33:12cd, "Others he curses and brings low, and expels them from their place," is that God curses some people because they have chosen the path of wickedness; it is not that they are wicked because God has cursed them.[68]

Di Lella thus sees a resolution here between the tension since God's blessing and cursing still, for Ben Sira, correspond to the choice of the individual of life (i.e., following Torah) or death (i.c., disobedience).[69] Thus the text seems to indicate more about God's judgment than about a predetermined path he has outlined for each individual and from which they have no opportunity to stray. The overall emphasis of the book focuses on human responsibility and the consequences for wickedness, and thus a resolution to these statements that accounts for the book's emphasis seems the best approach to the tension.

Psalms of Solomon. *Psalms of Solomon* 18, the final psalm of the collection, offers a benediction of sorts. Here the psalmist praises God for his mercy and goodness to Israel, "the descendants of Abraham," whose discipline of them is "as (for) a firstborn son" (*Pss. Sol.* 18:1-4). The psalmist again prays for the cleansing of Israel (*Pss. Sol.* 18:5). The author describes the cleansing as preceding the messianic reign, and thus Elliott suggests, "It is only reasonable to expect that the author would demand from apostate Israel the same experience of repentance and concern for

---

[67]See Grindheim, *Crux of Election*, p. 38.
[68]Patrick W. Skehan and Alexander A. Di Lella, OFM, *The Wisdom of Ben Sira: A New Translation with Notes*, AB (New York: Doubleday, 1987), p. 83.
[69]See also Goering, *Wisdom's Root Revealed*, pp. 64-65.

piety that he demanded from his own group. . . . 18:5 suggests that restoration is the *result* rather than the *cause* of this repentance and cleansing."[70]

The tension between statements of God's mercy toward and protection of Israel and assertions about the necessity of obedience and the place of works in God's judgment seem to create polarizing extremes in the collection.[71] We need not see, however, any opposition. God grants mercy/blessings to those who are faithful to the covenant (as defined here by the community). We should view these covenantal works as in keeping with the framework of the covenant that God himself established.[72] When viewed as a collection, the emphasis of the *Psalms of Solomon* seems clear. The Jews of Jerusalem and their leaders (i.e., the Hasmoneans and Sanhedrin)[73] have transgressed the Torah, profaned the temple and failed to repent. Their sins exceed even those of the Gentiles, and they developed a false confidence that God would protect them in spite of their sin. God used the Gentiles to punish the unrighteous. Though the righteous receive this punishment as discipline, the unrighteous multiply their sins and face judgment because of their wickedness.[74] The chief polemic of the *Psalms* comes against the Jews of

---

[70]Elliott, *Survivors of Israel*, p. 560; see also p. 325.

[71]See, e.g., Daniel Falk, "Psalms and Prayers," in *Justification and Variegated Nomism*, vol. 1, *The Complexities of Second Temple Judaism*, ed. D. A. Carson, Peter T. O'Brien and Mark A. Seifrid (Grand Rapids: Baker Academic, 2001), p. 38; Gathercole, *Where Is Boasting*, p. 67; Mark A. Seifrid, *Justification by Faith: The Origin and Development of a Central Pauline Theme* (Leiden: Brill, 1992), pp. 130-31; Preston M. Sprinkle, *Law and Life: The Interpretation of Leviticus 18:5 in Early Judaism and in Paul* (Tübingen: Mohr Siebeck, 2008), p. 93.

[72]Sprinkle suggests this in stating, "In sum, the *Psalms of Solomon* do not portray salvation through self-righteous works, and yet Sanders's category of covenantal nomism is not very helpful either. We should speak, rather, of a tension whereby God's mercy is held together with the necessity of obedience. The basis for future life is not purely covenant membership, nor is it merited by works. Participation in the righteous community is essential in order to inherit the covenant promises, and this participation is dependant [*sic*] both upon obedience and upon God's mercy" (Sprinkle, *Law and Life*, p. 93). This is contra Atkinson and Lane, who see primarily a theology of merit (Kenneth Atkinson, "Enduring the Lord's Discipline: Soteriology in the *Psalms of Solomon*," in Gurtner, *This World and the World to Come*, pp. 160, 162; William L. Lane, "Paul's Legacy from Pharisaism: Light from the Psalms of Solomon," *Concordia Journal* 8 [1982]: 133), and Sanders who sees only a theology of mercy (Sanders, *Paul and Palestinian Judaism*, p. 393). See also VanLandingham, *Judgment and Justification*, p. 44.

[73]See Elliott, *Survivors of Israel*, pp. 93-94.

[74]And so Grindheim writes, "Whereas the present punishments are a signal of rejection for the nation as a whole, the righteous accept this as discipline and thus demonstrate that they constitute the group for which the election-based promises are still valid" (Grindheim, *Crux of Elec-*

Jerusalem, and the author indicts the entire city, as the devout have escaped to the wilderness to avoid defilement. The fate of the individual is determined by their choice of the way of life (righteousness) or the way of death (wickedness), and though the author affirms the election of Israel through Abraham, they qualify the national language and title of "Israel" as applying only to the "true Israel," the devout community responsible for the collection.[75] The collection places its emphasis on human agency, though the community is dependent on God's mercy and faithfulness. The devout, though not sinless themselves,[76] will inherit the promises of God because of their repentant spirit and pursuit of righteousness.

Dead Sea Scrolls. 1QS is addressed to the "instructor," and seeks to equip the community[77] to do what is good, just, commanded, selected and true,[78] and "to welcome all those who freely volunteer to carry out God's decrees into the covenant of kindness" (1QS 1.1-8). Even at the beginning of the text, we must note the tension throughout 1QS. Here, those who join the community "freely volunteer" to "carry out God's decrees" (1QS 1.7). Thus Emmanuel Tukasi can state, commenting on the more deterministic language in the book, "The fact that the universal order is set beforehand is indisputable,"[79] while Alfred Leaney asserts that the "men of the sect, though God's chosen, must each make his own

---

tion, p. 51). See also Falk, "Psalms and Prayers," p. 44; Robert B. Wright, "Psalms of Solomon," in *The Old Testament Pseudepigrapha*, vol. 2, *Expansions of the "Old Testament" and Legends, Wisdom and Philosophical Literature, Prayers, Psalms, and Odes, Fragments of Lost Judeo-Hellenistic Works*, ed. James H. Charlesworth (1985; repr., Peabody, MA: Hendrickson, 2011), p. 643.

[75]Elliott, *Survivors of Israel*, pp. 556, 559; Falk, "Psalms and Prayers," p. 50; Sprinkle, *Law and Life*, p. 92.

[76]See Falk, "Psalms and Prayers," p. 42; Grindheim, *Crux of Election*, p. 51.

[77]For a discussion of the meaning and referent of יחד (*yahad*), see Arie van der Kooij, "The *Yahad*—What Is in a Name?," *DSD* 18 (2011): 109-28.

[78]Tukasi comments, "Hatred in both human beings and God is directed towards whatever falls outside of the divine choices as revealed in the scripture. Thus, human beings love and hate in accordance with what God chooses and what he rejects. It is this idea of divine choice (בחר) and reject (מאס) that forms the essence of טוב and רע respectively in the *Rule of the Community*" (Emmanuel O. Tukasi, "Dualism and Penitential Prayer in the *Rule of the Community* (1QS)," in *Dualism in Qumran*, ed. Géza G. Xeravits [New York: T&T Clark, 2010], p. 179).

[79]Emmanuel O. Tukasi, *Determinism and Petitionary Prayer in John and the Dead Sea Scrolls: An Ideological Reading of John and the Reading of the Community (1QS)* (New York: T&T Clark, 2008), p. 30.

decision to practise the Law of Moses as interpreted in their community."[80]

We find perhaps the most heavily discussed and most debated portion of 1QS in 3.17–4.26, where we find the so-called Treatise on the Two Spirits. The author states that the instructor is obligated to teach the sons of light about the designs of God. According to 1QS 3, this includes divulging when the sons of light "have come into being, at their appointed time, they will execute all their works according to his glorious design, without altering anything. In his hand are the laws of all things and he supports them in all their affairs" (1QS 3.13-17). Furthermore, within human beings God has placed two spirits—truth and deceit—which walk with him "until the moment of his visitation" (1QS 3.17-19). The spirit of deceit and the angel of darkness rule over the sons of deceit, while the spirit of truth and the prince of lights rule over the sons of justice. All sin, grief and affliction comes from the angel of darkness, even for the sons of light, but the prince of lights and the God of Israel aid the sons of light/justice in resisting these evil powers (1QS 3.19-26).

Some take God himself placing these spirits in humanity to indicate that he has predetermined the ultimate fate of each person.[81] Others have suggested, since truth itself can be defiled by injustice and "the spirits of truth and injustice feud in the heart of man" (1QS 4.23), that the spirits are simply the good and evil force inside of each person.[82] Others

[80]Alfred R. C. Leaney, *The Rule of Qumran and Its Meaning: Introduction, Translation and Commentary* (Philadelphia: Westminster, 1966), p. 119.

[81]Vermes, for example, takes this section to mean that the sect "insisted, moreover, on the individual election of each sectary" (Geza Vermes, *The Dead Sea Scrolls: Qumran in Perspective* [Cleveland: William Collins & World, 1978], p. 171). See also Alexander, "Predestination and Free Will," p. 31; Grindheim, *Crux of Election*, p. 57. Preben Wernberg-Møller compares the doctrine to Augustine's formulation of double predestination (Preben Wernberg-Møller, "A Reconsideration of the Two Spirits in the Rule of the Community (1 Q Serek III,13—IV,26)," *RevQ* 3, no. 3 [1961]: 424). Tukasi seems to agree in stating, "The universe as it now exists could not have been other than what it is. This is a cosmological type of determinism" (Tukasi, *Determinism and Petitionary Prayer*, p. 36), and, "Human activity is not actually theirs per se but is produced by the spirit which has the dominion over them" (ibid., p. 37), though he also notes elsewhere that "'the walk' of each person determines his or her category. Thus to walk in truth, light and righteousness is to fall in the lot of God, and to walk in darkness and deceit is to belong under the dominion of Belial" (ibid., p. 48).

[82]So Leaney writes, "The main doctrine at Qumran appears to have been that every individual man is a mixture of the two spirits, but the thought certainly oscillates between two sets of terms, truth/perversity, light/darkness; and from the metaphorical and inexact way of writing when the latter set is used, as from the fact that light/darkness seems to provide a fundamental antith-

still see them as more or less absolute categories.[83] Before returning to these options, a discussion of the remainder of the passage is necessary.

According to the author, those who follow the paths of true justice through the enlightenment of the spirit of truth—typified by meekness, patience, compassion, goodness, knowledge, wisdom, dependence on God and detesting of idols—will enjoy eternal life and blessings (1QS 4.2-7). Those, however, who are led by the spirit of deceit—typified by greed, lack of compassion, deceit, pride, cruelty, impatience, foolishness, lustful acts, blasphemy and stubbornness—will suffer eternal damnation and humiliation, with no remnant or survivor remaining (1QS 4.9-14).[84]

The dualism described here appears absolute in the sense that these two trajectories may encapsulate all of humanity, and "every deed they do (falls) into their divisions" (1QS 4.15-16). In God's visitation, the injustice perpetrated by the wicked will cease, and the upright will receive purification, with the spirit of injustice removed from them, and will receive the anointing of the spirit of truth (1QS 4.18-22). So the sons of light themselves cannot claim perfection since both spirits are at war within the heart of the individual (1QS 4.23).[85] In 1QS 4.25 we find that the righteous and the wicked have been sorted by God "into equal parts until the appointed end and the new creation." Paul Heger, contra Florentino García Martínez and following Geza Vermes, translates 4.25 as "For God has established the two spirits in equal measure until the determined end."[86] Thus the sons of man (i.e., humanity) know both good and evil, and God has "cast the lot of every living being according to his spirit in [. . . until the time of] the visitation" (1QS 4.26).

---

esis" (Leaney, *Rule of Qumran*, pp. 37-38; see also pp. 149, 155). See also Marco Treves, "Two Spirits of the Rule of the Community," *RevQ* 3, no. 3 (1961): 450.

[83]See Alexander, "Predestination and Free Will," p. 29; Merrill, *Qumran and Predestination*, p. 44; Preben Wernberg-Møller, *The Manual of Discipline: Translated and Annotated with an Introduction* (Grand Rapids: Eerdmans, 1957), p. 84.

[84]Gathercole writes, "The abundance of 'eternal' language here points toward an unending glorious state for the righteous, and the corresponding opposite for the wicked. From them there will be no remnant or survivor" (Gathercole, *Where Is Boasting*, p. 99).

[85]So Alexander writes, "There is a note of realism here: the elect are capable of sinning . . . [and] the righteous only become perfect at the eschaton" (Alexander, "Predestination and Free Will," p. 32).

[86]Heger, *Challenges*, p. 327.

To return to the question posed earlier, since we find both the spirit of darkness and the spirit of light influencing the sons of light, it seems most likely that the notion of the intermingling of the spirits best explains the passage. In keeping with the first column of 1QS, it seems reasonable, if not preferable, to understand this section as stating that God has defined the boundaries of good and evil, and that both impulses reside within each individual. God has also chosen a people (i.e., the community, the "true Israel"), and the members of this people are typified by the behaviors brought about by the influence of the spirit of light. This does not prevent the spirit of darkness from influencing them, but rather it seems that whatever spirit receives the dominant influence in the individual determines their lot. Thus Tukasi states correctly, "This struggle is inconsistent with the notion that a person's lot is determined. If a person's lot in truth or deceit were already fixed and unalterable, the struggle between the two spirits would be irrelevant."[87]

What appears, however, to be central in all of this development of the concept of different lots, spirits and God's declaration of what is good and evil is the definition of the boundaries of the true people of God. Thus Elliott suggests—and Heger agrees—that the Treatise on the Two Spirits "functioned within the context of intra-Jewish debate to legitimize and explain the division felt to exist *within Israel*, not to outline a doctrine of predestination."[88] The fundamental question this text answers is why not all of Israel can currently identify with the elect community. They have sinned, and the existence of the two spirits explains why they sinned. The clear presence of conditional elements for membership in the elect community, and the lack of any necessity to see ab-

---

[87]Tukasi, *Determinism and Petitionary Prayer*, p. 59. Heger likewise writes, "If some humans are condemned to be wicked, lacking faculty ever to repent and change, what would be the divine rationale for implanting in them some righteous spirit or inclination? Further, it is only reasonable to assume that Dual Predestination applies equally to the righteous: If they are chosen to be perpetually righteous, there would be no reason to implant in them bad inclinations. . . . Finally, it seems to me inconceivable that the highly intellectual Qumran scholars would have created a theology that contradicts the cardinal biblical doctrine of repentance and forgiveness" (Heger, *Challenges*, p. 328).

[88]Elliott, *Survivors of Israel*, p. 407; Paul Heger, "Another Look at Dualism in Qumran Writings," in Xeravits, *Dualism in Qumran*, pp. 75-76.

solute determinism as present in this section, along with the contextual factors mentioned above, all militate against understanding 1QS to be promoting a kind of double predestination.

Interestingly, though column 4 is so heavy with deterministic language, column 5 begins with the assertion that "this is the rule for the men of the Community who freely volunteer to convert from all evil and to keep themselves steadfast in all he commanded in compliance with his will" (1QS 5.1; as in CD!). This notion again nullifies the possibility of understanding what has preceded as referencing some kind of absolute determinism.[89] Those who enter this covenant community do so in submission to the sons of Zadok, the priests and the community itself, which entails submitting to their "decision by lot . . . in every affair involving the law, property and judgment" (1QS 5.2-3).

We frequently find deterministic language bookended with conditional clarifications, which appear incompatible.[90] I suggested, however, that the language primarily deals with the recognition that God has declared certain ways to be true and good, and others to be deceitful and evil,[91] and the spirits influence individuals in these ways. The individual, however, must *walk*, in one way or the other, and their choice ultimately determines their fate.[92]

Paul's "Both/And" View

The tendency among most interpreters of Paul gravitates toward the divine-initiative end of the spectrum when looking at Paul's thought and

---

[89]Timmer writes, "Since these voluntary elements are not consistently conditioned by an anthropology in which all human works are in need of purification, they suggest the possibility of a cooperative soteriology, something that comes more clearly into view in the *Community Rule*'s theology of atonement" (Daniel C. Timmer, "Variegated Nomism Indeed: Multiphase Eschatology and Soteriology in the Qumranite *Community Rule* (1QS) and the New Perspective on Paul," *JETS* 52, no. 2 [2009]: 347). This is contrasted with Schwartz, who suggests that new members must be thought of as "'sons of light' all along" (Schwartz, "To Join Oneself," pp. 445-46).

[90]Treves states succinctly, "It seems to me that our author's predestinarianism has been somewhat exaggerated" (Treves, "Two Spirits," p. 451).

[91]See Tukasi, *Determinism and Petitionary Prayer*, p. 62.

[92]See ibid., p. 61; Grindheim, *Crux of Election*, p. 65. Contra Dimant, who writes, "While the biblical covenant implies a real choice and acceptance, and the curses and blessings function as threats and rewards, the covenant of the sectaries asserts and reinforces a situation predetermined by God from the beginning" (Dimant, "Qumran Sectarian Literature," 2:500).

tends to minimize the extent to which Paul incorporates human responsibility. It seems to me, however, that Paul, like most of his Jewish contemporaries, asserts both realities in a manner that does not hamper one
for the sake of the other. By this I do not mean that Paul understands
divine and human action to be occurring on the same level or to the
same efficacy. But neither should we take Paul as asserting that God acts
in such a unilateral manner so as to make the presence of human responsibility either illusory or meaningless.

Romans 8:1-17. Many scholars have taken this section of Romans as
indicating Paul has a unilateral or meticulous view of divine agency, to the
extent the role humans play becomes minimal or nonexistent.[93] To tackle
Romans 8 we must first get a sense of its context. I cannot, of course, ex-
pound on Romans 7 in its entirety. Paul seems to argue in Romans 7 that
we must not view the law negatively since "sin" kept it from bringing life.
This does not represent a defect in the law, but rather a defect in those who
attempt to keep it; those hampered by the weakness of human flesh.[94] As
Paul closes the chapter (Rom 7:24-25), he asserts that God, through Jesus,
sets the body free from death (and assumedly sin), and Paul subsequently
raises the issue of serving the law on one hand and sin on the other.

Paul immediately turns his attention to this very issue in Romans 8. In
other words, it seems to me the address of Romans 8 deals with the tension
between obedience to God or to "sin." As Paul begins in Romans 8:1, he
asserts, "There is therefore now no condemnation for those who are in
Christ Jesus."[95] Paul explains how this lack of condemnation connects to

---

[93]Maston tends to emphasize the divine act in the Spirit as the ground for human agency, with
human agency more or less nonexistent while under the control of "Sin" (Maston, *Divine and
Human Agency*, pp. 159-68). Maston further states, "Additionally, it would be inaccurate to describe the believer's obedience as a 'response' to God's act in Christ. . . . For Paul, though, obedience is a continuation of God's act. There is no separation between God's deliverance of the
human in Christ and God's Spirit conforming believers into the image of Christ" (ibid., p. 169).
Sprinkle similarly concludes, "Christ and the spirit are the effective agents through whom God
unilaterally redeems and transforms his people" (Sprinkle, *Paul and Judaism Revisited*, p. 109
[emphasis mine]). Much of Sprinkle's argument rests on demonstrating that Paul favored a "prophetic" model rather than a "Deuteronomistic" model, which seems an unnecessary dichotomy.
[94]For a helpful treatment of "flesh" in Paul, see James D. G. Dunn, *The Theology of Paul the
Apostle* (Grand Rapids: Eerdmans, 1998), pp. 51-78; I. Howard Marshall, "Living in the 'Flesh,'"
BSac 159 (Oct–Dec 2002): 387-403.
[95]Or, those "in the realm" of Christ. See Constantine R. Campbell, *Paul and Union with Christ:*

God's work in Christ and the law of God in Romans 8:2, indicated by the conjunction γάρ. Thomas Schreiner says of Romans 8:1, "The reason believers are not under condemnation is because they have been freed from the tyranny of the law, for sin exercises dominion over those under the law."[96] It seems to me, however, that Paul understands not the law as the problem but rather "sin," which, when dealt with, allows believers to fulfill the law. The tyrant is "sin" and the law its co-opted hireling. Paul states as much in Romans 8:2, explaining that this condemnation comes in light of "the law of the Spirit of life" (ὁ νόμος τοῦ πνεύματος τῆς ζωῆς) setting them free from the "law of sin and death" (τοῦ νόμου τῆς ἁμαρτίας καὶ τοῦ θανάτου). Here two features stand out. First, the law here clearly refers to the Torah, and not to a "principle," as many commentators suggest.[97] The context demands as much given that the whole of Romans 7 focuses more or less on the law. Second, the "Spirit of life" here contains no mere abstract description but in all likelihood echoes back to Romans 7:10, which indicates that the purpose of the law was to bring life. Paul sees this purpose as fulfilled when the law functions in the realm of the Spirit and Christ rather than outside of it, where sin and death reign.

Paul further elaborates this point in Romans 8:3-4, where he asserts God accomplished what the law was unable to (because of sin) by condemning sin in the flesh of the Son so the "τὸ δικαίωμα τοῦ νόμου might be fulfilled in those who are walking not according to the flesh but according to the Spirit" (Romans 8:4).[98] Wright suggests that the inability of the law here includes its inability "not to produce mere ethical be-

---

An Exegetical and Theological Study (Grand Rapids: Zondervan, 2012), p. 128; Chuck Lowe, "'There Is No Condemnation' (Romans 8:1): But Why Not?," *JETS* 42, no. 2 (June 1999): 239.

[96]Thomas R. Schreiner, *Romans*, BECNT (Grand Rapids: Baker Academic, 1998), p. 398.

[97]E.g., Robert H. Mounce, *Romans*, NAC (Nashville: Broadman & Holman, 1995), pp. 174-75. See Klyne Snodgrass, "Spheres of Influence: A Possible Solution to the Problem of Paul and the Law," *JSNT* 32 (1988): 106.

[98]Or as McFadden states, "Paul's explanation of 8:1-2, then, is that the law was impotent to accomplish its goal of life, and because of this situation, God accomplished what the law could not: God condemned sin in the flesh of his Son, taking care of the reason for the law's impotency" (Kevin W. McFadden, "The Fulfillment of the Law's *Dikaiōma*: Another Look at Romans 8:1-4," *JETS* 52, no. 3 [2009]: 487). McFadden suggests that Paul understood the law to require perfect obedience, which seems unlikely in my mind given what we know of Judaism and what we see in Paul's own writings, and thus concludes that the fulfillment of this righteous requirement is a forward-looking, future event when Christians are resurrected (ibid., p. 494).

havior, but to give *life*—that is, the life of the new age, resurrection life."[99]
In its covenantal context, the intent of the law aimed at giving life to
Israel, but it brought, because of "sin," death instead. God does not jet-
tison his plan for the law to create life, but rather frees it from "sin," which
has been condemned because of Jesus, and places it in the realm of the
Spirit, where it can accomplish this original intent.[100] Klyne Snodgrass
summarizes quite well:

> Now in 8.2 the law functioning in the sphere of the life-giving Spirit frees.
> Again it is the genitive in each case that must be emphasized, but the law
> is still an actor on the stage. It is not the law itself that frees; 8.3 precludes
> such a thought. But the law is not left out of the picture. It has been too
> important in the discussion just to be forgotten. If the law is not involved
> in salvation, then sin is a victor because it defeated God's law which was
> for life (7.13, 10). But now the law is placed within the sphere of the Spirit
> (cf. 8.4), where it belongs (7.14). The law in the right sphere frees us from
> the tyranny of the law in the sphere of sin.[101]

Schreiner is correct that walking according to the Spirit under the law of
the Spirit in Christ refers to "the concrete working out of the law in the
lives of believers"[102] rather than to Christ's fulfilling the law and doing
away with it entirely.[103]

With the "law" here defined in terms of its relation to the power that
controls it, we should return to τὸ δικαίωμα τοῦ νόμου being fulfilled by
walking in the Spirit. It seems likely that Paul intended κατάκριμα (Rom
8:1) and δικαίωμα (Rom 8:4) to stand as contrasting terms, the first indicating the negative judicial verdict (decree of condemnation) and the
second declaring its opposite (decree of acquittal).[104] In other words,

---

[99]N. T. Wright, *The Climax of the Covenant: Christ and the Law in Pauline Theology* (New York:
T&T Clark, 1991), p. 202.

[100]So I take Paul's reference to the "law of the Spirit" here as in the sense of "the law under the
authority of the Spirit" rather than as metaphorical as Byrne and others suggest (Brendan
Byrne, "ΝΟΜΟΣ and the Relationship with Judaism in Romans," *CBQ* 62 [2000]: 305).

[101]Snodgrass, "Spheres of Influence," p. 107. See also Dunn, *Theology of Paul*, p. 646.

[102]Thomas R. Schreiner, *Paul, Apostle of God's Glory in Christ: A Pauline Theology* (Downers Grove,
IL: InterVarsity Press, 2001), p. 327; Schreiner, *Romans*, p. 406.

[103]See Sprinkle, *Paul and Judaism Revisited*, p. 106.

[104]Wright, *Climax of the Covenant*, p. 212.

God pronounces right-standing, grounded in the faithfulness of Jesus (see Rom 3), over those in Christ who keep the law by the empowerment of the Spirit. As Romans 8:3 indicates, the condemnation fell on "sin" (κατέκρινεν τὴν ἁμαρτία) and not the "law," allowing the law to fulfill its proper and always intended function. And so, as James Dunn states, "For Paul, the objective of God's saving action in Christ was to make possible the keeping of the law!"[105] For Paul this does not become a way to smuggle Gentiles under the Mosaic law and thereby require they submit to circumcision, something he argues adamantly against in Romans and Galatians. It seems, rather, that the law, at least as it relates to Gentiles, becomes transformed so the essential means of observing it, through the empowerment of the Spirit, becomes love of neighbor and love of God (see Rom 13:8-10; Gal 5:13-18, 23; 6:2). This does not mean Paul never uses the law to ground ethical imperatives for Gentile believers, since he does (Rom 13:9; 1 Cor 5:13; 9:9; 14:34; 2 Cor 6:16; Eph 5:31; 6:2-3). Rather, by loving God and others, through the foundation laid by Christ and the enabling work of the Spirit, we might then say Gentiles fulfill the true intent of the law. This is the essence of the requirements of the new covenant for Paul.[106]

In Romans 8:5-8, Paul expands on the contrast introduced in Romans 8:3-4 between the flesh and the Spirit. There Paul assured his readers that the weakness of the flesh prevented the law, because of sin, from fulfilling its purpose while the Spirit has provided the means by which it could accomplish that purpose. Here he reassures those who maintain their focus on the flesh rather than the Spirit will find death instead of life and peace (Rom 8:5-6). This reiteration of the Spirit as bringing "life and peace" should again call our minds to the fulfillment of the law's purpose

---

[105]Dunn, *Theology of Paul*, p. 646. This still accords with my reading of Galatians, wherein Paul is concerned with the fundamental way in which God's people are identified. It is clear that this renewed sense of the law does not entail that Gentiles keep certain aspects of the prescriptions of the Mosaic law, such as circumcision, but Paul can still call on the law elsewhere as an obligation for all believers, Jew and Gentile alike.

[106]As Wright comments on Rom 8:9-11, "The echoes of Ezekiel 37 in Romans 8.9-11 . . . make clear what this is about: resurrection indicates covenant restoration and renewal" (Wright, *Paul and the Faithfulness of God*, p. 720).

in the giving of the Spirit.[107] Paul may be echoing here Isaiah 63:10, where those who disobey God anger his Spirit and become his enemies (ἔχθραν) as they likewise do in Romans 8:7 (ἔχθρα). Simply put, the flesh cannot please God because "sin" and death still rule over it. It seems unlikely, as Schreiner has suggested, that Paul has in mind here an absolute division between believers (in the Spirit) and unbelievers (in the flesh).[108] First, the conditional sentences in Romans 8:9-11 indicate the possibility that some of the recipients of Romans may in fact not be "in the Spirit." Second, believers can walk "in the flesh" since Paul warns them against this very thing in Romans 13:14. Furthermore, Romans 8:12-13 seems to present an imperative of sorts to the Roman believers reminding them their obligation is to living according to the Spirit.[109]

In addition, Paul, as elsewhere in his letters, presents a tension between the "now" and the "not yet." In Romans 8:1, for example, he declares that there "is now no condemnation" for those in Christ. The present obligation of believers throughout Romans 8 emphasizes the need for them to walk/live "in the Spirit" and not "in the flesh," both of which Paul holds out as real possibilities. This walking anticipates a future event as those in whom the Spirit dwells *are* made alive (Rom 8:10) yet *will* receive life in their mortal bodies (Rom 8:11, 13).[110] Paul links this future aspect of their salvation with their relationship to the Spirit. That Paul views this as an ongoing necessity seems clear from 8:14, where "those who *are being led* by the Spirit" are God's children.[111] While many

---

[107]So Wright states, "When God by his Spirit works to bring life to a person (Romans 8.9-11), the desire and purpose of the Torah is thereby being fulfilled" (Wright, *Climax of the Covenant*, p. 209).

[108]See Schreiner, *Paul*, p. 135; Schreiner, *Romans*, pp. 411-12.

[109]Byrne states here, "Obedience is an integral element in the process. Salvation will not, of course, rest upon how many good works have been accomplished . . . but it will depend upon whether one has held fast and remained obedient to the new life in Christ communicated by the Spirit" (Brendan Byrne, "Living out the Righteousness of God: The Contribution of Rom 6:1-8:13 to an Understanding of Paul's Ethical Presuppositions," *CBQ* 43 [1981]: 577).

[110]Wright comments on Rom 8:10, "*dikaiosynē* refers to the verdict 'righteous' issued in the present over all those who believe, issued because of the Messiah's faithfulness, his self-giving to death . . . so Romans 8.10 indicates that 'righteousness'—the status which results from the verdict of the divine court, the polar opposite of 'condemnation' as in 8.1, the status which carries with it the notion of 'covenant membership' as in Romans 4—belongs at the heart of the exposition of 'being in Christ'" (Wright, *Paul and the Faithfulness of God*, p. 901).

[111]And so, "Those who thus obey Israel's God, the creator, will be acknowledged as 'God's son'" (ibid., p. 661).

have sought to place Paul's language here in a Greco-Roman context, his language fits more squarely in the context of Jewish theology. Paul asserts that those "who are being led by the Spirit" are "sons of God" (Rom 8:14), have "not received a spirit of slavery" (Rom 8:15), have "received a spirit of adoption" (Rom 8:15), "are children of God" (Rom 8:16) and "are heirs" and "fellow heirs with Christ" (Rom 8:17). The language here clearly harkens back to God's relationship with Israel, terminology we find in the Old Testament and Second Temple literature. As George Gianoulis notes of this language and its context, "Israel's sonship was closely associated with covenant and may be considered a metaphor of covenant itself. . . . As son, Israel was to revere and obey the commandments of Yahweh. Thus the honorific title 'son(s) of God' was pregnant with meaning for Israel, signifying the unique relationship Israel had with Yahweh as the people of the covenant."[112] Paul asserts that those who walk "in the Spirit" as a result of being "in Christ" are God's children. That Paul invokes the Jewish notion of election here, God choosing a people for himself to accomplish his purposes, seems beyond doubt. And Paul identifies those who walk in the Spirit and not the flesh as God's children. This possibility arises only from the initiative of God, but Paul presents this as no one-sided or unilateral activity in which God initiates, ensures the response and controls the process. Rather, a real responsibility exists since those who claim the name of Jesus *must* walk in the Spirit. Dunn summarizes this well:

> Yet if the Spirit-flesh antithesis were a thing of the past for the believer (as 8.2-9 might be taken to imply), then what meaning would there be in Paul advising his readers that they were "under no obligation to live in accordance with the flesh" (8.12)? How could he warn them that if they lived in accordance with the flesh, they would die (8.13)? How could he exhort them to put to death the deeds of the body and promise them life in consequence (8.13)? The only obvious answer is that the Spirit persons were still in danger of succumbing to the flesh, to its weakness and desires. They were not yet the ideal Spirit people, not yet the realized eschatological

---

[112]George C. Gianoulis, "Is Sonship in Romans 8:14-17 a Link with Romans 9?," *BSac* 166 (Jan–March 2009): 78.

hope of resurrected bodies. In the tension of the between times they had to be resolute in maintaining their alignment with the Spirit and in resisting the lure of sin in flesh.[113]

To summarize, in this train of thought in Romans 8, Paul contends that God has rescued the law, which "sin" prevented from fulfilling its purposes, has condemned "sin," and placed the law in the proper sphere of the Spirit. The Torah showed the path to the good life, but could not give eschatological life to God's people because of "sin's" sway. Now, however, those "in Christ" fulfill the law of the Spirit by walking in the enablement of the Spirit, which for Paul (in particular for Gentile believers) likely does not mean submitting to the requirements of the Mosaic law per se (e.g., circumcision), but rather fulfilling the law by loving God and loving others. This fulfillment comes through the enablement of the Spirit, but not at the removal of the actual responsibility of the individual. Those "in Christ" must persist in obeying the Spirit since Paul presents the possibility of succumbing to the flesh and thus to death as a real one. And those who submit themselves to the Spirit can truly be identified as God's children and the inheritors of his promises.

Ephesians 1:3–2:10. Another passage that is frequently called on in the discussion of divine and human agency in Paul is found in Ephesians. In Ephesians 1:4, Paul declares God "blessed" because he has "chosen us for himself in Christ before the foundation of the world that we might be holy and blameless before him in love, by choosing us beforehand for adoption as sons through Jesus Christ." First, Paul clearly envisions election as occurring within the sphere of Christ,[114] and so it appears that

---

[113]Dunn, *Theology of Paul*, p. 480.

[114]As Lincoln notes, "In many cases, Paul's 'in Christ' phrase involves the notion of the incorporation of believers into Christ, and this concept of the incorporation of many in one representative head, together with the use of ἐν, can be seen in the LXX in regard to other figures, such as Abraham (Gen 12:3) and Isaac (Gen 21:12), and in Paul in regard to Adam (1 Cor 15:22)" (Andrew T. Lincoln, *Ephesians*, WBC [Dallas: Word, 1990], p. 21). Lincoln suggests that "it is by explicitly linking the notion of election to that of being 'in Christ' that Ephesians takes further the discussion of election found in the undisputed Pauline letters" (ibid., p. 23), but as already shown above, this is quite consistent with what we have already examined. See also Stephen A. Fowl, *Ephesians*, NTL (Louisville: Westminster John Knox, 2012), p. 39; Carey C. Newman, "Election and Predestination in Ephesians 1:4-6a: An Exegetical-Theological Study of the Historical, Christological Realization of God's Purpose," *RevExp* 93 (Feb 1996): 238; Peter

he is thinking along the lines of "corporate election."[115] Second, God desires to create a blameless people set apart for him.[116] Third, God intends to accomplish the plan through his previous decision to adopt the elect as children through Jesus Christ.[117] While exegetes frequently hang much weight on προορίσας, as seen in Romans, the term simply means to decide beforehand, and does not contain any inherently deterministic value within the term itself.[118] The passage states that God decided beforehand for those elect in Christ to become adopted children of God through Christ.[119] We need not read this as God marking out certain individuals for salvation and thereby rejecting others, but rather determining the sphere and the means by which his people will be identified as his children.

S. Williamson, *Ephesians*, Catholic Commentary on Sacred Scripture (Grand Rapids: Baker Academic, 2009), p. 33.

[115]Contra O'Brien, who states that it "is inappropriate, however, to suggest that election in Christ is primarily corporate rather than personal and individual" (Peter Thomas O'Brien, *The Letter to the Ephesians*, Pillar New Testament Commentary [Grand Rapids: Eerdmans, 1999], p. 99). Patzia's view seems to pose a conflict between God's corporate election of Israel in the Old Testament and his view that God chooses specific individuals for salvation in the New Testament (Arthur G. Patzia, *Ephesians, Colossians, Philemon*, UBCS [Grand Rapids: Baker Books, 2011], p. 151). Schreiner objects to a corporate interpretation on several grounds. "First, the text does not specifically say that Christ was elected. The object of the verb 'chose' is 'us' in Eph 1:4. It is incorrect to see the emphasis on the election of Christ inasmuch as the verse stresses the election of people" (Thomas R. Schreiner, "Does Romans 9 Teach Individual Election unto Salvation? Some Exegetical and Theological Reflections," *JETS* 36, no. 1 [1993]: 37). "Second, when the text says 'he chose us in him' it probably means that God chose that the Church would experience salvation 'through Christ.' He is the agent and person through whom the electing work of God would come to fruition. When God planned to save some, he intended from the beginning that their salvation would be effected through the work of Christ. Third, thus it seems to me that those who stress that election is 'in Christ' end up denying that God chose a corporate group in any significant sense. All God's choice of a corporate group means is that God chose that all who put their faith in Christ would be saved. Those who put their faith in Christ would be designated the Church" (ibid., p. 38). Contra Schreiner, Abasciano writes, "The idea is rather that Jesus is the Elect One (Schreiner gets this point right) and the Church was chosen as a consequence of its being in Christ. Christ is the sphere of election. All who are in him share in his election just as all who were in Jacob/Israel were also elect" (Brian J. Abasciano, "Corporate Election in Romans 9: A Reply to Thomas Schreiner," *JETS* 49, no. 2 [2006]: 366).

[116]See Fowl, *Ephesians*, p. 41; Lincoln, *Ephesians*, p. 24; Thomas R. Yoder Neufeld, *Ephesians*, BCBC (Scottdale, PA: Herald, 2001), p. 60; Newman, "Election and Predestination," p. 240.

[117]Newman writes, "The election of those in Christ is made certain *because* of God's predestining work through Christ. Thus, *Paul sees that God's electing in, through, and by Christ lies within his predestining activity*" (Newman, "Election and Predestination," p. 240 [emphasis original]).

[118]Newman suggests that the timing is a result of the incarnational work of Jesus Christ (ibid., pp. 237-43).

[119]See Lincoln, *Ephesians*, p. 27.

We should also note that these promises of God originated as promises to Israel, and in the context here those promises should quite likely be associated with Jewish Christ followers. John McRay makes the point quite well:

> It is in the context of the role of Israel as the elect—chosen to provide the Messiah—rather than in the context of individual predestination to salvation, that Paul speaks of election. . . . Paul asserts in this chapter that the Jews, God's saints or holy ones, were "chosen" to bring the blessing of redemption to all nations in fulfillment of the promise to Abraham. It was the Jews who were foreordained unto adoption for this purpose (Eph. 1:5), chosen in the beloved (i.e., Messiah) for God's glory (i.e., to declare the sovereignty of monotheism, Eph. 1:6) before the foundation of the world to be "holy and blameless" (i.e., saints, Eph. 1:4) and to be the first to hope in the Messiah (Eph. 1:12).[120]

God thus determined that he would root his people in Christ.[121] God first called Israel as his children,[122] and thus God's choice for a family in Christ began with his adoption of Israel.[123] Since God's election occurred "before the foundation of the world," Paul may share the belief found in the Second Temple period that God's choice of a people for himself, specifically of Israel, occurred before creation (see *Jub.* 2:19; 1QM 13.9-10; *1 En.* 93:5; *Bib. Ant.* 60.2).[124]

---

[120]John McRay, *Paul: His Life and Teaching* (Grand Rapids: Baker Academic, 2003), pp. 339-40.

[121]So Yee states, "By saying that Christ is 'involved' in God's electing activity, the author of Ephesians is able to lay bare his claim that Christ is indeed the definitive self-expression of God's original purpose in electing his people" (Tet-Lim N. Yee, *Jews, Gentiles and Ethnic Reconciliation: Paul's Jewish Identity and Ephesians* [Cambridge: Cambridge University Press, 2005], p. 37). O'Brien does not see the continuity here and suggests that adoption belonged to Israel in the Old Testament, but "now it belongs to Christians" (O'Brien, *Letter to the Ephesians*, pp. 102-3).

[122]See Ben Witherington III, *The Letters to Philemon, the Colossians, and the Ephesians: A Socio-Rhetorical Commentary on the Captivity Epistles* (Grand Rapids: Eerdmans, 2007), p. 234; Klyne Snodgrass, *Ephesians*, NIVAC (Grand Rapids: Zondervan, 1996), p. 49.

[123]Bruce suggests that the backdrop of adoption here may be God's deliverance of Israel from Egypt and calling them as his sons; see Ex 4:22 (F. F. Bruce, *The Epistles to the Colossians, to Philemon, and to the Ephesians*, NICNT [Grand Rapids: Eerdmans, 1984], p. 257). Lincoln likewise notes that Paul, in Rom 9:4, lists adoption as one of Israel's privileges (Lincoln, *Ephesians*, p. 25). A Jewish background here seems more appropriate than Roman parallels (see, e.g., Fowl, *Ephesians*, p. 42), though it is difficult to say that those practices would have had no bearing on how the text was read.

[124]So while Lincoln and Newman are correct to note that the OT never speaks of Israel's election as having occurred "before the creation of the world" (Lincoln, *Ephesians*, p. 23; Newman, "Election and Predestination," p. 239), Jewish texts of the period do evidence the view.

We see further echoes of the "Jewishness" of the passage in Ephesians 1:7. Here Paul states that redemption has come through the blood of the Son, effecting the forgiveness of trespasses. The exodus certainly stands in the background here, God's paradigmatic act of salvation in the Old Testament by which he delivered Israel from Egypt, the sign of which was the blood over the doorpost.[125] So here, the new exodus occurs through the blood of the Lamb of God, who has redeemed the people of God.[126] In Ephesians 1:9, Paul affirms that God first revealed the secret of his will to the Jews, something done publicly in the incarnation of Christ.[127] In Ephesians 1:11, Paul states, "in whom also we have been chosen by lot, being determined beforehand according to the purpose of the one who is working all things according to the intention of his will." As Stephen Fowl notes, "Similar language, which also has connections to choosing by lot (cf. Num 26:55-56), is often used in Deuteronomy to speak of God's choosing Israel as God's special possession (Deut 4:20; 9:26, 29; 32:9)."[128] Paul contends in the beginning of Ephesians 1 Jewish believers stood in the line of God's choosing of Israel, and as God's plan unfolded, they became "the first to set our hope on Christ" (Eph 1:12).[129] In light of this, Ralph Martin aptly notes, "This short pericope . . . demonstrates to Gentile believers how they—with Israel's

---

[125]Lincoln notes, "The Pauline concept of redemption has its roots in the OT, where in particular the divine act of deliverance from Egypt was often described in terms of redemption (cf. Deut 7:8; 9:26; 13:5; 15:15; 24:18; 1 Chr 17:21)" (Lincoln, *Ephesians*, p. 27).

[126]Ralph P. Martin, *Ephesians, Colossians, and Philemon*, IBC (Louisville: John Knox, 1991), p. 17.

[127]Here Lincoln notes, "Against its Semitic background the terminology of 'making known a mystery' refers to the disclosure of a formerly hidden secret" (Lincoln, *Ephesians*, p. 30; see also Neufeld, *Ephesians*, pp. 49-50).

[128]Fowl, *Ephesians*, p. 49. Fowl does not see here Paul speaking of Israel or Jewish Christians but rather of believers in general. O'Brien recognizes the Old Testament background of the statement but seems to suggest some discontinuity in stating, "Now men and women *in Christ* are God's chosen people, having been claimed by him as his inheritance" (O'Brien, *Letter to the Ephesians*, pp. 115-16). Though he admits that Eph 1:11-12 focuses on Jewish believers (ibid., pp. 116-17), he interprets Eph 1:3-10 as applying to all believers though the language there is just as specific to Jews.

[129]Williamson states, "Paul celebrates the fact that *we*, meaning Jewish Christians, are God's people *chosen* (*klēroō*) in Christ, having been *destined* according to God's *purpose* to live for God's praise" (Williamson, *Ephesians*, p. 40). Though Lincoln applies the passage to believers in general, and does not see significance in the pronoun changes (Lincoln, *Ephesians*, p. 37), he notes, "God's purpose in choosing Israel had been expressed in similar terms, and the notion of God's acting for the sake of his name and his glory was an integral part of OT thinking" (ibid., p. 36).

remnant—are part and parcel of the new people which has inseparable roots in the Israel of the old covenant."[130]

In referring to the temporal priority by which the Jews received the gospel, Paul likely either references Israel's hope for a Messiah being first, and distinctly, a Jewish hope, or, in terms of historical sequence, how the Jews first heard and trusted the good news about Jesus. We also find this pattern in the book of Acts, where Jews, including those at Ephesus, have sequential priority in the preaching of the apostles.[131] Rather than an affirmation of individual election, Paul here has placed election within its historical context. Israel first received God's election, and with the incarnation of the Messiah, God had given Israel temporal priority in the hearing of the gospel. Those Jews who believed in the Messiah stand in the line of Israel's promises, which God transformed and fulfilled through the work of Christ.

Paul likely recognizes, then, in the turn in Ephesians 1:13 to the "you," the historic turn to the Gentiles.[132] Paul states, "in whom also *you*, having heard the word of truth, the gospel of our salvation, in which also having

---

[130]Martin, *Ephesians, Colossians, and Philemon*, p. 20. See also McRay, *Paul*, pp. 339-40.

[131]See Acts 2:5-11; 9:10-20; 11:19; 13:5, 14-52; 14:1-7; 16:20; 17:1-5, 10-14; 18:4-5, 19-21; 19:8-10, 17; 20:21; 26:23. See also Rom 1:16.

[132]Hoehner suggests that the first-person pronoun refers to Paul and his companions (Hoehner, *Ephesians*, pp. 231-33), but unlike his other letters, Paul says little here about his entourage, and thus this suggestion, especially in light of Eph 2, is unlikely. This also creates problems for his interpretation of προηλπικότας, which he regards as referring to "all believers reading this epistle" (ibid., p. 233). If this were the case, there would be no need for Paul to make a distinction between "we" and "you" since the "you" here are obviously reading the letter as well. Patzia suggests, oddly, that the pronouns move from "all Christians" in Eph 1:3-10, to Jewish Christians in Eph 1:11-12, to Gentile Christians in Eph 1:13, and to "all Christians" again in Eph 1:14 (Patzia, *Ephesians, Colossians, Philemon*, p. 156). Given the heavy Old Testament imagery in what precedes, it is more likely that the single referent in Eph 1:3-12 is Jewish Christians, the "saints." Lincoln denies any significance to the pronoun changes based, in part, on the fact that "the proposed distinction between 'we' as Jewish Christians and 'you' as Gentile Christians is one that simply does not hold for the rest of the letter" (Lincoln, *Ephesians*, p. 38). We should note, however, Paul builds a significant contrast between the two groups in Eph 1-2 and asserts, with the close of Eph 2, that all divisions have been broken down in Christ. It should be expected, then, after first building the divisions and then destroying them, that Paul would speak more universally in what follows with the distinctions no longer able to be maintained. In support of the recognition of the distinction made between we/you and Jew/Gentile, see Jack Haberer, "Ephesians 1:15-23," *Int* 62, no. 3 (2008): 312-14; Martin, *Ephesians, Colossians, and Philemon*, p. 19; McRay, *Paul*, pp. 340-42; Neufeld, *Ephesians*, p. 54; Gary E. Weedman, "Reading Ephesians from the New Perspective on Paul," *Leaven* 14, no. 2 (2006): 82; Williamson, *Ephesians*, p. 40.

believed, you were sealed by the Holy Spirit of promise, who is the down payment of our inheritance, unto the redemption of his possession, unto the praise of his glory" (Eph 1:13-14). While Paul's audience may have thought he spoke of the promises made to them in Ephesians 1:3-12, he makes it clear here that they are inheritors only because of Israel, whose promises through Christ came to the Gentiles.[133] We cannot precisely say whether the phrase "our inheritance" mentioned in Ephesians 1:14 refers to collective Jews and Gentiles, as Thomas Yoder Neufeld suggests,[134] or to Jews (first). The notion of an inheritance is, of course, a particularly Jewish notion, typically describing the blessings of God (primarily in the form of the land) for Israel or Israel as God's possession, and is frequently present in the Old Testament.[135] We also find the theme in Second Temple literature,[136] and Paul's use of the term in Galatians 3:18 clearly comes from a Jewish background. Regardless, if Paul intends Israel's inheritance, or Israel as God's inheritance, the blessings first promised to them now extend to Gentile believers as well. Furthermore, as Paul begins his prayer for the Ephesian believers in Ephesians 1:15, he notes his thankfulness for their faith in Jesus and their love "for all the saints." Based on the distinction noted earlier, it is possible here that by "saints" Paul is referring to Jewish believers. I would argue, then, that in Ephesians 1 Paul is not dealing with an abstract form of double predestination in which God has chosen some for redemption and others for condemnation.[137]

---

[133]So Weedman states, "The audience, mainly Gentile, is caught by surprise and is led to understand that while they live in God's favor because of Jesus Christ, they do so also by standing on the shoulders of Israel. It was Israel who was blessed, chosen, predestined, favored, redeemed, graced, recipients of the 'mystery,' the first to hope—all of these characteristics coming to fullness as they participated 'in Christ' (1.3-12)" (Weedman, "Reading Ephesians," p. 84). See also Martin, *Ephesians, Colossians, and Philemon*, pp. 4-5.

[134]Neufeld, *Ephesians*, pp. 54-55.

[135]E.g., Ex 15:17; Num 18:20, 23; 26:54, 56; 32:18; 34:2; 36:2-12; Deut 2:12; 3:20; 12:9; 32:9; 33:4; Josh 1:15; 11:23; 18:7; 1 Sam 10:1; 26:19; 2 Sam 14:16; 20:1, 19; 21:3; 1 Kings 8:36, 51-53; 1 Chron 16:18; 2 Chron 6:27; Ps 2:8; 21:12; 37:18; 46:5; 68:9-10; 73:2; 78:62, 71; 79:1; 94:5, 14; 105:5, 40; 110:6; 135:12; 136:21-22; Is 19:25; 47:6; 49:8; 54:17; 58:14; 63:17; Jer 2:7; 3:19; 10:16; 12:7-9, 14-15; 16:18; 27:11; 51:19; Lam 5:2; Ezek 11:15; 44:28; 45:1; 46:16-18; 47:14, 22-23; 48:28; Joel 2:17; 3:2; Mic 2:2; 7:14, 18.

[136]Jdt 8:22; 9:12; 13:5; 16:21; 1 Macc 2:56; 15:33-34; 2 Macc 2:4, 17; *Odes Sol.* 1:17; 2:9; Sir 23:12; 24:7, 12, 20, 23; 44:23; 45:20, 22, 25; 46:8-9; *Pss. Sol.* 7:2; 9:1; 17:23; *T. Benj.* 10:2.

[137]It should be noted that the "negative" side of double predestination is entirely missing in this passage.

Rather, he is dealing with the historic promises of Israel, now fulfilled in Christ and offered to the Gentiles who, like their Jewish brothers and sisters, may become inheritors if they receive God's Messiah by faith.[138] As Paul concludes his prayer, he expounds on the power God has exercised in Christ, through his resurrection and exaltation, a power the church now shares in as the body of Christ.[139]

Paul reminds the Ephesians, both in Ephesians 2:1-3 and Ephesians 2:11-12, of their former life apart from Christ.[140] Then they were "dead in transgressions and sins," walking according to the *aeon* of the world, under the power of "the ruler of the power of the air," living in the "desires of the flesh," and being "natural children of wrath" (Eph 2:1-3). Because they "lived" outside of the resurrection life of Christ, these believers were, in fact, formerly dead.[141] Some have suggested that Paul means they had "no capacity at all to respond to the gospel."[142] More likely, Paul meant they had not been invigorated with Christ's life prior to their incorporation into Christ through faith. Likewise, neither does their being "sons of disobedience" or "children of wrath" indicate a pre-

---

[138]So Haberer rightly summarizes, "The key to understanding this pericope is found in the use of the pronouns of personal address. Who is the 'I,' who are the 'we,' and who are the 'you' (plural) repeatedly referenced in these chapters? Scholars agree that one of the central issues addressed overall in this epistle is that of a burgeoning multiplication of Gentile converts who at best increasingly forget or at worst consciously dismiss the church's Jewish-Christian roots. What often gets overlooked is that the writer is tackling this matter right from the start. Indeed, these entire two chapters are less about individual soteriology than about communal ecclesiology, and in particular, the new converts' place in the church of Jesus Christ" (Haberer, "Ephesians 1:15-23," p. 312).

[139]Here Neufeld notes, "The use of Psalm 8 here and elsewhere in the NT illustrates this interplay between special individual and corporate experience, in this case between Christ and reconstituted humanity. In the NT, however, Psalm 8 (esp. v. 6) is used to celebrate the special status of the risen and exalted Christ (cf. 1 Cor. 15:27, where, as here, it sits alongside Ps. 110:1; Heb. 2:6; cf. use of Ps. 110:1 in Heb. 1:13). However, as stated in the notes, the Christ who is raised and exalted is never understood to be a solitary individual. Christ is humanity reconstituted. That basic connection allows the authors of 1 Corinthians, Ephesians, and Hebrews to use Psalm 8 messianically: the exaltation of Christ means the restoring of creation. In Ephesians that tradition is employed, not to stress the distance between Christ and saints, but to minimize it, indeed to render Christ and saints one whole—*head* and *body*" (Neufeld, *Ephesians*, p. 84).

[140]For a discussion of the possibility of Ezek 37 serving as the backdrop of Eph 2, see Robert H. Suh, "The Use of Ezekiel 37 in Ephesians 2," *JETS* 50, no. 4 (2007): 715-33.

[141]So Lincoln states, "If Christ's resurrection introduced the life of the age to come ahead of time, then one's state prior to participation in that resurrection life must, comparatively speaking, be viewed as death" (Lincoln, *Ephesians*, p. 92).

[142]Schreiner, *Paul*, p. 138; O'Brien, *Letter to the Ephesians*, p. 163.

determined judgment, since their fate changed once they responded to the gospel.[143] Rather, they lived outside of Christ and deserved God's judgment because of their own sins and disobedience.[144]

In Ephesians 2:4-10 and Ephesians 2:13-22, Paul further reminds them that their former state no longer defines them. God, because of his love and mercy, has made them "alive together with Christ" (Eph 2:5), and raised them up and seated them in the heavens with Christ (Eph 2:6). Just as God raised Christ and exalted him (Eph 1:20-22), so those who are in Christ share in his resurrection and exaltation.[145] Through being "in Christ," which occurs by faith(fulness), the Ephesians experience these blessings.[146] Accordingly, Paul describes their salvation (spoken of here in the perfect tense, which is the only occurrence of σῴζω in the perfect in the Pauline corpus[147]) as "by grace" (τῇ χάριτι) and "through faith(fulness)" (διὰ πίστεως), which "is not of yourselves" (οὐκ ἐξ ὑμῶν) and "is not from works" (οὐκ ἐξ ἔργων). So the source of their salvation

---

[143]It is often noted that these phrases are Hebraisms, emphasizing that their behavior made them deserving of God's wrath. See Lincoln, *Ephesians*, pp. 97-98. Witherington thus states, "It should be clear that Paul does not mean that people were destined for wrath, since he is talking about himself and in this case other Jewish Christians" (Witherington, *Letters*, p. 254). According to Martin, "The idiom is drawn from the Old Testament and means 'deserving of God's judicial condemnation.' In the history of exegesis and Christian doctrine the phrase has played a significant—if wrongly conceived—role. It has been used to support a teaching on original guilt (as distinct from original sin, which says that all are born with a tendency to wrongdoing, not as actual sinners needing baptism to cancel out their inherited birth sin). And it has from time to time given rise to the false characterization of God as 'angry.' . . . What the phrase *does* say is that all are under divine judgment by reason of the moral choices they have made and that these in turn are dictated by their warped nature. Moral accountability is at the heart of the Christian understanding of the human condition and must never be compromised" (Martin, *Ephesians, Colossians, and Philemon*, pp. 26-27).

[144]So Lincoln notes, "This explanation of sin does not, however, do away with human responsibility, for in the next breath the writer can say that not only the readers, but all believers, were at one time those who chose not to obey, who instead gave their consent to the inclinations of the flesh, and who therefore fully deserved God's wrath" (Lincoln, *Ephesians*, p. 117).

[145]See Thomas G. Allen, "Exaltation and Solidarity with Christ: Ephesians 1:20 and 2:6," *JSNT* 28 (1986): 104.

[146]Allen states, "Christ reveals God's decision to love man because he is God's decision to love man as God's chosen representative for man, Man-elect. . . . Christ, then, through his personhood and personal actions supplies to those who believe the necessary conditions, qualities, and relationships of a new life, a new corporate self-identity. . . . To be included in Christ's exaltation means also to enter into the corporate person that Christ is by virtue of providing through his own person and work a corporate self-identity to those with whom he is united" (ibid., p. 27). See also Fowl, *Ephesians*, p. 74.

[147]See Andrew T. Lincoln, "Ephesians 2:8-10: A Summary of Paul's Gospel?," *CBQ* 45 (1983): 620.

originates in God alone and occurs through faith(fulness).[148] Humans possess no quality or ability to effect their own resurrection from death. God alone can offer such a gift. In fact, as frequently noted, the τοῦτο of Ephesians 2:8 indicates grammatically that Paul has the entirety of salvation in view.[149] God only offers salvation from his mercy and grace because he owes no debt to humanity—or Israel for that matter—when they have rebelled against him.[150] God in his mercy, however, did not respond to human unfaithfulness with rejection, but with generosity. He calls into the realm of disobedience and offers salvation to those who will hear and respond.[151]

Paul primarily describes salvation here as a transfer of realms, from the realm of oppression to freedom in Christ.[152] Most suggest that Paul's statement that faith is not "from works" (οὐκ ἐξ ἔργων) is not the typical Pauline expression of "works of the law," but human effort in general.[153] We should first note that Paul does not have justification in view, where he shows concern about covenantal status and the sufficiency of πίστεως Χριστοῦ alone, but rather God's work of the transference of the sinner to new life in Christ. Second, Paul has no problem with "good works" (ἔργοις ἀγαθοῖς), which is clear since he affirms that those in Christ were

---

[148]Neufeld suggests here, in keeping with Rom 3:22, 26; and Gal 2:16, 20, that πίστις may refer here not to the individual faith of believers, but rather to Jesus' own faithfulness, as in Eph 3:12. As he states, "It is better to interpret *pistis* in the present instance as referring not so much to human trust in God, as important as that is, as to *God's faithfulness*. This meaning suggests that salvation by grace is God's way of keeping faith with the human community, including Gentiles, who have been under the oppression of evil. Such fidelity is, of course, more appropriate to covenantal relationships. *But God* reaches out to those who have either never been part of the covenantal relationship (Gentiles, 2:12) or who have broken it (Jews, 2:3; cf. the hymn fragment in 2 Tim. 2:13)" (Neufeld, *Ephesians*, pp. 99-100). Cf. Eph 3:12, 17. See also O'Brien, *Letter to the Ephesians*, pp. 174-75. The more common interpretation, however, is that individual faith is here in view.

[149]See Ernest Best, *Ephesians*, ICC (New York: T&T Clark, 2004), p. 226; Fowl, *Ephesians*, p. 78; Hoehner, *Ephesians*, p. 343; Lincoln, *Ephesians*, p. 112. Some have suggested this to mean that believers do not actually exercise faith apart from God regenerating them first. It is better, as Witherington suggests, that "the work of salvation, including the gift of faith, is all the work and gift of God to the believer, it is not our own doing or striving, though certainly believers must exercise that gift of faith and appropriate its benefit. God will not and does not have or exercise faith for us" (Witherington, *Letters*, p. 256).

[150]Fowl, *Ephesians*, p. 78; Lincoln, "Ephesians 2:8-10," p. 622.

[151]Neufeld, *Ephesians*, p. 96; Lincoln, *Ephesians*, p. 111.

[152]See Neufeld, *Ephesians*, pp. 98-99; Lincoln, "Ephesians 2:8-10," p. 620.

[153]Lincoln, "Ephesians 2:8-10," p. 623; O'Brien, *Letter to the Ephesians*, p. 177; Schreiner, *Paul*, p. 123.

created *for good works* (Eph 2:9),[154] echoing again the thought in Ephesians 1:4 of God's purpose for his people. We should not understand the preparation of these works beforehand as indicating a deterministic mindset since believers must still "walk in them" (περιπατήσωμεν).[155] Paul has thus established that humans, Jew and Gentile, do not "deserve" salvation, but God has graciously given it, through (his) faith(fulness), in order that his people might walk in a way fitting for those in Christ.

Throughout this passage we again see that Paul holds both the divine initiative of God and the responsibility of humans, both unbelievers who incur judgment because of their disobedience, and believers who must continue in obedience, together. That salvation comes by God's favor and through (Christ's) faith(fulness) does not eliminate human response. Neither does God's choice of a people in Christ mean he has determined the fates of individuals and marked out some for a predetermined condemnation. Paul's election language here, as elsewhere, must be seen in its Jewish context, a context that does not generate such interpretations.

SUMMARY

We saw in the Jewish literature of this chapter an emphasis on divine initiative *and* human responsibility. Often these themes present themselves within the same texts. I argued that the Jewish literature does not make human responsibility determinative apart from any action or initiative of God, and neither does the divine program eliminate the necessity of human response and obedience. So it is with Paul. Paul asserts that the divine rescue plan came from God's own initiative, and the resurrection afforded to believers through Jesus as well as the enablement of the Spirit do not come through human impetus. But neither does this mean that the fate of individuals is predetermined or that the obedience

---

[154]So Fowl states, "The grammar here makes it clear that it is the works, rather than the humans, which God prepared beforehand" (Fowl, *Ephesians*, p. 80).

[155]Thus Lincoln notes, "Even the living out of salvation in good works is completely by grace. But this is not a total determinism. God has prepared the good works in advance 'in order that we might live in them.' The human activity of 'walking' is still necessary; the actual living out of God's purpose in the world has to take place" (Lincoln, *Ephesians*, p. 116).

of believers stands assured, since they must walk in the Spirit and resist the flesh. Though God stands as the ultimate agent, this does not eliminate other forms of agency, involved in the process in ways that do not require a deterministic outlook. Paul can thus both assert that salvation comes through God's generosity as a gift and yet demand that those "in Christ" walk faithfully in accordance with their calling.

Rereading
Romans 8:26–11:36

Few passages in the Pauline corpus have received as much attention or garnered as much debate as Romans 8:26–11:36. Romans contains one of the fullest expressions (if not the fullest) of Paul's soteriological beliefs, but this expression occurs within the parameters of the letter as an occasional document rather than a theological treatise. Many see this section of Romans, and rightly so, as its climax.[1] Set against its Jewish background, we can see more clearly that Paul's argument here is fundamentally concerned with the fate of Israel and Gentile inclusion rather than double predestination, as some have argued. We must first admit, as N. T. Wright has remarked, that "Romans 9–11 is as full of problems as a hedgehog is of prickles."[2] As elsewhere, I will only address those issues pertinent to our discussion of Paul's election theology. We should also admit from the outset that Paul, as he specifically displays as early as Romans 9:3, addresses a particularly Jewish problem from a Jewish context, a context that I have more fully explored in previous chapters.[3]

---

[1]E.g., C. E. B. Cranfield, *Romans 9–16*, ICC (New York: T&T Clark, 1979), p. 445; James D. G. Dunn, *Romans 9–16*, WBC (Dallas: Word, 1988), pp. 519-20; Krister Stendahl, *Paul Among Jews and Gentiles* (Philadelphia: Fortress, 1976), p. 28.

[2]N. T. Wright, *The Climax of the Covenant: Christ and the Law in Pauline Theology* (New York: T&T Clark, 1991), p. 231.

[3]See Ben Witherington III, *Paul's Letter to the Romans: A Socio-Rhetorical Commentary* (Grand Rapids: Eerdmans, 2004), p. 246.

GOD'S PURPOSE IN CHRIST (ROMANS 8:26-39)

Paul's remarks at the end of Romans 8 serve as the transition to Romans 9, and in some ways bookend his argument. Paul's comments here come in the context of personal suffering (Rom 8:18-27), as is so often the case when reflections concerning election are found in Jewish literature.[4] Paul states,

> Now we know that, for those who love God, all things work together for good, to those who are called according to purpose,[5] because those whom he foreknew, he also decided beforehand to be conformed to the image of his Son, so that his Son would be the firstborn among many siblings; and those whom he decided beforehand [to be conformed to the image of his Son], these also he called; and those whom he called, these also he declared righteous; and those whom he declared righteous, these also he glorified. (Rom 8:28-30)

Paul first states of those whom God foreknew that he determined ahead of time they would be conformed to the image of Christ, with the purpose that Jesus would be the firstborn of many children of God. God's determination that the foreknown be conformed to the image of his Son, called, declared righteous and glorified all come after his foreknowledge of them.

Some have argued that this passage teaches that God has specifically chosen which individuals will be a part of his eschatological people, and has guaranteed that they will be so because of his "effectual call."[6] They

---

[4]In particular, *Jubilees*, *Testaments of the Twelve Patriarchs*, 1 Maccabees, *Psalms of Solomon*, the Dead Sea Scrolls, *Sibylline Oracles*, *1 Enoch* and *Testament of Moses* display such a connection. This alerts us to the fact that a function of election language is to comfort the afflicted.

[5]Witherington here recognizes "'His' is not in the text. Some commentators have urged that prothesis could refer to human beings here, in which case the text would mean 'those called according to (their own) choice,' or, as we would say, 'by choice,' the free act of choice by which those called respond to God's call" (Witherington, *Romans*, p. 227). Regardless, such an interpretation is still possible (and likely) in the passage even if the "his" is supplied, though reading the text without supplying the pronoun makes this clear.

[6]Schreiner states that this calling "must be understood as effectual. It is not merely an invitation that human beings can reject, but it is a summons that overcomes human resistance and effectually persuades them to say yes to God" (Thomas R. Schreiner, *Romans*, BECNT [Grand Rapids: Baker Academic, 1998], pp. 450-51). Likewise, Robert H. Mounce, *Romans*, NAC (Nashville: Broadman & Holman, 1995), p. 188; Colin G. Kruse, *Paul's Letter to the Romans*, Pillar New Testament Commentary (Grand Rapids: Eerdmans, 2012), p. 356. We have not seen individual

have furthermore described this foreknowledge as a "foreloving," a personal, covenantal knowledge.[7] The verb (προγινώσκω) occurs only twice in all of the Pauline writings, in Romans 8:29 and again in Romans 11:2. If Paul meant by the term that God had a covenant love for each individual in the elect before they came to exist, this causes problems (as will be seen) for his usage in Romans 11:2, where he refers to ethnic Israel. It makes better sense here to see the people as a whole in view and to recognize that the focus is on the kind of people God intends them to be.[8] Paul's discussion, as seen from what has preceded as well as what follows in Romans 8:30-39, intends to encourage the people of God in light of the current difficulties they experience.[9] Because God raised Jesus from the dead and vindicated him, those who are in him cannot be separated from God's love.[10] Furthermore, as shall be seen more explicitly in Romans 9–11, Paul's language here is the language of Israel's election in the Old Testament. Craig Keener states,

> Paul's own audience would think of Israel as the people God has chosen, and recognize that Paul's argument was designed to show that God was so sovereign that he was not bound to choose (with regard to salvation)

predestination in our examination of Jewish beliefs concerning election. Had Jews of the period held a firm concept of a divine election of the individual that was irresistible in nature, this would be more likely. But we have not seen this in the Judaism of Paul's time, and thus it is unlikely Paul speaks of such a phenomenon here.

[7]See Bruce Demarest, *The Cross and Salvation: The Doctrine of Salvation* (Wheaton, IL: Crossway, 1997), p. 128; Schreiner, *Romans*, p. 452. Curiously, BDAG and L&N list Rom 9–11 and 1 Pet 1:20 as the only instances of the gloss "forechoosing," while the customary meaning of the verb is "to know beforehand or in advance, *have foreknowledge (of)*." LSJ lists the meaning as "to know, perceive, learn, or understand beforehand."

[8]Holland writes, "'Foreknowledge' has to do with God's covenantal relationship, and, once the term has been put into its OT setting, it naturally conveys the idea of election—but it is an election of the nation" (Tom Holland, *Romans: The Divine Marriage* [Eugene, OR: Wipf & Stock, 2011], p. 283). See also B. J. Oropeza, *Jews, Gentiles, and the Opponents of Paul: Apostasy in the New Testament Communities* (Eugene, OR: Cascade, 2012), 2:168-69.

[9]So Ridderbos states, "This is not an abstract pronouncement concerning the immutability of the number of those predestined to salvation, but a pastoral encouragement for the persecuted and embattled church (cf. v. 36), based on the fixed and unassailable character of the divine work of redemption. . . . Fixity does not lie in a hidden *decretum*, therefore, but in the corporate unity of the church with Christ, whom it has come to know in the gospel and has learned to embrace in faith" (Herman N. Ridderbos, *Paul: An Outline of His Theology* [Grand Rapids: Eerdmans, 1975], pp. 350-51).

[10]See Frank J. Matera, *Romans*, Paideia Commentary on the New Testament (Grand Rapids: Baker Academic 2010), pp. 204-5.

based on Jewish ethnicity. Paul might ground predestination in fore-knowledge (8:29) to allow that God takes faith into account (in advance) in salvation (a question much debated by theologians). . . . Perhaps more importantly, Paul will use even the term "foreknow" for Israel (11:2), thus connecting this claim with his larger argument.[11]

It seems unlikely that Paul would here state something to contradict what follows in Romans 9–11. Keener rightly recognizes the Jewish context of Paul's descriptions and its place in the flow of thought in the text. We need not assume here that what Paul intends is that God's sovereignty has predetermined the specific individuals who will be a part of his people.[12] Simply put, this people who love God, whom God has fore-known, will receive future resurrection through their union with Christ, who is the first of many who will experience this glorification.[13] Paul has said nothing here that would contradict a corporate and conditional notion of election, and makes such a concept all the more explicit in Romans 9–11.

GOD'S FAITHFULNESS TO THE COVENANT (ROMANS 9:1-18)

Paul begins Romans 9 by recounting the personal anguish he experi-enced from his fellow Israelites' separation from Christ. The Jewish people had numerous advantages as descendants of Abraham (adoption

---

[11]Craig S. Keener, *Romans*, New Covenant Commentary Series (Eugene, OR: Cascade, 2009), p. 110.

[12]Mounce is incorrect to suggest that God's predestination could not be contingent on foreknowl-edge because "God would not be sovereign" (Mounce, *Romans*, p. 188). This, of course, depends on one's definition of sovereignty. God could determine whatever means and mode he sees fit, even if that means a conditional election, and still be properly sovereign. As Keener rightly recognizes, "Most ancient Jewish authors did not pit God's sovereignty against human choice (cf. e.g., Josephus *J. W.* 2.162-63; idem *Ant.* 18.13; *m.* 'Abot 3:16); a sovereign God could sover-eignly allow much choice and still accomplish his purposes" (Keener, *Romans*, p. 109 n. 45).

[13]So Marshall states, "First, God's purpose for those whom he 'foreknew' was that they might share the image of Jesus, that is, share in his glory. Second, God has already started the process: God has called the people for whom he has this purpose. Calling was followed by justification, obviously of those who believed and thereby responded to the call. And justification is followed by a glorification that has already begun (2 Corinthians 3:18). . . . The passage is not a statement about the effectual calling of those whom God foreknew. It is a guarantee that those who have responded to God's call with love (and faith) can be fully assured of his purpose of final glorifi-cation for them" (I. Howard Marshall, "The Problem of Apostasy in New Testament Theology," *PRSt* 14 [1987]: 77). See also Paul J. Achtemeier, *Romans*, IBC (Louisville: Westminster John Knox, 1986), p. 144; Witherington, *Romans*, p. 229.

as sons, the glory, the covenants,[14] the giving of the law, the temple service, the patriarchs and the human lineage of the Messiah; Rom 9:4-5).[15] Yet in spite of these advantages, they rejected the Christ, apparently prompting questions as to whether God's promises had failed. Paul responds to this query with a series of examples from the Scriptures in order to illustrate that "not all those who are descended from Israel are truly Israel" (Rom 9:6).[16] Here Paul clearly evidences a belief in a "true Israel." From the previous examination of Jewish literature, we should readily recognize that this limiting of the "true Israel" was quite common.[17] Paul has at this point suggested nothing controversial in light of the Judaism of his time.[18] What Paul will establish throughout is that these advantages of the Jew have amounted to little advantage at all, and have actually become a disadvantage to them and an advantage to the Gentiles. The whole thrust of Paul's argument in these chapters is that the Gentiles are full covenant members without submitting to the marks of Judaism, while most Jews, by pursuing the law apart from Christ,[19] are now outsiders. Paul's concern, as was the concern of many of his peers, was, as

---

[14]For a discussion on "covenants" here as singular or plural, see Ellen Juhl Christiansen, *The Covenant in Judaism and Paul: A Study of Ritual Boundaries as Identity Markers* (Leiden: Brill, 1995), pp. 219-22.

[15]Christiansen notes correctly that Paul is no doubt concerned with more than identity markers or Jewish privilege here: "*None* of the Jewish distinctive marks is mentioned: circumcision, Sabbath, festivals, purity marks such as food laws, ritual washings, or the temple as centre of holiness, or possession of the land" (ibid., p. 218).

[16]For a discussion on the various interpretations of this phrase, see Dunn, *Romans 9–16*, pp. 539-40. As Dunn notes, a shift takes place here in which Paul no longer refers to a contrast between Jews and Gentiles, but is focused on a new term: "Israel" (James D. G. Dunn, *The Theology of Paul the Apostle* [Grand Rapids: Eerdmans, 1998], p. 505). A fuller discussion of this terminology must be saved for Rom 11.

[17]Contra Eastman, who argues Paul's use of "Israel" in Rom 9–11 is to be equated with the Jews (Susan Grove Eastman, "Israel and the Mercy of God: A Re-Reading of Galatians 6.16 and Romans 9-11," *NTS* 56, no. 3 [2010]: 367-95).

[18]Thus, it is not, as Schreiner states, "astonishing . . . that most of ethnic Israel . . . are identified with Esau and Ishmael" (Schreiner, *Romans*, p. 502).

[19]Garlington correctly notes that Paul's operation from a Jewish covenantal and messianic framework is a part of his argument in the letter. As he states, "In Rom 1.3-4, then, Paul underscores to his readers that the subject of his gospel is a *thoroughly Jewish* Messiah, the Son of David prophesied, as it is commonly agreed, by Ps. 2.7f. (Ps 110), and, therefore, the fulfilment of Israel's eschatological expectations; he has now been 'installed' (ὁρίζειν) on none other than the throne of his father David (cf. Lk 1.32)" (Don B. Garlington, *The Obedience of Faith: A Pauline Phrase in Historical Context* [Tübingen: Mohr Siebeck, 1991], p. 236).

Michael Cranford describes, "to identify *which* group is in fact elected as God's people, and the criteria by which they are distinguished."[20]

As Paul makes clear in Romans 9:7, Jewish ethnic privilege did not guarantee that each Israelite would actually be a member of the covenant people, since not all of Abraham's children are of Abraham's seed.[21] His first example is that of Isaac and Ishmael, both descendants of Abraham, but only "through Isaac" would his descendants be counted (Rom 9:7). Paul explains that this meant it was only "the children of the promise" and not "the children of the flesh" who would be recognized as Abraham's descendants (Rom 9:8-9). As seen previously, being of the seed of Isaac was important both for the author of *Jubilees* (*Jub.* 1:7; 6:19; and especially 15:19) and for the author of the Epistle of Enoch (*1 En.* 93:5), and Isaac (along with Abraham and Jacob) also serves such a function in the *Testament of Levi* 15:4. Ishmael, in *Jubilees*, on the other hand, while blessed by God (*Jub.* 15:20), and even circumcised (15:23), was not a part of the covenant line, at least in part because his circumcision was not as prescribed in the law (15:26-30). Within these texts, both Isaac and Ishmael serve as corporate figures, or representative heads, of a type of people. Paul uses the Isaac/Ishmael contrast at this point to affirm that ethnicity or national identity is not a sufficient requirement for membership among the covenant people.[22]

Paul's next example contains even more force. He notes that before Jacob and Esau were even born "or had done anything good or evil (so

---

[20]Michael Cranford, "Election and Ethnicity: Paul's View of Israel in Romans 9:1-13," *JSNT* 50 (1993): 36.

[21]Tanner here is fundamentally correct in stating, "In other words being Jewish by birth did not guarantee a person a right standing with God. That had to be accompanied by 'circumcision of the heart' (Deut. 30:6) and partaking of the Holy Spirit—both being matters related to the New Covenant. Thus in Romans 9:6 Paul was saying that there is a 'true Israel' within 'ethnic Israel,' and this true Israel is the believing remnant of the nation. For God to fulfill His promises to Israel, He need not do so with every single physical descendant but only with the believing element within ethnic Israel" (J. Paul Tanner, "The New Covenant and Paul's Quotations from Hosea in Romans 9:25-26," *BSac* 162 [Jan–March 2005]: 96). See also Cranford, "Election and Ethnicity," pp. 27-41; Dunn, *Theology of Paul*, pp. 510, 540; Thomas H. Tobin, SJ, *Paul's Rhetoric in Its Contexts: The Argument of Romans* (Peabody, MA: Hendrickson, 2004), p. 327. This is contra the view espoused by Cranfield that God was distinguishing a special elect "hidden Church" within elect Israel (Cranfield, *Romans 9–16*, pp. 473-74).

[22]This may also be a subtle critique of circumcision as decisive in election.

that God's purpose in election would stand, not by works but by his calling)" that God had set Jacob apart (loved) but not Esau (hated) (Rom 9:10-13).[23] Jacob, even more prominently than Isaac, serves as a representative figure in numerous texts of the period (Sir 24:8; 36:11; 46:10; 47:22; Bar 3:30; *Jub.* 1:7; 2:20, 24; 6:19; 19:16, 23; 22:10-23, 28-30; 24:7-11; 25:14-23; 26:23-24; 27:22-27; 31:6-7, 15-20; 32:17-19; 1 Macc. 5:2; *T. Sim.* 6:2; *T. Levi* 4:3; *Pss. Sol.* 7:9).[24] In the book of *Jubilees*, Jacob represents the faithful Jews who observe the law correctly (i.e., as envisioned by the author of *Jubilees*) while Esau and Ishmael represent outsiders, particularly Jews who have been unfaithful to the covenant (though possibly Gentiles as well). Those "of Jacob" are within the boundaries of the covenant community because of their faithful observance of the law.[25] God did not choose Esau, however, because of his deeds. Esau, for example, gained wealth by evil means (*T. Gad* 6:7), was guilty of fornication and idolatry (*T. Benj.* 10:10), married foreign wives (*Jub.* 25:1; 27:8; 29:18) and was not chosen because God knew his unrighteous and violent ways (*Jub.* 15:30; 19:15; 35:9, 13; 36:10; 37:24; *Bib. Ant.* 32.5); while Jacob observed the Sabbath (*Jub.* 2:20-24) and festival of weeks (6:19), separated himself from the Gentiles, abstained from idolatry, did not marry Gentile wives and tithed to the Lord (22:16-23; 25:1-7; 27:10-11; 30:12; 32:9-10). The deeds envisioned in these Jewish texts are Torah deeds. Commentators reject this as a possibility in Romans 9 on the grounds that the law had not yet come,[26] but this rejection neglects the frequent view in Second Temple

---

[23] As Kaminsky has observed, it is not uncommon in the Old Testament (Jacob, Joseph and David serving as prime examples) for God's choosings to be against human intuitions (Joel S. Kaminsky, "Reclaiming a Theology of Election: Favoritism and the Joseph Story," *PRSt* 31, no. 2 [2004]: 135-52). Paul's emphasis on Jacob supports his contention that God's elective purposes are not predictable or according to human (i.e., here, Jewish) intuitions.

[24] This should not be surprising since Jacob also serves such a function in the Old Testament (e.g., Deut 32:9; 33:10, 28; Jer 10:16, 25; 30:7-10, 18; 31:7, 11; 46:27-28; 51:19; Ezek 28:25; 37:25; 39:25; Hos 10:11; 12:2; Mal 1:2; 2:12).

[25] Brian J. Abasciano, "Corporate Election in Romans 9: A Reply to Thomas Schreiner," *JETS* 49, no. 2 (2006): 355.

[26] Paul specifies that these "works" are "works of the law" in Rom 2:15; 3:20, 28, and implicitly in Rom 3:27; 4:2, 6; and thus it seems likely that such a designation would continue in Rom 9–11, especially in that he is focusing on the status of the relationship between Israel and God. Contra Kruse, who states, "The indications are that the 'works' the apostle denies had any effect upon God's choice are the 'good' or the 'bad' that people do. Clearly, such works are not the performance of, or the failure to perform, 'works of the law,' that is, those things that are prescribed

literature that the law was eternal and that the patriarchs observed it.[27] Thus, when Paul argues that God's purpose in election stands on his calling and not on works,[28] this quite possibly, given the backdrop, means he has "works of the law" in mind even though the phrase in its entirety is not present.[29] He does not offer a general polemic against "deeds" or "merit," as Paul does not oppose such activity.[30] His argument here is a matter of salvation history. One can anticipate, then (as Rom 10–11 will make clear), that Paul continues his faith-Christ/works-law contrast here.[31] We can suggest, furthermore, that Paul employs the

---

by the Mosaic law and understood by some as Jewish sociological markers, because Paul is speaking of the patriarchal period prior to the given of the law" (Kruse, *Romans*, p. 379). Grindheim also denies this possibility (Sigurd Grindheim, *The Crux of Election: Paul's Critique of the Jewish Confidence in the Election of Israel* [Tübingen: Mohr Siebeck, 2005], p. 144 n. 31).

[27] As stated or alluded to particularly in Ben Sira, *Jubilees*, and *Bib. Ant.*

[28] God's purpose in election, in its Old Testament context, is the blessing of Israel and the blessing of the nations (see Gen 12). Concerning the grammatical function of the phrase in Rom 9:11, Abasciano notes, "It is much simpler, clearer and straightforward to say that election fulfills God's purpose" (Brian J. Abasciano, *Paul's Use of the Old Testament in Romans 9.10-18: An Intertextual and Theological Exegesis* [New York: T&T Clark, 2011], p. 48).

[29] Cranford is basically correct in recognizing, "To claim that Paul is attacking individual merit here is to totally miss the flow of the argument, which deals with bounded communities and not individuals. Rather, Paul argues that the criteria associated with ethnic Israel (i.e., Torah observance as a boundary marker) was not a factor in God's election" (Cranford, "Election and Ethnicity," p. 39). Though Abasciano does not see this as a shorthand reference to "works of the law," he states that Paul "almost certainly has special (but not exclusive) reference to the works of the Law" and that such a referent "would be the natural focus of concern from the broader category for Paul and his readers" (Abasciano, *Paul's Use*, p. 52).

[30] Contra Grindheim, *Crux of Election*, p. 144. So Dunn states correctly, "Jews who insist on 'works of the law' as the indispensable mark of God's chosen people are actually denying not simply the gospel but also their *own* election" (Dunn, *Romans 9–16*, p. 549). Das is probably right to assert, contra the "new perspective," that "there is nothing to indicate that Paul has only ethnic boundary markers in mind. Paul uses the language of ἔργα νόμου to indicate the deeds or works that the Mosaic law requires *in general*" (A. Andrew Das, *Paul, the Law, and the Covenant* [Peabody, MA: Hendrickson, 2001], pp. 237-38). There is nothing in these chapters that would require a narrower view of "works of the law" limited only to circumcision, dietary regulations and the like. Rather, Paul likely has in mind, as will be clear in Rom 9:30–10:13, that Torah-keeping *apart from Christ* is worthless. Abasciano is correct, then, to assert, "Paul does seem to be countering a prevalent theological conviction among Jews . . . that took Jacob's election and Esau's rejection to have rested on their works. The salvation-historical observation that Paul makes gets to the core of Israel's election—for Jacob's election is the election of Israel—and destroys any notion that God is bound to call/name the seed of Abraham based on ethnicity or Law-keeping" (Abasciano, *Paul's Use*, p. 58).

[31] See Abasciano, *Paul's Use*, pp. 52, 64; Achtemeier, *Romans*, p. 157; Matera, *Romans*, p. 224. Schreiner argues from silence that Paul's "failure to insert human faith as the decisive and ultimate basis for God's election indicates that God's call and election are prior to and the ground of human faith" (Schreiner, *Romans*, p. 500). Contra Schreiner, Abasciano notes, "To admit that

Isaac/Ishmael and Jacob/Esau motifs, familiar already in Jewish literature, in order to describe them as representative heads of collective
groups.[32] This affirms his claim in Romans 9:6 that "not all those who
are descended from Israel are truly Israel," a claim with which Jews at the
time likely would have largely agreed. Paul's "twist," however, comes in
Romans 9:11-12, where, contrary to Jewish beliefs, he asserts their faithfulness to the Mosaic covenant does not stand as the "boundary marker"
of the covenant people.

Having declared that God had no necessity to base inclusion among
the elect on ancestry or keeping the law, Paul inquires, "What then will
we say? Is there unrighteousness with God? May it never be!" (Rom 9:14).
Paul's use here of ἀδικία, which is frequently translated as "injustice" (NIV,
NET, ESV, NASB, HCSB; "unfair" in NLT) rather than "unrighteousness,"
should clearly be set in the context of the covenant rather than as an abstract question of God's character, as many often take it to be. It seems
clear that Paul asks, probably reflecting the objection of an interlocutor
(whether real or imagined), "If God does not base election on ancestry or
keeping the law, has he not violated the covenant?"[33] Paul answers the
question by looking at the exodus and the example of Pharaoh. He states,

> For [God] says to Moses: "I will show mercy to whoever I show mercy,
> and I will have compassion on whoever I have compassion." Therefore,

---

Paul's doctrine of justification is implicit here demands that one admit that faith is implicit here
also, since his doctrine is justification *by faith*" (Abasciano, *Paul's Use*, p. 54).

[32]So Watson states, "Paul, however, is not interested in these individual life stories per se, but in
the scriptural precedents they establish for a divine electing purpose that takes *communal* form.
. . . His argument is that the divine turn from Jews to Gentiles is consonant with the scriptural
account of God's electing purpose, rather than flatly contradicting it (as his critics claim)"
(Francis Watson, *Paul, Judaism and the Gentiles: A Sociological Approach* [Cambridge: Cambridge
University Press, 1986], p. 314). In support of a collective view, see also Abasciano, *Paul's Use*,
pp. 59-60; Achtemeier, *Romans*, pp. 160-65; C. K. Barrett, *The Epistle to the Romans*, BNTC
(Peabody, MA: Hendrickson, 1991), p. 255; Cranfield, *Romans 9–16*, pp. 479-81; Dunn, *Theology
of Paul*, pp. 511, 544-45; Witherington, *Romans*, pp. 25, 255. Contra Demarest, who suggests
that this clearly shows that Paul's emphasis is on God's sovereignty and not human response
(Demarest, *Cross and Salvation*, p. 129). Likewise, contra Kruse, *Romans*, pp. 379-80. In recognizing the conflict between double predestination and the emphasis of Paul in his letters on
human responsibility, Schreiner appeals to "mystery" as a resolution (Schreiner, *Romans*, p. 501).
When the text is understood through the lens of Second Temple Judaism and the individuals
are seen as corporate representatives, such an appeal is unnecessary.

[33]See Abasciano, *Paul's Use*, pp. 171-72; Keener, *Romans*, p. 118.

then, it is not the one who is desiring or the one who is running but God who is showing mercy. For the Scripture says to Pharaoh, "For this very reason I raised you up, in order that I show my power in you and in order that my name be proclaimed in all the earth." Therefore then, he shows mercy to whomever he desires and he hardens whomever he desires. (Rom 9:15-17)

Paul's response here has been taken many times as a general theological principle, illustrating the presence of double predestination in Paul's thought.[34] As I argued above, and we will again see explicitly in Romans 9:23-24, Paul focuses here on the status of Israel's election, not the election of individuals. His corporate interest became obvious in the Isaac/Ishmael and Jacob/Esau contrasts, and no doubt continues here. Schreiner suggests that Paul's statement here indicates that he refers to the election and salvation of individuals as well as corporate groups or nations, citing the singular of the pronoun as evidence of a reference to individuals, and thus, "Those who say that Paul is only referring to corporate groups do not have an adequate explanation as to why Paul uses the singular again and again."[35] The singular, however, in Greek, frequently functions to mark a collective, particularly in the neuter or masculine, as we have here.[36] In addition, in the Old Testament context of the quotation, Moses addresses the restoration of the people, not an individual.[37] Schreiner's objection, then, both in the context in Romans and the original Old Testament quotation, does not obtain. Paul does not here declare, as a solution to the alleged problem of Israel's election, that

---

[34]See, e.g., Schreiner, *Romans*, p. 510.

[35]Schreiner, "Does Romans 9 Teach," p. 34.

[36]Rom 10:13 provides an example of how the singular can stand for a collective, though ἄν helps clarify the usage there. Another clear example occurs in Rom 11:2, where it is said that "God has not rejected his people whom [ὅν] he foreknew," clearly referring there to a collective entity by nature of the noun to which it refers. It is thus quite possible for a collective use, in light of what has preceded, to be in mind here.

[37]See Abasciano, "Corporate Election in Romans 9," p. 359; Abasciano, *Paul's Use*, pp. 174-75. Likewise, as Di Lella has noted, Paul here appears to borrow a phrase (ὅν θέλει) from Tob 4:19, which Tobit uses to affirm God's freedom to choose Israel over other nations. Tobit's statement is national/corporate in focus, and Paul's use of the phrase in this context again suggests it is the same (Alexander A. Di Lella, "Tobit 4,19 and Romans 9,18: An Intertextual Study," *Biblica* 90 [2009]: 260-63).

God has decided to save some individuals and to condemn, like Pharaoh, others. In fact, his specific connection of this example of hardening to Israel in Romans 11:7, 25, will make that clear.[38] Rather, Paul continues his line of argument that God can determine the basis of election however he chooses, and he has not violated the covenant by not basing it on ancestry or keeping the law.[39] Thus God stands under no constraint to show mercy to Israel by the manner of their choosing, but rather may freely show mercy on whatever basis he determines, and may freely harden on whatever basis he determines.[40] Neither did God harden Pharaoh in advance of any action on Pharaoh's part, as the narrative of Exodus suggests.[41] Again, as we will see in Romans 11, Paul sees Israel's unbelief (in Christ) as the reason they stand outside of the covenant now, and the reason for which they have been hardened.[42] Paul accuses Israel not only of taking the role of covenant outsiders, but also of resembling one of their most despised enemies (Pharaoh) more so than the people of God (those "in Christ"). The exodus was, no doubt, God's paradigmatic act of salvation for Israel in the Old Testament, and the deliverance from Pharaoh played a central part in the Jewish hope for deliverance from foreign oppressors among the Second Temple period (e.g., *Jub.*

---

[38]That Paul intends Pharaoh to represent Israel is widely recognized by commentators. Here, again, we see the notion of a representative head, with Pharaoh (!) representing Israel. In support, see Abasciano, *Paul's Use*, p. 204; Karl Barth, *Church Dogmatics*, ed. and trans. T. F. Torrance and Geoffrey W. Bromiley (New York: T&T Clark, 2004), II/2, p. 220; Dunn, *Romans 9–16*, p. 563; Watson, *Paul, Judaism and the Gentiles*, p. 317.

[39]Abasciano supports this in noting, "Paul's use of θέλω earlier in the epistle (7.15-21) suggests that the 'willing' of 9.16 specifically refers to desiring to keep the Law of God" and likewise τρέχω, in light of Ps 119:32 and likely also Prov 4:12, "probably suggests a vigorous and wholehearted keeping of the Law and the effort involved in it" (Abasciano, *Paul's Use*, pp. 188-89).

[40]See Tobin, *Paul's Rhetoric*, p. 331.

[41]Contra Schreiner, it is not the case that "it is an imposition on the text to conclude that God's hardening is a response to the hardening of human beings. One cannot elude the conclusion that Paul teaches double predestination here" (Schreiner, *Romans*, p. 510). Ben Sira, in fact, uses Pharaoh as an example of one whose evil deeds ("whose works were manifest under the heavens"; Sir. 16:15) were apparently the basis for God's hardening of his heart.

[42]So Morris is correct to note, "Neither here nor anywhere else is God said to harden anyone who had not first hardened himself" (Leon Morris, *The Epistle to the Romans*, Pillar New Testament Commentary [Grand Rapids: Eerdmans, 1988], p. 361). Likewise, Wright comments that "within normal Jewish apocalyptic thought-forms 'hardening' is what happens when people refuse the grace and patience of God, and is the prelude to a final judgment which will be seen to be just" (Wright, *Climax of the Covenant*, p. 247).

48:4; 1 Macc 4:9). Paul's argument here thus reverses Israel's role, or more specifically the role of those Jews who have rejected God's Messiah and, as we saw in Romans 8, defines all who oppose God's purposes in his Messiah, as enemies of God.

GENTILE INCLUSION IN GOD'S PEOPLE (ROMANS 9:19-33)

That Paul makes such a connection, no doubt, would alarm his Jewish brethren. This likely, then, provides the basis for the next part of Paul's argument in Romans 9:19-29. Paul begins here with a second question, asking, "Why does he still find fault? For who has resisted his will?" (Rom 9:19). He then invokes the image of a potter molding clay and asks, "Does the figure say to one who formed it, 'Why have you made me like this?' Or does the potter not have authority over the clay to make from the same lump a vessel of honor and another of dishonor?" (Rom 9:20-21). Here again, some take Paul's analogy as indicating strict double predestination and/or determinism.[43] As we have seen, however, Paul questions in this chapter, as Paul Achtemeier notes, "the place of Israel in God's plan of salvation. He is not dealing with the fate of individuals."[44]

The identity of the vessels here is of the utmost importance for properly interpreting the passage.[45] Paul references here a single lump of clay out of which God makes both vessels for honor/mercy and dishonor/wrath. Paul reveals the interpretive key, in part, in Romans 9:24, where he states these vessels of mercy are those whom God has called from out of the Jews and out of the Gentiles. In keeping with the analogies already presented, then, the vessels of dishonor/wrath here must be (primarily at least) unbelieving Israel. Part of the difficulty in this section lies with the

---

[43]Thus Schreiner seems to generalize the principles here, when clearly Paul has a specific problem in mind (Schreiner, *Romans*, pp. 514-15). Likewise, Demarest states that this means "God has the sovereign right to bestow more grace on one of his creatures than on another (v. 21)" (Demarest, *Cross and Salvation*, p. 130). Contra this view, Dunn notes, "That Paul intended a specific reference with the imagery (individuals and final judgment) is hardly as clear as Piper (173-86) argues: the imagery of creator and creation was used of Israel as well as of individuals, and it is Israel's sense of *national* distinctiveness which Paul seeks to counter" (Dunn, *Romans 9-16*, p. 557).

[44]Achtemeier, *Romans*, p. 165. Contra Kruse *Romans*, p. 383.

[45]As Abasciano notes, "It begs the question to assume that the singular vessel must refer to an individual person. It could just as well refer to a group of people like Israel or the Church" (Abasciano, "Corporate Election in Romans 9," p. 360).

fact that Paul seems to introduce a conditional sentence in Romans 9:22, but does not complete the thought with the consequence of an apodosis.[46] Furthermore, the difference in the verbs used to describe the preparation of the vessels (κατηρτισμένα and προητοίμασεν) is noteworthy. As Ben Witherington has suggested,

> Paul uses two different verbs when talking about the vessels of mercy and the vessels of wrath. . . . *Katērtismena*, used of the vessels of wrath, is a perfect passive participle. *Proētoimasen*, used of the vessels of mercy, is an aorist active indicative. This change cannot be accidental, and it suggests that Paul means that the vessels of wrath are ripe or fit for destruction. Indeed, one could follow the translation of John Chrysostom here and understand it in the middle voice: "have made themselves fit for" destruction. If so, this verse certainly does not support the notion of double predestination. Rather it refers to the fact that these vessels are worthy of destruction, though God has endured them for a long time.[47]

While this translation would certainly diminish the possible presence of double predestination here, even without it, Paul's sense seems clear. God may still rightly "find fault" because, as the potter, he molds the lump (his people) into whatever he wishes, even if this means he incorporates Gentiles in addition to Jews.[48] Thomas Tobin summarizes correctly, "The logic of the argument is that if God can do whatever God thinks best (the 'greater'), God can also, more specifically, show mercy not only to Jews but also to Gentiles (the 'lesser')."[49] As Paul makes clear in Romans 9:23-24, his point here argues for God's rightness both to define election as he chooses and to include Gentiles without the need to keep the law, even if this decision has meant that the majority of Jews, like Pharaoh, are now vessels of wrath, and thus enemies of God, though even their status could change.[50]

---

[46]See Matera, *Romans*, p. 228.

[47]Witherington, *Romans*, p. 258. See also Cranfield, *Romans 9–16*, pp. 496-97. Contra Kruse, *Romans*, p. 387.

[48]See Keener, *Romans*, p. 120. Grindheim states, "The edge of Paul's argument is to align the majority of Israel with the vessels of dishonor, prepared for destruction (v. 22). While they are still in God's plan, the role they are playing is that of Pharaoh" (Grindheim, *Crux of Election*, p. 147).

[49]Tobin, *Paul's Rhetoric*, p. 312.

[50]Furthermore, as Shellrude notes, "It is clear from 11:23-24 that this is not necessarily a perma-

Paul further elaborates on the inclusion of Gentiles by appealing to Hosea and Isaiah, whom he uses to support his argument. The first quotation, which forms a chiastic structure, states that those who were not God's people and unloved will become God's people, his beloved, and "sons of the living God" (Rom 9:25-26). As Sigurd Grindheim describes, "At the center of the chiasm [vv. 25-26], he emphasizes the love terminology. By highlighting the 'call' terminology and the 'love' terminology, Paul recalls the paragraph 9:10-13, where 'call' and 'love' also are the key terms. Paul thus forges a link between Jacob as the beloved and the elect and the Gentiles (with believing Jews) as the beloved and the elect."[51] While the quotation from Hosea supports Gentile inclusion, Paul calls on Isaiah to show that only a portion of Israel, the remnant, will be saved, "Just as Isaiah predicted" (Rom 9:27-29).[52] In doing so, however, Paul shows that God has been faithful to the covenant, and thus any claims of unrighteousness are unwarranted.[53] Paul's purpose throughout Romans 9:1-29 has thus been to affirm the inclusion of the Gentiles and to deny that God was unrighteous to define election as he has defined it.[54]

Paul's next section again opens with a question. He asks, "What, therefore, will we say? That the Gentiles who did not pursue righteous but obtained it, that is, a righteousness from faith, but Israel who pursued a law of righteousness did not reach the law? For what reason? Because

---

nent condition, that they can become 'vessels of mercy' by responding to God's free initiative in Christ" (Glen Shellrude, "The Freedom of God in Mercy and Judgment: A Libertarian Reading of Romans 9:6-29," *EvQ* 81, no. 4 [2009]: 315). Likewise, Oropeza argues, "The combined weight of Paul's use of Israel's scriptures and corporate language in Rom 9:22-33, along with his belief that God's patience is for the objects of wrath (i.e., Israelites) to repent (Rom 2:4; cf. Wis 12) and that the objects of wrath (i.e., Israelites) are not finally destroyed (Rom 11:26-32), and also that elsewhere in Pauline literature the objects of wrath can indeed become believers (e.g., Eph 2:3), argues rather pointedly against the view that the objects of wrath in Rom 9:22 are individuals who are irrevocably predestined to eternal damnation" (Oropeza, *Jews, Gentiles, and the Opponents of Paul*, pp. 189-90).

[51]Grindheim, *Crux of Election*, p. 148.

[52]In contrast with most commentators, Heil has argued these verses are to be taken more positively than usually interpreted, and suggests that Paul sees here that the remnant of Israel will be numerous in the future (John Paul Heil, "From Remnant to Seed of Hope for Israel: Romans 9:27-29," *CBQ* 64, no. 4 [2002]: 703-20). Contra Schnelle, who sees Paul advocating "double predestination, for salvation and destruction" (Udo Schnelle, *Apostle Paul: His Life and Theology* [Grand Rapids: Baker Academic, 2005], p. 346).

[53]See Matera, *Romans*, pp. 230, 240.

[54]See Achtemeier, *Romans*, p. 155; Shellrude, "Freedom of God," pp. 309-10.

it was not from faith but as from works; they stumbled over the stone of stumbling" (Rom 9:30-32). Paul again calls on Isaiah to affirm that this was predicted by the prophets, since Isaiah warned that a stone in Zion would "make them fall, yet the one who believes in him will not be put to shame" (Rom 9:33). Paul clarifies his point in Romans 10:1-4, noting that his Jewish brethren "have zeal for God, but not according to knowledge; for ignoring the righteousness from God and seeking to maintain their own, they did not become submissive to the righteousness of God. For Christ is the goal of the law unto righteousness for all who are believing" (Rom 10:2-4).

JESUS AND THE IDENTITY OF GOD'S PEOPLE (ROMANS 10:1-21)

I must reiterate here, first and foremost, that Paul does not hold a negative view of the law, as many have argued,[55] or of those who keep the law, but rather of those who keep the law apart from Christ and believe it will impart eschatological life.[56] Paul recognizes here that the Gentiles have obtained righteousness by faith,[57] but Israel, pursuing "a law of righteousness," did not because they pursued it "by works." Paul's association here of righteousness connected with the law and with works likely indicates that he has in mind here the now familiar contrast (see

---

[55]See Cranfield, *Romans 9–16*, p. 508.

[56]Tobin's observation is significant: "Paul is not—and this needs to be emphasized—referring to Israel's situation prior to Christ but to Israel's situation in the wake of Christ. There is a temporal orientation to the argument" (Tobin, *Paul's Rhetoric*, p. 341). Garlington here is correct, stating, "We affirm, then, that Paul's interaction with Judaism was an encounter with covenantal nomism. The question, however, is whether Paul was opposed in principle to such an understanding of God's dealings with his people. The answer must be no, because this was undoubtedly the teaching of the OT itself, which Paul sees as the anchorage for his gospel (Rom 1.2). Given both that Paul expected his converts to render faith's obedience and that Christ is the law's τέλος, our conclusion is that he opposed, to coin a phrase, '*Christless* covenantal nomism,' i.e., the position of his fellow Jews that since the law of Moses was eternally and unalterably fixed, fidelity to it was sufficient in itself to make one acceptable to God" (Garlington, *Obedience of Faith*, pp. 264-65).

[57]Abasciano suggests, "This implies that membership in the elect people of God being based on faith is what facilitates fulfilment of the purpose of incorporating Gentiles into the chosen people. . . . That this principle of faith is the primary condition by which God determines the membership of the elect people of God is shown by the fact that Paul goes on to explain that Gentiles who forsake faith will be cut off from God's people and Jews who come to faith will be grafted in (11.20d-24)" (Abasciano, *Paul's Use*, pp. 207-8).

Rom 2:15; 3:20, 28) of ἔργων νόμου and πίστεως Ἰησοῦ Χριστοῦ.[58] For
Paul the object and foundation of πίστις is obviously the Christ (see Rom
3:3, 22, 25, 26; 5:1; 10:17). We may best understand Paul's contrast here
between ἔργον and πίστις as a contrast between the modifiers of "law"
and "Christ." Paul is not principally concerned with the absence of faith
among the Jews in general. Obviously, those keeping the law believed in
God and were committed to faithful obedience to him. This should go
without saying. The πίστις they lacked was not because of their legalistic
attitude and attempt to merit their own salvation.[59] What they lacked was
πίστις in Christ, as Paul makes clear in Romans 9:33. Thus their zeal was
not according to *knowledge* because they did not *know* Christ (Rom
10:2).[60] Their works of the law apart from Christ, as Paul stated in Romans
3:20, only brought them ἐπίγνωσις ("knowledge") of sin. So their zeal
was misdirected in that they ignore the righteousness of God (τῇ

---

[58]Schreiner denies this connection and suggests "*works of the law* should be defined as the deeds
or actions *demanded by the law*, whereas the term *works* refers to all deeds or actions that are
done" (Thomas R. Schreiner, *Paul, Apostle of God's Glory in Christ: A Pauline Theology* [Downers
Grove, IL: InterVarsity Press, 2001], p. 112). To do so, however, is to ignore Paul's own mention
of the law in Rom 9:31. Likewise, contra Matera (*Romans*, p. 242), who interprets "works" here
as "human striving and exertion" and "an ethical notion of personal achievement." Similarly,
Das takes this as a righteousness of their own achievement rather than one based on trust in
God (Das, *Paul, the Law, and the Covenant*, pp. 245-47). These views apparently assume Jews of
the period did not exercise faith/trust in God. What they lacked, clearly, was faith *in Christ*.

[59]Schreiner here, in stating "when Paul says that Israel did not attain the law, the idea is that the
Israelites did not keep the law, they did not attain to the standard required, they fell short of the
goal. . . . No one becomes right with God through the pathway of the law since human sin in-
tervenes" (Schreiner, *Paul*, p. 121), seems to read too much into the text. Paul himself said that
he was blameless according to the law (Phil 3:6). This also overlooks the fact that the law made
provisions for dealing with sin for those who would recognize their sin, repent and offer sacrifices. To keep the law was *not* an impossible task. This misconstrues Judaism and the Old Testament covenants and incorrectly equates obedience to the law with moral perfection. Likewise,
contra Kruse, *Romans*, p. 394.

[60]Schreiner objects to a corporate view of election in Rom 10:1 by stating "if the reference to
Israel in Romans 9–11 is only corporate, then Israel's failure to pursue the law from faith, and
her attempt to be righteous by works (9:30-10:8), must be exclusively a corporate problem and
not an individual one" (Schreiner, "Does Romans 9 Teach," pp. 34-35). Likewise, Kruse objects
in stating, "Such a notion of election does not support an explanation of why some Jewish individuals accept the gospel while others do not, which is the reason Paul introduces it in chapter
9" (Kruse, *Romans*, p. 392). This is wrong on several accounts. First, Paul clearly uses "Israel" in
two senses in the passage as evidenced by Rom 9:6. Second, corporate election allows that unbelief or apostasy means the elect may lose their status. Thus, while most/many Jews in Paul's
thought may have been in right standing with God *before Christ*, their rejection of his Messiah
has meant they have forfeited that status. Third, by thinking of "Israel" here in a national/ethnic
sense and not in the sense of "true Israel," Paul can maintain the corporate perspective.

δικαιοσύνη τοῦ θεοῦ), and thus they lack true ἐπίγνωσις. Paul has used this phrase (τῇ δικαιοσύνῃ τοῦ θεοῦ) in Romans 1:17; 3:5, 21-22, 25-26, with reference to Christ and his gospel. The τῇ δικαιοσύνῃ τοῦ θεοῦ that the Jews have ignored, to which they have not submitted themselves by trying to maintain[61] their own righteousness through the law, is Jesus Christ.[62] It is in this way Christ is the τέλος of the law, for those who had being keeping covenant with God should have been the first to recognize him as their Messiah.[63] The law pointed to Jesus, the revealed righteousness of God, which the majority of Jews, having rejected him as Messiah, have stumbled over as the stumbling stone.

To support his claim, Paul connects Christ and the gospel with the giving of the law to Moses. Here he contrasts "the righteousness from the law" and "the from-faith-righteousness" (Rom 10:5). The context of these quotations in the Old Testament illustrates that Paul is showing the progression from Moses to Christ. Just as keeping the law *was not out of Israel's reach* (see Deut 30:11-20), so faith in Christ is as near as their heart and mouth (see Rom 10:6-8),[64] so that if they confess the faith that the

---

[61]So Dunn argues, "The verb ('establish') likewise denotes not an act of creation, a bringing about of something which previously did not exist, but a setting or establishing or confirming of something which is already in existence" (Dunn, *Romans 9–16*, p. 595).

[62]Schnelle comes close to this perspective (Schnelle, *Apostle Paul*, p. 346). Sanders is correct when he argues, "The simplest interpretation of the meaning of the quotation, and the one generally accepted, is probably correct: the 'stumbling-stone' is Christ, and those who believe in him are not put to shame. The explanation of 'not by faith but by works,' then, is 'they did not believe in Christ,' not 'they incorrectly tried for righteousness and by trying achieved only self-righteousness.' Israel's failure is not that they do not obey the law in the correct way, but that they do not have faith in Christ" (E. P. Sanders, *Paul, the Law, and the Jewish People* [Minneapolis: Fortress, 1983], p. 37). See also N. T. Wright, "Romans 9–11 and the 'New Perspective,'" in *Between Gospel and Election*, ed. Florian Wilk and J. Ross Wagner (Tübingen: Mohr Siebeck, 2010), p. 40; Wright, *Paul and the Faithfulness of God*, p. 1169.

[63]See Cranfield, *Romans 9–16*, pp. 505, 512, who sees Paul's thought here in terms of a destination, though he interprets the passage differently than has been argued above. Dunn recognizes the possibility of this interpretation (Dunn, *Romans 9–16*, p. 597). Matera sees the notion here as "goal" as well, though he emphasizes the element of human effort as a part of the contrast (Matera, *Romans*, p. 245). See also Robert Jewett, "The Law and the Coexistence of Jews and Gentiles in Romans," *Int* 39, no. 4 (1985): 352; Tobin, *Paul's Rhetoric*, p. 312.

[64]Dunson suggests, "Thus, just as Moses explained to Israel that the pathway to pleasing God was not to be found in an esoteric reality beyond her grasp (instead being located in the clear word of Torah), so also in the present, the word about Christ is equally available for all to hear and respond to. The content of this word of faith consists of a call to individual confession (ὁμολογήσῃς) of the Lord Jesus with one's mouth and individual belief" (Ben C. Dunson, "Faith in Romans: The Salvation of the Individual or Life in Community?," *JSNT* 34, no. 1 [2011]: 31).

apostles have preached to them and believe that God raised Jesus from the dead, they will be saved and declared righteous (Rom 10:9-10).[65] The gospel thus puts all on equal footing before God, eliminating any distinction, as was inherent in the law, between Jew and Gentile (Rom 10:12). Paul's contrast thus continues between the law and Christ since the law is inoperative outside of faith in Jesus and finds its true purpose in him.[66] And so, as James Dunn states clearly, "The one essential condition of salvation is faith."[67] Paul's brethren in Israel were not in unbelief for a lack of hearing the message, as he carefully develops in Romans 10:14-15. Rather, they heard the message and did not *obey the gospel* (Rom 10:16).[68] Here, again, Paul does not intend to set faith and works against each other, but rather contrasts the futility of the law outside of Christ and the reality that humanity now finds right-standing in the covenant only through obedience to the gospel.

PAUL'S HOPE FOR JEWISH UNBELIEVERS (ROMANS 11:1-16)

Paul affirms in Romans 10:18 that the Jews have indeed heard the gospel,

---

[65]And thus, "Here, 'God's righteousness' becomes a roundabout, allusive way of referring to 'the gospel of Jesus Christ,' on the basis of 3:21-31" (Wright, "Romans 9–11 and the 'New Perspective,'" p. 41). As Wright continues, he insightfully notes, "if Jesus was the Messiah . . . then Israel's God had in fact renewed the covenant through him. The present passage is one of the central pieces of evidence, along with Rom 4, Gal 3 and 2 Cor 3, for reading Paul's theology as essentially *covenantal*, in the sense that he believed that God had fulfilled the covenant promises to Abraham, and the promise of covenant renewal in Deuteronomy, in and through Jesus Christ" (ibid., p. 47).

[66]So Matera states, "The contrast, however, is not intended to criticize Moses or the law, nor is it meant to establish an opposition between 'doing' and 'believing.' Rather, having identified Christ as the goal of the law, Paul shows how the law finds its goal in Christ" (Matera, *Romans*, p. 249). Likewise, Dunn states, "It needs to be said yet again that there is no thought of 'achieving righteousness' here. . . . And the verb should *not* be emphasized, as though Paul was objecting to the idea of 'doing' the law" (Dunn, *Romans 9–16*, p. 601).

[67]Dunn, *Romans 9–16*, p. 616.

[68]Garlington, in examining the concepts of "faith" and "obedience" in Second Temple Judaism, notes, "The obedience of God's people, consisting in their fidelity to his covenant with them, is the product of a prior belief in his person and trust in his word" (Garlington, *Obedience of Faith*, p. 233), and so "not only the privileges of the covenant but also its responsibilities were part and parcel of 'the obedience of faith among all the nations for his name's sake': Jew and Gentile in Christ have been called to respond to the voice of God with believing obedience" (ibid., p. 249). Likewise, for Dunn, Paul's discussion shows "clearly the continuity Paul sees between God's covenant with Israel, the law, and the faith which he proclaimed; they confirm that for Paul obedience . . . is a fundamental aspect of covenant righteousness, as much for him as for his fellow Jews" (Dunn, *Romans 9–16*, p. 588).

and God intended the faith demonstrated by the Gentiles to bring about Israel's jealousy while God continues to hold "out [his] hands to this disobedient and stubborn people" (Rom 10:21; cf. Is 65:2). Paul's discussion now comes full circle to the questions of Romans 9. Paul identifies himself, "an Israelite, a descendent of Abraham, from the tribe of Benjamin," as an example of the fact that "God has not rejected his people whom he foreknew" (Rom 11:1-2).[69] Just as in Elijah's day (Rom 11:3-4), "there is in the present time a remnant according to election of grace; now if it is by grace, it is no longer by works, for grace would no longer be grace" (Rom 11:5-6). God's favor is thus on the remnant, as evidenced by their election, which is "no longer by works."[70] Thus Israel failed to obtain "what they sought for" (ἐπιζητεῖ), but the "elect obtained it" while "the rest were hardened." Dunn denies that the "what" that Israel sought for could be its election, which would be the closest referent and would correspond to the contrast with the "elect" who obtained it.[71] Paul may also reference here "righteousness" if he refers back to his statement in Romans 10:3, where they did not obtain the righteousness they sought

---

[69]It is not here, as Schreiner suggests, that "Israel's election as a nation functions as a type of the election of the church" (Schreiner, Romans, p. 578). Because he does not see election as corporate, it seems that Schreiner must postulate two elections by God, a theocratic election of Israel that apparently had only earthly consequences, and a spiritual election of those who will receive God's gift of salvation. As Oropeza states, "Paul's focus is not on the individual—God has chosen the people of Israel and the church 'in Christ,' and foreknowledge in 11:2 stresses the object of God's people as a corporate community" (Oropeza, Jews, Gentiles, and the Opponents of Paul, p. 171). See also Witherington, Romans, p. 265.

[70]Schreiner states works here must be taken as good works in general, not Torah-works, since Paul omits νομός (Romans, pp. 534-45). We need not expect, however, that Paul repeat the phrase in its entirety, especially when he is speaking specifically about Israel, whose identity was defined by the Torah. Does Paul's language here indicate that election was at one time "by works"? If so, clearly this would be "works of the law," that is, faithfulness to the Mosaic covenant. This should not be taken to mean, however, that election was meritoriously earned. Again, if one sees Paul's contrast between works of the law and faith in Christ, there is no need to deny any significance to "doing." Witherington is helpful here, stating, "Paul is not merely opposing a legalistic way of approaching the Mosaic Law or the Mosaic covenant. And in any case, he is all for his converts keeping the Law of Christ and tells them that they must avoid the deeds of the flesh and do the Law of Christ if they want to enter the kingdom (Galatians 5–6). . . . Paul affirms a sort of covenantal nomism, though it is grace-empowered and Spirit-driven. It is just not the Mosaic covenant that he wants Gentiles to keep. It is a mistake to call any demand or requirement to obey a law 'legalism' in a context where salvation is by grace and faith. The obedience that necessarily must follow on and depend on living faith is not legalism. Paul's problem is not with obedience or good works, or laws per se" (Witherington, Romans, p. 266).

[71]Dunn, Romans 9–16, p. 640.

(ζητοῦντες). If so, again, the reason they did not obtain it is because they did not have πίστις in Christ. The "elect" here are either the Gentiles or the remnant mentioned in Romans 11:5, which, due to its proximity, is the more likely choice.[72] We should also note that "elect" here is in the singular, in the form of the less commonly used term ἐκλογὴ (used only in Rom 9:11; 11:5, 7, 28; 1 Thess 1:4), which emphasizes the *collective* nature of Paul's understanding of the term. If those who were hardened have been hardened[73] because of their lack of faith (ἀπιστία; see Rom 9:31, 32-33; 10:2-4, 16; 11:23, 30-31),[74] then clearly those who are elect have shown πίστις in the Christ. Furthermore, the text makes clear that double predestination does not appear here by what follows.[75] Paul affirms that Israel "did not stumble into an irrevocable fall" (Rom 11:11 NET). If their state is reversible, then Paul surely does not mean that their hardening represents their consignment to eternal reprobation. Their trespass (unbelief) has brought salvation to the Gentiles, but Paul hopes this will provoke them to jealousy and belief (Rom 11:11-15).[76]

---

[72]Toews suggests that what they obtained is "inclusion in the end-time people God is creating" (Toews, *Romans*, p. 276), i.e., membership in the elect.

[73]It is worth recalling here the connection back to Pharaoh in Rom 9:17, where Paul argued it was not lineage or works of the law that was the condition of election, and by rejecting God's condition of faith in the Messiah Israel now played the role of Pharaoh. The validity of this interpretation is affirmed by Paul's explicit connection here. See Ridderbos, *Paul*, p. 345.

[74]There is nothing in the text here that requires, as Schreiner proposes, that Israel's hardening by God produced its unbelief (Schreiner, *Romans*, p. 587). The opposite phenomenon (unbelief followed by a hardening of the heart) was observed earlier both in the exodus narratives and in 2 Thess 2, and Oropeza has documented thoroughly that divine hardening in the New Testament is consistently a response to disobedience (see B. J. Oropeza, *Apostasy in the New Testament Communities* [Eugene, OR: Wipf & Stock], 3 vols.).

[75]Wright comments, "This was never an abstract 'doctrine of predestination,' attempting to plumb the mysteries of why some people (in general, without reference to Israel) hear and believe the gospel and others do not. . . . Rather, it was a way of saying, very specifically, that the fact of Israel's election . . . had always been there to deal with the sin of the world; that Israel's election had always involved Israel being narrowed down . . . to a single point, to the Messiah himself, *who would himself be 'cast away' so that the world might be redeemed*" (Wright, *Paul and the Faithfulness of God*, p. 1208 [emphasis original]).

[76]Allison's observation here is noteworthy. As he says, "Enlarging further on the distinctive presentation in Rom. 11:11-15, we may say that whereas for much Jewish eschatology the repentance of Israel makes possible and leads to the salvation of the Gentiles, in Paul this is turned around: the salvation of the Gentiles comes before that of Israel. And whereas in much Jewish eschatology the acceptance of the Gentiles (whose repentance is not set forth as a pre-condition of the new age) simply follows after the repentance of Israel, all this is reversed in Paul, for whom the acceptance of Israel (whose repentance is at most implicit in 11:14—'to stir emulation in the

Paul's Warning for Gentile Believers (Romans 11:17-36)

Paul again turns to analogy in the remainder of his discussion concerning the salvation of the Gentiles and the Jews' rejection of God's Messiah. He introduces two images in Romans 11:16: "Now if the firstfruit is holy, so is the batch of dough; and if the root is holy, so are the branches." Both of Paul's examples come from agriculture, with the same meaning intended, that if the initial portion ("firstfruit" or "root") is holy, then so are all parts of the entity ("batch of dough" or "branches"). That Paul has in mind here the validity of Gentile inclusion in the people of God again seems clear. As Paul continues, he states, "Now if some of the branches were broken off, but you, a wild olive tree, have been grafted in among them and become a sharer in the fatness of the root, do not boast over the branches; but if you boast, [remember that] you do not support the root, but the root supports you" (Rom 11:17-18).[77] The Gentiles are the "wild olive tree" that has been grafted into the root of God's people.[78] As Paul continues, he further argues that the Gentiles must take care not to boast over the Israelites, for just as they were broken off *because of their unbelief*, so the Gentiles may not be spared, assumedly if they fall into the same error (Rom 11:20-21).[79] Israel's condition of hardening and their

---

men of my own race') simply follows upon the salvation of the Gentiles. 'A hardening has come upon part of Israel until the full number of the Gentiles comes in, and so all Israel will be saved' (11:25-26). In short—and this is the presupposition of Rom. 11:11-15—the roles of Jew and Gentile have been exchanged. Although—and to this extent the traditional scheme is retained—it is the salvation of Israel that is the proximate cause of the onset of the consummation, the repentance required before the Kingdom's coming is being fulfilled not by the Jews but by the Gentiles" (Dale C. Allison Jr., "Romans 11:11-15: A Suggestion," *PRSt* 12 [1985]: 29).

[77] So Cranfield recognizes, "If the Gentile Christians insist on boasting over those who are the natural branches, that will never alter the fact that it is from his incorporation into the stock of Israel, the people of God's election, to whom the promise was given of the seed in whom all the nations should find blessing, that all his spiritual privileges derive. No amount of boasting on the part of the branches which have been grafted in can reverse their relation to the root" (Cranfield, *Romans 9–16*, p. 568).

[78] In the Old Testament, plant imagery is often used to refer to Israel (e.g., Ps 44:2; 80:8, 15; 92:13; Is 5:2; 60:21; 61:3; Jer 1:10; 2:21; 11:17; 12:2; 17:8; 18:9; 24:6; 31:27, 28; 32:41; 42:10; 45:4; Ezek 16:7; 17:4-10, 22, 23; 19:10, 13; Hos 2:23; Amos 9:15. This imagery is present in *1 Enoch* (10:16-17; 84:5-6; 93:5-10), where it is used to refer to the righteous remnant/the elect, and likewise in *Bib. Ant.* 12.8-9, where it refers to Israel as a nation (i.e., corporately).

[79] Here Shellrude argues, "If Israel's unbelief was indeed predestined by God, then Paul would be guilty of over-simplification in saying that the problem of Israel's unbelief can be easily resolved by a response of faith. It would also seem odd to suggest that God's unconditional election of some Gentiles to salvation can be easily undone by an arrogance that leads to being cut off from

exclusion from the people of God will, however, be reversed "if they do not persist in their unbelief" (ἐὰν μὴ ἐπιμένωσιν τῇ ἀπιστίᾳ; Rom 11:23).[80] Again, Paul's polemic clearly does not indicate that Israel has been hardened as a sign of their predestination to condemnation, nor that they were blinded by legalism or a merit-based theology, but that they have not believed in the Messiah of God! Paul's line of argument has thus been consistent throughout. Election does not stand on ancestry or keeping the law (though those things are good!), but on whether or not one, Jew or Gentile, obeys the gospel and, by faith, becomes right with God through Jesus Christ. As Brian Abasciano argues, "Paul's olive tree metaphor in Rom 11.17-24 evidences the view of the corporate election perfectly. Individuals get grafted into the elect people (the olive tree) and participate in election and its blessings by faith or get cut off from God's chosen people and their blessings because of unbelief, while the focus of election clearly remains the corporate people of God, which spans salvation history."[81]

Paul's next statement, no doubt, represents one of the most heavily debated passages in all of Paul's letters. He states that he wants his readers to be aware of the following mystery, "that a hardening of a part of Israel has taken place until the fullness of the Gentiles comes in, and thus [οὕτως], all Israel [πᾶς Ἰσραὴλ] will be saved" (Rom 11:25-26). Paul then supports his claim with quotations from Isaiah 59[82] and Isaiah 27, passages largely concerned with the sin of Israel and God's deliverance of

---

salvation. It is hard to imagine that a theologian operating within a strongly deterministic framework would express himself in this way" (Shellrude, "Freedom of God," p. 308).

[80]See Matera, Romans, pp. 270-71. Schreiner is correct in noting that "Paul does not contemplate the regrafting of Israel apart from faith, because he says specifically that they will be grafted in again 'if they do not remain in unbelief'" (Schreiner, Romans, p. 612). That these arguments cause problems for those who hold to double predestination is clear from Schreiner's discussion: "The warnings are grammatically hypothetical but are seriously intended for believers" (ibid., p. 608). Nothing about Paul's discussion here suggests this is hypothetical or those who were "in" were never really "in" at all. By speaking of grafting, Paul clearly speaks of inclusion in the people of God, and thus it is possible, both for Jew and Gentile, that those who have once been included among the people of God can be excluded for unbelief, specifically for denial of Jesus as Lord and Messiah.

[81]Abasciano, Paul's Use, pp. 60-61; Abasciano, "Corporate Election in Romans 9," p. 362.

[82]Paul quotes here the LXX, and the differences between the LXX and the MT are substantial. Compare Is 59:20 in the MT: "The Redeemer will come to Zion, to those in Jacob who repent of their sins," with the LXX: "And the deliverer shall come for Zion's sake, and shall turn away ungodliness from Jacob."

corporate Jacob from its enemies. In Isaiah 27, Jacob repents of their idolatry and subsequently God gathers and rescues them. For Paul, no doubt, it will be when the unbelieving Jews cease their unbelief concerning Jesus that they will be regrafted into the people of God. So what, then, does Paul have in mind in stating that that "all Israel will be saved"? As C. E. B. Cranfield has summarized, this may include (1) all the elect (Jews and Gentiles), (2) all the elect from the nation of Israel, (3) all of the nation of Israel, composed of every individual Israelite, or (4) the nation of Israel as a whole, but not every individual Israelite.[83] The overwhelming majority of recent interpreters have opted for the fourth option, that Paul has in mind here Israel as a whole, and not every individual Israelite.[84] This seems to suggest, then, that Paul speaks of Israel in two senses in Romans 11:25-26 as he did in Romans 9:6, of Israel as a nation and of Israel in the sense of a "true Israel."[85] Most commentators also agree that one should not see here a special dispensation for end-time Israel by which God saves them by any means other than repentance and faith in Christ.[86] Debate persists as well as to whether Paul views this as an end-time event at all.[87] Regardless of the correct interpretation, Paul speaks of a "true Israel" as defined by faith in Christ. He has not gone so far as to say explicitly that Gentile believers too are

---

[83]Cranfield, *Romans 9–16*, p. 576.

[84]Kruse is representative, stating, "The election of the nation did not mean that every individual Israelite would enjoy God's blessings irrespective of their response to his word, something dramatically illustrated by the fact that virtually an entire generation was refused entry to the promised land (Numbers 14)" (Kruse, *Romans*, p. 446). See also Dunn, *Romans 9–16*, p. 681; Tobin, *Paul's Rhetoric*, p. 372; Christopher Zoccali, "'And So All Israel Will Be Saved': Competing Interpretations of Romans 11.26 in Pauline Scholarship," *JSNT* 30, no. 3 (2008): 289-318.

[85]Harvey and Wright both support the possibility (Graham Harvey, *The True Israel: Uses of the Names Jew, Hebrew, and Israel in Ancient Jewish and Early Christian Literature* [Leiden: Brill, 1996], p. 232; Wright, *Climax of the Covenant*, p. 250).

[86]So Tobin writes, "Given Paul's insistence throughout Romans on the significance of Christ for both Jews and Gentiles and on the equality of Jews and Gentiles in both sin and salvation, it is almost impossible to imagine that he could think of Israel's ultimate salvation as somehow apart from Christ" (Tobin, *Paul's Rhetoric*, p. 374).

[87]For a representative of the view, see Matera, *Romans*, p. 273. Contra the end-time interpretation, see Kruse, *Romans*, p. 451. Likewise, Wright does not take this as a reference to the parousia, but rather that "'Whenever' God takes away their sins, i.e. whenever Jews come to believe in Christ and so enter the family of God, in that moment the promises God made long ago to the patriarchs are being reaffirmed" (Wright, *Climax of the Covenant*, p. 251).

"Israelites,"[88] but he envisions one people of God, the boundary of which is defined by faith in Jesus Christ, and he holds out hope for the conversion of his own people, which will come through faith in the Messiah. And again, he clearly has corporate intentions since he can speak of Israel as a collective entity without requiring that every individual Jew or Israelite is a part of God's elect, a status given only to those who exercise faith in Christ.[89]

As Paul closes the chapter, he again recognizes the reversal of roles among the Jews and Gentiles and the basis of exclusion from the people of God. He states, "For just as you formerly were disobedient to God, but now have been shown mercy by their disobedience, in this manner also they are now disobedient resulting in your receipt of mercy, so that they also might be shown mercy. For God has enclosed them all in disobedience, in order that they all may be shown mercy" (Rom 11:30-32). If disobedience (assumedly to the gospel; see Rom 10:16) entails exclusion, it follows that obedience to the gospel is what defines those who are included in God's people.[90]

SUMMARY

To summarize briefly, in Romans 8:28–11:36, Paul has not argued that God has predetermined certain individuals to eternal life and others to eternal death. Rather God foreknew that he would form a people and determined the goal of their development, which is conformity to

---

[88]Kim argues that the referent here is all Jewish and Gentile believers (Dongsu Kim, "Reading Paul's καὶ οὕτως πᾶς Ἰσραὴλ σωθήσεται (Rom. 11:26a) in the Context of Romans," *Calvin Theological Journal* 45 [2010]: 317-34). Harvey and Keener both deny this possibility (Harvey, *True Israel*, p. 231; Keener, *Romans*, p. 136).

[89]Guthrie's summary can thus be wholeheartedly affirmed: that Paul's argument, contra to traditional interpretations, is less about individuals than groups, emphasizes the unity and continuity of the people of God, rather than hard distinctions between the church and Israel, and focuses on the many rather than the few (Shirley C. Guthrie, "Romans 11:25-32," *Int* 38 [1984]: 286-91).

[90]And so Staples summarizes, "It is not that the rules have changed or that God has rejected his people. Quite the opposite, God is cutting off only those of Israel who have forfeited their standing through covenantal unfaithfulness—those from Judah who are indeed 'inward Jews' (2:27-29) remain. As Paul has already pointed out, this is not the first time the majority of Israel has rejected God, but God has always preserved a remnant through it all (11:2-5)" (Jason A. Staples, "What Do the Gentiles Have to Do with 'All Israel'? A Fresh Look at Romans 11:25-27," *JBL* 130, no. 2 [2011]: 384). As such, it may be more appropriate to speak of a "renewed" covenant than a "new" covenant. There is much continuity between the "old" and the "new" in Paul's thought.

Christ. Furthermore, God has not defined inclusion among the elect people of God in terms of ancestry or keeping the law, but has defined the "boundary marker" of God's people as faith in Jesus the Messiah. Those who obey the gospel are incorporated into the one people of God. The majority of Jews in Paul's day, however, had rejected Jesus as their Messiah and thus, for Paul, had rejected the covenant and its subsequent blessings. Their unbelief, their rejection of the righteousness of God found through Jesus Christ, meant that they were cut off from the people of God, though if they should cease in their rejection, they would once more receive the blessings found in life in the covenant. Paul thus agrees with his contemporaries that election is primarily corporate (not nationalistic) and includes those who are faithful to the covenant. He has, however, argued that faithfulness to the covenant does not mean, for the Jew, faithfulness to the law apart from Christ. Rather, as it is for the Gentile, Paul's Jewish brothers and sisters would share in "election," in identification in God's people, through obeying the good news and responding in faith(fulness) to God through the faithfulness of Christ. Paul's redefinition thus does not result in the individualization of election, but rather the conviction that the renewal of the covenant brought a redefinition of the "boundary marker" based on God's work in the Messiah and the full inclusion of Gentiles.

Where Do We Go
from Here?

I hope to have demonstrated the value and necessity of placing Paul's election language back in its original context, which was a decidedly Jewish one. As we reviewed the Jewish literature, we discovered a view of election that was grounded in God's promises to the patriarchs. This overwhelmingly emphasized the collective nature of election as a concept that applied to a bounded community. When individuals were in view, their role, their character or their representation of a group was emphasized, never their being chosen for a particular soteriological standing. Likewise, the Jewish literature was decidedly conditional, with the various authors defining who was "in" and who was "out" by different means and markers. This typically meant Gentiles were excluded, along with many or most Jews, from the people of God. We can thus express these tendencies as described below:

1. At times, the description of individuals or a group as "elect" emphasizes primarily their character or piety rather than a particular, predetermined, soteriological standing (Ben Sira, *Testaments*, Additional Psalms of David, *1 Enoch*).

2. When individuals are mentioned as "elect," the identification either (1) recognizes them as such because they represent or mediate for a corporate group (*Jubilees, Testaments*, DSS, *1 Enoch*), or (2) describes a vocational calling (king, priest, etc.; see Ben Sira, *Psalms of Solomon*).

The picture of election is primarily conditional, either implicitly (Tobit, Ben Sira, Baruch, Wisdom of Solomon, *Sibylline Oracles*, pseudo-Philo) or explicitly (*Jubilees, Testaments*, 1 Maccabees, 2 Maccabees, *Psalms of Solomon*, DSS), in that a number of Jews, whether a majority (*Jubilees, Testaments*, 1 Maccabees, *Psalms of Solomon*, DSS, *1 Enoch, Testament of Moses*) or an undefined number (Tobit, Ben Sira, Baruch, 2 Maccabees, Wisdom of Solomon, *Sibylline Oracles*, pseudo-Philo), were presently apostate and outside of the covenant. The concept was thus not nationalistic or ethnic, but primarily remnant-oriented.

1. The conditions of the covenant *emphasized* vary throughout the literature, and included circumcision, general piety, Sabbath observance, ritual purity, abstinence from sexual immorality, avoidance of intermarriage with Gentiles, proper calendrical and festival observances, resistance of Hellenization and idolatry, support for the Hasmoneans, rejection of the Hasmoneans, honesty, humility, proper interpretation and application of the law, rejection of the corrupt leadership in Jerusalem (e.g., the priests, Pharisees, Sadducees, Sanhedrin, Maccabees or Hasmoneans), and association with/allegiance to a particular community and its understanding of the law or its specially received revelation.

2. In spite of the conditional nature, God's election of Israel was still primarily presented as a corporate, not an individual, concept. This is clear from the many uses of corporate or national terminology and imagery, such as use of the moniker "Israel" or "Judah" when referring only to the pious, vine and plant imagery, association with a righteous person (e.g., Enoch or Noah) or an explicit invocation of the remnant motif.

Some texts make an allowance for the possible inclusion of Gentiles in the eschatological people of God (*Sibylline Oracles, 1 Enoch*, pseudo-Philo), though largely Gentiles are considered to be wicked and sinful by nature.

God's mercy and human obedience do not exist in mutually exclusive terms. The recognition of Israel's sin is widespread throughout the literature. At times, God's mercy means his decision not to reject Israel completely, though they are deserving of such a fate. This does not create, however, carte blanche for Israel to be licentious, as they needed to remain faithful to the covenant (as variously defined) in order to receive the covenant blessings.

1. God's sovereignty and human freedom do not exist in mutually exclusive terms. While certain things, such as the declaration of what is good and what is evil, the final judgment and its rewards or punishments, and the election of Israel/the remnant are described as being predetermined, in no text does this negate human freedom and the responsibility to be faithful to the covenant with God. That God has an overarching plan is clear, but that every nuance within that plan, including the individual actions of humans, is preordained, is not.

2. There is a real possibility, except once the final judgment comes, for the apostates to repent and commit themselves to keeping the covenant as well as for those in the "true Israel" to commit apostasy and reject the covenant and its blessings.

As we looked at Paul's letters, we did not find a drastically different picture. Paul similarly worked within a collective and conditional framework. Like his contemporaries he viewed the elect as a restricted group. In his most explicit election texts, Paul never concerns himself with God choosing specific individuals to receive eschatological salvation. Rather, in his most explicit election texts (in particular Gal 2–3; Rom 3; 8–11; and Eph 1–2), Paul *always* concerns himself with what it means for Gentiles to be a part of God's people. Recognizing this aspect alone should cause us to step back and ask what exactly Paul is doing. When we see these sociological divisions and Paul's attempt to bring a theological resolution to the problem of Gentile inclusion and majority Jewish exclusion, we recognize that Paul does not explore an abstract theological doctrine of God determining each individual's eschatological fate, but rather wrestles with how to make sense of God's actions in light of the covenant with the patriarchs. Paul deals in detail with how to resolve this dilemma, adamant that God has freedom to work how he chooses, has indeed fulfilled his promises to bless the nations through Israel and has renewed the covenant through his faithful and loving act in the Messiah. This public display of Jesus and miraculous vindication through the resurrection act as the sign that God himself has truly intervened. And through this act, the law took its proper place in the realm of the risen Jesus and the Spirit, where God's people, those who identify with his Messiah and submit to his Spirit, receive the enablement to fulfill this law and thus receive the promised eschatological life. For Paul, as for his contemporaries, election controversies were more about *who* God's people were than *how* they were God's people.

Among Jews of the period, the concept of election came to signify the "true Israel" or "remnant," meaning those Israelites who remained faithful to the covenant. For Paul the terminology takes on quite the same meaning. In referring to those who have trusted in Jesus as "elect" or "chosen" or "called," Paul claims that it is those who have been united with God's Messiah who are actually in right-standing with God. Torah-faithfulness apart from obedience to the good news of God expressed through Jesus has become useless. For Paul, obedience to God comes only through identification with Jesus. Thus Jesus' own faithfulness both grounds the faithfulness of the believer and brings God's declaration of "rightness" to them.

So What?

Occasionally I am asked something to the effect of "What difference does it make how we think about election?" or "What does this view 'do' that others don't?" It seems to me that this view better fits within the thought-world of Second Temple Judaism. The more we immerse ourselves in that world, the better we will make sense of Paul, a Jewish follower of a Jewish Messiah, and his letters. Several very practical implications also arise from this view. Space does not permit me to articulate these more fully, though we have touched briefly on each at various points in our discussion.

Much of the early Jewish discussion of the "elect" concerned their piety more than whether or not they were, or would be, "saved." They shared a deep concern, though expressed in different and competing ways, with living faithfully to God's commands as expressed in his covenant with them. Paul expresses a similar concern in his articulation of the faithfulness required of God's people in Christ. For Paul, this faithfulness is enabled through the gift of God's Spirit, but not at the elimination of the responsibility and commitment of the individual. Paul still calls God's people to obedience to his law, though he expresses this in a more condensed formula based on the emulation of the Savior and the love of God and others.

Paul's Jewish contemporaries also shared a common concern to distinguish God's people from the rest of the world. This sometimes resulted in extremes, as we saw at Qumran or in the Maccabees. Each group, however, wrestled with how to remain faithful to God and resist the attractions and temptations of the world. This came, after all, from God's own declaration for his people to be set apart for service to him. When Paul declares believers, including Gentiles (!), elect, holy, righteous and called, he calls on this rich history of God's covenantal people. Those in God's Messiah would likewise need to live in a way that distinguished them from the world, for this was their calling. And again the Messiah himself emulated this lifestyle and God's Spirit will enable those who belong to him to reflect Jesus. As it was for Israel, this meant living in ways counterintuitive to the larger culture, dying to their own desires that they might live for God, and subsequently, and perhaps ironically from a human perspective, in doing so actually live life as God had intended all along.

The various Jewish sects of the period represented in our literature had deep convictions about how to define the boundaries of God's people. This likewise fostered an important sense of unity in those communities. Paul too, perhaps more adamantly even, held a deep concern for the unity of God's people, especially in light of the reconciliation of Gentiles to God. When competing identity markers, such as circumcision or collective cultural wisdom, challenged the centrality of the Messiah and his cross and resurrection, Paul felt compelled to strip those things of their significance. In doing so, he both continued to elevate the primacy of obedient commitment to Jesus as the central marker of identity and sought to promote the unity of God's people around the primary marker.

This unity required people from differing racial and socioeconomic backgrounds to learn to function together as a united, reformed, renewed people of God. In the case of Jews and Gentiles, long held religious beliefs and animosities created tensions and hostilities among God's people. Paul would not allow these problems to continue to fester but rather dismantled any notion, whether an idea, a practice or a person, that might be exalted to the status which Jesus alone held. Paul would allow God's people in Christ to be defined by no other means than the Messiah's life, death and resurrection.

Finally, election from its inception in the biblical text through much of the Second Temple literature, and certainly in Paul, held a central position in the mission of God's people. God chose Israel for his special possession in order to bring the Abrahamic blessing to the nations. This missional aspect of Israel's calling is echoed through the prophetic literature of the Old Testament and through many Second Temple texts. For Paul this blessings in one sense had been accomplished since God had brought the Gentiles into his people as full members through Christ. In another sense, both as it pertains to unbelieving Gentiles, and paradoxically to unbelieving Jews, this missional call of God's people to bless the nations still endured and had not yet found its final fulfillment since there still existed those "outside the camp."

WHAT ELSE?

We have been able only to scratch the surface of this topic in our examinations and reflections of these texts. I hope through this discussion that we might increase our awareness of the Jewish context of the New Testament and the ways in which we can better understand its message within that context. I have attempted to offer an account of the relationship between Paul's thought and his Jewish background, which is both contextually sensitive and recognizes the connecting points and the divergences between them. In doing so, I have developed a view that attempts to deeply appreciate the continuity between Paul's thought, the covenantal theology of the Old Testament and his background as a first-century Jew. I have aimed at providing a "thick description" of Paul's theology of election, accounting for these various contexts as important influences on his theological articulations. These contexts act as spotlights that, when shown on their subject, allow us to appreciate the details of what we view. My study has also aimed at a rich theological description of these beliefs set within the ancient thought world rather than our own. Such a view also, as I have summarized briefly, creates important practical implications for how we understand human responsibility, Christian unity, faithful obedience to God and the core identity of God's people. Though we face challenges in how we apply these ideas in our own context, which is in some ways very different from Paul's and in others quite similar, by seeing Paul's convictions in their historical and cultural contexts we can better allow them to shape our own.

I do not anticipate this to be the final word on this subject. I am grateful for the opportunity to offer a contribution to this area of Christian thought, which has been contentious for millennia. I do believe sincerely that when we aim at a more robust view of Paul's world we can likewise grasp a more robust view of Paul's letters. I also believe that what we see in Paul's letters, specifically in terms of how he thinks about election from a Jewish framework, accords well with what we see in the rest of the New Testament. I have not, of course, developed this here, but I believe further work can illuminate it in a way that effectively accounts for both the world of the New Testament and the place of the New Testament in that world.

Select Bibliography

Abasciano, Brian J. "Corporate Election in Romans 9: A Reply to Thomas Schreiner." *JETS* 49, no. 2 (2006): 20-31.

———. *Paul's Use of the Old Testament in Romans 9.10-18: An Intertextual and Theological Exegesis*. New York: T&T Clark, 2011.

Achtemeier, Paul J. *Romans*. IBC. Louisville: Westminster John Knox Press, 1986.

Alexander, Philip S. "Predestination and Free Will in the Theology of the Dead Sea Scrolls." In *Divine and Human Agency in Paul and His Cultural Environment*, edited by John M. Barclay and Simon J. Gathercole, pp. 27-49. New York: T&T Clark, 2006.

Allison, Dale C., Jr. "Romans 11:11-15: A Suggestion." *PRSt* 12 (1985): 23-30.

Atkinson, Kenneth. "Enduring the Lord's Discipline: Soteriology in the *Psalms of Solomon*." In *This World and the World to Come: Soteriology in Early Judaism*, edited by Daniel M. Gurtner, pp. 145-66. New York: T&T Clark, 2011.

———. "Taxo's Martyrdom and the Role of the *Nuntius* in the *Testament of Moses*: Implications for Understanding the Role of Other Intermediary Figures." *JBL* 125, no. 3 (2006): 453-76.

Baird, William. "Visions, Revelation, and Ministry: Reflections on 2 Cor 12:1-5 and Gal 1:11-17." *JBL* 104, no. 4 (1985): 651-62.

Barrett, C. K. *The Epistle to the Romans*. BNTC. Peabody, MA: Hendrickson, 1991.

———. *The First Epistle to the Corinthians*. BNTC. Peabody, MA: Hendrickson, 1968.

Barth, Karl. *Church Dogmatics*. Vol. II/2. Edited and translated by Geoffrey W. Bromiley and T. F. Torrance. Edinburgh: T&T Clark, 1957.

Barth, Markus. *Israel and the Church: Contribution to a Dialogue for Peace*. Eugene, OR: Wipf & Stock, 2005.

Bartlett, John R. *The First and Second Books of the Maccabees*. Cambridge: Cambridge University Press, 1973.

Bauckham, Richard. *The Jewish World Around the New Testament*. Tübingen: Mohr Siebeck, 2008.

Beale, G. K. *1-2 Thessalonians*. IVP New Testament Commentaries. Downers Grove, IL: InterVarsity Press, 2003.

Belleville, Linda L. *Second Corinthians*. IVP New Testament Commentaries. Downers Grove, IL: InterVarsity Press, 1996.

Bergsma, John S. "Qumran Self-Identity: 'Israel' or 'Judah'?" *DSD* 15 (2008): 172-89.

Best, Ernest. *1 and 2 Thessalonians*. BNTC. Peabody, MA: Hendrickson, 2003.

———. *Ephesians*. ICC. New York: T&T Clark, 2004.

Bickerman, Elias. *The God of the Maccabees: Studies on the Meaning and Origin of the Maccabean Revolt*. Leiden: Brill, 1979.

Bird, Michael F. "Incorporated Righteousness: A Response to the Recent Evangelical Discussion Concerning the Imputation of Christ's Righteousness in Justification." *JETS* 47, no. 2 (2004): 253-75.

Black, Matthew. *The Book of Enoch or I Enoch: A New English Edition*. Leiden: Brill, 1985.

Blackwell, Ben C. "Immortal Glory and the Problem of Death in Romans 3.23." *JSNT* 32, no. 3 (2010): 285-308.

Blomberg, Craig. *1 Corinthians*. NIVAC. Grand Rapids: Zondervan, 1994.

Bruce, F. F. *The Epistles to the Colossians, to Philemon, and to the Ephesians*. NICNT. Grand Rapids: Eerdmans, 1984.

———. *The Epistle to the Galatians*. NIGTC. Grand Rapids: Eerdmans, 1988.

Buitenwerf, Rieuwerd. *Book III of the Sibylline Oracles and Its Social Setting*. Leiden: Brill, 2003.

Byrne, Brendan. *Galatians and Romans*. Collegeville, MN: Liturgical Press, 2010.

———. "Living Out the Righteousness of God: The Contribution of Rom 6:1-8:13 to an Understanding of Paul's Ethical Presuppositions." *CBQ* 43 (1981): 557-81.

———. "The Problem of NOMOΣ and the Relationship with Judaism in Romans." *CBQ* 62 (2000): 294-309.

Campbell, Constantine R. *Paul and Union with Christ: An Exegetical and Theological Study*. Grand Rapids: Zondervan, 2012.

Campbell, W. S. "Romans III as a Key to the Structure and Thought of the Letter." *NovT* 23.1 (1981): 22-40.

Capes, David B. "Interpreting Ephesians 1–3: 'God's People in the Mystery of His Will.'" *SwJT* 39 (1996): 20-31.

Capes, David B., Rodney Reeves and E. Randolph Richards. *Rediscovering Paul:*

An Introduction to His World, Letters and Theology. Downers Grove, IL: Inter-Varsity Press, 2007.

Christiansen, Ellen Juhl. *The Covenant in Judaism and Paul: A Study of Ritual Boundaries as Identity Markers.* Leiden: Brill, 1995.

Clarke, Ernest G. *The Wisdom of Solomon.* Cambridge: Cambridge University Press, 1973.

Collins, John J. *The Apocalyptic Imagination.* Grand Rapids: Eerdmans, 1998.

———. *Jewish Wisdom in the Hellenistic Age.* Louisville: Westminster John Knox, 1997.

———. *The Sibylline Oracles of Egyptian Judaism.* Missoula: University of Montana Press, 1972.

Collins, Raymond. *First Corinthians.* Sacra Pagina. Collegeville, MN: Liturgical Press, 1999.

Cosgrove, Charles H. "Justification in Paul: A Linguistic and Theological Reflection." *JBL* 106 (1987): 653-78.

Cousar, Charles B. "II Corinthians 5:17-21." *Int* 35 (1981): 180-83.

Cranfield, C. E. B. *Romans 9–16.* ICC. Edinburgh: T&T Clark, 1979.

Cranford, Michael. "Abraham in Romans 4: The Father of All Who Believe." *HTR* 41 (1995): 72-73.

———. "Election and Ethnicity: Paul's View of Israel in Romans 9:1-13." *JSNT* 50 (1993): 27-41.

Crenshaw, James L. *Old Testament Wisdom: An Introduction.* Louisville: Westminster John Knox, 1998.

Das, A. Andrew. *Paul, the Law, and the Covenant.* Peabody, MA: Hendrickson, 2001.

Davies, Philip R. "Eschatology at Qumran." *JBL* 104, no. 1 (1985): 39-55.

DeSilva, David A. *Introducing the Apocrypha: Message, Context, and Significance.* Grand Rapids: Baker Academic, 2002.

Donaldson, Terence L. "Proselytes or 'Righteous Gentiles'? The Status of Gentiles in Eschatological Pilgrimage Patterns of Thought." *JSP* 7 (1990): 3-27.

Doran, Robert. *Temple Propaganda: The Purpose and Character of 2 Maccabees.* Washington, DC: Catholic Biblical Association of America, 1981.

Dunn, James D. G. *The New Perspective on Paul.* Grand Rapids: Eerdmans, 2005.

———. *Romans 9–16.* WBC. Dallas: Word, 1988.

———. *The Theology of Paul's Letter to the Galatians.* Cambridge: Cambridge University Press, 1993.

Dunson, Ben C. "Faith in Romans: The Salvation of the Individual or Life in Community?" *JSNT* 34, no. 1 (2011): 19-46.

Eastman, Susan Grove. "Israel and the Mercy of God: A Re-Reading of Galatians 6.16 and Romans 9–11." *NTS* 56, no. 3 (2010): 367-95.

Elias, Jacob W. *1 and 2 Thessalonians*. BCBC. Scottdale, PA: Herald, 1995.

Elliott, Mark Adam. *The Survivors of Israel: A Reconsideration of the Theology of Pre-Christian Judaism*. Grand Rapids: Eerdmans, 2000.

Eshel, Hanan. *The Dead Sea Scrolls and the Hasmonean State*. Grand Rapids: Eerdmans, 2008.

Evans, Craig A. *Ancient Texts for New Testament Studies: A Guide to the Background Literature*. Peabody, MA: Hendrickson, 2005.

Fee, Gordon D. *The First Epistle to the Corinthians*. NICNT. Grand Rapids: Eerdmans, 1987.

Fitzmyer, Joseph A. *First Corinthians*. AYB. New Haven, CT: Yale University Press, 2008.

Flusser, David. *Judaism of the Second Temple Period*. Vol. 1. Grand Rapids: Eerdmans, 2007.

Forman, Mark. "The Politics of Promise: Echoes of Isaiah 54 in Romans 4.19-21." *JSNT* 31, no. 3 (2009): 301-24.

Fowl, Stephen A. *Ephesians*. NTL. Louisville: Westminster John Knox, 2012.

Franklyn, Paul N. "The Cultic and Pious Climax of Eschatology in the Psalms of Solomon." *JSJ* 18, no. 1 (1987): 1-17.

Fuller, Michael E. *The Restoration of Israel: Israel's Re-Gathering and the Fate of the Nations in Early Jewish Literature and Luke-Acts*. Berlin: de Gruyter, 2006.

Fung, Ronald Y. K. *The Epistle to the Galatians*. NICNT. Grand Rapids: Eerdmans, 1988.

Garland, David E. *1 Corinthians*. BECNT. Grand Rapids: Baker Academic, 2003.

Garlington, Don B. *An Exposition of Galatians: A Reading from the New Perspective*. Eugene, OR: Wipf & Stock, 2007.

———. *The Obedience of Faith: A Pauline Phrase in Historical Context*. Tübingen: Mohr Siebeck, 1991.

———. "Paul's 'Partisan ἐκ' and the Question of Justification in Galatians." *JBL* 127, no. 3 (2008): 567-89.

———. "Role Reversal and Paul's Use of Scripture in Galatians 3.10-13." *JSNT* 65 (1997): 85-121.

Gathercole, Simon J. *Where Is Boasting? Early Jewish Soteriology and Paul's Response in Romans 1–5*. Grand Rapids: Eerdmans, 2002.

George, Timothy. *Galatians*. NAC. Nashville: Broadman & Holman, 2001.

Gianoulis, George C. "Is Sonship in Romans 8:14-17 a Link with Romans 9?" *BSac* 166 (January-March 2009): 70-83.

Goering, Greg S. *Wisdom's Root Revealed: Ben Sira and the Election of Israel.* JSJSup 139. Leiden: Brill, 2009.

Goldstein, Jonathan A. *I Maccabees: A New Translation with Introduction and Commentary.* AB. New York: Doubleday, 1976.

———. *II Maccabees.* AB. New York: Doubleday, 1983.

Gombis, Timothy G. "Ephesians 2 as a Narrative of Divine Warfare." *JSNT* 26, no. 4 (2004): 403-18.

Grabbe, Lester. *Wisdom of Solomon.* New York: T&T Clark, 1997.

Green, Gene L. *The Letters to the Thessalonians.* Pillar New Testament Commentary. Grand Rapids: Eerdmans, 2002.

Grierson, Fiona. "The Testament of Moses." *JSP* 17, no. 4 (2008): 265-80.

Griffin, Patrick J. *The Theology and Function of Prayer in the Book of Tobit.* PhD diss., Catholic University of America, 1984.

Grindheim, Sigurd. "Apostate Turned Prophet: Paul's Prophetic Self-Understanding and Prophetic Hermeneutic with Special Reference to Galatians 3:10-12." *NTS* 53 (2007): 545-65.

———. *The Crux of Election: Paul's Critique of the Jewish Confidence in the Election of Israel.* Tübingen: Mohr Siebeck, 2005.

———. "Not Salvation History, but Salvation Territory: The Main Subject Matter of Galatians." *NTS* 59 (2013): 91-108.

Hanneken, Todd R. *The Subversion of the Apocalypses in the Book of Jubilees.* Atlanta: Society of Biblical Literature, 2012.

Harrington, Daniel J. *Invitation to the Apocrypha.* Grand Rapids: Eerdmans, 1999.

———. "'Saved by Wisdom' (Wis 9.18): Soteriology in the Wisdom of Solomon." In *This World and the World to Come: Soteriology in Early Judaism*, edited by Daniel M. Gurtner, pp. 181-90. New York: T&T Clark, 2011.

Harris, Murray J. *Prepositions and Theology in the Greek New Testament: An Essential Reference Resource for Exegesis.* Grand Rapids: Zondervan, 2012.

———. *The Second Epistle to the Corinthians: A Commentary on the Greek Text.* NIGTC. Grand Rapids: Eerdmans, 2005.

Harvey, Graham. *The True Israel: Uses of the Names Jew, Hebrew, and Israel in Ancient Jewish and Early Christian Literature.* Leiden: Brill, 1996.

Hays, Richard B. *First Corinthians.* IBC. Louisville: Westminster John Knox, 1997.

———. "Have We Found Abraham to Be Our Forefather According to the Flesh?" *NovT* 28, no. 1 (1985): 76-98.

————. "Psalm 143 and the Logic of Romans 3." *JBL* 99, no. 1 (1980): 107-15.

Heger, Paul. *Challenges to Conventional Opinions on Qumran and Enoch Issues.* Leiden: Brill, 2012.

Heil, John Paul. "From Remnant to Seed of Hope for Israel: Romans 9:27-29." *CBQ* 64, no. 4 (2002): 703-20.

Hellerman, Joseph. "Purity and Nationalism in Second Temple Literature: 1-2 Maccabees and *Jubilees*." *JETS* 46, no. 3 (2003): 401-21.

Henten, Jan Willem van. *The Maccabean Martyrs as Saviours of the Jewish People: A Study of 2 and 4 Maccabees.* Leiden: Brill, 1997.

Hoehner, Harold W. *Ephesians: An Exegetical Commentary.* Grand Rapids: Baker Academic, 2002.

Hogan, Karina Martin. *Theologies in Conflict in 4 Ezra: Wisdom, Debate, and Apocalyptic Solution.* Leiden: Brill, 2008.

Hollander, Harm W., and Marinus de Jonge. *The Testaments of the Twelve Patriarchs: A Commentary.* Leiden: Brill, 1985.

Hooker, Morna D. "On Becoming the Righteousness of God: Another Look at 2 Cor 5:21." *NovT* 50 (2008): 358-75.

Horgan, Maurya P. *Pesharim: Qumran Interpretations of Biblical Books.* Washington, DC: Catholic Biblical Association of America, 1979.

Howard, George. "Romans 3:21-31 and the Inclusion of the Gentiles." *HTR* 63 (1970): 223-33.

Jacobson, Howard. *A Commentary on Pseudo-Philo's Liber Antiquitatum Biblicarum with Latin Text and English Translation.* Vol. 1. Leiden: Brill, 1996.

Jewett, Robert. "The Law and the Coexistence of Jews and Gentiles in Romans." *Int* 39, no. 4 (1985): 341-56.

————. *The Thessalonian Correspondence: Pauline Rhetoric and Millenarian Piety.* Minneapolis: Fortress, 1986.

Jipp, Joshua W. "Rereading the Story of Abraham, Isaac, and 'Us' in Romans 4." *JSNT* 32, no. 2 (2009): 217-42.

Johnson, Luke Timothy. "Rom 3:21-26 and the Faith of Jesus." *CBQ* 44 (1982): 77-90.

Johnston, J. William. "Which 'All' Sinned? Rom 3:23-24 Reconsidered." *NovT* 53 (2011): 153-64.

Jonge, Marinus de. "The Future of Israel in the Testaments of the Twelve Patriarchs." *JSJ* 17, no. 2 (1986): 196-211.

Kaminsky, Joel S. "Reclaiming a Theology of Election: Favoritism and the Joseph Story." *PRSt* 31, no. 2 (2004): 135-52.

Keck, Leander E. "God the Other Who Acts Otherwise: An Exegetical Essay on 1 Cor 1:26-31." *WW* 26, no. 4 (1996): 437-43.

Keener, Craig S. *Romans.* New Covenant Commentary. Eugene, OR: Cascade, 2009.

Kistemaker, Simon J. *Exposition of the First Epistle to the Corinthians.* New Testament Commentary. Grand Rapids: Baker Books, 2001.

Kittel, Bonnie. *The Hymns of Qumran.* Atlanta: Scholars Press, 1981.

Knibb, Michael A. "The Book of Enoch or Books of Enoch? The Textual Evidence for 1 Enoch." In *The Early Enoch Literature,* edited by Gabriele Boccaccini and John J. Collins, pp. 21-40. Leiden: Brill, 2007.

———. *The Qumran Community.* Cambridge: Cambridge University Press, 1987.

Kruse, Colin G. *Paul's Letter to the Romans.* Pillar New Testament Commentary. Grand Rapids: Eerdmans, 2012.

Lambrecht, Jan. "Critical Reflections on Paul's Partisan 'ἐκ' as Recently Presented by Don Garlington." *ETL* 85, no. 1 (2009): 135-41.

Lane, William L. "Paul's Legacy from Pharisaism: Light from the Psalms of Solomon." *Concordia Journal* 8 (1982): 130-40.

Leaney, Alfred R. C. *The Rule of Qumran and Its Meaning: Introduction, Translation and Commentary.* Philadelphia: Westminster, 1966.

Lincoln, Andrew T. "The Church and Israel in Ephesians 2." *CBQ* 49 (1987): 605-24.

———. "Ephesians 2:8-10: A Summary of Paul's Gospel?" *CBQ* 45 (1983): 617-30.

———. *Ephesians.* WBC. Dallas: Word, 1990.

Lohr, Joel N. *Chosen and Unchosen: Conceptions of Election in the Pentateuch and Jewish-Christian Interpretation.* Winona Lake, IN: Eisenbrauns, 2009.

Longenecker, Bruce W. "ΠΙΣΤΙΣ in Romans 3.25: Neglected Evidence for the 'Faithfulness of Christ'?" *NTS* 39 (1993): 478-80.

Lowe, Chuck. "'There Is No Condemnation' (Romans 8:1): But Why Not?" *JETS* 42, no. 2 (1999): 231-50.

Macatangay, Francis M. *The Wisdom Instructions in the Book of Tobit.* Berlin: de Gruyter, 2011.

Mack, Burton L. *Wisdom and the Hebrew Epic: Ben Sira's Hymn in Praise of the Fathers.* Chicago: University of Chicago Press, 1986.

Maier, Walter A. "Paul's Concept of Justification, and Some Recent Interpretations of Romans 3:21-31." *Springfielder* 37 (1974): 248-64.

Mangan, Celine. "Christ the Power and the Wisdom of God: The Semitic Background to 1 Cor 1:24." *PIBA* 4 (1980): 21-34.

Marshall, I. Howard. *1 and 2 Thessalonians*. NCB. Grand Rapids: Eerdmans, 1983.

———. "Living in the 'Flesh.'" *BSac* 159 (October-December 2002): 387-403.

———. "The Problem of Apostasy in New Testament Theology." *PRSt* 14 (1987): 65-80.

Martin, Michael D. *1, 2 Thessalonians*. NAC. Nashville: Broadman & Holman, 1995.

Martin, Ralph P. *Ephesians, Colossians, and Philemon*. IBC. Louisville: Westminster John Knox, 1991.

Martínez, Florentino García. *Echoes from the Caves: Qumran and the New Testament*. Leiden: Brill, 2009.

———. "The Heavenly Tablets in the Book of Jubilees." In *Studies in the Book of Jubilees*, edited by Matthias Albani, Jörg Frey and Armin Lange, pp. 243-60. Tübingen, Mohr Siebeck: 1997.

Martínez, Florentino García, and Eibert J. C. Tigchelaar. *The Dead Sea Scrolls: Study Edition*. Vol. 1-2. Grand Rapids: Eerdmans, 1997.

Maston, Jason. *Divine and Human Agency in Second Temple Judaism and Paul*. Tübingen: Mohr Siebeck, 2010.

Matera, Frank J. *Romans*. Paideia Commentary on the New Testament. Grand Rapids: Baker Academic 2010.

Matlock, R. Barry. "The Rhetoric of πίστις in Paul: Galatians 2.16, 3.22, Romans 3.22, and Philippians 3.9." *JSNT* 30, no. 2 (2007): 173-203.

McFadden, Kevin W. "The Fulfillment of the Law's *Dikaiōma*: Another Look at Romans 8:1-4." *JETS* 52, no. 3 (2009): 483-97.

McKnight, Scot. *Galatians*. NIVAC. Grand Rapids: Zondervan, 1995.

McRay, John. *Paul: His Life and Teaching*. Grand Rapids: Baker Academic, 2003.

Merrill, Eugene H. *Qumran and Predestination: A Theological Study of the Thanksgiving Hymns*. Leiden: Brill, 1975.

Moo, Douglas J. *Galatians*. BECNT. Grand Rapids: Baker Academic, 2013.

Moore, Carey A. *Daniel, Esther, and Jeremiah: The Additions*. AB. New York: Doubleday, 1977.

———. *Tobit: A New Translation with Introduction and Commentary*. AB. New York: Doubleday, 1996.

Morris, Leon. *The Epistles of Paul to the Thessalonians: An Introduction and Commentary*. TNTC. Grand Rapids: Eerdmans, 1984.

———. *The Epistle to the Romans*. Pillar New Testament Commentary. Grand Rapids: Eerdmans, 1988.

Mounce, Robert H. *Romans*. NAC. Nashville: Broadman & Holman, 1995.

Murphy, Frederick J. *Pseudo-Philo: Rewriting the Bible.* Oxford: Oxford University Press, 1993.

———. "Retelling the Bible: Idolatry in Pseudo-Philo." *JBL* 107, no. 2 (1988): 275-87.

Najman, Hindy. *Past Renewals: Interpretive Authority, Renewed Revelation, and the Quest for Perfection in Jewish Antiquity.* Leiden: Brill, 2010.

Nickelsburg, George W. E. "1 and 2 Maccabees—Same Story, Different Meaning." *CTM* 42 (1971): 52.

———. *1 Enoch.* Vol. 1. Hermeneia. Minneapolis: Fortress, 2001.

———. "The Apocalyptic Message of *1 Enoch* 92-105." *CBQ* 39 (1977): 309-28.

———. "Enochic Wisdom: An Alternative to the Mosaic Torah?" In *Hesed Ve-Emet: Studies in Honor of Ernest S. Frerichs,* edited by Jodi Magness and Seymour Gitin, pp. 123-32. Atlanta: Scholars Press, 1998.

———. *Jewish Literature Between the Bible and the Mishnah.* Minneapolis: Fortress, 2005.

———. *Resurrection, Immortality, and Eternal Life in Intertestamental Judaism and Early Christianity.* Cambridge, MA: Harvard University Press, 2006.

———. "Tobit." In *The HarperCollins Bible Commentary,* edited by James L. Mays, pp. 719-31. New York: HarperCollins, 1988.

O'Brien, Peter Thomas. *The Letter to the Ephesians.* Pillar New Testament Commentary. Grand Rapids: Eerdmans, 1999.

O'Day, Gail R. "Jeremiah 9:22-23 and 1 Corinthians 1:26-31: A Study in Intertextuality." *JBL* 109, no. 2 (1990): 263-64.

Pascuzzi, Maria. "Baptism-Based Allegiance and the Divisions in Corinth: A Reexamination of 1 Corinthians 1:13-17." *CBQ* 71 (2009): 813-29.

Patzia, Arthur G. *Ephesians, Colossians, Philemon.* Understanding the Bible Commentary. Grand Rapids: Baker Books, 2011.

Ridderbos, Herman N. *Paul: An Outline of His Theology.* Grand Rapids: Eerdmans, 1975.

Ringgren, Helmer. *The Faith of Qumran: Theology of the Dead Sea Scrolls.* New York: Crossroad, 1995.

Rowley, H. H. *The Biblical Doctrine of Election.* London: Lutterworth, 1964.

Sanders, E. P. *Paul and Palestinian Judaism.* Minneapolis: Fortress, 1970.

———. *Paul, the Law, and the Jewish People.* Minneapolis: Fortress, 1983.

Sanders, James A. *The Dead Sea Psalms Scroll.* Ithaca, NY: Cornell University Press, 1967.

Schiffman, Lawrence H. *The Eschatological Community of the Dead Sea Scrolls.* Atlanta: Society of Biblical Literature, 1989.

———. *Qumran and Jerusalem: Studies in the Dead Sea Scrolls and the History of Judaism*. Grand Rapids: Eerdmans, 2010.

———. *Reclaiming the Dead Sea Scrolls: Their True Meaning for Judaism and Christianity*. New York: Doubleday, 1995.

Schnelle, Udo. *Apostle Paul: His Life and Theology*. Grand Rapids: Baker Academic, 2005.

Schofield, Alison. *From Qumran to the Yahad: A New Paradigm of Textual Development for the Community Rule*. Leiden: Brill, 2009.

Schreiner, Thomas R. "Does Romans 9 Teach Individual Election unto Salvation? Some Exegetical and Theological Reflections." *JETS* 36, no. 1 (1993): 25-40.

———. *Galatians*. Exegetical Commentary on the New Testament. Grand Rapids: Zondervan, 2010.

———. *The Law and Its Fulfillment: A Pauline Theology of the Law*. Grand Rapids: Baker Books, 1993.

———. *Paul, Apostle of God's Glory in Christ: A Pauline Theology*. Downers Grove, IL: InterVarsity Press, 2001.

———. *Romans*. BECNT. Grand Rapids: Baker Academic, 1998.

Schuller, Eileen. "Petitionary Prayer and the Religion of Qumran." In *Religion in the Dead Sea Scrolls*, edited by John J. Collins and Robert A. Kugler, pp. 29-45. Grand Rapids: Eerdmans, 2000.

Schultz, Brian. *Conquering the World: The War Scroll (1QM) Reconsidered*. Leiden: Brill, 2009.

Schwartz, Daniel R. *2 Maccabees*. Berlin: de Gruyter, 2008.

Scott, J. Julius, Jr. "Paul and Late-Jewish Eschatology—A Case Study, I Thessalonians 4:13-18 and II Thessalonians 2:1-12." *JETS* 15, no. 3 (1972): 133-43.

Segal, Michael. *The Book of Jubilees: Rewritten Bible, Redaction, Ideology, and Theology*. Leiden: Brill, 2007.

Seifrid, Mark A. *Justification by Faith: The Origin and Development of a Central Pauline Theme*. Leiden: Brill, 1992.

Shellrude, Glen. "The Freedom of God in Mercy and Judgment: A Libertarian Reading of Romans 9:6-29." *EvQ* 81, no. 4 (2009): 306-18.

Shemesh, Aharaon. "Expulsion and Exclusion in the Community Rule and the Damascus Document." *DSD* 9, no. 1 (2002): 44-74.

Shillington, V. G. *2 Corinthians*. BCBC. Scottdale, PA: Herald, 1998.

Shogren, Gary S. *1 and 2 Thessalonians*. Exegetical Commentary on the New Testament. Grand Rapids: Zondervan, 2012.

Skehan, Patrick W., and Alexander A. Di Lella, OFM. *The Wisdom of Ben Sira: A New Translation with Notes*. AB. New York: Doubleday, 1987.

Slingerland, Dixon. "The Nature of *Nomos* (Law) Within the *Testaments of the Twelve Patriarchs*." *JBL* 105, no. 1 (1986): 39-48.

Snodgrass, Klyne. *Ephesians*. NIVAC. Grand Rapids: Zondervan, 1996.

———. "Spheres of Influence: A Possible Solution to the Problem of Paul and the Law." *JSNT* 32 (1988): 93-113.

Soards, Marion L. *1 Corinthians*. UBCS. Grand Rapids: Baker Books, 2011.

Sprinkle, Preston M. "The Hermeneutic of Grace: The Soteriology of Pseudo-Philo's *Biblical Antiquities*." In *This World and the World to Come: Soteriology in Early Judaism*, edited by Daniel M. Gurtner, pp. 50-67. New York: T&T Clark, 2011.

———. *Paul and Judaism Revisited: A Study of Divine and Human Agency in Salvation*. Downers Grove, IL: IVP Academic, 2013.

Staples, Jason A. "What Do the Gentiles Have to Do with 'All Israel'? A Fresh Look at Romans 11:25-27." *JBL* 130, no. 2 (2011): 371-90.

Stegman, Thomas D., SJ. "Paul's Use of *dikaio-* Terminology: Moving Beyond N. T. Wright's Forensic Interpretation." *TS* 72 (2011): 496-524.

Stendahl, Krister. *Paul Among Jews and Gentiles*. Philadelphia: Fortress, 1976.

Stokes, Ryan E. "The Origin of Sin in the Dead Sea Scrolls." *SwJT* 53, no. 1 (2010): 55-67.

Stowers, Stanley K. "*Ek pisteos* and *dia tes pisteos* in Romans 3:30." *JBL* 108, no. 4 (1989): 665-74.

Stubbs, David L. "The Shape of Soteriology and the *Pistis Christou* Debate." *SJT* 61, no. 2 (2008): 137-57.

Stückenbruck, Loren T. *1 Enoch 91–108*. Berlin: de Gruyter, 2007.

Suh, Robert H. "The Use of Ezekiel 37 in Ephesians 2." *JETS* 50, no. 4 (2007): 715-33.

Tanner, J. Paul. "The New Covenant and Paul's Quotations from Hosea in Romans 9:25-26." *BSac* 162 (2005): 95-110.

Thiselton, Anthony C. *The First Epistle to the Corinthians: A Commentary on the Greek Text*. NIGTC. Grand Rapids: Eerdmans, 2000.

Thompson, James W. *Moral Formation According to Paul: The Context and Coherence of Pauline Ethics*. Grand Rapids: Baker Academic, 2011.

Thornhill, A. Chadwick. "'Spheres of Influence' in the Epistle to the Galatians." *HBT* 36, no. 1 (2014): 21-41.

Tiller, Patrick A. *A Commentary on the Animal Apocalypse of I Enoch*. Atlanta: Scholars Press, 1993.

Timmer, Daniel C. "Variegated Nomism Indeed: Multiphase Eschatology and Soteriology in the Qumranite *Community Rule* (1QS) and the New Perspective on Paul." *JETS* 52, no. 2 (2009): 341-56.

Tobin, Thomas H., SJ. *Paul's Rhetoric in Its Contexts: The Argument of Romans.* Peabody, MA: Hendrickson, 2004.

Toews, John E. *Romans.* BCBC. Scottdale, PA: Herald, 2004.

Treves, Marco. "Two Spirits of the Rule of the Community." *RevQ* 3, no. 3 (1961): 449-52.

Tromp, Johannes. *The Assumption of Moses: A Critical Edition with Commentary.* Leiden: Brill, 1993.

Tso, Marcus K. M. *Ethics in the Qumran Community.* Tübingen: Mohr Siebeck, 2010.

Tukasi, Emmanuel O. *Determinism and Petitionary Prayer in John and the Dead Sea Scrolls: An Ideological Reading of John and the Reading of the Community (1QS).* New York: T&T Clark, 2008.

———. "Dualism and Penitential Prayer in the *Rule of the Community* (1QS)." In *Dualism in Qumran*, edited by Géza G. Xeravits, pp. 166-87. New York: T&T Clark, 2010.

Van Rooy, Herrie F., ed. *Studies on the Syriac Apocryphal Psalms.* JSSSup 7. Oxford: Oxford University Press, 2000.

VanderKam, James. *The Book of Jubilees.* Sheffield: Sheffield Academic, 2001.

VanLandingham, Chris. *Judgment and Justification in Early Judaism and the Apostle Paul.* Grand Rapids: Baker Academic, 2006.

Vermes, Geza. *The Dead Sea Scrolls: Qumran in Perspective.* Cleveland: William Collins & World, 1978.

———. *An Introduction to the Complete Dead Sea Scrolls.* Minneapolis: Fortress, 2000.

Wacholder, Ben Zion. *The New Damascus Document: The Midrash on the Eschatological Torah of the Dead Sea Scrolls: Reconstruction, Translation and Commentary.* Leiden: Brill, 2007.

Wanamaker, Charles A. *The Epistles to the Thessalonians: A Commentary on the Greek Text.* NIGTC. Grand Rapids: Eerdmans, 1990.

Wardle, Timothy. *The Jerusalem Temple and Early Christian Identity.* Tübingen: Mohr Siebeck, 2010.

Watson, Francis. *Paul, Judaism and the Gentiles: A Sociological Approach.* Cambridge: Cambridge University Press, 1986.

Weedman, Gary E. "Reading Ephesians from the New Perspective on Paul." *Leaven* 14, no. 2 (2006): 81-92.

Wernberg-Møller, Preben. *The Manual of Discipline: Translated and Annotated with an Introduction.* Grand Rapids: Eerdmans, 1957.

———. "A Reconsideration of the Two Spirits in the Rule of the Community (1 Q Serek III,13–IV,26)." *RevQ* 3, no. 3 (1961): 413-41.

Westerholm, Stephen. "Paul's Anthropological 'Pessimism' in Its Jewish Context." In *Divine and Human Agency in Paul and His Cultural Environment*, edited by John M. Barclay and Simon Gathercole, pp. 71-98. New York: T&T Clark, 2006.

Williams, David J. *1 and 2 Thessalonians.* UBCS. Grand Rapids: Baker Books, 2011.

Williamson, Peter S. *Ephesians.* Catholic Commentary on Sacred Scripture. Grand Rapids: Baker Academic, 2009.

Winninge, Mikael. *Sinners and the Righteous: A Comparative Study of the Psalms of Solomon and Paul's Letters.* Stockholm: Almqvist & Wiksell International, 1995.

Winston, David. *The Wisdom of Solomon: A New Translation with Introduction and Commentary.* New York: Doubleday, 1979.

Wisdom, Jeffrey R. *Blessing for the Nations and the Curse of the Law: Paul's Citation of Genesis and Deuteronomy in Gal 3.8-10.* Tübingen: Mohr Siebeck, 2001.

Witherington, Ben, III. *1 and 2 Thessalonians: A Socio-Rhetorical Commentary.* Grand Rapids: Eerdmans, 2006.

———. *Conflict and Community in Corinth: A Socio-Rhetorical Commentary on 1 and 2 Corinthians.* Grand Rapids: Eerdmans, 1995.

———. *Jesus the Sage: The Pilgrimage of Wisdom.* Minneapolis: Fortress, 1994.

———. *The Letters to Philemon, the Colossians, and the Ephesians: A Socio-Rhetorical Commentary on the Captivity Epistles.* Grand Rapids: Eerdmans, 2007.

———. *Paul's Letter to the Romans: A Socio-Rhetorical Commentary.* Grand Rapids: Eerdmans, 2004.

———. *The Problem with Evangelical Theology: Testing the Exegetical Foundations of Calvinism, Dispensationalism and Wesleyanism.* Waco: Baylor University Press, 2005.

Wright, N. T. *The Climax of the Covenant: Christ and the Law in Pauline Theology.* New York: T&T Clark, 1991.

———. *Jesus and the Victory of God.* Minneapolis: Fortress, 1996.

———. *Paul and the Faithfulness of God.* Minneapolis: Fortress, 2013.

———. "Paul and the Patriarch: The Role of Abraham in Romans 4." *JSNT* 35, no. 3 (2013): 207-9.

———. "Romans 9–11 and the 'New Perspective.'" In *Between Gospel and Election*, edited by Florian Wilk and J. Ross Wagner, pp. 37-54. Tübingen: Mohr Siebeck, 2010.

Yadin, Yigael. *The Scroll of the War of the Sons of Light Against the Sons of Darkness*. Oxford: Oxford University Press, 1962.

Yee, Tet-Lim N. *Jews, Gentiles and Ethnic Reconciliation: Paul's Jewish Identity and Ephesians*. Cambridge: Cambridge University Press, 2005.

Yoder Neufeld, Thomas R. *Ephesians*. BCBC. Scottdale, PA: Herald, 2001.

Zeitlin, Solomon. *The Second Book of Maccabees*. New York: Harper & Bros., 1954.

Author Index

Subject Index

Scripture Index

Ancient Texts Index